COMPARATIVE REGIONAL INTEGRATION

Comparative Regional Integration: Governance and Legal Models is a ground-breaking comparative study on regional or supranational integration through international and regional organizations. It provides the first comprehensive and empirically based analysis of governance systems by drawing on an original sample of eighty-five regional and international organizations. The authors explain how and why different organizations select specific governance processes and institutional choices, and outline which legal instruments – regulatory, organizational or procedural – are adopted to achieve integration. They reveal how different objectives influence institutional design and the integration model, for example a free trade area could insist on supremacy and refrain from adopting instruments for indirect rule, while a political union would rather engage with all available techniques. This ambitious work merges different backgrounds and disciplines to provide researchers and practitioners with a unique toolbox of institutional processes and legal mechanisms, and a classification of different models of regional and international integration.

In the study "Lead, follow or get out of the way? International secretariats in comparative perspective," Sender takes a close look at international secretariats, with the principal objective of providing distilled hard data on how secretariats are structured and what it is, precisely, that they do.

CARLOS CLOSA is Professor at the Institute for Public Goods and Policies (IPP) and former Director of the Research Area European, Transnational and Global Governance at the Global Governance Programme/RSCAS at the European University Institute (EUI).

LORENZO CASINI is full Professor of Administrative Law in the Faculty of Law at the University of Rome "Sapienza" and at IMT of Lucca. He is a Research Fellow at New York University for the Global Administrative Law Project and has written several articles and books on comparative and global administrative law.

OMRI SENDER is counsel for the World Bank and a consultant in public international law. He is currently pursuing a doctoral degree in international law at the George Washington University Law School, and frequently writes and publishes in the field of public international law.

INTEGRATION THROUGH LAW

The Role of Law and the Rule of Law in ASEAN Integration

General Editors
J. H. H. Weiler, European University Institute
Tan Hsien-Li, National University of Singapore

The Association of Southeast Asian Nations (ASEAN), comprising the ten member states of Brunei Darussalam, Cambodia, Indonesia, Lao PDR, Malaysia, Myanmar, Philippines, Singapore, Thailand and Vietnam, has undertaken intensified integration into the ASEAN Community through the Rule of Law and Institutions in its 2007 Charter. This innovative book series evaluates the community-building processes of ASEAN to date and offers a conceptual and policy toolkit for broader Asian thinking and planning of different legal and institutional models of economic and political regional integration in the region. Participating scholars have been divided up into six separate thematic strands. The books combine a mix of Asian and Western scholars.

Centre for International Law, National University of Singapore (CIL-NUS)

The Centre for International Law (CIL) was established in 2009 at the National University of Singapore's Bukit Timah Campus in response to the growing need for international law expertise and capacity building in the Asia-Pacific region. CIL is a university-wide research centre that focuses on multidisciplinary research and works with other NUS or external centres of research and academic excellence. In particular, CIL collaborates very closely with the NUS Faculty of Law.

COMPARATIVE REGIONAL INTEGRATION

Governance and Legal Models

CARLOS CLOSA AND LORENZO CASINI

With a Study by Omri Sender on International Secretariats in Comparative Perspective

CAMBRIDGE
UNIVERSITY PRESS

CAMBRIDGE
UNIVERSITY PRESS

University Printing House, Cambridge CB2 8BS, United Kingdom

Cambridge University Press is part of the University of Cambridge.

It furthers the University's mission by disseminating knowledge in the pursuit of education, learning and research at the highest international levels of excellence.

www.cambridge.org
Information on this title: www.cambridge.org/9781107578586

First published 2016

A catalogue record for this publication is available from the British Library

Library of Congress Cataloguing in Publication data
Names: Closa, Carlos, author. | Casini, Lorenzo, 1976–, author. | Sender, Omri, author. | National University of Singapore. Centre for International Law, sponsoring body.
Title: Comparative regional integration: governance and legal models / Carlos Closa and Lorenzo Casini; with a study by Omri Sender on international secretariats in comparative perspective.
Description: Cambridge, United Kingdom: Cambridge University Press, 2016. | Series: Integration through law: the role of law and the rule of law in ASEAN integration; 10 | Includes bibliographical references and index.
Identifiers: LCCN 2015040098 | ISBN 9781107578586 (Paperback)
Subjects: LCSH: Regionalism (International organization) | International agencies.
Classification: LCC KZ1273 .C56 2016 | DDC 341.24–dc23 LC record available at http://lccn.loc.gov/2015040098

ISBN 978-1-107-57858-6 Paperback

CONTENTS

FIGURES

TABLES

GENERAL EDITORS' PREFACE

This monograph is published within the context of a wide-ranging research project entitled, Integration Through Law: The Role of Law and the Rule of Law in ASEAN Integration (ITL), undertaken by the Centre for International Law at the National University of Singapore and directed by J. H. H. Weiler and Tan Hsien-Li.

The Preamble to the ASEAN Charter concludes with a single decision: "We, the Peoples of the Member States of the Association of Southeast Asian Nations. [h]ereby decide to establish, through this Charter, the legal and institutional framework for ASEAN." For the first time in its history of over four decades, the Legal and the Institutional were brought to the forefront of ASEAN discourse.

The gravitas of the medium, a Charter: the substantive ambition of its content, the creation of three interlocking Communities, and the turn to law and institutions as instruments for realization provide ample justification for this wide-ranging project, to which this monograph is one contribution, examining ASEAN in a comparative context.

That same substantive and, indeed, political ambition means that any single study, illuminating as it may be, will cover but a fraction of the phenomena. Our modus operandi in this project was to create teams of researchers from Asia and elsewhere who would contribute individual monographs within an overall framework which we had designed.

The project framework, involving several thematic clusters within each monograph, is thus determined by the framework and the place of each monograph within it.

As regards the specific content, however, the authors were free, indeed encouraged, to define their own understanding of the problem and their own methodology and reach their own conclusions. The thematic structure of the entire project may be found at the end of this Preface.

The project as a whole, and each monograph within it, display several methodological sensibilities.

First, law, in our view, can only be understood and evaluated when situated in its political and economic context. Thus, the first studies in the overall project design are intended to provide the political, economic, cultural and historical context against which one must understand ASEAN and are written by specialists in these respective disciplines. This context, to a greater or lesser degree, also informs the sensibility of each monograph. There are no "black letter law" studies to be found in this project and, indeed, even in the most technical of areas we encouraged our authors to make their writing accessible to readers of diverse disciplines.

Comparative experience suggests that the success of achieving some of the more ambitious objectives outlined in Article 1 of the Charter will depend in no small measure on the effectiveness of legal principles, legal rules and legal institutions. This is particularly true as regards the success of establishing "an ASEAN Community comprising the ASEAN Security Community, the ASEAN Economic Community and the ASEAN Socio-Cultural Community as provided for in the Bali Declaration of ASEAN Concord II". Article 2(2)(n) stipulates the commitment of ASEAN Member States to act in accordance with the principle of "adherence to multilateral trade rules and ASEAN's rules-based regimes for effective implementation of economic commitments and progressive reduction towards elimination of all barriers to regional economic integration." The ASEAN Member States therefore envisage that rules of law and the Rule of Law will become a major feature in the future of ASEAN.

Although, as seen, the Charter understands itself as providing an institutional and legal framework for ASEAN, the question of the "role of law and the rule of law" is not advocacy but a genuine enquiry in the various substantive areas of the project as to:

- the substantive legal principles and substantive rules of the various ASEAN communities;
- the procedural legal principles and rules governing institutional structures and decision-making processes;
- implementation, enforcement and dispute settlement.

One should not expect a mechanical application of this scheme in each study; rather, a sensibility that refuses to content itself with legal enactments as such and looks to a "living" notion of law and institutions is ubiquitous in all the studies. Likewise, the project is sensitive to "non Law." It variously attempts to locate the appropriate province of the law in this experience. That is, not only the role of law, but also the areas that are and should remain outside the reach of legal institutionalization with due sensitivity to ASEAN and Asian particularism and political and cultural identities.

The project, and the monographs of which it is made, are not normatively thick. They do not advocate. They are designed, for the most part, to offer reflection, discuss the pros and cons, and in this way enrich public awareness, deepen understanding of different options and in that respect contribute indirectly to policymaking.

This decisive development of ASEAN has been accompanied by a growing Asian interest in various legal and institutional forms of transnational economic and political cooperation, notably the various voices discussing and showing an interest in an East Asia Integration project. The number of Free Trade Agreements (FTAs) and Regional Trade Agreements (RTAs) has increased from six in 1991 to 166 in 2013, with a further 62 in various stages of negotiations.

Methodologically, the project and many of the monographs are comparative in their orientation. Comparative law is one of the few real-life laboratories that we have in which to assess and understand the operation of different legal and institutional models designed to tackle similar objectives and problems. One should not need to put one's own hand in the fire to learn that it scorches. With that in mind a couple of monographs offer both conceptual reflection and pragmatic "tool boxing" on some of the key elements featuring in all regional integration systems.

Comparative law is in part about divergence: it is a potent tool and means to understand one's own uniqueness. One understands better the uniqueness of Apples by comparing them to Oranges. You understand better the specialness of a Toyota by comparing it to a Ford.

Comparative law is also about convergence: it is a potent tool and means to understand how what are seemingly different phenomena are part of a broader trend, an insight which may enhance both self-understanding and policy potentialities.

Although many studies in the project could have almost immediate policy implications, as would the project as a whole, this is not its only or even principal purpose. There is a rich theory of federalism which covers many countries around the world. There is an equally rich theory of European integration, which has been associated with the advent Union. There is also considerable learning on Free Trade Areas and the like.

To date, the study of the legal aspects of ASEAN specifically and other forms of Asian legal integration has been derivative of, and dependent on, theoretical and conceptual insight which were developed in different contexts.

One principal objective of ITL and these monographs will be to put in place the building blocks for an authentic body of ASEAN and Asian integration theory developed in, and with sensitivity to, the particularities and peculiarities of the region and continent. A theory and conceptual framework of Asian legal integration will signal the coming of age of research of and in the region itself.

Although the monographs form part of an overarching project, we asked our authors to write each as a "standalone" – not assuming that their readers would have consulted any of the other titles. Indeed, the project is rich and few will read all monographs. We encourage readers to pick and choose from the various monographs and design their own menu. There is, on occasion, some overlap in providing, for example, background information on ASEAN in different studies. That is not only inevitable but desirable in a project of this amplitude. The world is increasingly witnessing a phenomenon of interlocking regional organization where the experience of one feeds on the others. In some way, the intellectual, disciplinary and comparative sensibility of this project is a microcosm of the world it describes.

The range of topics covered in this series comprises:

The General Architecture and Aspirations of ASEAN The Governance and Management of ASEAN: Instruments, Institutions, Monitoring, Compliance and Dispute Resolution Legal Regimes in ASEAN
The ASEAN Economic Community
ASEAN and the World
The Substantive Law of ASEAN

States formalize their cooperative relations with the aim of providing, together, certain public goods that they cannot provide in isolation. The range of these goods is greatly varied, encompassing security, identity and religion; and development, infrastructure and regulatory frameworks for trade, labor or air transport, for instance. To this end, States accept to be bound by formal arrangements whereby they commit to deliver these goods, but also to respect the agreements concluded. Formal institutions respond precisely to these needs for provision and commitment.

Globalization has underlined the inability of States to provide goods in isolation and has hence accelerated legal integration at international and supranational levels: the number of international institutions – now over 60,000 – began growing after the Second World War and is still rising; the relations between State administrations and international institutions are becoming ever more numerous;[1] forms of regional organization have been spreading; new

[1] See S. Cassese, *Relations between International Organizations and National Administrations*, International Institute of Administrative Sciences, Proceedings of the XIXth International Congress of Administrative Sciences (London: Kluwer Law and Taxation Publishers, 1983).

forms of global networks and global "administrations" have been developing.[2]

As a consequence, scholars worldwide have devoted themselves to studying global governance,[3] international organizations (IOs)[4] and regionalism.[5] From these various perspectives, what has emerged clearly is that a mono-disciplinary approach is not capable of capturing all the implications related to these issues, which means that it becomes crucial to combine different fields of research. In this context, the use of concepts derived from both political science

[2] A.-M. Slaughter, *A New World Order* (Princeton University Press, 2004); E. Kinney, "The Emerging Field of International Administrative Law: Its Contents and Potential," 54 *Administrative Law Review* 415 (2002); B. Kingsbury, N. Krisch and R. B. Stewart, "The Emergence of Global Administrative Law," 68 *Law and Contemporary Problems* 15 (2005).

[3] For a multidisciplinary approach, see K.-H. Ladeur (ed.), *Public Governance in the Age of Globalization* (Aldershot: Ashgate, 2004); D. Held and M. Koenig-Archibugi (eds.), *Taming Globalization: Frontiers of Governance* (London: Polity Press, 2003).

[4] J. Klabbers, *An Introduction to International Institutional Law* (Cambridge University Press, 2nd edn, 2009); H. G. Schermers and N. M. Blokker, *International Institutional Law, Unity Within Diversity* (Leiden: Martinus Nijhoff, 5th edn., 2011); J. E. Alvarez, *International Organizations as Law-Makers* (Oxford University Press, 2005).

[5] *Inter alia*, A. Acharya, "The Emerging Regional Architecture of World Politics," 59:4 *World Politics* 629–652 (2007); P. J. Katzenstein, *A World of Regions: Asia and Europe in the American Imperium* (Ithaca, NY: Cornell University Press, 2005); E. D. Mansfield and E. Solingen, "Regionalism," 13:1 *Annual Review of Political Science* 145–163 (2010); A. Panagariya, "The Regionalism Debate: An Overview," 22:4 *The World Economy* 477–512 (1999).

and law has turned out to be extremely effective,[6] such as in the case of regime theory being used to explain the formation of global regulatory systems.[7] This is why this book presents these two perspectives jointly, in its endeavor to define models of international and supranational legal integration.

Our aim, therefore, is threefold. First, we map and outline models of regional integration by studying their institutional design and processes of governance. Second, we extend our analysis to IOs and other international regimes, to identify which techniques are capable of governing complex global legal systems. Third, we offer a toolbox of institutional processes and legal mechanisms, which may be adopted by current or new projects of international and supranational integration, such as ASEAN. We address these

[6] W. Mattli and N. Woods (eds.), *The Politics of Global Regulation* (Princeton University Press, 2009); also, J. Pauwelyn, R. Wessel and J. Wouters (eds.), *Informal International Lawmaking: Mapping the Action and Testing Concepts of Accountability and Effectiveness* (Oxford University Press, 2012).

[7] See J. G. Ruggie, "International Responses to Technology: Concepts and Trends," 29 *International Organization* 557 (1975); and S. D. Krasner (ed.), *International Regimes* (London: Cornell University Press, 1983), particularly S. D. Krasner, "Structural Causes and Regime Consequences: Regimes as Intervening Variables," pp. 1 *et seq.*, and R. O. Keohane, "The Demand for International Regimes," pp. 141 *et seq.*; and B. Simma, "Self-Contained Regimes," 16 *Netherlands Yearbook* 111 (1985). See also B. Simma and D. Pulkowski, "Of Planets and the Universe: Self-Contained Regimes in International Law," 17 *European Journal of International Law* 483 (2006); A. Hasenclever, P. Mayer and V. Rittberger, *Theories of International Regimes* (Cambridge University Press, 1997); and V. Rittberger (ed.), *Regime Theory and International Relations* (Oxford: Clarendon Press, 1993).

aims in two chapters, both based on the idea that integration is a formal process.[8]

Chapter 1 assesses the empirical models of formalization, based on a large sample of existing organizations across all continents. The chapter unveils the structure of formal commitments used in integration and other international organizations. It focuses on the formal mechanisms that secure "credible commitments." Credible commitments result from institutional design which comprises a number of instruments: the regulation of membership; the institutional structure of integration organizations; the decision-making procedure; the nature of derived norms and the mechanisms for their incorporation into national orders; and the mechanisms of jurisdictional control, supervision and scrutiny. Each of these serves to "lock" participants into integration schemes, and restricts their freedom to withdraw from accepted commitments. The chapter does not explore the causality link between informal/formal integration, nor does it "measure" informal integration or consider the achievements gained under informal integration. The chapter examines the structure of formalized institutional commitments, by looking at the organs for decision-making, the procedures for taking decisions and the model of derived norms. It also provides a classification of the different integration schemes by examining the relationship between an integration organization's

[8] See the seminal work by M. Cappelletti, M. Seccombe and J. H. H. Weiler (eds.), *Integration Through Law: Europe and the American Federal Experience* (Berlin and New York: Walter de Gruyter, 1985) (6 vols.) (see especially vol. I entitled *Methods, Tools, and Institutions*).

objectives and the formal instruments available to it for generating credible commitments. As the thesis of this chapter is that the objectives of regional integration organizations inspire a given institutional structure, it will also examine the kind of objectives existing within integration organizations. A data set comprising the institutional features of eighty-five integration and/or international organizations provides the empirical evidence underlying the arguments of this chapter. The analysis will show that States entering regional (and other) organizations accept formal commitments to achieve their goals with the expectation that other participant States will reciprocate, and it will also examine how this happens.

Chapter 2 focuses on the legal mechanisms and instruments that drive the development of international regimes, their institutional features and their functioning. To outline and critically describe the typology of international organizations and their regimes, and to identify the main legal techniques of governance, the analysis will cover most of the eighty-five international and regional organizations examined in Chapter 1 (such as the EU, ECOWAS, MERCOSUR and ASEAN), as well as other international institutions of both intergovernmental and hybrid public–private nature (such as the ISO and ICANN).[9] In this chapter, the perspective

[9] Union of International Associations, *Yearbook of International Organizations* (Brussels: Union of International Associations, 48th edn., 2011); B. Kingsbury, N. Krisch and R. B. Stewart, "The Emergence of Global Administrative Law," 68 *Law and Contemporary Problems* 15 (2005); and on the 100-odd cases examined in S. Cassese *et al.*, *Global Administrative Law: The Casebook* (Rome, New York and Edinburgh:

adopted is essentially a "managerial" one, which seeks to avoid bias connected to any given political objective. International regimes have increasingly been using accountability mechanisms, but principally to ensure their own efficiency and effectiveness rather than to address any democratic gaps. In other words, the need to enhance the legitimacy and accountability of IOs has a functional reason; this is confirmed by the fact that all regimes tend to adopt similar mechanisms regardless of the degree of "democracy" they may present. The focus will therefore be on a classification of IOs, and on the common threads in the development of international regimes and their mechanisms for ensuring accountability: the increasing differentiation and separation of functions – the "legislative" (norm-making), "judicial" (dispute settlement) and executive-administrative ones; the emergence of intra- and inter-IO institutional pluralism; the growing degree of proceduralization; the need for multiple forms of legitimacy and the adoption of different mechanisms for accountability. These threads may not all occur simultaneously in every regime, and there are many asymmetries. One thread may be more common than another. See, for example, the different ways in which international administrations emerge: these are stronger in global private regimes or in political unions (such as the EU), but weaker in free trade areas. This analysis will enable the main techniques of governance and models of legal integration beyond the State to be

IRPA-IILJ, 3rd edn., 2012); A. Berman, S. Duquet, J. Pauwelyn, R. Wessel and J. Wouters (eds.), *Informal International Lawmaking: Case Studies* (The Hague: TOAE, 2012).

identified: indirect rule, role-splitting and normative supremacy.[10] All these techniques can be productively adopted at various levels, in the pursuit of international and supranational legal integration.[11]

This book offers the first comprehensive overview and conceptualization of different models of international and supranational integration. It illustrates which governance processes and institutional choices – and how and why – are developed by regional organizations. It also displays which legal instruments – regulatory, organizational, procedural – are adopted to achieve integration. It explains how different objectives can influence institutional design and the integration model: for example, a free trade area could insist only on supremacy and refrain from adopting instruments for indirect rule, while a political union would rather engage with all available techniques in all their possible declinations: from the most sophisticated (such as preliminary ruling by domestic judges) to the most effective (such as "higher law" clauses). Finally, this book aims to provide academics and practitioners with a toolbox of concepts that may be fruitfully used

[10] G. Scelle, "Le droit public et la théorie de l'État," in G. Scelle *et al.* (eds.), *Introduction à l'étude du droit*, vol. I (Paris: Arthur Rousseau, 1951), pp. 32 *et seq.*; and S. Cassese, "Le droit tout puissant et unique de la société. Paradossi del diritto amministrativo," *Rivista Trimestrale di Diritto Pubblico* 895 (2010).

[11] For a similar approach in the context of the European Community, see the chapters by G. Gaia, P. Hay and R. Rotunda, in M. Cappelletti, M. Seccombe and J. H. H. Weiler (eds.), *Integration Through Law: Europe and the American Federal Experience* (Berlin and New York: Walter de Gruyter, 1985) (6 vols.), vol. I, Book 2, *Political Organs, Integration Techniques and Judicial Process*, pp. 113 *et seq.*

regardless of whether the "pendulum" swings towards "nationalism" or "transnationalism, federalism, or [a] broad grouping of states."[12]

The book further includes, as a study by Omri Sender, a detailed comparative overview of the design and role of secretariats serving selected regional organizations. Secretariats are the organs to which supra-State delegation happens (when it actually happens), and in trying to understand the potential and constraints of institutionalized international cooperation, their role should not be overlooked. The detailed parallels of operating experiences provided in the study offer a wealth of empirical evidence, and some general observations, to consider together with the thesis presented in Chapters 1 and 2.

Carlos Closa and Lorenzo Casini
Madrid and Rome

[12] M. Cappelletti, "Foreword" to P. Hay and R. D. Rotunda, *The United States Federal System* (Milan: Giuffrè, 1982), p. xi.

ABBREVIATIONS

AAEU	Agreement on Arab Economic Unity
ACP	Africa, Caribbean, Pacific Group of States
ACS	Association of Caribbean States
AEC	African Economic Community
AFTA	African Free Trade Area
AfTA	Asian Free Trade Area
ALADI	Asociación Latinoamericana de Integración
ALBA	Alternativa Bolivariana de las Américas
ANZCERTA	Australia New Zealand Closer Economic Agreement
APEC	Asia Pacific Economic Cooperation
APSA	African Peace and Security Architecture
ASEAN	Association of South East Asian Nations
ATJ	Andean Tribunal of Justice
AU	African Union
BMC	Budget and Management Committee (APEC)
CACJ	Central American Court of Justice
CACM	Central American Common Market
CAN	Community of Andean Nations
CARICOM	Caribbean Community
CCJ	Caribbean Court of Justice
CDS	South American Defense Council
CEFTA	Central European Free Trade Agreement

CEMAC	Communauté Économique et Monétaire de l'Afrique Centrale
CEN-SAD	Community of Sahel-Saharan States
CENTO	Central Treaty Organization
CFA	Communauté Financière Africaine
CHF	Swiss francs
CIS	Commonwealth of Independent States
CJEU	Court of Justice of the European Union
CLACS	Community of Latin American and Caribbean States
CMA	Common Monetary Area
CMC	Common Market Council (MERCOSUR)
CO	Coordinated Organizations
CoE	Council of Europe
COMESA	Common Market for Eastern and Southern Africa
DFAIT	Department of Foreign Affairs and International Trade
DLS	Department of Legal Services
EA Summit	East Asian Summit
EAC	East African Community
EACJ	East African Court of Justice
EAEC	East Asia Economic Caucus
EALA	East African Legislative Assembly
EASA	European Aviation Safety Agency
EC	European Community
ECCAS	Economic Community of Central African States

ECHA	European Chemicals Agency
ECJ	European Court of Justice
ECLAC	UN Economic Commission for Latin America and the Caribbean
ECO	Economic Cooperation Organization
ECOWAS	Economic Community of West African States
EEA	European Economic Area
EEC	European Economic Community
EES	European Economic Space
EFSA	European Food Safety Authority
EFTA	European Free Trade Association
EPO	European Patent Organization
ESO	EFTA Statistical Office
EU	European Union
EUI	European University Institute
FAO	Food and Agriculture Organization
FMSN	Frente Farabundo Martí de Salvación Nacional
FOCEM	Structural Convergence Fund for MERCOSUR
FSA	Financial Services Authority
GAFTA	Greater Arab Free Trade Area
GATT	General Agreement on Tariffs and Trade
GCC	Cooperation Council for the Arab States of the Gulf
GMC	Common Market Group (MERCOSUR)
GUAM	Organization for Democracy and Economic Development (ODED-GUAM)

IAEA	International Atomic Energy Agency
ICANN	Internet Corporation for Assigned Names and Numbers
ICAO	International Civil Aviation Organization
ICES	International Council for the Exploration of the Sea
IDA	International Development Agency
IGAD	Intergovernmental Authority on Development
IGO	intergovernmental organization
IHO	International Hydrographic Organization
ILO	International Labour Organization
IMF	International Monetary Fund
IMO	International Maritime Organization
IMSO	International Mobile Satellite Organization
INTERPOL	International Criminal Police Organization
IO	international organization
IOC	International Olympic Committee
IOM	International Organization for Migration
IOR-ARC	Indian Ocean Rim Association for Regional Co-operation
IOSCO	International Organization of Securities Commissions
ISO	International Organization for Standardization

ITRA	Inter-American Treaty for Reciprocal Assistance
ITSO	International Telecommunications Satellite Organization
ITU	International Telecommunication Union
KEDO	Korean Peninsula Energy Development Organization
LAFTA	Latin America Free Trade Area
LAIA	Latin American Integration Association (previously ALAC)
MERCOSUR/ MERCOSUL	Mercado Común del Sur / Mercado Comum do Sul / Common Market of the South
NAAEC	North American Agreement on Environmental Cooperation
NAALC	North American Agreement on Labor Cooperation
NAFTA	North American Free Trade Agreement
NATO	North Atlantic Treaty Organization
NCP	National Contact Point
NGO	non-governmental organization
OAS	Organization of American States
OAU	Organization of African Unity (now the AU)
OBSEC	Organization of Black Sea Economic Cooperation
OCAS	Organization of Central American States (ODECA)

ODECA	Organization of Central American States
ODED	Organization for Democracy and Economic Development (ODED-GUAM)
OECD	Organisation for Economic Co-operation and Development
OECS	Organization for Eastern Caribbean States
OEI	Organization of Iberoamerican States
OHADA	Organisation pour l'Harmonisation en Afrique du Droit des Affaires
OIC	Organization of the Islamic Conference
OIF	Organisation Internationale de la Francophonie
OPCW	Organization for the Prohibition of Chemical Weapons
OPEC	Organization of the Petroleum Exporting Countries
OSCE	Organization for Security and Co-operation in Europe
PACE	Parliamentary Assembly of the Council of Europe
PEIP	Planning and Evaluation of Individual Performance
PICES	North Pacific Marine Science Organization
PMU	Project Management Unit (APEC)
PSU	Policy Support Unit (APEC)
SAARC	South Asian Association for Regional Cooperation
SACU	Southern African Customs Union

SADC	Southern African Development Community
SADCC	Southern African Development Cooperation Conference
SAFTA	South Asia Free Trade Agreement
SCO	Shanghai Cooperation Organization
SEAFTA	Southeast Asia Free Trade Area
SEATO	South East Asia Treaty Organization
SICA	Sistema de la Integración Centroamericana
SOM	Senior Officials' Meeting (APEC)
SPA	Secretariat for Political Affairs (OAS)
SPS	Sanitary and Phyto-Sanitary Agreement (WTO)
TATF	Technical Assistance and Training Facility (APEC)
TBT	Technical Barriers to Trade Agreement (WTO)
TJCA	Tribunal de Justicia de la Comunidad Andina
TRIPS	Trade-Related Aspects of Intellectual Property Rights Agreement (WTO)
TTA	Treaty on the Andean Tribunal
UA	Units of Account
UEMOA/ WAEMU	West African Economic and Monetary Union
UMA	Union of the Arab Maghreb
UN	United Nations
UNASUR	Union of South American Nations

UNESCO	United Nations Educational, Scientific and Cultural Organization
UNICEF	United Nations Children's Fund
UNWTO	(UN) World Tourism Organization
UPU	Universal Postal Union
WAEMU/ UEMOA	West African Economic and Monetary Union
WAHO	West African Health Organization
WAMZ	West African Monetary Zone
WCO	World Customs Organization
WEU	Western European Union
WHO	World Health Organization
WIPO	World Intellectual Property Organization
WTO	World Trade Organization

Chapter 1

Governance structures and processes in integration organizations

Formalization of institutional credible commitments for governance

Carlos Closa*

1.1 Introduction: credible commitments and formalization

This chapter proposes the following thesis: States entering regional (and other) organizations accept *formal commitments* to achieve their goals with the expectation that other participant States will reciprocate.[1] The legal and institutional

* IPP-CSIC, Madrid, and Global Governance Program at the Robert Schumann Centre, European University Institute

[1] In the opposite sense, Kahler and Lake argue that personal, cultural or institutional ties between actors facilitate through reciprocity the making of credible commitments over time and space. Reciprocity acts as the enforcement mechanism. M. Kahler and D. A. Lake, "Explaining Regulatory Change in the Global Economy," in W. Mattli and N. Woods (eds.), *Explaining Regulatory Change in the Global Economy* (Princeton University Press, 2009). They follow A. Greif, *Institutions and the Path to the Modern Economy: Lessons from Medieval Trade* (Cambridge University Press, 2006) (available at http://books.google.com/books?id=2cwCxLAogNQC&pgis=1) and J. E. Rauch and A. Casella, *Networks and Markets* (New York: Russell Sage Foundation, 2001) (available at https://www.russellsage.org/publications/networks-and-markets).

features of the organization create credibility by locking participants into a system which regulates their behavior and restricts their ability to release themselves from the commitments accepted. By locking themselves into specific policy choices, States reduce the margin of action for future governments, and thus the risk that they will change them. My thesis is that the intensity and extent of the formal commitments depend directly on the kind of objectives/regional public goods that the organizations pursue. The larger the number of objectives, and the more ambitious in relation to the current *status quo*, the more robust the institutional commitments need to be if the organization is to succeed in attaining them. There is a trade-off between yielding sovereignty (that is, accepting credible commitments) and entering into complex integration schemes. Less ambitious objectives may be attained with a lower level of institutional commitment.

This study will focus on the formal mechanisms that secure "credible commitments." Credible commitments result from institutional design which comprises a number of instruments: the regulation of membership; the institutional structure of integration organizations; the decision-making procedure; the nature of derived norms and the mechanisms for their incorporation into national orders; and the mechanisms of jurisdictional control, supervision and scrutiny. Each of these serves to "lock" participants into integration schemes, and restricts their freedom to withdraw from accepted commitments.

By focusing on institutional design, this study adopts a clear position on regional integration: it considers that integration is a formal process. Current scholarship has consolidated a conceptual difference between "regionalization" and "regionalism."[2] These two concepts correspond to what in the 1990s W. Wallace insightfully named "informal" and "formal" integration respectively. Regionalization, or informal integration, refers to a spontaneous process of interaction between public or private actors, creating networks and directing flows towards each other in economic, security and cultural domains, among others.[3] On these lines, Álvarez proposes studying the alternative to traditional international organizations which comprises transgovernmental networks of regulators, non-binding inter-State institutions; public/private consortia and standard setting by private actors.[4] Similarly, Mansfield and Solingen refer to societal, bottom-up and often economically driven processes in constant flux, and Breslin and Higgott speak of processes of integration which, albeit seldom unaffected by State policies, derive their driving force from markets, from private trade and investment flows, and

[2] T. Behr and J. Jokela, *Regionalism and Global Governance: The Emerging Agenda*, Notre Europe Studies and Research No. 85 (2011) (available at www.notre-europe.eu/en/axes/europe-and-world-governance/works/publication/regionalism-global-governance); S. Breslin and R. Higgott, "Studying Regions, Learning from the Old, Constructing the New," 5:3 *New Political Economy* 344 (2000); L. Fawcett and H. Gandois, "Regionalism in Africa and the Middle East: Implications for EU Studies," 32:6 *Journal of European Integration* 617–636 (2010).

[3] W. Wallace, *The Dynamics of European Integration* (London: Pinter Publishers for the Royal Institute of International Affairs, 1992).

[4] J. E. Álvarez, "Institutionalised Legalization and the Asia-Pacific 'Region'," 5:1 *New Zealand Journal of Public and International Law* 9–28 (2007), p. 19.

from the policies and decisions of companies, rather than from predetermined government plans.[5]

In contrast, regionalism or formal integration is normally associated with a political project,[6] a top-down process which is highly institutionalized and State-led and which is channeled through formal instruments (that is, treaties).[7] The relationship between both forms, regionalization/informal integration and regionalism/formal integration, is a complex one. Sandholtz and Stone Sweet argue the existence of "the rule centre logic of institutionalisation," which leads transactors to demand clearer and more predictable rules as interdependence increases.[8] Logically also, the aim of formal integration is precisely to trigger informal integration or regionalization. Hence, the relationship between both can be construed as a circular one in which informal integration may trigger formal integration, and this in turn aims to provoke further informal integration or regionalization.

This study assesses the empirical models of formalization based upon a large sample of existing organizations across all continents. It does not explore the causality link

[5] E. D. Mansfield and E. Solingen, "Regionalism," 13:1 *Annual Review of Political Science*, 145–163 (2010) and S. Breslin and R. Higgott, "Studying Regions, Learning from the Old, Constructing the New," 5:3 *New Political Economy* 344 (2000).

[6] L. Fawcett and H. Gandois, "Regionalism in Africa and the Middle East: Implications for EU Studies," 32:6 *Journal of European Integration* 617–636 (2010), p. 619

[7] S. Breslin and R. Higgott, "Studying Regions, Learning from the Old, Constructing the New," 5:3 *New Political Economy* 344 (2000).

[8] W. Sandholtz and A. Stone Sweet, *European Integration and Supranational Governance* (New York: Oxford University Press, 1998).

between informal/formal integration, nor is this study interested in "measuring" informal integration or the achievements under informal integration. It rather explores the relationship between the type of objectives and public goods that an organization seeks to provide and the kin of institutional commitments designed for achieving them.

Despite criticism of this "soulless" process that lacks support from public opinion and/or citizens,[9] the focus of this study is formalization. Formalization means providing a treaty form for framing interactions and flows with the objective of fostering them and/or organizing already existing ones. Formalization provides a legal form for political

[9] In relation to Africa, Matthews argues that public sector organizations have driven regionalism from above and that it has lacked the support and involvement of the private sector and the general public (A. Matthews, *Regional Integration and Food Security in Developing Countries* (Rome: Food and Agriculture Organization of the United Nations, 2003)). In the case of MERCOSUR, Pena and Rozemberg point out that, unlike other integration experiences, the private sector and legislative representatives have not managed to become relevant forums of consultation for MERCOSUR institutions, nor have they substantively contributed to promoting the integration initiative within their respective societies (C. Pena and R. Rozemberg, *MERCOSUR: A Different Approach to Institutional Development* (The Canadian Foundation for the Americas (FOCAL), 2005) (available at www.focal.ca)). Lamy writes that regional integration processes have suffered from a lack of political and democratic involvement of public opinion. Integration processes habitually remain a top-down and in some respects technocratic exercise, with fairly little in the way of legitimacy (P. Lamy, "Regional Integrations in Africa: Ambitions and Vicissitudes/Intégrations Régionales en Afrique: Ambitions et Vicissitudes," Notre Europe Policy Paper No. 43 (2005), p. 33 (available at www.eng.notre-europe.eu/media/policypaper_43_lamy_02.pdf?pdf=ok)).

commitments and, through this form, increases their credibility. This is true whether these produce a transfer of powers or, conversely, represent a commitment to prevent power transfer. The tendency towards formalization is growing, with a significant number of treaties signed every year among different groups of actors. Behind this mushrooming lies the belief that treaties are a good instrument for promoting stated goals in regional (and indeed other kinds of) cooperation schemes.

Formalization reflects the strongest point along the scale composed of the three components of the legalization paradigm[10] (that is, obligation).[11] Obligation means that States (or other actors) are legally bound by rules or other forms of commitment. In formal integration schemes, treaties fulfill the function of creating a legal obligation which is subject to scrutiny under the general rules, procedures and discourses of international law.[12] Whilst informal integration (that is, regionalization) goes beyond the scope of this study, it may be

[10] K. W. Abbott *et al.*, "The Concept of Legalization," 54:3 *International Organization* 401–419 (2000).

[11] Another component of the legalization paradigm, delegation (i.e. existence of third parties with authority to implement, interpret and apply the rules, to resolve disputes and – possibly – to make further rules) is examined under a slightly different construction in section 1.2 below. The third component, precision (i.e. unambiguous definition of the conduct that rules require, authorize or prescribe) is not directly examined in this study. For a strong criticism of the legalization paradigm, see J. E. Álvarez, "Institutionalised Legalization and the Asia-Pacific 'Region'," 5:1 *New Zealand Journal of Public and International Law* 9–28 (2007).

[12] K. W. Abbott *et al.*, "The Concept of Legalization," 54:3 *International Organization* 401–419 (2000).

hypothesized that it is also subject to legalization, but of a very different kind: whenever flows of goods, people, money, services and so on exist, they rely on the existing domestic law (and politics) of the origin, transit and destination. Whilst operating on a legal enabling structure of domestic law, a formalized overarching structure may not have emerged for these flows.

Formalization means a formal (i.e. treaty) legal framework created either for existing informal interactions or else to promote them. Formalization does not necessarily imply rigidity or inflexibility though, nor indeed uniformity or homogeneity. In practice, formalization covers a wide array of practices spanning integration schemes and international organizations. Importantly, formalization does not imply "freezing" organizations at the foundational moment. Rather, formalization serves to adapt organizations to changing circumstances and objectives. Nor does formalization require uniformity and/or single institutional structure; it does not remit to a Cartesian structure of single organizations per geographical area and sector of activity. Rather, formalization has served to create a thick web of overlapping institutions and organisms. Formalization does not result in an inflexible design either; instead it accommodates flexible membership (accommodating acceding States, but also allowing for withdrawal) and differentiated geometry through a variety of mechanisms. In short, formalization does not lead to a world of uniformity, but rather to one of plurality. This variety, evolution overlapping, flexibility and differentiation is examined in the following sections.

Sections 1.3 to 1.7 examine the structure of formalized institutional commitments by looking at the organs for decision-making, the procedures for taking decisions and the model of derived norms. Section 1.8 then provides a classification of the different integration schemes by examining the relationship between an integration organization's objectives and the formal instruments available to it for generating credible commitments. As the thesis of this chapter is that the objectives of regional integration organizations inspire a given institutional structure, Section 1.3 examines the kind of objectives existing within integration organizations.

1.2 Methodological considerations

The analysis of the formal characteristics of integration organizations derives from a data set specifically built for this project. The data set comprises institutional features of eighty-five integration and/or international organizations. Comparative integration being the object of this project, the sample includes all organizations that define integration either as one among several or their main objective. The sample also includes organizations which do not have integration as one of their objectives and have alternative ones. This makes the sample richer and, moreover, increases variation, which, in turn, permits identifying models. This book does not focus on agreements or treaties, but rather on organizations, since its objective is to assess the institutional modalities existing within formal organizations. An agreement may or may not generate organs (i.e. formal institutions). Naturally, integration may also result from the combination of a set of overlapping treaties without a strong structure of formal institutions behind them. Capturing this reality will require a different research design, but the research question emerging would be slightly different (that is, how integration happens).

The sample selected permits dealing with the main research question (that is, what is the relation between the objectives of a given organization and the institutional design chosen?). The introduction of variation in terms of objective allows observing divergence in terms of institutional design. And this relates to the main purpose, which is to substantiate analytical models of "integration organizations." The organizations in the sample are listed in the abbreviations at the start of this book. These organizations may have either regional or global reach; they may aim at extensive or punctual objectives, and these can be highly specific or grossly undefined. Two specific cases are given special treatment. On the one hand, we do not discuss ASEAN extensively since the *specifics of its governance, legal order and community building* are the topic of most of the studies in the series. Furthermore, a specific volume will discuss in detail the ASEAN model in relation to the comparative template that this book proposes. This treatment does not imply conceding credit to the arguments on the *sui generis* nature of ASEAN: all organizations possess formal institutions and ASEAN is no exception. The EU is the other special case. A significant number of comparative studies take the EU as the explicit or implicit model followed in other cases (for instance, the so-called diffusion paradigm[13]). Unavoidably, some normative conclusions are drawn out of the comparison, making the EU the standard of integration to achieve. This has prompted strong

[13] T. A. Börzel and T. Risse, "From Europeanisation to Diffusion: Introduction," 35:1 *West European Politics* 1–19 (2012).

reactions against "eurocentrism."[14] In order to control this methodological bias, the EU is taken as a case among others in every section and, for the purposes of illustrating the argument, other cases will usually be presented as examples. This methodological caution is particularly relevant for matters of design of organizations' bodies, and the introduction to Section 1.5 will reassert the case. Epistemologically, this research questions the plea for recognizing the uniqueness of different integration organizations. This advocates underlining idiosyncratic explanations which exist in any other case (from SADC to MERCOSUR). Idiosyncrasy precludes comparison, which is the very reason for a project on comparative regional integration. Hence, we believe that the plea to take into account idiosyncratic features does not make much sense in epistemological terms. Rather, research on comparative regionalism/regional integration needs to be mainstreamed.[15]

1.3 Objectives: creating commitments to achieving public goods

The commitment to certain objectives, principles and values acts as meta-orienter of the organization. These serve to

[14] F. Söderbaum and A. Sbragia, "EU Studies and the 'New Regionalism': What Can Be Gained from Dialogue?," 32:6 *Journal of European Integration* 563–582 (2010); P. Murray, "Comparative Regional Integration in the EU and East Asia: Moving Beyond Integration Snobbery," 47 *International Politics* 308–323 (2010); A. Acharya, "Comparative Regionalism: A Field Whose Time Has Come?," 47:1 *International Spectator: Italian Journal of International Affairs* 3–15 (2012).

[15] C. Closa, *Mainstreaming Regionalism*, EUI RSCAS Working Paper 2015/12, Global Governance Programme-158.

"lock" participants into integration schemes (whilst restricting their freedom to back away from accepted commitments). Specifically, objectives identify the purpose of a given organization: the purpose of its creation should in theory be readily understood just by reading its objectives. Naturally, drafters may not faithfully translate the real objectives behind given organizations, and organizations may have implicit (that is, derived but not explicitly mentioned) or undeclared objectives. Moreover, objectives may evolve through time and/or organizations may add new goals to the original ones. What is relevant from the point of view of this inquiry is that objectives, *prima facie*, set commitments to attain specific public goods that the organization aims to achieve.

The objectives of an organization define the completeness of its contract, that is, its degree of precision and absence of need for interpretation. Marks *et al.*[16] differentiate the completeness of organizational contracts according to the objectives. Thus, a relatively complete contract commits Member States to a fixed objective under clearly specified conditions. Intermediate contracts (that is, less complete ones) commit to vague objectives such as enhancing peaceful coexistence among Member States, or fostering their economic and social development. A highly incomplete contract commits Member States to vague purposes such as, according to them, a "community of peoples" or an "even closer union," to be achieved by unspecified actors through an open-ended

[16] G. Marks *et al.*, *Discovering Cooperation: A Contractual Approach to Institutional Change in Regional International Organizations*, EUI RSCAS Working Paper 2014/65, Global Governance Programme-113.

process. These authors establish a relationship between the completeness of the contract and institutional change: organizations resting on highly incomplete contracts (that is, those involving unspecified obligations that are open to interpretation) are much more likely to undergo endogenous institutional change than institutions based on relatively complete contracts. Without testing the validity of the dynamic relationship between objectives and institutional design, this chapter develops a static version of the same: incomplete contracts with wide and underspecified objectives would *prima facie* require a more complex set of institutions and procedures to implement them and to give them more specific content. Hence, complex, vague and extensive objectives correlate with a larger and more complex institutional design. Whilst this section presents a typology of objectives, Section 1.8 will relate them to institutional design.

Table 1.1 proposes a typology for the classification of objectives that follows its "*ratione materiae*" based on the declared ones. The classification is not dichotomous and the table does not include the subset of IOs which have specific sectoral/functional objectives, such as the ILO or the WHO, and it restricts itself to organizations that may be loosely associated with the notion of integration.

Economic objectives prevail among those organizations that are associated, however loosely, with "integration." These organizations can be positioned along the Bela Balassa successive stages.[17] Free trade is the objective of those

[17] B. Balassa, *The Theory of Economic Integration* (Homewood, IL: Richard D. Irwin, 1961).

Table 1.1 *Typology of objectives in regional integration and international organizations*

Objectives	Organizations
Free trade	AFTA, ASEAN, ECO, EFTA, GAFTA, IOR-ARC, NAFTA, OECD, SEAFTA
Customs union	AfTA, Eurasian Community
Market	ASEAN, BEU, LAFTA, LAIA, MERCOSUR, Pacific Alliance, UMA
Economic union	AAEU, AU, CARICOM (very specific objectives), CEN-SAD, ECCAS, WAEMU
Integration	AFTA (economic), ALBA, APEC Forum (economic), AU (socioeconomic), CAN (integration as means to development), ECCAS (human plus physical, economic and monetary integration), ECOWAS (economic), GUAM (European), OCAS (Central America), OECS (economic East Caribbean), SICA, UNASUR
Cooperation/harmonization of policies	ACS, Arab League, ASEAN, CIS, EAC, ECCAS, ECO, GCC, GUAM, IDA, IOR-ARC, MERCOSUR, NATO, OAS, OBSEC, OECS, SAARC, SCO
Development	AEC, APEC Forum (sustainable economic growth), CAN, CIS, COMESA (sustainable growth), ECO, IDA, IOR-ARC, LAIA, OAS, OCAS, OECD, SAARC, SADC, SICA, UNASUR
Security/peace	ASEAN, AU, CENTO, CIS, COMESA, EA Summit, ECCAS, GUAM, IDA, NATO, OAS, SEATO, SICA, UMA
Defense of sovereignty, territorial integrity and independence	Arab League, AU, OECS, OIC
World role	ASEAN, AU, CAN, ECO, OECS, OIC, UNASUR

Table 1.1 (*cont.*)

Objectives	Organizations
Rights and freedoms/ democracy, rule of law and human rights	CIS, CoE, COMESA, GUAM, OAS, OIC, SADC, SICA

Source: Own elaboration

organizations which call themselves "free trade areas/agreements," a designation that immediately conveys a lack of interest in formalization and institutionalization. A clear exception is the Economic Cooperation Organization (ECO), which lists free trade among its objectives, when this would be better understood as a derived or secondary objective. In fact, *a characteristic of "free trade associations" is that they do not have additional objectives beyond this specific economic one.*

Prima facie, global trade and regional integration/ regionalism seem to embody contradictory principles: whilst the first assumes total openness of national markets to any State, the second restricts this openness to specific regional clusters of States. To solve this dichotomy, a number of authors and even the UN ECLA sponsored the notion of "open regionalism" which seeks to reconcile the potential conflict between "free trade" and "preferential free trade" (inherent to regional agreements).[18] A number of devices

[18] See CEPAL, *Open Regionalism in Latin America and the Caribbean: Economic Integration as a Contribution to Changing Production Patterns with Social Equity* (UN ECLA, 1994) (available at www.eclac.cl); and

make this possible, but contradictions still remain.[19] The APEC embraced the concept at its inception in 1989 and has championed it ever since, most clearly with the Bogor 1994 Declaration. The reference to the objective of "world role" or "world insertion" provides an additional interpretative clue: thus, ASEAN's objective can be coherently linked to the notion of "open regionalism," whilst in the case of UNASUR, or even CAN or MERCOSUR, the organization's world role has a more defensive character.

Following the Bela Balassa stages of economic integration, the second category of objectives comprises the creation of a "customs union." Only two organizations adhere to this as a final and single objective: the African Free Trade Area (AFTA) and the Eurasian Community (EAEC). However, AfTA defines customs union as a previous step (and hence subordinate objective) of the common African market for three African communities: COMESA, EAC and SADC. This leaves the Russia-led EAEC as the only one placing sole emphasis on a customs union. One may deduce from this that, whilst "free trade" inspires a significant number of international arrangements, the creation of a customs union in itself is not a determinant objective for international organizations overall. An explanation may be that "customs union" is in the main perceived as a transitional and therefore provisional stage in the path towards the two upper stages in the

C. F. Bergsten, *Open Regionalism*, Peterson Institute for International Economics Working Paper 97/3, 1997 (available at www.iie.com/publications/wp/wp.cfm?ResearchID=152).

[19] Bergsten, *ibid.*

Bela Balassa construction: the creation of a "market" and/or an "economic union." When these two objectives are considered, the number of cases in which organizations hold them as their aim enlarges significantly. According to Bela Balassa, a "common market" represents a "lower" integration threshold.

However, organizations having the (common or single, and so on) market as their driving objective may simultaneously pursue political objectives; this is the case of ASEAN and UMA (in both cases, the political objective is security and peace promotion) and it could easily be argued that MERCOSUR has also adhered to political objectives (that is, the protection of democracy). Organizations declaring economic union as their main objective may also refer simultaneously to the overarching objective of "integration." This is the case for AU and ECCAS. Surprisingly, not many organizations define "integration" as an explicit objective. Moreover, when they do, they do not mean exactly the same. For instance, "integration" objectives may mean socioeconomic (AU), economic (APEC Forum), human plus physical, economic and monetary integration (ECCAS) or integration as a means to development (CAN). It would thus be difficult to define "integration" were one to use these organizations' shared objectives as a starting point. As an alternative to integration, several organizations use the objective of "cooperation and/or harmonisation of policies." The list of organizations subscribing to these goals generally includes those with less commitment to a higher level of integration (with three exceptions: ECCAS, ECO and EAC).

A significant number of organizations define "*development*" as a driving objective; for instance, CAN sees "integration" as a means of achieving "development." Development implies a socioeconomic dimension which concerns improving living conditions for the population as an active policy, rather than as a by-product of trade. In some schemes (for instance, APEC Forum or COMESA), development is associated with "sustainable growth." Whatever the meaning given to it, development appears as a meaningful objective which is counterposed to the notion of "open regionalism" in several integration schemes. This happens in contexts as different as Latin America and Africa. In the former, UNASUR has been described as post-liberal regionalism whose characteristics are, on the one hand, a rejection of the neoliberal policies of the Washington consensus – which some regional leaders identify expressly with "open regionalism" and with groups such as MERCOSUR and CAN[20] – and, on the other, a strategy at the service of the developing State. In Africa, regional integration remains a key component of the *development strategy* for countries in Southern Africa. Comparing the South East Asian and African models, Draper *et al.* write that, for the former, the overriding adherence to the linear textbook model of regional integration means that the central focus continues to be trade in goods, with much energy still devoted to negotiations on tariffs issues.[21] These authors also

[20] J. A. Sanahuja, "Multilateralismo y regionalismo en clave sudamericana: El caso de UNASUR," 33 *Pensamiento Propio* 115–157 (2011), p. 122.

[21] P. Draper, D. Halleson and P. Alves, *SACU, Regional Integration and the Overlap Issue in Southern Africa: From Spaghetti to Cannelloni?*, Trade Policy Report No. 15, South African Institute of International Affairs, 2007, p. 2 (available at http://sarpn.org/documents/d0002411/SACU_SAIIA_Jan2007.pdf).

noticed that it is increasingly agreed that the real challenge to regional integration for South East Asia lies behind the borders. In contrast with South East Asia, regional integration in Southern Africa continues to be focused on intraregional matters.

Political or non-economic objectives also feature within integration schemes with three prevalent categories: (i) peace and security (singled out as an objective by a significant number of organizations); (ii) the defense of sovereignty, territorial integrity and independence (AU, Arab League, OECS, OIC); and (iii) the respect of human rights and freedoms, democracy and the rule of law (CIS, GUAM, OAS, OIC, SICA, SADC). Whilst peace and security may be conceived of as regional public goods, the latter two groups of concepts differ from the former in that they may also be enunciated by a large number of organizations as principles inspiring their functioning rather than as goals to be attained. Moreover, they raise some contradictory issues which shine light on the nature of the organization. On the one hand, entering into a regional/international organization may be in contradiction with a complete assertion of sovereignty and independence. On the other hand, democracy and human rights make sense in the case of associations of democratic States, but appear contradictory if the Member States are not democratic. As will be illustrated below, States increasingly perceive regional integration as a powerful framework for locking in commitments to democracy and human rights in the face of threats of domestic revolution. This works both for States with a weak democracy and also for more robust democracies which aim to create a supra-State "straitjacket" for the organization's membership.

Objectives, though, do not remain static and unchanged through time. Member States usually update them, either by adding new ones or adapting old ones to new needs. This process of changing objectives is of utmost importance to the nature of organizations, since it is determinative of the preference of States for sticking to (upgraded) existing organizations.

1.3.1 Evolving objectives

Organizations do not necessarily freeze around the specific set of objectives initially agreed. In fact, formal change to treaties remains an instrument used to accommodate change, be it to help achieve the original objectives, include new ones, acquire new members, change ideological orientation, and so on. *Ceteribus paribus,* the cost of adding new objectives to existing organizations is lower than creating new organizations for these new goals, and this explains both the permanence and the change of organizations. Adding new objectives to existing organizations is a less costly and less risky strategy (in terms of uncertainty) than creating new ones.

Examples of this use of existing organizations to accommodate new objectives and relaunch original designs exist in both Latin America and Africa. Latin American States created the initial integration organizations in the 1960s[22]

[22] The intellectual sources diverged widely between the three regions (Andean, South Cone and Central America). Two of these (Andean and Central America) had brief experiences of political integration in the nineteenth century. Andean integration in the 1960s was propelled by

by means of treaties which they revised in the 1990s; and this happened both in the Andean area[23] and in Central America.[24] MERCOSUR is a more recent product, but it has a similar evolutionary history through successive treaties.[25]

the ECLA and the influential thesis of its first general director, Raúl Prebistch, on the "import substitution" paradigm. Central American integration, in turn, owed much to US promotion of the creation of a buffer against Communist Cuban influence in the area. Integration in the South Cone derives from the need to accommodate rivalry and cooperation between Argentina and Brazil. A similar influence was exerted by the UN in Africa: the UN Economic Commission for Africa (UNECA) became the champion of regional integration, already in the mid-1960s, proposing the division of Africa into regions for the purposes of economic development. The subsequent Abuja Treaty, signed in 1991, divided the continent into five regional areas, the north, west, south, east and center, in preparation for establishing the AEC.

23 The *Acuerdo de Cartagena* (1969) launched the Andean Community, and the Protocol of Trujillo (1997) adapted the original scheme to changes in the international system.

24 In Central America, the 1991 *Protocolo de Tegucigalpa* created the SICA over the preexisting Central American Common Market (MCC) created by two successive treaties: *the Tratado Multilateral de Libre Comercio e Integración Económica Centroamericana* (1958) and the *Tratado de Integración Económica Centroamericana* (1960).

25 MERCOSUR's origins lie in the bilateral agreement between Argentina and Brazil called *Acta para la integración Argentino-Brasileña* (1986), which was substituted in 1988 by a *Tratado de Integración, Cooperación y Desarrollo* (Treaty of Integration, Cooperation and Development) with the objective of creating an area of free trade within ten years. The founding treaties of MERCOSUR are the *Tratado de Asunción* (1991) (whose declared objective was the creation of a common market) and the Protocols of Ouro Preto (1994) and Olivos (2002). The former defined MERCOSUR institutions and their role and functions, whilst the latter regulated the system of dispute resolution.

Initially, demands for institutionalization were limited because of the combination of low interdependence and the relative concentration of power in just two members (Argentina and Brazil).[26] In parallel, MERCOSUR drafters adopted a "gradualist" approach which meant that organizations were created only as and when the process required them. The Asunción Treaty established the institutions that would govern MERCOSUR during the transition period (from 1991 to 1994), leaving open the possibility of creating new institutions or modifying the intergovernmental organization.[27] The same approach towards institutional framework inspired the Ouro Preto Protocol, which, once again, was temporary.

A similar pattern of updating preexisting organizations in order to adapt them to changing circumstances and/or objectives also exists on the African continent. Thus, the initial three customs unions of the 1960s[28] did not become the foundational stones of regional integration. It was rather the OAU-sponsored Lagos Plan that promoted the formalization of regional integration. The plan encompasses three

[26] C. Pena and R. Rozemberg, *MERCOSUR: A Different Approach to Institutional Development* (The Canadian Foundation for the Americas (FOCAL), 2005) (available at www.focal.ca).

[27] *Ibid.*

[28] These are the Customs Union of West African States (UDEA, 1966), the Economic and Customs Union of Central Africa (UDEAC, 1964) with the associated Bank of Central African States (BEAC, 1961), and the Southern African Customs Union (SACU, 1969) with the associated Common Monetary Area (CMA).

regional arrangements aimed at the creation of separate but convergent and overarching integration arrangements in three sub-Saharan sub-regions. The Treaty of Lagos (1975) established the Economic Community of West African States (ECOWAS) with a basic institutional structure which the Cotonou Treaty (1993) then reinforced. A number of protocols complemented provisions on the Parliament and the Court of Justice. For Central Africa, the 1983 Treaty of the Economic Community of Central African States (ECCAS) remains to be fully ratified. Finally, East and Southern Africa comprises a wide geographical area in which a number of overlapping treaties formalized forms of cooperation and evolved afterwards. Thus, in 1993 the Common Market for Eastern and Southern Africa (COMESA) replaced the initial Preferential Trade Area (PTA), which had been established in 1981. In East Africa, the East African Community (EAC) Treaty (signed in November 1999 and which entered into force on July 7, 2000) resurrects the original Community of the same name which existed from 1967 to 1977. After Rwanda and Burundi joined in November 2006, the EAC approved its *Development Strategy 2006–2010*, which exemplifies evolving formalization to adapt to new objectives. This strategy aims, specifically, to amend the founding Treaty, particularly the provisions that deal with the definition of the Community. It is designed to address issues such as: definition of the EAC as a subject of international law; timetable for achievement of objectives; partner States' commitment to the treaty; decision-making process within the EAC; separation of powers of the organs of the EAC; composition of the East African Legislative Assembly (EALA); election of members of the EALA and the related functions; and jurisdiction of the East African Court of Justice (EACJ), among others.[29]

Outside the master design of the Lagos Plan, the SADC provides another example of how formalization evolves to adapt to changing circumstances, transforming and enlarging original objectives. Originally, the SADCC Treaty (1979) provided a collective response of Southern African States to the South African apartheid regime. SADCC focused on reducing economic reliance on the apartheid government and promoting economic cooperation among its members, and, because of this, it has been termed the economic pillar of the anti-colonial and anti-apartheid struggle of the region.[30] It had a loose institutional structure, no legal binding framework, a decentralized structure where each Member State was allocated a sector for coordination, and each Member State took responsibility for the implementation of policy decisions. But, once the apartheid regime ended in 1992, the SADCC evolved into the SADC, including its former adversary, South Africa. Strong formalization in strong contrast with its previous looseness marked this evolution: whilst a *Memorandum of Understanding* which promoted the independence and sovereignty of Member States and a minimum level of institutionalization regulated the original SADCC, the new SADC Treaty enlarged the

[29] *Proposed Review and Amendment of the Treaty for the Establishment of the East African Community* (Arusha: EAC Secretariat, 2007).

[30] L. Fawcett and H. Gandois, "Regionalism in Africa and the Middle East: Implications for EU Studies," 32:6 *Journal of European Integration* 617–636 (2010).

objectives of the Community to new areas not covered by the previous SADCC. It also removed the optional character of treaty obligations. Within the same geographical area, SACU offers a model of radical upgrading. Created by the colonial power (Great Britain) in 1910 in order to facilitate economic transactions in the Southern Africa region, SACU Member States concluded a new agreement in 1969 and the 2002 SACU Treaty (which has not been fully implemented).

Democracy and respect for human rights is an increasingly common objective in integration schemes and it exists in almost all geographical areas. Most of these provisions emerged after 1989, when geopolitical change allowed the principle of democracy to acquire normative hegemony.[31] Several cases illustrate this development: in collaboration with Chile and Bolivia, MERCOSUR elaborated the *Democratic Compromise* (1996), and later the *Ushuaia Protocol* (1998). In Africa, ECOWAS adopted the 2001 *Protocol on Democracy and Good Governance*, and SADC adopted in 2004 the *Principles and Guidelines Governing Democratic Elections*. Mansfield and Milner have argued that democratic leaders seek free trade agreements since this enhances their prospects of retaining power.[32] They illustrate their argument precisely with the cases of SADC and MERCOSUR, arguing that newly

[31] C. Closa, *Institutional Design of Democratic Conditionality in Regional Organizations*, EUI RSCAS Working Paper 2013/45, Global Governance Programme-54.

[32] E. D. Mansfield and H. V. Milner, *Votes, Vetoes, and the Political Economy of International Trade Agreements* (Princeton University Press, 2012).

democratic governments in these States sought to freeze their commitment with free trade, releasing it from the control of their domestic constituencies. But a more convincing argument is that newborn democracies seek membership in regional organizations (and, in general, in international agreements) as a pre-commitment strategy: they seek to anchor the newborn regime in the set of norms provided by regional organizations as a mechanism to prevent domestic actors overturning democracy. In accordance with this strategy, regional integration organizations have simultaneously constructed a democratic requirement for membership (see Sections 1.4.1.1 and 1.4.1.3 below).

Adding new objectives to existing formal agreements plays a very important role: it reinforces States' commitment to formalization with institutional structures. In fact, one of the most common objectives of treaty revision is precisely the strengthening of preexisting institutional structures. In parallel, the repetition of formalization also serves the seemingly contradictory purpose of changing and/or updating objectives. Repetition contributes to creating a path: since the costs of using existing organizations to provide new public goods are lower than creating new ones, States find it more logical to use and reuse existing structures rather than facing the costs of creating new ones.

1.3.2 *Overlapping objectives among institutions and organizations*

Integration rarely happens by means of a single institutional structure per geographical area and sector of activity. In fact, virtually every integration scheme is inserted in a thick web of overlapping, competing and completing alternative structures, which generate the very descriptive but analytically frustrating notion of a "spaghetti bowl."[33] Figures 1.1 to 1.4 depict the web of regional (and other) organizations, providing thus an image of the density of organizational relations among States.

Three types of organization may overlap (both in objectives and/or membership) at any given moment in time and in a particular geographical area. First, organizations with the same objectives and even identical membership may coexist. This phenomenon is particularly acute in the domain of trade and economic integration. Second, integration schemes may be framed by overarching organizations that express some form of identity (be this geographical, cultural or even religious). Third, in Latin America and Africa, overlapping responds partially to an *ad hoc* design and cumulative efforts but also to the different (and even competing) ideological inspiration behind the various schemes. Whilst free trade permeates several integration organizations, development (Africa) and post-liberal integration (Latin America) also inform the creation of some alternative ones.

[33] According to A. Sbragia, "Review Article: Comparative Regionalism: What Might It Be?," 46 *Journal of Common Market Studies* 29–49 (2008), p. 37. J. Bhagwati, "Regionalism and Multilateralism: An Overview" in J. D. Melo and A. Panagariya (eds.), *New Dimensions in Regional Integration* (Cambridge University Press, 1993), coined the now universally used image of a "spaghetti bowl" to symbolize the complex set of trade agreements that jeopardized global free trade.

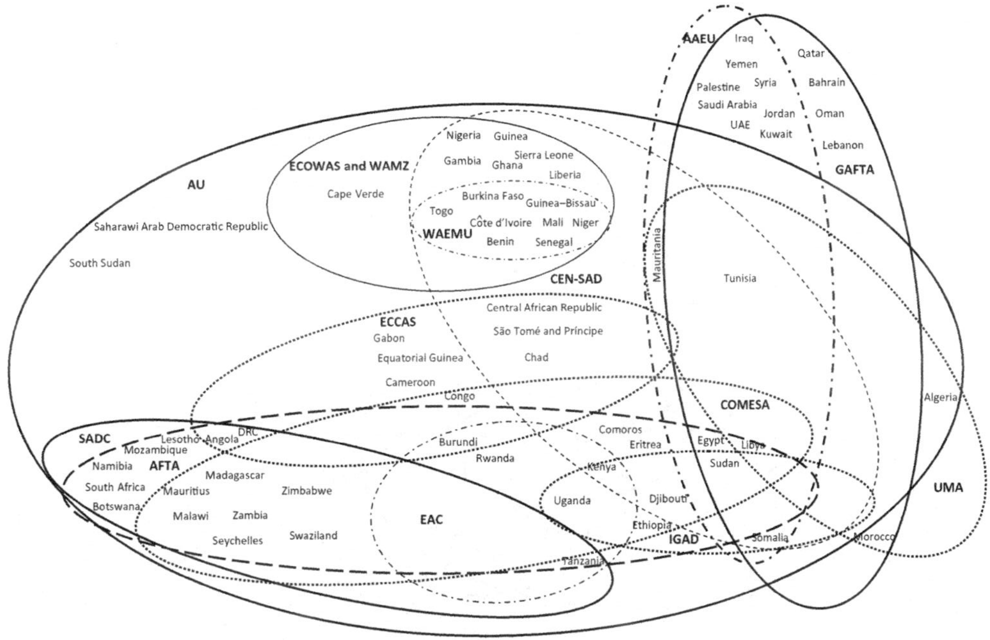

Figure 1.1 Regional integration schemes in Africa

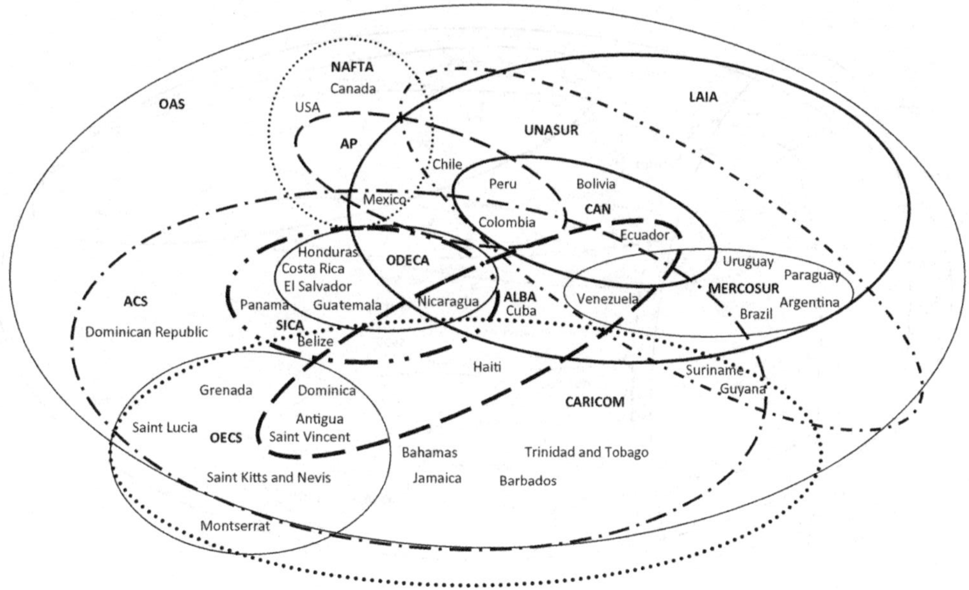

Figure 1.2 Regional integration schemes in America

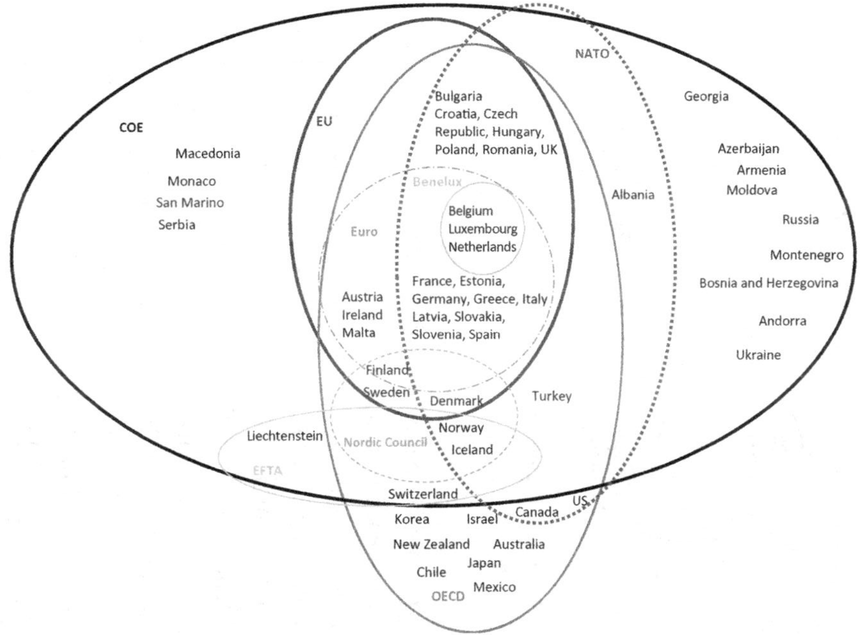

Figure 1.3 Regional integration schemes in Europe

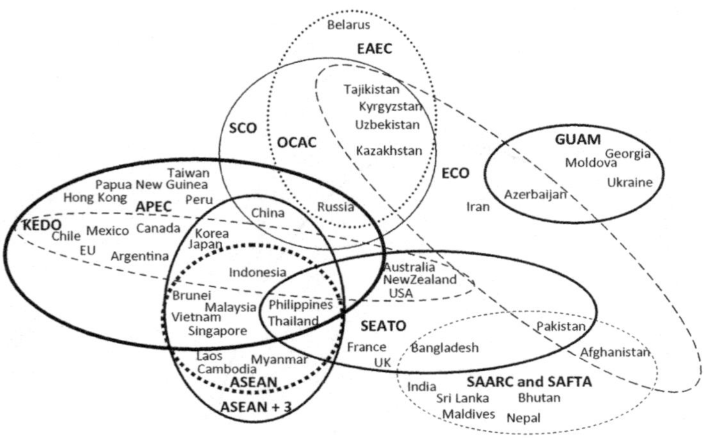

Figure 1.4 Regional integration schemes in Asia

1.3.2.1 Competing organizations: same objectives, different institutions

Organizations with similar objectives and/or aims exist around all integration schemes. Thus, in Europe, the initial European Communities competed with the EFTA. Nowadays, the existence of the EES accommodates non-EU members within a common market structure led by the EU. In the Americas, the Free Trade Area of the Americas tried to create a dense web of bilateral trade agreements, which in turn overlaps with existing integration organizations. It also overlaps with the Latin America ALADI, which was created as a promoter of integration via bilateral agreements, and as an umbrella for any emerging "integration" scheme. In recent decades, a competing paradigm has sought to provide alternative ideological hegemony for integration efforts: the

Venezuela-sponsored ALBA, which is basically a scheme for the exchange of State-owned goods. Lately, UNASUR has also assumed a role in the coordination of existing economic agreements: CAN and MERCOSUR. Although UNASUR's geopolitical orientation seems more evident, it also aims to create a free trade area between both schemes.

The overlapping of organizations with similar objectives is particularly acute in Africa, where no fewer than fourteen regional integration schemes coexist.[34] Further, each geographical region has a minimum of two groups, and States often belong to a minimum of two regional organizations. The problems resulting from multiple and overlapping memberships hinder regional integration by creating a complex entanglement of political commitments and institutional requirements which may affect informal integration processes. For example, in East and Southern Africa, COMESA coexisted with two other integration schemes: the SADC[35]

34 S. Cleary, "Variable Geometry and Varying Speed: An Operational Paradigm for SADC," in C. Clapham, G. Mills, A. Morner and E. Sidiropoulos (eds.), *Regional Integration in Southern Africa: Comparative International Perspectives* (Pretoria: South African Institute of International Affairs, 2001), pp. 87–104; P. Draper, D. Halleson and P. Alves, *SACU, Regional Integration and the Overlap Issue in Southern Africa: From Spaghetti to Cannelloni?*, Trade Policy Report No. 15, South African Institute of International Affairs, 2007.

35 All SACU members are members of SADC, while Swaziland is a member of both SADC and COMESA (subject to an annual derogation from the other four SACU members). Four of the five countries are also members of the Common Monetary Area (CMA), with Botswana being the exception.

and the EAC (first created in 1967). Membership between these organizations overlapped, and, to add further confusion, in 2008 the twenty-six-Member States comprising these three organizations agreed to establish a free trade area.

But why does overlapping happen? Part of the answer may be that the maintenance of a large number of competing and overlapping intergovernmental regional organizations is deliberate in order to increase the possibilities for rhetorical and discursive regionalism. One related hypothesis in need of further research is that weak political regimes are particularly prone to such behavior and may search for as many arenas as possible to satisfy their quest for formal status and recognition.[36]

External actors have acted as promoters of a certain "rationalization," eliminating dual membership of existing organizations whilst simultaneously promoting patterns of regionalization. In Africa, both the AU, through its African Economic Community, and the EU have adopted initiatives in this direction. In 1991, the AEC designed an overarching project for already existing regional integration communities. The treaty envisaged, as the first stage in the creation of an African Community, strengthening the existing regional economic communities, and establishing new communities where these did not exist, in order to ensure the gradual establishment of the African Community (Article 28). The AU consciously stimulates integration along regional blocks

[36] F. Söderbaum, *What's Wrong with Regional Integration? The Problem of Eurocentrism*, EUI RSCAS Working Paper 2013/64, Global Governance Programme-63.

as part of the pan-African identity, and it also stimulated some rationalization of the membership between the three communities (ECOWAS, ECCAS and COMESA). The AEC's power as "rationalizer" is greatly enhanced by the fact that it has the competence to act as "norm provider" for a subcontinental regional organization: AEC's Decisions and Regulations are binding on the regional economic communities (Articles 10 and 13 AEC Treaty).[37] In parallel, the EU has acted in the same way, although not in an entirely converging direction. The EU has used the negotiation of the Economic Partnership Agreements (EPAs) to demand a similar rationalization and eliminate overlapping. However, configurations of States in EPA negotiations are not coterminous with existing regional economic schemes and this makes it difficult for constituent countries to agree on common negotiating positions. The EUI allocated European Development Funds to the groupings negotiating EPAs rather than existing regional organizations in the period (2008–2013). This places considerable pressure on countries to consolidate their

[37] This role does not go totally unchallenged. Thus P. Draper, D. Halleson and P. Alves, *SACU, Regional Integration and the Overlap Issue in Southern Africa: From Spaghetti to Cannelloni?*, Trade Policy Report No. 15, South African Institute of International Affairs, 2007, p. 35, argued that "SACU members should not be overly concerned with developments at the continental or AU level. It is doubtful whether the AU will have the political legitimacy or clout to impose its vision of economic integration on the disparate economic regions; nor is the African Economic Community a feasible medium-term objective. However, the problems inherent in overlapping memberships are real and need to be tackled at the regional level because that is where their ill effects are directly experienced."

memberships if they are to access those regional resources; it also places pressure on the secretariats to justify their existence, given that they will not actually allocate the funding.[38]

1.3.2.2 Identity-framing organizations: continental, ethnic and religious

Narratives of the existing continental and/or subcontinental identities based on cultural, historical, social and other kinds of factors have been instrumental to the processes of regional integration. European, American/Latin American, African and Arab and/or Islamic identities have been appealed to in order to strengthen the case for integration. Pan-Americanism, pan-Africanism and pan-Arabism were founded on shared conceptions of history and culture (sometimes imagined) and a common project for the advancement of decolonization.[39] Notably, Asia is the only area that lacks both a narrative on identity and a continental or supra-regional organization.

Identity by itself does not explain integration, but it provides a useful framing narrative for the creation of specific organizations. Europe, Africa and (Latin) America share a similar paradox: identity rhetoric inspires moves towards greater integration, but, in parallel, an equally powerful rhetoric and conviction in the value of national sovereignty limits the transfer of power to integration organizations.

[38] *Ibid.* pp. 19–20.

[39] A. Acharya, "Comparative Regionalism: A Field Whose Time Has Come?," 47:1 *The International Spectator* 3–15 (2012), p. 5.

In Europe, actors appeal occasionally to the ongoing rhetoric on European identity and Europeanness (which is sometimes premised on essentialist arguments) in order to justify and/or explain integration. Arguably, European integration schemes and organizations do not respond to this identity-promotion, or the purpose of formalizing identity, even though these identity traits may be found in some of the institutions. This applies not only to the European Union but also to the Council of Europe, which, together with democracy and human rights, has culture as a central concern.

Two parallel and contradictory identity patterns have inspired integration schemes in America. On the one hand, the United States has sought hegemonic leadership over the continent since the time of the *Monroe* doctrine (that is, America for the Americans) (1823). A number of successive updates, such as the *Manifest Destiny* doctrine (1904), extended this pan-American vision well into the twentieth century. This background is essential to understanding US-led organizations, such as the OAS or the AFTA. But US dominance, in parallel, has been a constant reference for the constitution of Latin American identity, values and political culture.[40] The discrediting of US-led organizations such as OAS and ITRA is due to the fact that they were perceived as purely anti-communist instruments of the US during the Cold War. Furthermore, Latin American States resented the fact that the US privileged relations with other partners over

[40] J. A. Sanahuja, "Multilateralismo y regionalismo en clave sudamericana: El caso de UNASUR," 33 *Pensamiento Propio* 115–157 (2011), p. 116.

Latin American ones (for example, during the Falklands/ Malvinas conflict). This has stimulated attempts to create autonomous organizations such as the Río Group and Esquipulas Process in Central America. The Community of Latin American and Caribbean States (CLACS) represents the latest development in this tendency to create a distinctive Latin American identity (separate from the US and Canada).

In parallel, subcontinental regions also formulated their own identity and created organizations crystallizing this. Thus, in Central America, perception of identity can be traced back to the nineteenth century, and the attempts to create a Unified Central American Republic. In 1951, Central American States signed the Charter of the ODECA (Organization of Central American States), and SICA was in fact constructed as an appendix to ODECA, which acts as the framing institution. In South America, a number of attempts at treaties and confederations in the nineteenth century foreshadowed the later integration schemes (in particular the CAN). More recently, UNASUR aims to flesh out an existing South American identity as the basis for cooperation, defining regionalism as a South American rather than a Latin American project.[41]

In Africa, pan-Africanism, as an expression of continental identity and coherence, distinguishes regional integration in Africa from that of other regions in the developing world.[42] Pan-Africanism inspired the creation of the OAU,

[41] *Ibid.*, p. 123.

[42] C. McCarthy, "Regional Integration: Part of the Solution or Part of the Problem?," in S. Ellis (ed.), *Africa Now: People, Policies, and Institutions* (London: James Currey; Portsmouth: Heinemann, 1995), p. 14.

which expresses a rejection of the colonial fragmentation of the continent.[43] The OAU's founding principles of functional economic cooperation and integration clearly orientate towards "integration," whilst other founding principles, such as respect for national sovereignty, non-interference and territorial integrity provide a counterweight, limiting, *a priori*, its ability to advance in that direction. In a considerable shift from the OAU, the AU explicitly recognized the "responsibility to protect," and with that preserved for itself the right of intervening in the affairs of its Member States on humanitarian and human rights grounds.[44] Contrary to the debate in Europe, the political teleology of African regionalism has remained very much at a rhetorical level, as concerns about national sovereignty for these newly independent nations framed the debate differently than in Europe. Nevertheless, pan-Africanism and the idea that "Africa must unite" remain a dominant narrative of African politics even today. Identity (more specifically, pan-Africanism) and also economics were behind the creation of ECOWAS and SADC.[45] Pan-Africanism had a very pragmatic utility in stimulating regional integration: the OAU designed the Lagos Plan (1980) which promoted a number of regional integration communities (see Section 1.3.1 above). Later on, the AU stimulated the creation of the AEC. Often a rhetorical tool, pan-Africanism has nevertheless

[43] T. Murithi, *The African Union: Pan-Africanism, Peacebuilding, and Development* (Burlington, VT: Ashgate, 2005).

[44] *Ibid.*

[45] L. Fawcett and H. Gandois, "Regionalism in Africa and the Middle East: Implications for EU Studies," 32:6 *Journal of European Integration* 617–636 (2010), p. 620.

played a legitimizing role in the creation of African regional organizations, as well as their revival, with the slogan "African solutions to African problems."[46]

As for the Arab world, the "pan" idea, as the explicit rejection of the colonial legacy, was important in early discussions about the design of the Arab League. Amid a large and heterogeneous group of States, it was the sovereignty-first formula that triumphed, and the League emerged as a highly State-centric institution. Though pan-Arabism never entirely lost its salience domestically or at the regional level, there has been no single identity script that is widely shared in the Middle East since then.[47]

In Asia, there is a conspicuous lack of continental or even regional (that is, subcontinental) institutions/organizations. This may be due to the lack of formulation of some sort of "Asian identity" different from Africa, America and Europe. In continental terms, Asia embraces a vast cultural, linguistic, religious and ethnic diversity, unmatched in any other continent. It also comprises all kinds of political and economic regimes, ranging from quasi-theocracies to multicultural democracies, and from State-led economies to some of the more open economies in the world. Similar arguments (with only minor adjustments) apply on the subcontinental scale when the focus turns towards regions such as the Asia-Pacific.

[46] *Ibid.*, pp. 620 and 629.

[47] A. Gomaa, *The Foundation of the League of Arab States* (London: Longman, 1977); L. Fawcett and H. Gandois, "Regionalism in Africa and the Middle East: Implications for EU Studies," 32:6 *Journal of European Integration* 617–636 (2010), p. 622.

Moreover, questions about belonging and borders remain an open issue for existing cooperation organizations. Against this background, the historical heritage of conflicts adds explanatory weight to the lack of an overarching identity which frames organizations such as those in existence in the American, African, European, Arab and Islamic environments.

1.3.2.3 Security and peace objectives: "framing" organizations

In the early stages of regionalism/regional integration (that is, in the aftermath of the Second World War and until the end of the Cold War), the creation of specialized security organizations served to frame integration organizations and/or acted as a trigger for integration. NATO epitomizes this model, but SEATO (which ceased to exist in 1977) aimed at fulfilling a similar function in relation to South East Asia,[48] although several countries rejected US leadership in the organization. In fact, ASEAN's insistence on sovereignty and non-intervention may also relate to the experience of SEATO. Among the Cold War security organizations, CENTO (1955–1979, which operated in the Middle East with the aim of preventing

[48] SEATO's objectives were to settle any international disputes in which they might have been involved by peaceful means, in such a manner that international peace, security and justice were not endangered; to refrain in their international relations from the threat or use of force in any manner inconsistent with the purposes of the United Nations; to maintain and develop their individual and collective capacity to resist armed attack; and to prevent and counter any external subversive activities directed against their territorial integrity and political stability.

communist incursions and fostering peace in the region) did not frame parallel economic integration schemes. Since Iran and its privileged partnership with the US was a central component of CENTO, the arrival of the Shia regime put an abrupt end to the organization.

In America, US-led OAS organized security via the Inter-American Treaty for Reciprocal Assistance (ITRA, 1947). However, Latin American States resented the traditional heavy-handed US policy towards security in the continent (see above), as well as what they perceived as its lack of real commitment to Latin America. In 1982, Argentina invoked ITRA's mutual assistance clause in its dispute with Britain over the Falklands, but the US sided with Britain, arguing that Argentina was, in fact, the aggressor State and hence the Treaty could not be activated. In 2002, Mexico renounced the Treaty, and in June 2012, ALBA States (Bolivia, Ecuador, Nicaragua and Venezuela) also denounced it. Hence, even though ITRA security provisions resembled NATO's (in particular, the mutual assistance clause), their roles as "framers" of integration diverge sharply between Latin America and Europe.[49]

This background may explain why security goals increasingly permeate South American integration efforts. Next to rationalization of economic integration (that is, structuring the relationships between MERCOSUR and CAN),

[49] C. Malamud, "Los frenos a la integración regional en América Latina," Real Instituto Elcano ARI No. 134/2005 (available at www.realinstitutoelcano.org/wps/portal/rielcano/Imprimir?WCM_GLOBAL_CONTEXT=/elcano/Elcano_es/Zonas_es/ARI%20134-2005).

security concerns prompted the creation of UNASUR. Brazil, in particular, conceived of it as an alternative to US hegemony (which, in the view of some, is more of a destabilizing factor than anything else). In fact, UNASUR has acted as a substitute for the OAS in times of crisis, as the Bolivian and Ecuadorean domestic political crises and the Colombia–Venezuela conflict exemplify, and this move triggered anxious warnings from Colombia's President Uribe, demanding that UNASUR not distance itself from OAS, or indeed go against it. As a result, the initial economic and trade objectives of UNASUR have been diluted among a large number of additional objectives, in particular security ones given the early salience of the South American Defense Council (CDS). The CDS responds to a Brazilian initiative expressing the will to secure a peaceful environment both *vis-à-vis* regional instability, and border problems triggered by guerrillas, paramilitary groups and drug cartels.[50] States' preference for UNASUR preeminence may help to explain why MERCOSUR has not developed any meaningful security dimension, even though, since the Treaty of Asunción, cooperative military activity has flourished throughout the region, and all the MERCOSUR members have engaged in a series of confidence-building measures that have included military secondments, informational exchanges and joint exercises.[51]

[50] J. A. Sanahuja, "Multilateralismo y regionalismo en clave sudamericana: El caso de UNASUR," 33 *Pensamiento Propio* 115–157 (2011), p. 135.

[51] D. Pion-Berlin, "Will Soldiers Follow? Economic Integration and Regional Security in the Southern Cone," 42:1 *Journal of Inter-American Studies and World Affairs* 43–69 (2000), p. 47.

Africa offers a slightly different approach: the AU has assumed the leading role in security on the continent, but existing economic integration schemes have also developed strong security. This is particularly true for ECOWAS, but SADC has also taken some steps towards developing a security dimension with the creation of the Organ on Politics, Defense and Security Cooperation, which is responsible for the promotion of peace and security, prevention of the breakdown of law and order, development of common foreign policies, enforcement of action in line with international law, and promotion of the development of democratic institutions among Member States (Protocol on Politics 2001, Article 2). However, realistic assessments warn against any naïve enthusiasm for the identity of the values and purposes presumed to exist among the Member States in the aftermath of apartheid, which led to serious mistakes, and later clashes, in this area. In the case of the Democratic Republic of Congo, the SADC Organ has failed spectacularly, with presidents Mugabe, dos Santos and Nujoma treating the SADC as though a mutual defense pact had been constituted and the president of the Organ had the authority to deploy forces in SADC's name without reference to the Summit or to the other Member States.[52]

[52] S. Cleary, "Variable Geometry and Varying Speed: An Operational Paradigm for SADC," in C. Clapham, G. Mills, A. Morner and E. Sidiropoulos (eds.), *Regional Integration in Southern Africa: Comparative International Perspectives* (Pretoria: South African Institute of International Affairs, 2001), pp. 87–104, p. 91.

1.4 Membership and its forms

Formal integration refers to organizations made up of Member States. In integration schemes, States are normally considered parties to the organization. The only partial exception is the scarcely formalized and institutionalized Asian Pacific Economic Community (APEC), which refers to "*Member Economies*," an expression that allowed it to bypass former problems relating to Hong Kong statehood, as well as the disputed status of Taiwan. The following sections will review the issues of membership (accession and withdrawal, as well as other status and the temporary suspension of membership) and two forms of accommodating membership: differentiated participation and institutional opt-out. Membership poses a key dilemma: size versus intensity of cooperation, a dilemma which is particularly acute in relation to the decision to accept new members: broadening the membership of any regional grouping inherently complicates the process of deepening integration.[53]

1.4.1 Flexible membership: accession and withdrawal

As a common feature, integration schemes keep a flexible policy on membership. Both accession and withdrawal remain open, which means that the organizations adapt

[53] C. F. Bergsten, *Open Regionalism*, Peterson Institute for International Economics Working Paper 97/3, 1997 (available at www.iie.com/publications/wp/wp.cfm?ResearchID=152).

through the increase and/or reduction in the number of members through time. At the same time, several integration schemes also allow some form of different membership (that is, associated status).

1.4.1.1 Accession

Integration schemes and international organizations almost invariably open membership to new States. This has permitted a large movement in terms of accession. The EU may be the extreme case, with its membership increasing more than fourfold between 1957 and 2005. ASEAN has doubled membership from the original five.[54] In Africa, COMESA started with an initial sixteen members, and gained five new members in 1994.[55] Egypt joined on January 6, 1999, followed by Seychelles (2001), Libya (2005) and South Sudan (2011). A parallel process of withdrawals pursuing "rationalization" (see below) followed, bringing current membership to twenty States. Other schemes, such as CAN (Venezuela joining in 1972), MERCOSUR (Venezuela in 2012 and Bolivia in 2015) or EAC (Burundi and Rwanda joined in 2006), show similar, though more modest patterns of membership growth. APEC originally had twenty-one members and another twelve States have applied to join. But despite the commitment to openness, no other State has so far been admitted. This reflects a contradiction inherent to open regionalism: despite its

[54] Original members were Singapore, the Philippines, Thailand, Indonesia and Malaysia (1967). Subsequently, Brunei (1984), Vietnam (1995), Laos (1997), Myanmar/Burma (1997) and Cambodia (1999) joined ASEAN.

[55] Angola, Lesotho, Mozambique, Namibia and Tanzania.

commitment to open membership, this cannot translate to *unlimited* membership.[56]

Much of the literature assumes a trade-off between the number of members and the effectiveness of regional organizations.[57] Growing size can have an impact on the ability of any organization to perform effectively and may limit informal cooperation: stating the obvious, a larger size requires more specific and formal rules. Other arguments point out that a greater number of actors involved make monitoring and enforcement more difficult. Also, the more States that accede to an organization, the more likely it is that diversity increases, making policy convergence tougher to achieve and decision-making more difficult. Slapin and Gray argue that the effectiveness of integration organizations is independent of their size. They argue that the number of countries involved tends to produce agreement with greater ambition and more expansive scope: organizations with more members tend to have broader goals.[58]

[56] C. F. Bergsten, *Open Regionalism*, Peterson Institute for International Economics Working Paper 97/3, 1997 (available at www.iie.com/publications/wp/wp.cfm?ResearchID=152), p. 4.

[57] G. Downs *et al.*, "Managing the Evolution of Multilateralism," 52:2 *International Organization* 397–419 (1998); M. J. Gilligan, "Is There a Broader-Deeper Trade Off in International Multilateral Agreements?," 58:3 *International Organization* 459–484 (2004); R. Stone *et al.*, "Choosing How to Cooperate," 52:4 *International Studies Quarterly* 335–362 (2008).

[58] J. B. Slapin and J. Gray, "Depth, Ambition and Width in Regional Economic Organizations," 21:5 *Journal of European Public Policy* 730–745 (2014).

This is so because the chances for heterogeneity of goals among States increases, and agreements tend to become more far-reaching.

In most cases, membership has grown in most of the existing and new organizations and this explains the overlapping issue: States retain membership in old organizations whilst acceding simultaneously to new ones. In fact, there are very few organizations that have reduced membership. EFTA and, to a lesser extent, CAN provide the clearest examples of "shrinking organizations." In both cases, absorption by competing neighboring integration (the EU and MERCOSUR/UNASUR respectively) explains this trend.

In general, even where a distinction exists between original and subsequent members, this distinction lacks any legal significance. However, original or current members may act as a club in their regulation of the acceptance of new members: they may seek to preserve the advantages of the organization for the existing members whilst transferring costs to acceding members, for instance, by means of long transition periods before being able to enjoy the full benefits of the organization.

Organizations usually preserve "clubness," imposing certain criteria for membership (see Table 1.2). Leaving aside functional global organizations and the UN, sub-global organizations normally restrict membership. The option to limit accession has appeared even within the paradigm of "open regionalism," and its intellectual inspirers argue that membership is not necessary for non-members of a regional arrangement to escape discriminatory economic treatment. Moreover, broadening membership of any

Table 1.2 *Membership requirements*

Requirement		International organization
Structural	Geographic area	ACS, AEC, **ASEAN**, **AU**, CAN, **CARICOM**, **CoE**, COMESA, **EAC**, **ECO**, ECOWAS, **EU**, GCC, IOR-ARC, LAFTA, **MERCOSUR**, NATO, **OAS**, OAU, OBSEC, OECS, OEI, **SCO**, **SICA**, UEMOA, **UNASUR**, WAMZ
	Cultural/religious	**AAEU**, **Arab League**, **OIC**, **OIF**, **UMA**
Political	Democracy and human rights (express mention in the treaty or protocol)	**AU**, **CoE**, **EAC**, **EU**, GUAM, **MERCOSUR**, **OAS**, **UNASUR (implicit)**
	Commitment to respect the objectives and principles	**ASEAN**, **CARICOM**, CIS, EAEC, **ECO**, GUAM, IOR-ARC, KEDO, NATO, OECD, **SCO**, **SICA**
No specific requirement		IAEA, ICES, ILO, IMF, IMO, IMSO, ITSO, OPCW, PICES, UN, UPU, WCO, WHO, WIPO

Source: Own elaboration. Integration schemes with more than a membership requirement are shown in bold.

regional grouping inherently complicates the process of deepening its integration.[59]

[59] And, according to Bergsten, restricting membership was crucial for the APEC to implement its Bogor Declaration (C. F. Bergsten, *Open Regionalism*, Peterson Institute for International Economics Working Paper 97/3, 1997 (available at www.iie.com/publications/wp/wp.cfm?ResearchID=152).

The acceding State's location within the geographical area defining the region is usually the main criterion for accession, to the point that geography may dictate the exclusion of an applicant (as happened with Morocco's application for EU membership in 1987). This confirms the intuitive perception that regional integration is connected to geographical contiguity. A few organizations declare themselves either implicitly or explicitly to be rim organizations where a sea or ocean acts as the nexus of union (for example, the Black Sea Economic Cooperation, the Indian Ocean Rim Association of Regional Cooperation, the Union for the Mediterranean or APEC). Less often, schemes based on cultural or religious identity demand this kind of attachment in order to accept a new member (for example, being an Arab or an Islamic country).

Conditioning and/or restricting membership points to the question of why States organize cooperation regionally rather than globally. The answer again links back to the nature of the objectives pursued. States enter into international/regional agreements/organizations in order to achieve certain objectives. These are the public goods that States cannot provide on their own and which become the *objectives* of the organization. This raises the question as to the level at which the public good is provided: why do States choose the global or the regional level?

The distinction between international/global and regional public goods is not an obvious one. Regional public goods have a more limited geographical reach to the benefits afforded: they benefit regional communities whose size depends on the issue addressed. On the other hand, their production typically requires cross-border collective action. Given that the costs increase with the size and given that benefits may have a cross-border dimension, the rationale for regional integration emerges. The cautious approach towards open-ended membership is visible even in those organizations more committed to "openness," such as APEC: the Subic summit in November 1996 directed APEC officials to develop criteria for considering accession bids,[60] but sixteen years later, no new member has been admitted to the paradigmatic organization of open regionalism.

Increasingly, organizations have made certain political requirements a prerequisite for membership, and chief among these is the requirement of being a democratic State.[61] Democratic credentials may be a powerful leveler for accession, as Venezuela's application for MERCOSUR membership shows. After abandoning CAN, Venezuela applied for admission to MERCOSUR. Although Member States agreed on this in 2006, the Senate of Paraguay blocked its accession. Whilst the government of Fernando Lugo and the Congress supported accession, the *Partido Colorado*, which controlled the Senate, consistently rejected ratifying the accession treaty, arguing that Venezuela was not a fully democratic State. Senators appealed to the democratic imperative written into

[60] C. F. Bergsten, *Open Regionalism*, Peterson Institute for International Economics Working Paper 97/3, 1997 (available at www.iie.com/publications/wp/wp.cfm?ResearchID=152).

[61] C. Closa, *Institutional Design of Democratic Conditionality in Regional Organizations*, EUI RSCAS Working Paper 2013/45, Global Governance Programme-54.

MERCOSUR's Democratic Compromise and the Ushuaia Protocol. Similarly, Sudan saw its application for EAC membership declined because Tanzania and Uganda objected on the grounds of its mistreatment of and discrimination against black Africans, and other human rights violations, religious intolerance, blatant racism and warmongering.[62] Conversely, membership of integration organizations including respect for democracy and human rights as criteria for belonging may greatly enhance the credentials of an acceding State and reinforce domestic democratic processes.

There is an interesting connection between geographical and democratic criteria: integration organizations establish geographical belonging as a precondition to accession in all cases in which democracy and respect for human rights are also required. GUAM, an organization of former Soviet States, is the only exception, as it covers both European and Asian States, although it has a distinct regional character. On the other hand, if the democratic requirement is combined with the objectives of the organization, as described in Table 1.1, the result is that most of the organizations requiring their members to be democratic commit themselves to the objective of "integration," whilst, on the other hand, no free trade area *explicitly* requires its members to be democratic (although this may be implicit in NAFTA and EFTA).

[62] "EAC Split on Khartoum's Bid to Join Community, Serious Opposition from Tanzania and Uganda" (see www.jamiiforums.com/jukwaa-la-siasa/174141-eac-split-on-khartoum%92s-bid-to-join-community-serious-opposition-from-tanzania-and-uganda.html).

1.4.1.2 Other status related to membership

Formalized integration schemes sometimes offer the possibility of a form of membership which falls short of full membership. These (associated, partial, affiliated or observer) variations pragmatically accommodate either the unwillingness of current members to accept new members, or the unwillingness of potential members to fully accede to the organization or, alternatively, serve as a "waiting room" for full membership. Associated membership usually appears as a form of membership with limited rights, possibly leading to full membership.[63] This exists in the EU, in SICA and in MERCOSUR. After the accession of Greece, the EU has stopped using the status of associated member. In MERCOSUR, Chile, Colombia and Peru became associated members, which allowed them to join the free trade area without adopting the common external tariff systems. Bolivia and Venezuela were former associated members before becoming full members, as also happened with the Dominican Republic in SICA. These developments supported the idea that associated status is a preliminary stage on the road to full membership. The precise meaning of "observer" varies greatly among organizations and, in general, they do not participate in votes nor pay dues. SICA has one of the most extensive lists of observer States. Table 1.3 illustrates some modalities of alternatives to membership open to third States.

[63] J. Klabbers, *An Introduction to International Institutional Law* (Cambridge University Press, 2nd edn. 2009), p. 99.

Table 1.3 *Status other than membership*

Status	Organizations
Associated status	EU: Greece,[a] Turkey MERCOSUR: Bolivia,[a] Chile, Colombia, Ecuador, Peru, Venezuela[a] SICA: Dominican Republic[a]
Observer status	GUAM: Turkey and Latvia SAARC: Australia, China, Burma, EU, Japan, Iran, Mauritius, South Korea and US SICA (regional observers): US, Mexico, Argentina, Chile, Peru and Brazil SICA (extra-regional observers): Australia, Spain, Taiwan, Germany, Italy and Japan

Source: Own elaboration
Note
[a] Joined as full member

1.4.1.3 Withdrawal

Withdrawal is not uncommon in integration schemes, some of which explicitly provide for this possibility. Table 1.4 summarizes the three types of clauses encountered in integration organizations and some others considered in the larger sample.

Most organizations foresee that members may withdraw unilaterally, and in all cases, withdrawal is unconditional.[64] In relatively few cases, withdrawal is forbidden

[64] In the early 1980s, withdrawal was debated in relation to the EU, with some authors such as Schermers arguing that unilateral withdrawal was not compatible with international organizations (H. G. Schermers, *International Institutional Law* (The Hague: Sijthoff and Noordhoff International Publishers, 1980), p. 29). The inclusion of an explicit provision in the Lisbon Treaty has settled this dispute.

Table 1.4 *Typology of withdrawal clauses*

Effect of clause	Organizations
Withdrawal is allowed at any time	ACS, AEC, Arab League, AU, CAN, CIS, CoE, COMESA, EAC, EAEC, ECCAS, ECO, ECOWAS, EFTA, EU, GUAM, IGAD, ILO, IMF, IMSO, IOM, ITSO, KEDO, LAFTA, LAIA, MERCOSUR, NAFTA, OAS, OAU, OBSEC, OECD, OECS, OIC, OIF, OPCW, OPEC, PICES, SADC, SAFTA, SCO, UNASUR, UPU, WAEMU, WAMZ, WCO, WIPO, WTO
Denunciation/ withdrawal is precluded for a fixed number of years	AAEU (five years after expiry of transitional period), Helsinki Convention (five years after the entry into force), ICES (two years after entry into force), IHO (five years after entry into force), IMO (one year after entry into force), NATO (after the Treaty has been in force for twenty years)
No explicit provision	ASEAN, Benelux, CARICOM, GCC, IAEA, INTERPOL, IOR-ARC, ODECA, SAARC, SICA, UMA, UN, WHO

Source: Own elaboration. Typology adapted from L. R. Helfer, "Exiting Treaties," 91 *Virginia Law Review* 1579–1648 (2005). In his analysis of *treaties*, Helfer proposes a typology of six different cases. In the sample of integration and related *organizations* that is used in this study, three of these types do not have any real-life examples. These are (a) denunciation/ withdrawal is allowed at fixed time intervals; (b) denunciation/withdrawal is allowed on a single occasion; (c) denunciation/withdrawal follows automatically from ratification of a new superseding treaty.

before a certain period of time elapses following admission, with NATO, the most demanding case, requiring twenty years before withdrawal is permitted.[65] In almost all cases,

[65] In 1966, France withdrew from NATO's integrated military structure. The French government legally justified its move by distinguishing

the withdrawing State does not need to provide justification, the two exceptions being OPCW and OECS. In both cases, the right of withdrawal derives from a State deciding that extraordinary events, related to the subject matter of the Conventions, have jeopardized the supreme national interest (Articles 16 and 24 respectively). Most organizations contain certain procedural requirements: as a general rule, they require a "preparation" or "cooling-off" period between the announcement of withdrawal and the effective withdrawal, and this period varies between ninety days (KEDO) and two years (OAS), with one year being the most common time period.[66] The EAC stands alone in setting a procedural requirement that impinges upon the domestic constitutional order: an EAC partner State may withdraw if two-thirds of the National Assembly members support the decision (Article 145). This provision constructs a domestic check on unilateral moves by government executives.

A second category of withdrawal clauses precludes denunciation for a certain number of years, which varies between one (IMO) and twenty years (NATO). This is not very common and the Agreement on Arab Economic

between the original treaty (to which it remained a party) and the organization founded by it. Withdrawal occurred before the legal reservation period established by the Treaty.

[66] This cooling-off period has the function of allowing the withdrawing State to change its position. Thus, Spain decided not to withdraw from the League of Nations in 1928 shortly before its notice to do so would have taken effect.

Union (AAEU) is alone among integration organizations in having such a clause (with a cautionary period of five years – Article 19). Finally, the last category comprises those organizations whose treaties do not contain a specific withdrawal clause. Although it is smaller than the first group, it comprises several integration schemes (such as ASEAN, CARICOM or SICA). Lacking a specific clause, the assumption would be that the Vienna Convention on the Law of Treaties applies and that withdrawal is allowed under the conditions set therein (Articles 61 and 62 on supervening impossibility of performance and fundamental change of circumstances respectively).

Whilst these are the written regulations, there are few practical examples of withdrawal (see Table 1.5 below). In Africa, a number of States have withdrawn from integration organizations following the "rationalizing" pull of the African Economic Community. Mozambique (1997), Lesotho (1997), Tanzania

Table 1.5 *Cases of withdrawal and suspended membership*

Case	Organizations
Withdrawing States	CAN: Chile (1976) and Venezuela (2006) COMESA: Mozambique (1992), Lesotho (1997), Tanzania (2000), Namibia (2004) ECOWAS: Mauritania (2000) GUAM: Uzbekistan (2005)
Suspended membership	AU and SADC: Madagascar (2009) ECOWAS: Guinea (2008), Niger (2009) and Côte d'Ivoire (2009) following either *coups d' état* or fraudulent elections MERCOSUR and UNASUR: Paraguay (2012)

(2001), Namibia (2004) and Angola (2007) left COMESA. Similarly, in December 2000, Mauritania withdrew from ECOWAS, having announced its intention to do so in December 1999. However, these are cases with no political relevance, since, as mentioned, they responded to the master plan for integration of the African Union and their incorporation into other regional organizations.[67] Seychelles withdrew from SADC on July 1, 2004 for purely financial reasons: economic reforms in the country required a rationalization of the cost of membership of international organizations, balanced against the economic benefits for the people.[68] It rejoined in 2008.

There are cases of withdrawal of much larger political significance. In the late 1960s, the Council of Europe threatened the Greek military regime with expulsion because of its "neglect" of human rights. The Greek government chose withdrawal before the expulsion materialized. In 1976, Chile withdrew from CAN following the *coup d'état* of General Pinochet. Probably, Venezuela's withdrawal from CAN (and immediate application for membership of MERCOSUR) has been the most significant event of this kind, since it triggered a change in the

[67] Greenland's withdrawal from the European Communities in 1985 falls into the same category (i.e. withdrawal without real political significance).

[68] Address by Mr. James Alix Michel, President of the Republic of Seychelles, August 17, 2008, Summit of the South African Development Community Heads of State and Government, Sandton, South Africa, August 16–17, 2008 (available at www.Sadc.Int/Index/Browse/Page/217).

equilibrium between States, groups of States and, above all, integration schemes. Venezuela withdrew from CAN in 2006, arguing that the free trade agreements that Colombia and Peru had negotiated with the US contravened its integration spirit. Disputes centered on the political and ideological interpretation of FTAs.[69] Both countries argued that CAN Decision 598 allowed for these bilateral agreements, since it provided that in the event that negotiations as a community were not possible, bilateral relations could take place. Article 2 of Decision 598 sets out the requirements to be respected in these bilateral negotiations: preserving Andean law, taking into consideration the sensitivities of other Andean parties with regard to free trade, and maintaining an adequate exchange of information and consultation through talks within a framework of transparency and solidarity. Both Colombia and Peru claimed that they respected these requirements. Finally, Uzbekistan illustrates another case of political withdrawal: in 2005, it withdrew from GUAM in response to a shift from a pro-Russian to a pro-Western approach in the organization's policies.[70]

[69] C. Malamud, "Los frenos a la integración regional en América Latina," Real Instituto Elcano ARI No. 134/2005 (available at www.realinstitutoelcano.org/wps/portal/rielcano/Imprimir?WCM_GLOBAL_CONTEXT=/elcano/Elcano_es/Zonas_es/ARI%20134-2005), pp. 1–5.

[70] C. J. Chivers, "Uzbekistan: GUUAM loses a 'U'," *New York Times*, May 7, 2005 (available at http://query.nytimes.com/gst/fullpage.html?res=9800E2DC1530F934A35756C0A9639C8B63).

1.4.1.4 Suspension of membership

The most common situation regarding suspension of membership is for treaties to remain silent on this point, and the safest conclusion is that suspension is excluded. In a number of instances, organizations permit suspension due to a failure to comply with financial obligations (that is, paying dues), although this is barely contentious in political terms. A number of schemes contain clauses that allow for suspension of membership either as a consequence of not fulfilling "general obligations" (which may leave a wide margin for interpretation), or, more specifically, if Member States violate certain key conditions, the respect of human rights and democracy being the most important of these. Table 1.6 offers a four-category typology of suspension clauses.

The practice of suspension is highly relevant to understanding the nature of integration organizations. Few organizations have suspended membership rights because of a failure to fulfill financial obligations. The WHO has suspended the voting rights of eight members and it is considering suspension of a further nine, whilst the IAEA has suspended fourteen others. In the past, the UN deprived Haiti (1963) and the Dominican Republic (1968) of their voting rights, but in 2012 it accepted the voting rights of six member countries in arrears.

The most interesting cases are those of suspension of membership because of breaches in respect of human rights, rule of law and democracy.[71] These are more common in

[71] See C. Closa, *Institutional Design of Democratic Conditionality in Regional Organizations*, EUI RSCAS Working Paper 2013/45, Global Governance Programme-54.

Table 1.6 *Typology of suspension clauses*

Type of suspension clause	Organizations
Suspension as a consequence of non-fulfillment of general obligations	AEC, CIS, CoE, COMESA, EAC, EAEC, ECOWAS, EU, GUAM, IAEA, IMF, IOM, OPCW, SADC, SCO, UN, UNWTO
Suspension as a consequence of non-fulfillment of financial obligations	AEC, AU, CAN, CoE, COMESA, ECCAS, IAEA, IGAD, IHO, ILO, IMO, INTERPOL, IOM, OIC, OPCW, PICES, SADC, UN, UNWTO, UPU, WHO, WIPO
Suspension as a consequence of offenses against human rights/rule of law/democracy	AU, CAN, ECOWAS, EU, MERCOSUR, OAS, OIF, UNASUR
No specific provision on suspension	AAEU, ACS, Arab League, ASEAN, Benelux, CARICOM, ECO, EFTA, EPO, GCC, Helsinki Convention, ICES, IMSO, IOR-ARC, KEDO, LAIA, NAFTA, NATO, ODECA, OECD, OECS, OEI, OPEC, SAARC, SAFTA, SICA, UMA, WAEMU, WAMZ, WCO, WEU, WTO

Source: Own elaboration

identity-framing organizations, in particular in the last decades. The African Union is the most active organization in using suspension against these breaches: it has done so in eleven cases between 2001 and 2015, and this has prompted similar measures in African regional integration schemes: SADC (Madagascar, 2009), ECOWAS (Togo, 2001, and Mali, 2009) and OIF (Mauritania, 2008, Madagascar, 2009, and Guinea, 2009). ECOWAS has *unilaterally* suspended membership for three

States (Guinea, 2008, Niger, 2009, and Côte d'Ivoire, 2009), following either *coups d'état* or fraudulent elections.

In Latin America, OAS's leadership as a guarantor of human rights, rule of law and democracy has progressively retreated. In 1962, it decided on the exclusion of Cuba from participation in the Inter-American System, arguing that "the present Government of Cuba, which has officially identified itself as a Marxist-Leninist government, is incompatible with the principles and objectives of the inter-American system."[72] Suspension was lifted in 2009 after a vote by the foreign ministers of OAS member countries.[73] In 2009, the OAS also suspended Honduras following a *coup d'état*, and this led SICA to adopt a similar measure. Aside from OAS, there are other examples of regional schemes in Latin America adopting decisions on suspension. Thus, CARICOM suspended Haiti after the ousting of President Aristide (2004). In 2012, MERCOSUR governments appealed to the Protocol of Ushuaia on the Democratic Compromise (1998) to deal with the decision of the Senate of Paraguay to remove President Lugo. This decision was perceived as unlawful and undermining the country's constitutional order, and in response, governments activated the provision that allowed for suspension of attendance to block meetings of the offending State. UNASUR, which had a similar

[72] Resolution VI: Exclusion of the Present Government of Cuba from Participation in the Inter-American System, Eighth Meeting of Consultation of Ministers of Foreign Affairs, Punta del Este, January 1962 (see www.cidh.oas.org/countryrep/Cuba79eng/intro.htm).

[73] UN General Assembly Resolution AG/RES. 2438 (XXXIX-O/09).

clause, although with deeper reach, adopted the same measures as MERCOSUR.[74]

Tellingly, the practice of suspending membership as a reaction to severe breaches in human rights and/or democracy extends even to regional schemes lacking a specific provision on the issue. These are the cases of SADC in relation to Madagascar in 2009, or SICA in relation to Honduras. Also, the normally sovereignty- and non-intervention-oriented Arab League applied suspension of membership in relation to Libya and Syria, both in 2011. Even in ASEAN, which lacks a specific provision, the possibility of using this threat came up informally during internal discussions prior to Myanmar's move towards political and economic liberalization.[75] This may indicate a growing perception of regional and integration organizations as mechanisms for guaranteeing respect for human rights and democracy.

1.4.2 Differentiated integration within integration schemes

Integration schemes may offer the option for States to participate flexibly in different areas which target different

[74] Decisión No. 26/2012, Reunión Extraordinaria del Consejo de Jefas y Jefes de Estado y de Gobierno de UNASUR. In fact, Paraguay had not ratified the *Protocolo Adicional sobre Compromiso con la Democracia* and, furthermore, some of its parliamentarians had denounced it: "Parlamentarios de Paraguay cuestionan cláusula democrática de la UNASUR," Comunicado de prensa de la Delegación de Paraguay del Parlamento del MERCOSUR (available at www.parlamentodelmercosur.org).

[75] I owe this observation to Pek Koon Heng.

objectives. Differentiated integration may comprise a *hard nucleus* of countries (those sharing more intense integration among themselves); *concentric circles* (a variation on the former which sets different levels of integration for different groups of countries); *variable geometry* (differentiated participation in different policy areas) and *multi-speed* (which implies achieving the same objective but at different speeds for different countries).

These theoretical categories have been constructed along the European model and in other geographical areas. Variable geometry is the most conspicuous form of differentiated integration. The Central American Integration System (SICA) provides an example. The system has four differentiated subsystems, each of them regulated by its own treaty and its own differentiated functional scope: economic integration,[76] social matters,[77] sustainable development[78] and democratic security.[79] Whilst the latter three retain SICA membership, Panama does not take part in the subsystem of economic integration. Each of these has a differentiated secretariat and bodies.

[76] *Protocolo al Tratado General de Integración Económica Centroamericana (Protocolo de Guatemala)* (1993); *Enmienda al Protocolo al Tratado General de Integración Económica Centroamericana (Protocolo de Guatemala)* (2003).

[77] *Tratado de la Integración Social Centroamericana* (1995) (Treaty of El Salvador).

[78] *Acuerdo sobre la Alianza para el Desarrollo Sostenible de Centroamérica* (ALIDES) (1994).

[79] *Tratado Marco de Seguridad Democrática en Centroamérica San Pedro Sula* (1995).

SADC has formalized a similar model of variable geometry creating subsystems that can be derived from the Community. For this, the Treaty identifies eight areas for cooperation[80] for which different groups of States may conclude protocols. Accession to these protocols is voluntary and they enter into force when two-thirds of Member States have ratified them, and they apply only to those Member States which have ratified them. So far, SADC States have completed twenty-three protocols, but they are unevenly implemented,[81] and few have entered into force.[82] In fact, Member States signed the Trade Protocol only in 1996, and in 2003 they agreed a Regional Indicative Strategic Program

[80] SADC Treaty, Article 21: "The Council may decide new areas for cooperation." SADC institutions are used for each of the protocols.

[81] P. Draper, D. Halleson and P. Alves, *SACU, Regional Integration and the Overlap Issue in Southern Africa: From Spaghetti to Cannelloni?*, Trade Policy Report No. 15, South African Institute of International Affairs, 2007, p. 21.

[82] Article 22 establishes that, once a protocol has entered into force, a Member State may only become a party thereto by accession. Each protocol shall be approved by the Summit on the recommendation of the Council. Protocols on shared watercourse usage, the Southern African power pool, transport, communications, meteorology and illicit drug trafficking have been approved by the SADC Heads of State. South Africa has ratified protocols on education and training and mining, but these have not yet achieved three-quarter majorities, while protocols on the development of tourism, wildlife, conservation, law enforcement, health, and immunities and privileges have been signed, but not ratified (S. Cleary, "Variable Geometry and Varying Speed: An Operational Paradigm for SADC," in C. Clapham, G. Mills, A. Morner and E. Sidiropoulos (eds.), *Regional Integration in Southern Africa: Comparative International Perspectives* (Pretoria: South African Institute of International Affairs, 2001), pp. 87–104, p. 90).

for Development (RISDP), with the aim of achieving a free trade area by 2008, a customs union by 2015, and monetary union by 2016. Some authors argue that protocols have an important advantage over the general treaty, since they place definite responsibility on signatory Member States and create a binding legal obligation.[83] SADC has another feature which comes close to the model of differentiated integration: the Parliamentary Forum of SADC. A constitution of its own regulates the Forum, which is a separate international organization with legal personality (Article 4 of the SADC Forum Constitution, as amended, 2010). Its relationship with the SADC Secretariat is at arm's length, and its activities are not necessarily coordinated or integrated with those of the SADC Secretariat. The operations of the two organizations are often disjointed.[84] Rather than resulting in a negative assessment, differentiated integration may be a remedy for circumventing a lack of progress. Thus, discussing the SADC, Cleary concludes that it is unlikely that all Member States will progress in unison towards a common, desirable end state.[85] Hence, those States

[83] A. Afadameh-Adeyemi and E. Kalula, "Re-examining the Legal and Institutional Anatomy of the Southern Africa Development Community," in A. Bös, A. D. Pisani, G. Erasmus, T. Hartzenberg and R. Sandrey (eds.), *Monitoring Regional Integration in Southern Africa Yearbook 2010* (Tralac/Konrad Adenauer Stiftung, 2011), p. 9 (available at www.tralac.org).

[84] S. Kingah and A. Cofelice, *EU's Engagement with African (Sub)Regional Parliaments of ECOWAS, SADC, the EAC and the AU*, UNU-CRIS Working Paper W-2012/8, p. 9.

[85] S. Cleary, "Variable Geometry and Varying Speed: An Operational Paradigm for SADC," in C. Clapham, G. Mills, A. Morner and E. Sidiropoulos (eds.), *Regional Integration in Southern Africa:*

that share a common purpose and demonstrate the will and the ability to progress more swiftly than others should not be hampered by the requirement of consensus and collective ratification of all programs by three-quarters of the fourteen Member States. "Variable geometry and varying speed" is simply the characterization of this "common-sense" approach.

A similar mode of differentiated integration exists in ASEAN, whose instruments (comprising declarations, agreements, conventions, concords, protocols, treaties and other ASEAN instruments) usually contain implementation clauses which allow for flexible participation of Member States. Thus, among the several implementation modalities, these instruments may require ratification by a specific number of ASEAN Member States; they may add to the former a waiting period of varying length or, using any of the previous two specifications, they may establish that they are binding only upon those States ratifying them.

Plans for monetary unification associated with African regional integration have led to further internal differentiation within the respective integration schemes. Thus, within ECOWAS, there are two competing schemes, namely, French-speaking and English-speaking members of the Community. The former created the Treaty on the West African Economic and Monetary Union (WAEMU) (1996), which uses the CFA[86] franc which is pegged to the euro.

Comparative International Perspectives (Pretoria: South African Institute of International Affairs, 2001), pp. 87–104, p. 88.

[86] Designation of the CFA varies between WAEMU and CEMAC (see below).

The Treaty created a whole set of differentiated institutions,[87] and its goals go well beyond purely monetary unification to encompass, *inter alia*, the creation of a common market (including freedom of circulation for all production factors) and insuring convergence of economic policies through multilateral surveillance. In 2000, English-speaking ECOWAS members responded to this plan with the creation of the West African Economic Zone (WEMAZ) and its own proposal for creating a common West African currency, the *eco* by 2009 (subsequently postponed to 2015). Within ECCAS (and despite its limited achievements), States have also formalized plans for a Central African Economic and Monetary Community (CAEMC/CEMAC), which comprises six countries[88] sharing the CFA franc. COMESA contains the Southern African Customs Union (SACU), with its associated monetary union (the Common Monetary Area, CMA). Table 1.7 illustrates some cases of sub-organizations within larger organizations (i.e. nested subsystems).

1.4.3 Institutional opting-out

Opting-out normally applies to specific policy areas, but at least one integration scheme has a specific variety of

[87] Article 16: "Les organes de l'Union sont constitués par la Conférence des Chefs d'État et de gouvernement, telle que définie à l'article 5 du Traité de l'UMOA; le Conseil des ministres, tel que défini à l'article 6 du Traité de l'UMOA; la Commission; la Cour de justice; la Cour des comptes."

[88] Cameroon, the Central African Republic, Chad, the Republic of Congo, Equatorial Guinea (which joined in 1985 and is the only non-former-French colony) and Gabon.

Table 1.7 *"Nested" subsystems*

Communities within AEC (54 members)	"Nested" subsystems
Community of Sahel-Saharan States (CEN-SAD)	Common Monetary Area (projected)
Common Market for Eastern and Southern Africa(COMESA) (20 members)	SACU (5 members)
East African Community (EAC) (5 members)	Economic and Monetary Community of Central Africa (CEMAC) (6 members)
Economic Community of Central African States (ECCAS/CEEAC) (11 members)	West African Economic and Monetary Union (WEAMU/ UEMOA) (8 members)
Economic Community of West African States (ECOWAS) (15 members)	West African Monetary Zone (WAMZ) (6 members)
Intergovernmental Authority on Development (IGAD) (7 members)	Southern African Customs Union (SACU) (5 members)
Southern African Development Community (SADC) (15 members)	Common Monetary Area (CMA) (3 members)

Source: Own elaboration

opting-out: institutional opting-out. Some States may not accept delegation and/or commitments to specific organs of the integration scheme. Thus, within SICA, Costa Rica and Panama are not members of the Central American Court of Justice, and Costa Rica and Belize are not members of the Central American Parliament (Parlacen). Moreover, the government of Panama attempted to withdraw from Parlacen in 2009. Following the critical position of President Martinelli towards Parlacen (see below), in 2009 Panama's parliament approved a law withdrawing from the Central American Parliament.[89] The government of Panama appealed specifically to Article 56 of the Vienna Convention. However, the Central American Court of Justice ruled that Panama could not withdraw from the parliament, a decision that the government of Panama rejected, arguing that the Court did not have jurisdiction over this decision, which, in any case, was a sovereign (and irrevocable) decision of Panama. In January 2012, the Panama Supreme Court ruled that the withdrawal had been unlawful and ordered the government to reinstate Panama's membership of Parlacen.

In relation to the Court, Costa Rica has strongly asserted that it does not recognize its jurisdiction. Thus, in November 2011, the government of Nicaragua took Costa Rica to the CACJ for environmental damage provoked by the construction of a road on the border between the two countries. In January 2012, the Court produced a unanimous ruling, with immediate and obligatory application, which required that Costa Rica suspend construction of the road. The government of Costa Rica rejected the judgment, and its foreign affairs minister forcefully argued that the Court did not have any jurisdiction whatsoever over Costa Rica, and hence the judgment was both irrelevant and null. He argued that the Costa Rican Congress had not ratified the *Estatutos de la Corte Centroamericana de Justicia* in 1995. From the CACJ's standpoint, the fact that Costa Rica had ratified the SICA agreements which referred to the Court implied acceptance of

[89] *Ley 78, de 11 de diciembre de 2009 que deroga las leyes que aprueban los instrumentos internacionales relativos al Parlamento Centroamericano.*

its jurisdiction.[90] The government of Panama endorsed Costa Rica's stance, and its foreign affairs minister argued that the CCJ was distorting its role and that of the SICA organs.[91]

A final variety of institutional opt-out refers to the validity of the norms: some organizations allow their Member States to decide that certain norms are not binding upon them. This is the case in the Arab League, where majority decisions are binding only upon those States that accept them (Article 7). This issue is reviewed again in Section 1.6, which concerns derived norms.

1.5 The institutional structure of integration organizations

International organizations, and by extension *integration* organizations (whether expressly defined as such or perceived implicitly as such), may adopt a variety of institutional forms.

[90] "Costa Rica ignora una orden de la Corte Centroamericana de Justicia," *El País*, January 18, 2012 (available at http://internacional.elpais.com/internacional/2012/01/18/actualidad/1326926845_688633.html). According to former Magistrate of the CACJ, Rafael Chamorro Mora, a number of rulings from the Costa Rica Constitutional Court (4638–96, 4640–96, 6619–99 and 1999–6619) endorse CACJ jurisdiction and competence in Costa Rica. "La Corte Centroamericana de Justicia y Costa Rica," *El Nuevo Diario*, February 2, 2012 (available at www.elnuevodiario.com.ni/opinion/240396). Based on the wording of these sentences, the interpretation seems a bit far-fetched, though.

[91] "Panamá y Costa Rica denuncian que Corte Centroamericana lesiona integración," *La Prensa*, February 2, 2012 (available at www.laprensa.com.ni/2012/02/02/ambito/89362-panama-costa-rica-denuncian).

Explanations for these institutional choices vary according to their theoretical orientation.

From a rational choice approach,[92] international organizations facilitate cooperation among States. They provide a stable structure for international relations, allowing actors to predict their respective behavior and increase mutual understanding. They reinforce the credibility of State commitments. They are also a source of relative gains that cannot be obtained by other means. Hence, the cost–benefit calculations of actors shape institutional choices. Factors influencing these calculations include the type of cooperation problem, the number of actors involved (and hence, the associated transaction costs), and the level of uncertainty. Other scholars argue that institutional choices require explanations that take into account the ideas and identities of actors, as well as history.[93] Supporting this eclectic approach, Rittberger argues that institutions often reflect normative obligations or cultural-cognitive schemes, which either serve as normative and moral constraints or as devices through which actors interpret the menu of legitimate or conceivable

[92] B. Koremenos *et al.*, "The Rational Design of International Institutions," 55:4 *International Organization* 761 (2001); R. O. Keohane, *Power and Governance in a Partially Globalised World* (London: Routledge, 2002); R. O. Keohane and A. Buchanan, "The Legitimacy of Global Governance Institutions," 20:4 *Ethical and International Affairs* 405 (2006).

[93] A. Acharya, "How Ideas Spread: Whose Norms Matter? Norm Localization and Institutional Change in Asian Regionalism," 58:2 *International Organization* 239–275 (2004).

alternatives.[94] Although this study does not aim to explain the origins of institutional choice, but rather to compare the institutional design of integration schemes/organizations, it takes into consideration both approaches (the rationalistic and the ideational cultural) in framing this comparison, as both calculus and ideas/culture are meaningful for understanding institutional design. In any case, ideas must be translated into institutional design and this implies a rational choice guided by these ideational inspirations.

Comparison must avoid what comparative institutional analysis considers a common but fatal analytical trap: perfectionism or single institutionalism. This analytical position usually highlights the panoply of defects of existing institutions and then assumes that the ideal alternative solution would be better. The proposed or potential alternatives are often ideal forms, or at least subject to much less examination than that applied to reject existing forms. But, on the contrary, any institutional alternative is highly imperfect.[95] This does not mean that institutional design results are irrelevant for producing given effects. In fact, depending on their design, institutions for regional cooperation can serve as a driver or as a brake on regional cooperation. Strong and autonomous regional institutions not only help to consolidate

[94] B. Rittberger, "Institutionalizing Representative Democracy in the European Union: The Case of the European Parliament," 50:1 *Journal of Common Market Studies* 18–37 (2012), p. 21.

[95] N. Komesar and M. Maduro, "Governance Beyond the States: A Constitutional and Comparative Institutional Approach for Global Governance" (EUI mimeo, on file with the authors, 2012).

gains for integration, by preventing any backsliding of participating actors, but they can also promote a deepening and widening of integration processes by removing barriers to integration and by establishing policy regimes in new areas.[96] The correlation between design and effects, however, goes beyond the scope of this study.

The warning against institutional "idealism" characterizes comparative institutional analysis, and its results are crucial in the case of comparative regional integration, since the European Union has brought about mimesis by other world regions as a political and intellectual project because of the strength of European integration and its institutional structure.[97] A legion of authors have questioned

[96] ADB, "Institutions for Regional Integration: Towards an Asian Economic Community" (Manila: ADB, 2010), in T. Behr and J. Jokela, *Regionalism and Global Governance: The Emerging Agenda*, Notre Europe Studies and Research No. 85 (2011) (available at www.notre-europe.eu/en/axes/europe-and-world-governance/works/publication/regionalism-global-governance).

[97] E. Best, "The European Integration Process: An Example for Other Regions?," in A. Ott and E. Vos (eds.), *Fifty Years of European Integration. Foundations and Perspectives* (T. M. C. Asser Press, 2009); Y. Kodama, *Asia Pacific Economic Integration and the GATT-WTO Regime* (The Hague: Kluwer Law International, 2000). P. Lamy, "Regional Integrations in Africa: Ambitions and Vicissitudes," Notre Europe Policy Paper No. 43 (2010), p. 35 (available at www.notre-europe.eu/en/axes/europe-and-world-governance/works/publication/regional-integrations-in-africa-ambitions-and-vicissitudes/), distinguishes between "Africa, Latin America and Central Asia, or the Arab world, where the process rests on architectural concepts marked by an irresistible urge to institutionalize, probably inherited from a European constitutional and political culture of messianic inspiration and an Asian

the status of the EU and European integration as the reference model on which other schemes *should* converge,[98] and new regionalism has emerged, precisely, out of the criticism of Eurocentrism.[99] Whilst the caution is valuable for normative positions (that is, what an integration scheme should be), comparative institutional analysis needs to be mindful of the possible institutional mimesis (or indeed the opposite wish to avoid mimesis) that may have inspired institutional design of integration structures.[100] In fact, some studies have traced the EU influence on

model that is much more pragmatic, where the question of the final purpose arises only once action has been taken, where progress is made step by step as consensus is reached and new priorities emerge. Institutions are created only where necessary to achieve objectives. No one really worries about where the process is ultimately leading."

98 J. E. Álvarez, "Institutionalised Legalization and the Asia–Pacific 'Region'," 5:1 *New Zealand Journal of Public and International Law* 9–28 (2007); L. Fawcett and H. Gandois, "Regionalism in Africa and the Middle East: Implications for EU Studies," 32:6 *Journal of European Integration* 617–636 (2010), p. 632; F. Peña, *MERCOSUR as a Regional and Global Protagonist*, EUI RSCAS Working Paper 2012/01, Global Governance Programme.

99 See a review on new regionalism in C. Closa, *Mainstreaming Regionalism*, EUI RSCAS Working Paper 2015/12, Global Governance Programme-158.

100 Comparisons between cases other than the EU are scarce. One of these, S. Cleary, "Variable Geometry and Varying Speed: An Operational Paradigm for SADC," in C. Clapham, G. Mills, A. Morner and E. Sidiropoulos (eds.), *Regional Integration in Southern Africa: Comparative International Perspectives* (Pretoria: South African Institute of International Affairs, 2001), pp. 87–104, compares the SADC and MERCOSUR (to the latter's advantage).

other regional integration scheme institutions (that is, courts) and their rulings.[101]

There are good explanations for actors' use of existing schemes as models (either to copy or reject): they offer a ready-for-use instrument whose calculus of utility has already been realized and, in some cases, tested. However, since this study does not explore the origins of institutional design, it proposes to organize the evidence along constant parameters rather than taking any given construction as the "model." These parameters allow for identification of the commitments that States accept in order to achieve their objectives, based on the premise that other participants will follow suit. In order to construct this structure of institutional commitments, the model will be based on a broad analytical and comparative focus, pulling together evidence from different regions and practices.[102] The EU will not be taken as the implicit comparison, nor will it provide the categories for comparison. Naturally, the taxonomy and analysis of the available toolkit of institutional procedures and

[101] *Inter alia*, T. Lenz, "Spurred Emulation: The EU and Regional Integration in MERCOSUR and SADC," 35:1 *West European Politics* 155–173 (2012); K. J. Alter, *The Multiple Roles of International Courts and Tribunals: Enforcement, Dispute Settlement, Constitutional and Administrative Review*, Buffett Center for International and Comparative Studies Working Paper 12-002, 2012; A. A. Leistenschneider, "Reflejos del derecho comunitario en las decisiones de la Corte Centroamericana de Justicia," *Revista General de Derecho Europeo*, num. 25 (2011).

[102] L. Fawcett, "Exploring Regional Domains: A Comparative History of Regionalism," 80:3 *International Affairs* 429–446 (2004), p. 435.

mechanisms does not itself account for the success or failure of a given integration process.[103]

In practice, though, the EU is often mentioned as a model to be either copied or avoided: a number of integration organizations explicitly refer to the EU as the model not to follow. For instance, MERCOSUR design had in mind avoiding the neighboring CAN model, which replicated the EU one. According to Pena and Rozemberg, MERCOSUR has adapted these principles to conform to the needs of an association among developing countries.[104] MERCOSUR's institutional structure is an intergovernmental one, with the goal of making the integration scheme more flexible and gradual. Also, explicit rejection and questioning of the EU model is a constant in discussions on the so-called ASEAN model. However, institutional mimesis does exist: unavoidably, integration institutional designs will look at the EU model and use it, albeit adapted to local circumstances, either preventing or promoting its central features. This is so because the number of institutional alternatives for formalizing regionalization and/or integration is finite. In relation to organs, delegation to international organizations oscillates between two poles: fully independent organs and typically intergovernmental bodies with strict mandates from their domestic principals. As we will see, the

[103] Causes may be elsewhere; see L. Fawcett and H. Gandois, "Regionalism in Africa and the Middle East: Implications for EU Studies," 32:6 *Journal of European Integration* 617–636 (2010).

[104] C. Pena and R. Rozemberg, *MERCOSUR: A Different Approach to Institutional Development* (The Canadian Foundation for the Americas (FOCAL), 2005) (available at www.focal.ca).

prevalent model between both comes closer to the second. This section examines the organs of regional integration schemes, paying attention to the decision-making organs (Section 1.5.1), the role of delegated agencies (secretariats) (Section 1.5.2), the role of jurisdictional organs (Section 1.5.3) and the function of supra-State parliamentary organs (Section 1.5.4).

1.5.1 Institutional structures and decision-making

A constant characteristic among all integration organizations, which extends also to international organizations without the need for further qualification, is that intergovernmental organs assume delegated functions/powers. Usually, the two constant organs in decision-making are the one gathering heads of State and a council of ministers (either foreign affairs ministers and/or sectoral, that is, policy-specific, councils). In general, these are the organs competent to make binding and/or authoritative decisions for the organization and its Member States (the scope of these decisions will depend on the kind of norms adopted).

1.5.1.1 Intergovernmental decision-making

Decision-making in integration organizations, generally speaking, follows an intergovernmental pattern. Intergovernmentalism means that national executives take all relevant decisions in the integration scheme, whilst any supra-State institution and/or agency created will be devoid of any decision-making power. Usually, intergovernmentalism is associated with a unanimity voting requirement (even though consensus is as dominant a procedure as unanimity in intergovernmental schemes). This study treats both (decision-making and voting requirements) separately. Whilst national executive dominance is the constituent feature of intergovernmentalism, empirical models show some nuances that allow for distinctions along certain lines. Thus, intergovernmentalism may exist with some delegation of legislative initiative to specific agencies/institutions. This can be labeled *intergovernmentalism with initiative delegation*. In cases where there is no agency entrusted with legislative initiative, there may still be specialized bodies with the same function, or, alternatively, the organ of members of the executive (a council of ministers) may take upon itself the function of initiating proposals. Table 1.8 groups integration schemes and some international organizations in these categories.

Cases of delegation of initiative power are the minority, although they do exist under intergovernmentalism. Strictly speaking, only two organizations (apart from the EU) vest in integration institutions/agencies the sole power to initiate proposals: ECOWAS and LAFTA. The former is perhaps the most salient, since proposals may lead to the adoption of secondary legislation. Whilst in these two cases the competence is unqualified, CAN's Secretary General has a similar vast power in scope, but with two significant practical limitations: first, the Andean Community Commission (made up of Plenipotentiary Representatives of Member States) filters proposals, and, second, Member States also retain the right to initiate proposals for derived norms (Article 30.c). In two other integration organizations, GCC and IGAD, the

Table 1.8 *Initiative under intergovernmentalism*

Intergovernmentalism with delegation of initiative		AAEU (Permanent Technical Bureau) AU (any institution) CAN (General Secretariat) CARICOM (Secretary General) EAEC (Interparliamentary Assembly) ECOWAS (Executive Secretary) GCC (General Secretariat) IGAD (Secretariat) LAFTA (Executive Committee) WAEMU (Commission) WAMZ (Technical Committee)
Concentrated intergovern-mentalism	**Specialized organ**	MERCOSUR (Common Market Group) OBSEC (Committee of Senior Officials) UNASUR (Council of Delegates)
	Non-specialized (council of ministers)	ACS AEC ASEAN CIS COMESA EAC ECCAS GCC IGAD OAS OECS SADC SICA UMA

Source: Own elaboration

Secretary General/Secretariat may initiate proposals, although this is not an exclusive right, since other organs may also do so. Agencies play a role in two integration schemes specifically concerned with monetary integration, WAEMU and WAMZ, and in the AAEU. In addition, two cases have a peculiar configuration: in the African Union, any institution may take initiatives, and in the EAEC, the Interparliamentary Assembly is the competent organ.

Among the cases of *concentrated intergovernmentalism*, very few rely on a specialized organ made up of national delegates, and, by and large, the organ of members of the executive (almost universally a council of ministers) is the one initiating proposals. Thus, they concentrate initiative and decision-making, acting as a general reinforcement of governments.

1.5.1.2 Presidential intergovernmentalism: the organ of top executives (heads of State and/or prime ministers)

All integration schemes have an organ that gathers either presidents and/or prime ministers, depending on whether States have a presidential or parliamentary system. The organ is most commonly formalized (that is, regulated in the treaties), even though in some cases, such as the European Council, it only emerged as an institution after a progressive process of institutionalization. Even in those cases in which such an organ is not formalized at all, as is the case of MERCOSUR, presidents play a very important role, enhanced by the informal character of their interactions.[105] Most commonly, foundational treaties formalize the organ, though in some cases, such as SICA, the organ (that is, the Presidents' Meeting) precedes the creation of the organization (SICA) itself. Some authors have associated this organ with organizations involving non-democratic countries, as these are usually less prone to devolve power away from the heads of State.[106] However, its ubiquitous character seems to disprove this view.

The range of functions and powers assigned to these organs is vast and treaties normally enumerate them.[107] The most common typology of functions would comprise those listed in Table 1.9, which differentiates between ordinary and structural functions (that is, those powers that may be used in order to alter the structure of the organization). The latter refer to decisions on the creation of new organs, accepting new members and reforming the organization.

105 A. Malamud, "Presidentialism and Mercosur: A Hidden Cause for a Successful Experience," in F. Laursen (ed.), *Comparative Regional Integration: Theoretical Perspectives* (Aldershot: Ashgate, 2003), pp. 53–73, and A. Malamud, "Presidential Diplomacy and the Institutional Underpinnings of Mercosur. An Empirical Examination," 40:1 *Latin American Research Review* 138–164 (2005).

106 T. Behr and J. Jokela, *Regionalism and Global Governance: The Emerging Agenda*, Notre Europe Studies and Research No. 85 (2011) (available at www.notre-europe.eu/en/axes/europe-and-world-governance/works/publication/regionalism-global-governance), p. 16.

107 For instance, AEC (Article 8); OECS (Article 6.4); AU (Article 4); EAC (Article 11); ECAS (Article 9); ECOWAS (Article 9); ASEAN (Article 7); GCC (Article 8); SCO (Articles 4–6).

Table 1.9 *Powers of heads of State and governments (summary)*

Powers		International organization
Ordinary	Political guidance	ACS, AEC, ASEAN, AU, CAN, CARICOM, CIS, COMESA, EAC, EAEC, ECCAS, GCC, GUAM, IGAD, OAU, OECS, SADC, SCO, SICA, UEMOA, UNASUR
	Decision-making	AEC, AU, CAN, CARICOM, COMESA, EAC, EAEC, ECCAS, GCC, GUAM, IGAD, OAU, OECS, OIC, SADC, SCO, UNASUR
	Budgetary powers	AEC, AU, CARICOM, CIS, GCC, IGAD, SCO
	Implementation	AEC, AU, COMESA, EAEC, ECCAS, OECS, OIC, SADC, SICA
	Appointments	AEC, ASEAN, AU, COMESA, EAC, ECCAS, GCC, IGAD, SADC
Structural	Establishment of subsidiary organs	ASEAN, AU, CARICOM, CIS, EAEC, SADC, SCO, UNASUR
	Amendments	GCC, SICA
	Admission of new members	AU, GUAM, SADC, SICA

Source: Own elaboration

Political guidance. All integration schemes grant heads of State and government the definition and orientation of the process and of the organization itself. The efficiency of this function depends on a number of additional factors, the first being the existence of a proper organ implementing political guidance via decision-making. Since most schemes do assign the organ of heads of State decision-making power, this is consistently secured.

Decision-making. Seemingly the most important power is that of decision-making. Some integration schemes explicitly present the organ of heads of State as the supreme policy-making institution.[108] However, there are not many cases in which this organ is entrusted with adopting secondary legislation. African schemes contain a formula which reflects what can be considered customary practice elsewhere: the organ of heads of State delegates the norm-making role to the council of ministers (on the assumption that the substantive decision has already been taken).[109]

Budgetary powers. *A priori*, the organ of heads of State is not the one typically entrusted with budgetary powers and only some institutions confer it explicitly. In any case, heads of State may be behind decisions on the budget.

Implementation. Several African schemes entrust the organ of heads of State/government with the function of *monitoring compliance* with decisions, with a procedure of remission to their respective courts.[110] In Latin America, the SICA Treaty (Article 15.e) assigns the same function to the heads of State, whilst dispute resolution has an explicit function in the same organ within CARICOM.

[108] This kind of formulation appears in CARICOM (Article 12); OECS (Article 6); COMESA (Article 82); SADC (Article 10.2); ASEAN (Article 7.2); whilst CIS (Article 14) restricts this function to issues of defense and guarding the external frontiers of Member States.

[109] ECAS (Article 9.i); ECOWAS (Article 9.i); SADC (Article 10.1).

[110] See AEC (Article 8k); ECAS (Article 9.j); ECOWAS (Article 9j).

Significantly, the three African cases require a majority instead of consensus (which is the general rule). This gives more teeth to the compliance monitoring procedure. Presidents act not only as decision-makers, but also as dispute-settlers and guarantors of the commitments, in some cases going beyond the treaties themselves. Thus, Malamud has shown how presidents acted as a dispute settlement organ in cases of bilateral disputes to the point that no partner has ever mentioned the possibility of appealing to the Protocol of Brasilia, the institutional instrument by which MERCOSUR partners are supposed to resolve their disputes.[111]

Appointments. Last but not least, the organ of heads of State/government normally retains the power to appoint top officials in the organization, such as the secretary general (AEC, ECAS, ECOWAS, ASEAN, GCC); president of the Commission (AU); commissioners (ECAS); and/or members of the Court of Justice (AU, COMESA, EAC). This may combine with the power to establish and/or dissolve other institutions and bodies (Article 12.f CARICOM, Article 7.g ASEAN, Article 4 SCO). This reinforces the position of the body which may even mistreat other integration institutions.

As for the powers with a structural reach, presidents may:

[111] A. Malamud, "Presidential Diplomacy and the Institutional Underpinnings of Mercosur. An Empirical Examination," 40:1 *Latin American Research Review* 138–164 (2005).

- *Establish new organs.* In a number of schemes, the organ of presidents may create new organs within the integration schemes or even regulate existing ones. This latter competence may have disruptive effects and SADC provides an example of what may happen: in August 2010, the Summit decided to suspend the activity of the SADC Tribunal and commissioned a study from the Secretariat on the mandate of the Tribunal, its operation, its role and responsibility, its jurisdiction, its power to review decisions of domestic courts and so on. The decision resulted from the displeasure of the Republic of Zimbabwe on the Tribunal decision in the case of *Mike Campbell and others* v. *Republic of Zimbabwe* (2007), where the Tribunal ruled in favor of the applicants and against Zimbabwe.[112] The Summit decided to stop the Tribunal from taking new cases for a period of six months. The suspension placed a question mark over the credibility and independence of the Tribunal. While it is acknowledged that the Summit has the capacity to review the mandate, suspension of its activities cast a doubt. In May 2011, an extraordinary meeting of the Summit decided not to appoint new judges and to extend the moratorium on reviewing new cases until the SADC Protocol on the Tribunal is reviewed. Comparative evidence does not show

[112] A. Afadameh-Adeyemi and E. Kalula, "Re-examining the Legal and Institutional Anatomy of the Southern Africa Development Community," in A. Bös, A. D. Pisani, G. Erasmus, T. Hartzenberg and R. Sandrey (eds.), "Monitoring Regional Integration in Southern Africa," in *Yearbook*, vol. 10 (Tralac/Konrad Adenauer Stiftung, 2011) (available at www.tralac.org), p. 16.

an extended practice of granting to the presidents' organ such an extensive power of regulating or derogating other existing organs.

- *Admit new members.* Not many integration organizations refer explicitly to this function.[113] However, in practice, the decision whether to accept new members into the "club" will always be in the hands of the top authorities, and hence, it will be performed by the organ of heads of State/government.
- *Revise the treaties.* The same consideration applies to treaty revision. Few organizations assign this to the presidents (Arab League; Association of Caribbean States and Central American Integration System). But again, even when this function is not explicitly mentioned, it seems obvious that their revision will be always approved by heads of State/government.

Leaving aside specific technicalities, the organ of heads of State/government emerges as the most powerful institution within integration schemes. This may have some advantages: for instance, it guarantees that, once decisions are made, they carry broad support; it allows for arbitration at the highest level and creates opportunities for trade-offs; and it ensures a speedy process of decision-making.[114] In a specific study on MERCOSUR, A. Malamud has argued that whatever success MERCOSUR has attained is due to its ability to resort to

[113] I.e. ASEAN (Article 6.3); SADC (Article 8); SICA (Article 15.d).

[114] T. Behr and J. Jokela, *Regionalism and Global Governance: The Emerging Agenda*, Notre Europe Studies and Research No. 85 (2011) (available at www.notre-europe.eu/en/axes/europe-and-world-governance/works/publication/regionalism-global-governance), p. 16.

direct negotiations between presidents every time a crucial decision needs to be made.[115] Presidents concentrate powers and have a high degree of autonomy because of domestic institutional features. This is called "interpresidentialism,"[116] presidential diplomacy or "summitry regionalism" (in the new regionalism literature).[117] This, however, is not conceptually different from the role of the prime minister in parliamentary democracies.

There are, however, some negative dimensions to the dominance by heads of the executive. First, being a personal office, the efficiency of the collective organ may depend greatly on the presidents' attitudes towards integration and their personal skills. Second, the strong parliamentary organ at the domestic level may facilitate specific sectoral interests capturing the support of the president and gaining access to the organ. Third, lack of alignment between the president's preferences and that of the national parliament may provoke deadlock if integration decisions require domestic transposition (as is the case, for instance, of MERCOSUR). Last but not least, concentration of decision-making on the organ of

[115] A. Malamud, "Presidential Diplomacy and the Institutional Underpinnings of Mercosur. An Empirical Examination," 40:1 *Latin American Research Review* 138–164 (2005).

[116] A. Malamud, "Presidentialism and Mercosur: A Hidden Cause for a Successful Experience," in F. Laursen (ed.), *Comparative Regional Integration: Theoretical Perspectives* (Aldershot: Ashgate, 2003), pp. 53–73.

[117] F. Söderbaum and A. Sbragia, "EU Studies and the 'New Regionalism': What Can Be Gained from Dialogue?," 32:6 *Journal of European Integration* 563–582 (2010).

heads of State/government means its effectiveness may be affected by the substantive overcrowding of presidential agendas with a multiplicity of summits. In a very critical review of African regionalism, Söderbaum concludes that "Summitry" has become part of "discursive" and "symbolic" regionalism. The summits of heads of States of the main intergovernmental regional organizations, such as AU, COMESA, ECOWAS and SADC, are gigantic events, where the political leaders can show to the world and their citizenry that they are promoting the cause of African regional cooperation, and at the same time show that their "State" is important (or at least "visible") on the international diplomatic scene. These summits and conferences are crucial elements in a discursive and even imaginary construction of regional organizations, and this social practice is then repeated and institutionalized at a large number of ministerial and other meetings, which in reality involves little debate and no wider consultation within or between Member States.[118]

Assuming the universal presence of the organ of heads of State/government, two institutional alternatives follow. The first is a highly concentrated one in which decision-making remains centered in the summit. According to Behr and Jokela, this tends to be the case of organizations involving non-democratic countries, as they are less prone to

[118] F. Söderbaum, *What's Wrong with Regional Integration? The Problem of Eurocentrism*, EUI RSCAS Working Paper 2013/64, Global Governance Programme-63.

devolve powers away from the head of State.[119] The second model develops an intergovernmental institutional structure integrated in a hierarchical line by councils of ministers and, next, committees of top- and lower-rank governmental officers. The next subsection explores this institutional alternative.

1.5.1.3 The councils of ministers

Councils of ministers are a conspicuous organ within most integration organizations. But, by and large, they are subordinate to the organ of heads of State/government, regardless of whether the Member States have presidential or parliamentary constitutional structures. In fact, the EU is the only case in which the Council operated in the absence of an organ for heads of State/government, and this happened only for a brief period (1951–1969). Regardless of this consideration, institutional design normally overloads councils with a large number of functions (see Table 1.10) and this may offer a distorted picture. Councils of ministers may have a general competence (and they are staffed by foreign affairs/economics ministers) or, more commonly, they may have sectoral competence, and in this case, their composition depends on the subject area.

Some notes regarding councils' functions are of interest. First, contrary to expectations, the organ of ministers is seldom entrusted with preparing the meetings of the organ of

[119] T. Behr and J. Jokela, *Regionalism and Global Governance: The Emerging Agenda*, Notre Europe Studies and Research No. 85 (2011) (available at www.notre-europe.eu/en/axes/europe-and-world-governance/works/publication/regionalism-global-governance), p. 16.

Table 1.10 *Powers of councils of ministers (summary)*

Power	International organization
Decision-making	AU, Benelux, COMESA, EAC, ECO, GCC, GUAM, MERCOSUR, OBSEC, OIC, SAFTA, UNASUR
Appointments	ACS, AEC, ASEAN, ECCAS, ECOWAS, GCC, LAIA, OIC, SADC
General policies	ACS, AEC, ASEAN, CAN, CARICOM, CIS, CoE, COMESA, EAC, ECCAS, ECOWAS, GCC, GUAM, IGAD, IOR-ARC, LAIA, MERCOSUR, OBSEC, ODECA, OECS, SAARC, SADC, UNASUR
Implementation	ASEAN, AU, CAN, CARICOM, CEN-SAD, EAC, GUAM, IGAD, OAU, OECS, OIC, OIF, SADC, SAFTA, SICA, UNASUR
Budgetary powers	ACS, AEC, CARICOM, COMESA, EAC, ECCAS, ECOWAS, GUAM, IGAD, OIC, SICA, UNASUR
Amendments	ACS, GCC, LAIA
Admission of new members	ACS, LAIA, OBSEC, SICA
Conclusion of international agreements	ACS, CAN, CoE
Establishment of organs	EAC, IOR-ARC, OBSEC, OIC, SADC, UNASUR
Preparatory organ of the meetings of the heads of State	ASEAN, CARICOM, GCC, GUAM, IGAD, OAU, SCO, SICA
Open clause	ACS, AEC, ASEAN, CAN, CARICOM, COMESA, EAC, ECCAS, ECOWAS, GCC, IGAD, OBSEC, OIC, SADC

Source: Own elaboration

presidents, and this may indicate something about the domestic structure of delegation. What is much more common is that councils of ministers implement the Presidents' decisions. Second, the councils of ministers retain (at least formally) decision-making powers in few organizations. This happens mainly in organizations related to economic integration. Third, councils generally have a looser entitlement to conduct or direct "general policies," which makes them the organ that drives the organization between summits. The large number of organizations that charge councils with driving general policies, and the significant number granting them powers by means of an "open clause" (that is, the treaty contains a specific provision stating that the council of ministers may have any other functions as may be provided in the treaty or delegated by the summit or similar), confirms this role. In any case, their ability to perform depends heavily on the position and attitude of the organ of presidents. On the other hand, and with few exceptions, councils do not normally possess structural powers, such as revising the treaties, accepting new members or creating new organs in the integration organization.

1.5.2 Delegation to agencies: the role of secretariats

Delegation to organs which are independent or autonomous from the control of Member States serves both to underline their commitment to the organization and also to increase its efficiency. The latter argument dominated functionalism's approach to international organization: technical bodies, chosen because of their technical capacity, could deliver efficient policies within strictly delimited fields. As for the former, States' commitment to independent technical bodies signals their willingness to delegate, hence, *prima facie* they renounce their ability to freely dispose of their treaty commitments. Empirical evidence, however, does not entirely substantiate the second argument. Agencies and, specifically, secretariats, have scarce powers in virtually all organizations. In fact, the original selection of the name "Secretariats" in the League of Nations responded to the wish to indicate a purely administrative, secondary organ,[120] and, even though their functions have increased ever since, their perceived status as subordinate organs remains, even in integration organizations. The bulk of their function concerns the implementation of decisions (meaning follow-up rather than a specific executive function), the coordination of activities and assistance to decision-making organs. Generally speaking, secretariats do not have decision-making functions, even though, in some cases, preparation of and participation in meetings may act as a proxy for "involvement" in decision-making. Table 1.11 lists the different types of functions that secretariats may assume within international/regional organizations.

1.5.3 Jurisdictional organs: courts and ad hoc *dispute settlement mechanisms*

The establishment of courts and *ad hoc* dispute settlement mechanisms in regional integration organizations greatly

120 H. G. Schermers and N. M. Blokker, *International Institutional Law: Unity Within Diversity* (Leiden: Martinus Nijhoff, 5th edn., 2011), p. 321.

Table 1.11 *Functions of general secretariats*

Power	International organization
Secretary general – legal representation	AEC, APEC, ASEAN,[a] AU, CARICOM, CEN-SAD, COMESA, ECOWAS, GCC, IOR-ARC, OAS, OIF, OPEC, SICA, UNASUR, UNWTO
Secretary general as chief administrative officer	ASEAN, CEN-SAD, CoE, ECCAS, ECO, GCC, Helsinki Convention, IMO, OAS, OECS, OIC, OPEC, SICA, UN, WHO
Secretary general as chief executive officer	CARICOM, CEN-SAD, COMESA, EAC, ECOWAS, IGAD, OAS, OIF, OPEC
Coordination of activities and assistance	ACS, APEC, AU, Benelux, CARICOM, CEN-SAD, CoE, COMESA, EAC, ECO, EFTA, GUAM, IGAD, IHO, INTERPOL, IOR-ARC, MERCOSUR, NAFTA, OAS, OECD, OECS, OPCW, OPEC, SAFTA, SCO, UNASUR, WCO, WHO
Recruitment/ appointments	AEC, Arab League, ASEAN, Benelux, ECCAS, ECOWAS, GCC, IMO, OAS, OECS, OIC, OIF, SADC, SICA, UNWTO, WHO, WTO
Implementation (follow-up)	ACS, AEC, ASEAN, Benelux, CARICOM, CEN-SAD, COMESA, EAC, ECCAS, ECO, ECOWAS, GCC, IGAD, INTERPOL, IOR-ARC, MERCOSUR, OECS, OIC, OPCW, SADC, SICA, UNASUR
Draft budget / financial activities	ACS, AEC, APEC, Arab League, Benelux, CARICOM, CoE, COMESA, EAC, ECOWAS, GCC, IGAD, IMO, INTERPOL, OAS, OIC, OIF, OPCW, SADC, SCO, SICA, UNASUR, UNWTO, WHO, WTO
Submission of reports and studies	ACS, AEC, ASEAN, CARICOM, COMESA, EAC, ECCAS, ECO, ECOWAS, GCC, GUAM, IGAD, INTERPOL, MERCOSUR, OAS, OECS, OIC, OPCW, OPEC, SADC, SICA, UN, UNASUR, UNWTO

Table 1.11 (*cont.*)

Power	International organization
Preparation of programs of action and development of proposals	AEC, CARICOM, EAC, ECCAS, ECOWAS, EFTA, IGAD, INTERPOL, OECD, OIF, SICA
Cooperation agreements	ACS, IGAD, IHO
Preparatory organ of the meetings	ACS, AEC, CARICOM, EAC, ECO, ECOWAS, GCC, IGAD, IOR-ARC, OAS, OECS, OIC, OPCW, SADC
Participation in meetings	ASEAN, INTERPOL, SICA, UN, UNASUR
Custody of documents	Arab League, IGAD, IOR-ARC, OAS, UNASUR
Open clause[b]	CARICOM, EAC, ECO, GCC, Helsinki Convention, ICES, IGAD, IMO, OIC, PICES, SADC, SICA, UN

Source: Own elaboration

Note

[a] According to Art. 11(d), the Secretary General presents the views of ASEAN and participates in meetings with external parties in accordance with approved policy guidelines and mandate given to the Secretary General.

[b] The treaty contains a specific provision stating that the secretariat may have any other functions as provided in the treaty or delegated by the organs.

reinforces the credibility of the commitments that States accept, to the point that they are one of the vital components of the sustainability of the process of regional integration. By accepting that other actors – whether States, companies or individuals – have a right to sue them in front of these regional judicial institutions, States engaged in regional cooperation thereby accept some limits to their own sovereignty.[121] However, it may be noticed that, in some cases, courts and *ad hoc* dispute settlement institutions are alternative mechanisms to purely political or diplomatic negotiations. Thus, the Protocol of Olivos (MERCOSUR) gives priority to direct negotiations among State parties and allows that controversies may be subject to the WTO system or any other preferential trade area's mechanism to which MERCOSUR members may be parties. Equally, ECOWAS parties may access the ECOWAS Court when consultations among them do not resolve the dispute.

Both models (courts and *ad hoc* mechanisms) exist in international/integration organizations, and they express a delegation which diminishes States' discretionary ability to interpret their commitments and, hence, ties their hands. Perhaps because of this, courts are not very common institutional structures in international organizations. Alter has identified twenty-five permanent (and operative) international courts, seventeen of which are international economic courts associated with integration schemes.[122] Their

[121] T. Behr and J. Jokela, *Regionalism and Global Governance: The Emerging Agenda*, Notre Europe Studies and Research No. 85 (2011) (available at www.notre-europe.eu/en/axes/europe-and-world-governance/works/publication/regionalism-global-governance), p. 17.

[122] K. J. Alter, *The Multiple Roles of International Courts and Tribunals: Enforcement, Dispute Settlement, Constitutional and Administrative Review*, Buffett Center for International and Comparative Studies Working Paper 12-002, 2012, identified three additional categories: international human rights courts (five courts, of which three also had

limited number, their concentration on the economic domain, and their relatively recent creation (nineteen of these were created in the 1990s or later) convey a view of the scarce propensity of States to lock themselves into an external jurisdiction where decisions may be binding upon them.

Beyond their mere existence, a court's functions and institutional design help us to understand their position within integration schemes and IOs in general. Alter distinguishes the following functions:

- law enforcement (80 percent of courts, that is, twenty courts out of twenty-five)
- administrative review (48 percent; that is, twelve courts)
- constitutional review (40 percent, that is, ten courts)
- dispute settlement (76 percent; that is, nineteen courts).

What appears highly relevant is the finding that economic integration courts make up the bulk of the latter two functions, and that these same courts usually also have administrative and law enforcement functions.

Design comprises the following features: compulsory jurisdiction (and, according to Alter, nearly all international courts today have compulsory jurisdiction) and the kind of subjects entitled to appeal to the court (whether States, individuals and/or supranational agents). She explored the functional thesis that court design responds to the functions that

competence on economic issues); international criminal tribunals (three) and specialized jurisdiction (i.e. the International Tribunal for the Law of the Sea). See also Chapter 2 below.

States delegate to them. In other words, international courts have the design features that they need to credibly play their delegated role. But her conclusions provided no confirmation of this: international courts with similar design do not necessarily share a record for legal activism and/or judicial law-making. Hence, the reasons behind court performance seem to be exogenous to the institutional design itself, and this finding may also apply to other elements of the institutional design. Table 1.12 contains a comprehensive description of the different functions performed by supranational regional courts and tribunals.

1.5.4 *Parliaments*

International or supra-State parliaments have varied formats and designations. Most of them adopt the form of national parliamentary delegations, meeting within an assembly format[123] which is normally associated with intergovernmental organizations.[124] The function of parliaments in international politics and within international organizations varies greatly, but can generally be associated with an ideational justification:

[123] *Inter alia*, Inter-Parliamentary Union, NATO Parliamentary Assembly, Latin American Parliament (Parlatino), Baltic Assembly, OSCE Parliamentary Assembly, Inter-Parliamentary Assembly of the CIS, Inter-Parliamentary Assembly of the Eurasian Economic Community, Arab Parliament, Asian Parliamentary Assembly, Euro-Mediterranean Parliamentary Assembly, Euro-Latin Parliamentary Assembly and PACE (Parliamentary Assembly of the Council of Europe).

[124] The Latin American Parliament (Parlatino) is an exception, since it is not linked to any existing international organization.

Table 1.12 *Domains, functions and institutional design of courts*

Court (date of creation)	Dispute settlement				Enforcement				Administrative review				Constitutional review			
	Cj	Sa	P	Sup	Cj	Sa	P	Sup	Cj	Sa	P	Sup	Cj	Sa	P	Sup
Economic systems: Europe																
European Court of Justice ECJ (1952/1988)	•	•	IO		•	•	I	C	•		•		•	•	•	AO
Benelux Court (1974)																
European Free Trade Area Court (EFTAC) (1992)	•	•	•		•			Sur	•	•	•					
Economic systems: Eurasia																
Economic Court of the Commonwealth of Independent States (ECCIS) (1992)	U	•														
Economic systems: America																
Andean Tribunal Of Justice (ATJ) (1984)	•	•	IO		•	•	•	S	•	•	•		•	•	•	S
Central American Court of Justice (CACJ) (1994)	•	•	•	O	•	•	•	AO	•	•	•	AO	•	•	•	AO
Caribbean Court of Justice (CCJ) (2001)	•	•	CbC						•	•	•		OP		•	
Southern Common Market (MERCOSUR) (2002)	•	•			•	•										
Economic systems: Asia																
Association of Southeast Asian Nations (ASEAN) Dispute Settlement Mechanisms (2004)	•	•	IO		•	•										
Economic systems: Africa																
West African Economic and Monetary Union (WAEMU) (1994)	•	•			•	•	I	C	•	•	I		•	•	•	AO
Common Court of Justice and Arbitration for the Organization for the Harmonization of Corporate Law in Africa (OHADA) (1997)	•	• Ad	•													

Table 1.12 (*cont.*)

Court (date of creation)	Dispute settlement				Enforcement				Administrative review				Constitutional review			
	Cj	Sa	P	Sup	Cj	Sa	P	Sup	Cj	Sa	P	Sup	Cj	Sa	P	Sup
Court of Justice for the Common Market of Eastern and Southern Africa (COMESA) (1998)	•	•	IO		•	•	I	S	•	•	•		•	•	•	
Central African Monetary Community (CEMAC)(2000)	•	•	IO		•	•	•	AO	•	•	•	AO	•	•	•	AO
East African Community Court of Justice (EACJ) (2001)	•	•	IO		•	•	•	S	•		•		•	•	•	Ad.
Court of Justice of the Economic Community of West African States (ECOWAS) (2001)	•	•	IO	C	•	•	HR	S	•	•	•		•	•		AO
Southern African Development Community Court (SADC Court) (2005)	•	•	•	O	•	•	•						•	•	•	AO
Economic systems: world																
World Trade Organization Appellate Body (WTO) (1994)	•	•			•	•										
Human rights: Europe																
European Court of Human Rights (ECtHR) (1958)					•	•	•									
Human rights: America																
Inter-American Court of Human Rights (IACtHR) (1979)					OP	•		C								
Human rights: Africa																
African Court on Human and Peoples' Rights (ACtHPR) (2005)					OP	•										
International criminal courts: Europe																
International Criminal Tribunal for the Former Yugoslavia (ICTY) (1993)					•			Pr								
International criminal courts: Africa																

International Criminal Tribunal for Rwanda (ICTR) (1994)				•	Pr			
International criminal courts: world								
International Criminal Court (ICC) (2002)				•	Pr			
General jurisdiction and other: world								
International Court of Justice (ICJ) (1945)	OP	•	Ad					
International Tribunal for the Law of the Sea (ITLOS) (1996)	OP	•				•	•	I

Source: Adapted from K. J. Alter, *The Multiple Roles of International Courts and Tribunals: Enforcement, Dispute Settlement, Constitutional and Administrative Review*, Buffett Center for International and Comparative Studies Working Paper 12-002, 2012.

Key:

Cj: compulsory jurisdiction
OP = optional protocol
U = unclear
Sa: State access
Ad = advisory opinions only
P: private litigant access
IO = IO employees and firms with disputes regarding goods and services supplied to the IO
CbC = case by case
HR = human rights only
Sup: supranational actor access
O = Community officials
C = Commission
AO = any Community organ
S = Secretariat
Pr = prosecutor
Sur = surveillance authority
I = indirect via national courts

rather than being required by the logic of delegation and efficiency, parliaments bring to the international arena (regardless of their specific powers) the ideals of representation and democracy inherent to domestic policy-making.

Whilst the self-designated free trade areas (with the single exception of EFTA) keep a low level of institutionalization which excludes any form of parliamentary assemblies, parliaments are a fairly common institutional feature in integration schemes (see Table 1.13). In some cases, such as MERCOSUR, they have evolved from previous organs for the coordination of national parliaments (for example, Comisión Parlamentaria Conjunta). Some institutions currently stick to the model of committees of national parliaments as exemplified by the SADC Parliamentary Forum; the Inter-Parliamentary Union of IGAD Member States (IPU-IGAD), founded in February 2004; REPAC (the Network of Parliamentarians of the Economic Community of Central African States (ECCAS)) (2002); and the Parliament of UEMOA (P-UEMOA) (2003). However, some of the integration schemes lacking parliamentary assemblies have discussed plans for creating them, as is the case of the SADC.[125]

[125] The SADC has a Parliamentary Forum, established in 1996 and loosely conceived of as a consultation forum for national parliamentarians interested in integration. Despite its pale life, it developed a Draft Protocol on the SADC Parliament. However, experts consider the creation of this institution a highly unlikely development in the near future. T. Musavengana, *The Proposed SADC Parliament. Old Wine in New Bottles or an Ideal Whose Time Has Come?* (Pretoria: Institute for Security Studies, 2011) (available at www.issafrica.org/uploads/Mono181web.pdf).

Table 1.13 *Supranational parliaments*

Name of parliament	Date of creation/ revision	Associated organization	Direct election of members	Size	All delegations the same size regardless of population	Consultative	Legislative	Budgetary	Appointments
European Parliament (EP)	1952/1979	EU	Yes	754	No		•	•	•
Nordic Council	1952		No	87	Yes[a]		•		
EFTA Parliamentary Committee	1977	EFTA	No	18	No	•	•		•
Inter-Parliamentary Committee of the West African Economic and Monetary Union (IPC)	1994/2003	WAEMU	Yes	40	Yes	•		•	•
Latin American Parliament (Parlatino)	1964/1987	(CLACS[b])	No[c]	264	Yes		•	•	•
Andean Parliament (Parlandino)	1979/1984	CAN	Yes[d]	20	Yes	•	•	•	•
Central American Parliament (Parlacen)	1986/1991	SICA	Yes	140	Yes		•		•
MERCOSUR Parliament (Parlasur)	1991/2006	MERCOSUR	Yes	99	Yes[e]	•	•	•	
Baltic Assembly	1991		No	60	Yes	•		•	
OSCE Parliamentary Assembly	1992	OSCE	No	320	No				

Table 1.13 (*cont.*)

Name of parliament	Date of creation/ revision	Associated organization	Direct election of members	Size	All delegations the same size regardless of population	Consultative	Legislative	Budgetary	Appointments
Inter-Parliamentary Assembly of the Commonwealth of Independent States	1992	CIS	No			•	•		
Parliamentary Assembly of the Black Sea Economic Cooperation (PAOBSEC)	1993	OBSEC	No	76	Yes[f]	•		•	
Assembly of Caribbean Community Parliamentarians (ACCP)	1994/1996	CARICOM	No		Yes[g]	•			
SADC Parliamentary Forum	1997	SADC	No	60	Yes	•	•	•	•
Parliamentary Union of the OIC Member States	1999	OIC	No	52[h]	No[i]	•			
Assemblée Parliamentaire de la Francophonie	1997	OIF	No	78[h]		•			

Asian Parliamentary Assembly	2006		No	206	No[j]				
Parliamentary Confederation of the Americas (COPA)	2000	(associated to the summits of Heads of State and Government of the Americas)	No	Size decided *ad hoc* for each meeting				•	•
East African Legislative Assembly (EALA)	2001	EAC	No	45	Yes		•	•	•
Inter-Parliamentary Assembly of the Eurasian Economic Community	2001/2006	EEC	No	106	No	•	•	•	•
ECCAS Parliamentary Network (REPAC)	2002	ECCAS	No/Yes[k]	50	Yes	•			
Commonwealth Parliamentary Association (CPA)	2003	Commonwealth of Nations	No					•	
Pan-African Parliament (PAP)	1991/2004	AU/AEC	No	235	Yes	•	Envisioned	•	•
Inter-Parliamentary Assembly EAEC		EAEC	No	70			•		
Arab Parliament	2004	Arab League	No	88	Yes				
ECCAS Parliament	2004	ECCAS	Yes	60	Yes	•	•		

Table 1.13 (*cont.*)

Name of parliament	Date of creation/ revision	Associated organization	Direct election of members	Size	All delegations the same size regardless of population	Consultative	Legislative	Budgetary	Appointments
ECOWAS Parliament	1994/2006	ECOWAS	Yes[m]	120	No[n]			•	
South American Parliament	2008 (pending)	UNASUR							

Notes

[a] Twenty from each of the four bigger countries, seven from Iceland.

[b] Parlatino is in the process of becoming the assembly of CLACS.

[c] In 2012, Venezuela elected directly its twelve members.

[d] By January 2013, Bolivia had not yet elected directly the members of the Parliament.

[e] As from 2011, the MERCOSUR Parliament was to have been composed following a criterion of citizen representation. However, member governments have so far failed to reach agreement. Hence, each State Party has eighteen seats, except for Venezuela, which provisionally has nine seats. By 2015, only Argentina and Paraguay had directly elected their members of Parlasur.

[f] Each Member State shall be represented by at least four seats in the Assembly. Any increase in the number of seats shall be based on the population criteria.

[g] Maximum of four for each Member State, minimum of two.

[h] The number of delegates varies.

[i] Speaker plus a maximum of four parliamentarians from each Member of the Union.

[j] Each Member parliament has a specific number of seats in the Assembly based on the size of their population.

[k] The ECCAS Network has not been constituted as yet. In the long term, its transformation into a directly elected assembly is envisaged.

[l] Not yet in operation. In 2000, an Inter-Parliamentary Commission (CIP-CEMAC) was created to cover the period until the Parliament is fully operative.

[m] During a transition period, National Assemblies of Member States or their equivalent institutions or organs are empowered to elect members from among themselves.

[n] Each of the fifteen Member States has five seats at least. The remaining seats are shared in proportion to the population.

Two different reasons may explain why States wish to establish parliaments in addition to other organs. The first is the wish to increase the legitimacy of the integration process by creating a popular representation organ within the institutional structure. The second is the nature of the functions that parliaments may perform within integration organizations and their contribution to a more efficient functioning.

1.5.4.1 Supra-State democratic organs

Parliaments are associated with democratic representation, so their appearance in the institutional structure may be related to the programmatic objective of investing integration with some sort of low-level "democratic legitimacy" by proxy. Theoretically at least, democratically elected parliaments will bring a larger legitimacy input, and several schemes foresee this requirement: the EU, the three Latin American schemes (CAN, SICA and MERCOSUR) and two African cases (ECOWAS and ECCAS). In other cases, national parliaments elect members of the supra-State assembly.[126] Direct elections have advanced more in CAN, albeit slowly.[127] By 2011, all

[126] The Speaker of the Kenyan National Assembly has opposed even the vague plans for a direct election of the EALA. He questioned their feasibility because of their costs and the difficulties for drawing electoral circumscriptions. See "Marende Says Direct Election of EALA MPs Not Feasible" (available at www.kbc.co.ke/news.asp?nid=73760).

[127] *Acuerdo de Cartagena* (Article 10); *Tratado Constitutivo del Parlamento Andino* (1979); and *Protocolo Adicional sobre Elecciones Directas y Universales de sus Representantes* (1997). Decision 551 (2003) created the *Consejo Electoral Andino* (Andean Electoral Council), which is made up of members of the electoral bodies of each of the States of the Andean Community. The *Acta de San Francisco de Quito* (2004) requested from

Member States had held direct elections, but they started at different moments. Venezuela held three elections before its withdrawal,[128] Ecuador and Peru two,[129] and Colombia[130] and Bolivia[131] one. SICA started earlier, directly electing the members of Parlacen, although only two countries, El Salvador and Guatemala, have held elections.[132] MERCOSUR

Andean States the ratification of the Protocol on Direct Elections (*Protocolo sobre Elecciones Directas del Parlamento Andino*) and asked national parliaments to hold direct elections to the Andean Parliament at the same time as legislative elections. The *Declaración de Santiago de León Caracas* (2005) reiterated the commitment of the Andean Electoral Council to direct elections, and the Decision on Electoral Cooperation (*Decisión Andina de Cooperación Electoral Horizontal*) (2008) sought to boost direct elections, but it did not produce any regulation.

128 In 1998, July 30, 2000 and December 4, 2005.

129 Ecuador on October 20, 2002 and June 14, 2009; and Peru on April 9, 2006 and April 10, 2011. In both countries, electoral legislation combines the elections with presidential and congressional elections (Ecuador, Article 5 of the Constitution; Peru, Law 28360/2004). However, in 2009, the electoral body separated the elections in order to avoid overload.

130 Article 227 of the Colombian Constitution grants the law the possibility of regulating direct elections to the Andean Parliament (Law 1157). Elections were held on March 14, 2010. There were 1.5 million voting forms with no vote marked on them, and this prompted demands for annulling the elections and holding them again. However, the Colombian Electoral Council rejected the demand and proclaimed the elected posts. *Consejo Nacional Electoral Resolución No. 1509 de 2010* (July 6, 2010)

131 October 16, 2011. Article 266 of the Bolivian Constitution provides: "The representatives of Bolivia to the supra-State parliamentary bodies emerging from the integration processes shall be elected by universal vote."

132 El Salvador's citizens have voted five times, even though the first of these, in 1989 (before the peace agreements with the FMSN), is not

designed a two-stage process: after the transitional phase in which national parliaments would designate members, citizens would directly elect parliamentarians for the period 2011–2014. However, only Paraguay implemented these provisions, and elections were held on April 20, 2008 and again on April 21, 2013. Argentina held elections in 2015 for the first time. For the second phase, the distribution of seats among Member States depends on a principle of proportional representation, which should be established by a decision of the MERCOSUR Common Market Council, based on a proposal from the Parliament itself.[133] Member States have so far failed to reach an agreement on the parliamentary proposal.

In Africa, no supra-State parliament has reached the stage of being directly elected. National legislative assemblies of Member States elect the ECOWAS assembly, which was constituted in 2001 and is considered "in transition" at present. The duration of the transitional period has not yet been

considered a free and fair election. Since then, El Salvador's citizens have voted in 1994 (taking their positions in 1996), in 2000 (2001), 2006 and 2009. Article 80 of the Constitution establishes direct election of the members of the Parlacen. Guatemala voted on September 11, 2011.

[133] Transitional Disposition 2 of the *Protocolo Constitutivo del Parlamento de MERCOSUR*. The decision should be approved before December 31, 2007. The Parliament approved the *Acuerdo Político de 28 de abril de 2009*, which establishes an "attenuated proportionality." Parliament must also work towards proposing a common date for the holding of elections (Article 6.4 of the Protocolo Constitutivo del PM provides: "On a proposal from the Parliament, the Council of the Common Market will establish the *Day of MERCOSUR Citizen*, for the simultaneous election in all Member States of the members of the parliament.")

determined; it is subject to the approval of the authority of heads of State and government. States initially planned to introduce direct elections in 2010, but this has been delayed. The *ad hoc* committee on elections by universal suffrage and enhancement of powers of the parliament submitted its report to the Assembly in October 2009.

In summary, supra-State parliaments are composed either of directly elected members or designated members from national assemblies. Two specific oddities with regard to their composition are the EAC and SICA. In the first, national assemblies designate nine members who should not be members of the domestic parliament and includes seven *ex officio* members who cannot vote. These are the national ministers responsible for regional cooperation and the two top EAC executives. The treaty left it to the respective national assemblies to develop their own legislation and guidelines on how to elect their representatives to the East African Legislative Assembly (EALA). Domestic implementation raised criticism regarding the lack of involvement of civil society and gender bias in the composition of delegations.[134] In particular, Kenya failed to fulfill the gender requirement inserted in the treaty. Requested to rule on the matter, the EAC Court declared that Kenya's rules for the election of the EALA members did not comply with Article 50 of the treaty.[135] Kenya's failure to implement treaty requirements triggered further action by the EALA, which approved the

[134] F. Ang'ila (ed.), *Processes for Elections to the East African Legislative Assembly* (Nairobi: Friedrich-Ebert-Stiftung, 2004).

[135] EACJ, Doc. EACJ Ref. No. 1 of 2006.

2011 Election Bill. This establishes a uniform rule and procedure to be followed by national parliaments when selecting the members of EALA.

SICA's Parlacen includes any ex-president or ex-vice presidents of the Member States as natural members. This composition has attracted strong objections: Panama's President Martinelli sharply criticized the immunities that membership affords former presidents, and the excessive, unnecessary and non-transparent expenditures and privileges granted. He further argued that the Parlacen had not fulfilled the responsibilities assigned to it due to its inability to be a forum for the analysis of common political, economic, social and cultural issues. He also argued that the reforms proposed in 2008[136] were insufficient and that, even if they were approved, Parlacen would still lack credibility, legitimacy and productivity.

1.5.4.2 Efficiency: the functions of supra-State parliaments

Besides democratic legitimacy, efficiency considerations may explain the creation of supra-State parliaments: if integration organs adopt derived norms which require domestic transposition, having representatives from national parliaments may *a priori* secure a smoother transmission. In four cases, integration parliaments have a recognized capacity to *promote harmonization of national legislation* (whether by

[136] *Protocolo de reformas al Tratado constitutivo del Parlamento Centroamericano y otras instancias políticas*, San Salvador, February 20, 2008.

transposition or otherwise). In all cases, though, the wording of the provisions is weak,[137] to the point that their real value may be questioned.[138]

Regional parliaments have limited powers in comparison to national ones. Thus, the traditional legislative power is an oddity rather than the rule among regional parliaments. Leaving aside the well-developed co-legislative position of the European Parliament, only six other Treaties regulate some form of legislative competence for the parliaments and, among these, only two of them (both in Africa) grant full legislative power to their assemblies. These are the AEC and the EAC, although the former considers full competence as an "ultimate objective," which in the transitional

[137] Thus, the AEC Parliament "works towards the harmonization or co-ordination of the laws of Member States" (Article 11.3 of the Protocol establishing the Parliament); the OBSEC may urge "national parliaments of the Member States to enact legislation needed for implementation of the decisions by the Council of the Ministers of Foreign Affairs" (Article 1.2); the Andean Parliament "promotes the harmonization of Member Country legislation" (Article 43.f of the Cartagena Agreement); and the EAEC Parliament "considers issues of harmonization (approximation, unification) of the national laws of the Contracting Parties" and it also "adopts standard drafts as the basis for development of national legal acts" (Article 7 of the EAEC Treaty).

[138] In relation to MERCOSUR, for instance, Á. Macías and M. Victoria, "Dos años de funcionamiento del Parlamento del MERCOSUR: una evaluación preliminary," *Revista Integración y Cooperación Internacional* No. 1 (October/December 2009), p. 5, write that the limitation of legislative powers of Parlasur creates doubts about its real ability to advance objectives of harmonization of national legislation and incorporation of MERCOSUR norms into domestic legal orders.

period is limited to "consultative powers."[139] Only the EALA has the power to adopt acts that are directly binding at the national level, although two factors weaken its legislative autonomy: drafted bills require assent by the heads of State or government;[140] and they should not have budgetary implications for the Community. Furthermore, it generally only meets once per year to deal with matters of enormous magnitude.[141] The parliaments of CAN and MERCOSUR have a similar consultative position, and both of them have a soft initiative competence, and the record for the second is poor: until 2009, it had proposed two projects of MERCOSUR norms and only one project of national norms.[142]

[139] The ultimate aim of the Parliament is to evolve into an institution with full legislative powers; however, in the meantime, it only has consultative powers (Article 2.3 of the Protocol to the Treaty Establishing the African Economic Community (AEC) Relating to the Pan African Parliament, March 2, 2001). The AEC Treaty (Article 14) stipulates that, to enhance the involvement of African people in the economic integration process, a parliament shall be created.

[140] Articles 59–64 of the EAC Treaty.

[141] S. Kingah and A. Cofelice, *EU's Engagement with African (Sub)Regional Parliaments of ECOWAS, SADC, the EAC and the AU*, UNU-CRIS Working Paper W-2012/8, p. 10.

[142] Parliament "participates in the law-making process by suggesting to the System bodies draft provisions on subjects of common interest, for incorporation in Andean Community Law" (Article 42.e of the Cartagena Agreement); Parliament "elaborates opinions on all the projects of norms of the Mercosur that require legislative approval in one or several States Parties; it also may propose projects of norms of the Mercosur for consideration by the CMC" (Articles 4.12 and 13 of the Protocol). Á. Macías and M. Victoria, "Dos años de funcionamiento del Parlamento del MERCOSUR: una evaluación preliminary," *Revista*

As far as other traditional parliamentary powers such as budgetary powers and approval of appointments for top offices, the general landscape is very limited. Only the EAC Parliament formally has the power to approve the Community budget; but this does not include entitlements to draw up or review budgets, which effectively reduces the assembly to a "rubber stamping institution."[143] In two other cases (CAN and AEC), the parliaments can make recommendations on the budget proposal. Likewise, the ECOWAS Parliament issued a resolution in September 2002 calling for the enhancement of its powers to make consultation on the adoption of the community budget obligatory.[144] As regards approving appointments, regional parliaments lack this competence, with the single exception of the Parlacen (SICA), which can elect the highest-rank officers of the organizations created by the treaties.[145]

Some regional integration organizations grant their assemblies a specific and, to a certain extent, *sui generis* power: that of *democratic oversight*. This is not specific to integration organizations, since other international organizations, such as

Integración y Cooperación Internacional No. 1 (October/December 2009), p. 9.

143 H. O. Morara, "The Inauguration of the East African Legislative Assembly – Time to Rejoice?," in *Mambo!* (the newsletter of the French Institute for Research in Africa) (2001), p. 2.

144 ECOWAS-P, Resolution relating to the enhancement of the powers of the community parliament, Ordinary Session, 03-13.09.2002, Parliament of the Economic Community of West African States (available at www.iss.co.za).

145 Article 5.c of the Treaty establishing the Parliament and other political institutions.

PACE, have similar endeavors. The extent to which this power is vested in these assemblies varies greatly and does not correspond to a specific geographical level. At a minimum, assemblies are recognized as being able to act in this arena (for instance, the ECOWAS Parliament can consider issues concerning human rights and fundamental freedoms of citizens), and a specific duty to promote and guarantee respect for human rights is expected from them.[146] More precisely, the Pan-African Parliament of the AEC is entitled to make recommendations on matters pertaining to human rights, and consolidating democratic institutions and the culture of democracy, as well as the promotion of good governance and the rule of law.[147] In two other cases, parliaments have expressly obtained the power to address the state of democracy in Member States.[148]

Given that democracy promotion is an implicit or explicit objective among integration parliaments, the MERCOSUR Parliament has explicitly been conceived as a guarantee against counter-democratic revolution, since it is charged with ensuring the preservation of the democratic regime of the Member States

[146] CAN, Articles 12.b and 12.c of the La Paz Treaty.

[147] Article 11.1 of the Protocol to the Treaty Establishing the African Economic Community relating to the Pan-African Parliament.

[148] Thus, Article 1.3 of the Rules of Procedure on the Declaration on the Establishment of the Parliamentary Assembly of OBSEC states that it provides assistance to national parliaments of the Member States so as to strengthen parliamentary democracy in the Member States, whilst for SICA, Article 5.f of the Treaty Establishing the Parliament and other Political Institutions declares that Parlacen promotes the consolidation of the democratic system in the Member States.

(Article 4.2 of the Protocol). Although its practical instruments are not numerous and some bemoan its limited role,[149] the Protocol (Article 4.3) requires that it elaborate an annual Report on Human Rights in the Member States. In particular, the Parliament has used its hearings to boost its power to bring pressure to bear. In two cases, Venezuela and Paraguay, the preparation of the report ignited political controversy.[150]

Similar developments have taken place elsewhere; for instance, the SADC Parliamentary Forum adopted the Benchmarks for Democratic Legislatures in Southern Africa in 2010. This has become a useful reference document as member countries embark on parliamentary reform programs. Moreover, the ASEAN Inter-Parliamentary Myanmar Caucus was inaugurated in 2004 to call on the military government in Myanmar to bring about changes and democratic reforms in the country.

In summary, parliaments are, by and large, a weak and underdeveloped institution in almost all integration schemes (with the single exception of the European Parliament). In some cases, some design elements indicate a bolder ambition

[149] Á. Macías and M. Victoria, "Dos años de funcionamiento del Parlamento del MERCOSUR: una evaluación preliminary," *Revista Integración y Cooperación Internacional* No. 1 (October/December 2009).

[150] Issues raised with regard to Venezuela included the political disqualification of some candidates and the media policy of the Chávez government in 2008, whilst in Paraguay the *Movimiento Campesino Paraguayo* denounced violations of human rights and the MERCOSUR Parliament instituted a temporary commission of inquiry (see www.parlamentodelmercosur.org).

which remains be accomplished, if at all. Viewed overall, the impact of parliaments in integration schemes is largely negligible. One argument cited for explaining the diminished role of parliaments refers to the fact that American, African and Asian integration systems are composed of presidential systems which do not depend on parliaments for the selection of the executive.[151] Institutional isomorphism (that is, the mirroring of the domestic institutional design in the integration organization, with a strong dominance of presidential organs) may explain their limited role. In addition, the weakness of parliamentary organs at the regional level may actually be a symptom of systemic weaknesses faced by national parliaments in the area of treaty-making in developing countries.[152] The current state of affairs demonstrates that African regional parliaments and parliamentary assemblies are in many ways at an infant stage of development and are still far from exercising the roles that fully fledged parliaments play in democratic setups. However, this stage must be seen as part of a larger, continuous process to complement economic integration with the broader political dimension of regional integration.[153]

151 A. Malamud and S. Stavridis, "Parliaments and Parliamentarians as International Actors," in B. Reinalda (ed.), *The Ashgate Research Companion to Non-State Actors* (London: Ashgate, 2012).

152 S. Kingah and A. Cofelice, *EU's Engagement with African (Sub)Regional Parliaments of ECOWAS, SADC, the EAC and the AU*, UNU-CRIS Working Paper W-2012/8, p. 6.

153 U. Terlinden, "African Regional Parliaments/Parliamentary Bodies as Engines of Integration: Current State and Challenges," Roundtable on "The Interface between Regional Parliamentary Bodies and the Pan-African Parliament," SADC Parliamentary Forum/Friedrich-Ebert-Stiftung, Namibia and Lusaka, August 8–9, 2005.

1.6 The voting rule for decision-making

A key decision in institutional design concerns the selection of the voting rules for international/integration organizations. Voting requirements fall into one of the three following categories: unanimity, consensus or majority (with different requirements). The meaning of unanimity (all voting agents agree) is self-evident, whilst the meaning of majority is intuitive, in that the number of votes to take a decision is less than the number of members and/or the total of votes granted to all members and more than half of all existing votes. Consensus has a more ambiguous meaning. Whilst it is used in many international organizations, few of these define its meaning.

Unanimity. The geographical scope of unanimity proves its universality: organizations in Europe (Benelux Decisions and EFTA Decisions and Recommendations), Latin America (OECS Authority Decisions and Decisions of the Authority of Heads of State of CARICOM) and Asia (the Interstate Council of the Eurasian Economic Community Decisions or the SAARC Decisions), as well as Arab organizations (Decisions of the Presidency Council of the Union of the Arab Maghreb) and even some functional organizations such as OPEC (all Decisions of the Conference of Ministers) apply unanimity as the general decision-making rule.

Consensus is the most common decision-making rule and it appears in every geographical area and type of organization. European (OBSEC), Eurasian (CIS), Latin American (CAN, MERCOSUR, SICA and UNASUR), African (COMESA Decisions of the Authority of Heads of State and the Council and Decisions of SADC institutions) and Asian (SCO) organizations explicitly prescribe decision by consensus. Within this universe, ASEAN refers explicitly to both *consensus* and (mutual) *consultation*.[154] Whether they make it explicit or not, both procedures are inherent to the decision-making procedures of most integration and international organizations. In general, treaties do not describe what consensus means, with two exceptions: the WTO Charter establishes that "the body concerned shall be deemed to have decided by consensus on a matter submitted for its consideration, if no Member, present at the meeting when the decision is taken, formally objects to the proposed decision" (Article IX.1 at footnote 1). The ODED (Article 12.1) defines consensus as achieving agreement without voting.[155] By and large, all organizations applying consensus seem to rely on this explicit definition: there is no formal vote and a decision is taken if no formal opposition is expressed. Thus, in general, consensus could be defined as "unanimity without voting." MERCOSUR decision-making rules prove this interpretation right: whilst MERCOSUR organs take decisions by consensus (Article 16), approval of applications for accession of new Member States requires the unanimous decision of the State parties (Article 20). The difference seems to be that members need to vote explicitly on the admission of new

[154] As a rule, decision-making shall be based on *consultation and consensus* (Article 20.1), including amendments to the treaty (Article 48.2).

[155] A similar definition is that of GUAM: Decisions in GUAM bodies shall be adopted with participation of all Parties on the basis of *consensus* by achieving agreement without voting (Article 12.1).

members. This understanding of consensus as unanimity without voting can likely be extended to any other international organization and regional integration scheme.

The unanimity/consensus rule has **exceptions** to limit its blocking potential (see below): **majorities** and **quorums; differentiating application of unanimity/consensus according to the organ taking the decision** and/or ***ratione materiae***. Table 1.14 summarizes the voting procedures in several integration schemes.

Unblocking mechanisms derogate unanimity. In this way, it is possible to overcome deadlock. Thus, the two-thirds majority works as a method to avoid deadlocks in the decisions and regulations of the African Economic Community,[156] the African Union[157] and the decisions of the COMESA Council.[158] It is also the default procedure for the Organization of the Islamic Conference.[159]

[156] Article 10.4: decisions of the Assembly of Heads of State and Government shall be adopted by **consensus**, failing that, by a two-thirds majority of Member States. Regulations of the Council of Ministers shall be adopted by **consensus** or, failing that, by a two-thirds majority of Member States (Article 13.4).

[157] Decisions of the Assembly of Heads of State and Government shall be adopted by *consensus*, failing that, by a two-thirds majority of Member States (Article 7.1). The same applies to decisions of the Executive Council (Article 7.1).

[158] Decisions of the Council shall be taken by consensus, failing which by a two-thirds majority of the members of the Council (Article 9.6).

[159] Decisions shall be taken by *consensus*. If consensus cannot be obtained, decisions shall be taken by a two-thirds majority of members present and voting unless otherwise stipulated in the Charter (Article 33.2).

Table 1.14 *Voting requirements*

	General rule	Unlocking procedure (two-thirds, three-quarters or simple majority) to bypass blockade under unanimity/consensus	Distinction between unanimity/consensus and majority *ratione materiae*	Distinction between unanimity/consensus and majority according to the organ making decisions
Unanimity	Arab League, Benelux, CARICOM, CoE, EAEC, ECO, EFTA, EPO, GCC, ODECA, OECS, OPEC, SAARC, UEMOA,[a] UMA	EU[b]	CoE, EFTA, OPEC	Benelux, CARICOM, CoE, EAEC, ODECA, UEMOA
Consensus	ACS, AEC, APEC, ASEAN, AU, CAN, CIS, COMESA, EAC, ECCAS, ECOWAS, GUAM, IGAD, IOR-ARC, KEDO, MERCOSUR, OBSEC, OECD, OIC, OPCW, PICES, SADC, SCO, SICA, UNASUR, WTO	AEC, ASEAN,[c] AU, COMESA, IGAD, KEDO,[d] OBSEC, OIC, OPCW, PICES,[e] WTO[f]	AEC, AU, IGAD, MERCOSUR, OECD, OPCW,[g] SADC, WTO[h]	CAN, EAC, OPCW
Majority	AAEU, EU, ICES, IHO, ILO, IMF, IMO, IMSO, INTERPOL, IOM, ITSO, LAFTA, LAIA, OAS, OAU, UNWTO, WHO, WIPO	EAEC[i]	IHO, ILO, IMO, INTERPOL, IOM, LAIA, OAS (changes the size of the majority)	OAS, OAU, WIPO (changes the size of the majority)

Table 1.14 (*cont.*)

Source: Own elaboration

Notes

[a] Decisions of the Conference ("*actes de la Conference*") require unanimity (Art. 114), but decisions of the Council, as a general rule, require two-thirds.

[b] Where the Treaty on the Functioning of the European Union or Title V of this Treaty provides for the Council to act by unanimity in a given area or case, the European Council may adopt a decision authorizing the Council to act by a qualified majority in that area or in that case. This subparagraph shall not apply to decisions with military implications or those in the area of defense (Art. 48.7).

[c] Where consensus cannot be achieved, the ASEAN Summit may decide how a specific decision can be made (Art. 20.2).

[d] If a consensus is not achievable at the Executive Council, by a majority vote (Art. 6.e).

[e] If consensus is not possible, decisions may be taken by three-quarters majority.

[f] Except as otherwise provided, where a decision cannot be arrived at by consensus, the matter at issue shall be decided by voting (. . .). Decisions of the Ministerial Conference and the General Council shall be taken by a majority of the votes cast, unless otherwise provided in this Agreement or in the relevant Multilateral Trade Agreement (Art. IX.1).

[g] Only applicable to decisions of the Executive Council on matters of substance (Art. 29).

[h] The decision to adopt an interpretation shall be taken by a three-quarters majority of the Members. Art. IX.2.

[i] Only applicable to the Integration Committee.

In very few cases, requiring a quorum serves to contain the blocking potential of unanimity[160] and consensus. If the quorum is achieved, decisions can be taken by the unanimous decision of less than the total of all Member States (in practice, a form of majority). However, the quorum requirement seems to create an incentive to attend rather than an alternative decision-making requirement. Thus, in UNASUR, the decisions of the Council of Heads of State and Government, the Resolutions of the Council of Ministers of Foreign Affairs and the Provisions of the Council of Delegates may be adopted with the presence of at least three-quarters of the Member States (Article 12).

Unanimity/consensus may apply *ratione materiae*, that is, treaties may distinguish between different types of issues, reserving unanimity for the most serious ones[161] and applying some form of qualified majority in others, or even simple majority. A clear case is the Council of Europe which, apart from reserving "important matters" for a unanimous decision of the Committee of Ministers, establishes that all other resolutions of the Committee will be taken by two-thirds

[160] Thus, in the GCC, Resolutions of the Supreme Council in substantive matters shall be carried by *unanimous* approval of the Member States participating in the voting (Article 9), and the meeting of the Supreme Council shall be considered valid if attended by two-thirds of Member States (Article 7). The same quorum applies to the Ministerial Council.

[161] For instance, the Council of Ministers of the Association of Caribbean States decides by consensus on the substantive matters submitted to it for consideration. Procedural matters shall be determined by a two-thirds majority of the Members present and voting (Article 11.4).

majority.[162] Surprisingly, the Committee decides on inviting new members (an important decision, taking into account the conditionality involved) by a two-thirds majority. This majority provision in the Committee of Ministers may be applied only if taken by a majority of the representatives entitled to sit on the Committee. The Arab League prescribes unanimity of the Council for decisions to repel aggression against a Member State and decisions to separate a State from the League. Similarly, the SADC uses a three-quarters majority instead of the usual consensus for what could be considered very serious decisions: dissolving the Community itself or any of its institutions or amending the treaties. Organizations using consensus may also use qualified majority (usually two-thirds) for the appointment of some top officials of the organization's agencies[163] and for procedural decisions.[164]

[162] See Articles 20 and 29.

[163] The Arab League requires a two-thirds majority to appoint the Secretary General (Article 12).

[164] EFTA requires unanimity (see above), but decisions to establish the rules of procedure of the Council and of any other bodies of the Association are taken by majority (with at least three States voting) (Article 44.a). The Arab League requires a simple majority for matters relating to personnel, the adoption of the budget of the League, the establishment of the administrative regulations for the Council, the committees and the Secretariat General and the decision to adjourn sessions (Article 16). The Council of Europe rules of procedure or financial and administrative regulations require a *simple majority* (Article 20). In the African Union, procedural decisions are taken by simple majority (Article 7.1). Decisions on procedural issues by the SICA Council of Ministers require a simple majority (Article 21).

Usually, different organs of the same organization apply the same voting requirement.[165] But cases in which different organs made up of national representatives apply different voting requirements are not uncommon. Thus, CARICOM requires unanimity for the decisions of the Conference of Heads of State, whilst the Community Council and Ministerial Councils take decisions by a qualified majority vote and such decisions shall be binding. Qualified majority means no less than three-quarters of the membership. Two additional dimensions of this differentiated voting requirement relate to decisions on procedural issues in Community organs (simple majority of Member States) and non-binding recommendations of Community organs (a two-thirds majority of Member States). Quorum is defined as a simple majority (Article 27) and applies to all organs. The COMESA Treaty establishes that the Council shall take decisions by consensus, and, failing that, by two-thirds majority of the members of the Council. This fallback provision does not apply to the Authority of Heads

The GCC Supreme Council and the Ministerial Council make resolutions on procedural matters by *majority vote* (Articles 9 and 13).

[165] The EAC requires consensus for decisions of the Summit (Article 12.3) and the Council of Ministers (Article 15.4). ECCAS prescribes also that, unless otherwise provided, decisions and directives of the Conference of Heads of State are adopted by *consensus* (Article 11.4), and the same applies to the Council (Article 15.3). ECOWAS establishes that decisions of the Authority shall be adopted by *consensus*, as a general rule (Article 9.2), and the same applies to the Council of Ministers (Article 12.2). Equally, SICA establishes that decisions of the Meeting of Presidents shall be adopted by *consensus* (Article 14), and decisions of the Council of Ministers on substantial issues shall be adopted by consensus (Article 21).

of State. Within integration organizations, agencies may also apply some sort of majority in taking their decisions.[166]

Some international organizations do not apply unanimity or consensus as the general rule, and instead work by some form of ***majority***. These are rare but significant exceptions: two of them are the pan-continental organizations in America and Africa, the OAS and the OAU. The first requires an absolute majority of the General Assembly or a two-thirds majority.[167] As for the OAU, it requires two-thirds of the Assembly of Heads of State and a majority from the Council of Ministers in order to take decisions.[168] Finally, the only

[166] The CAN Commission shall adopt its Decisions by affirmative vote of the *absolute majority* of the Member Countries. In some cases, an affirmative vote of the members with no negative vote is required (Article 26). In the Eurasian Economic Community, the Interstate Council shall take all of its decisions by *unanimous* vote. The Integration Committee shall take its decisions by a two-thirds majority of votes. Where four Contracting Parties vote in favor of a decision, but where there is still no two-thirds majority, the issue will be referred to the Interstate Council (Article 13.2).

[167] Decisions of the General Assembly shall be adopted by the affirmative vote of an *absolute majority* of the Member States, except in those cases that require a two-thirds majority vote (Article 59) and decisions on budgetary matters require the approval of two-thirds of the Member States (Article 55). Regarding the settlement of disputes, the decisions of the Permanent Council shall be taken by an affirmative vote of two-thirds of its Members except for such decisions as the rules of procedure provide shall be adopted by a *simple majority* (Article 89). Finally, the removal of the Secretary General or the Assistant Secretary General requires two-thirds of the Assembly (Article 116).

[168] For the Assembly of Heads of State and Government, all resolutions shall be determined by a two-thirds majority of the Members of the Organization; questions of procedure shall require a *simple majority*

other international organization *stricto sensu* using majority is the Latin American Integration Association (LAIA/ALADI), although an implicit veto power exists in this case.[169]

International agencies with functional scope normally use some form of majority vote, whether an unspecified majority (for example, Article 5.c of the IMF), a majority of present and voting members (IMO, Article 57.b) or merely a "simple majority" (IHO, ILO or Interpol). All these are technical authorities with very clear and delimited tasks and with low levels of politicization.

Prima facie, unanimity removes decision-making from the control of individual States, whilst unanimity allows them to control any and every outcome of decision-making. Behr and Jokela had made the case against majority and in favor of consensus. According to them, majority systems run the risk of producing persistent minorities that dislike the outcome of the voting process.[170] These discontented minorities have an incentive to loosen their commitment to regional organizations if there is little prospect that their priorities will be taken into consideration in the future.

(Article 10). For the Council of Ministers, all resolutions shall be determined by a *simple majority* (Article 14).

169 The Council, the Conference and the Committee shall adopt their decisions by the affirmative vote of two-thirds of the member countries (Article 43); some decisions shall be adopted by a two-thirds *affirmative vote, provided there is no negative vote* (see Article 43, second paragraph).

170 T. Behr and J. Jokela, *Regionalism and Global Governance: The Emerging Agenda*, Notre Europe Studies and Research No. 85 (2011) (available at www.notre-europe.eu/en/axes/europe-and-world-governance/works/publication/regionalism-global-governance), p. 18.

Consensual decision-making processes have the advantage of protecting all minorities, as they naturally constrain the powers of the largest and most powerful actors. Thus, the avoidance of structural minorities is the most powerful argument in favor of consensus/unanimity.

However, unanimity presents serious obstacles from the point of view of efficient decision-making. Unanimity permits unilateral blockades and does not incentivize the search for agreement via pay-offs, log-rolling and so on. In fact, unanimity greatly limited EU decision-making until the 1986 reforms under the Single European Act. Similar difficulties have been recorded in other geographical areas and organizations; thus, Afadameh-Adeyemi and Kalula record the SADC summit's inability to make decisions when the interest of a single country is affected. They warn that, if this trend continues, the summit could single-handedly undo all the efforts towards regional integration.[171]

Research on the operation of unanimity has shown its limitations. Thus, Buchanan and Tullock differentiated between two levels of collective action with different but interlinked decision rules.[172] The lower level is "ordinary

[171] A. Afadameh-Adeyemi and E. Kalula, "Re-examining the Legal and Institutional Anatomy of the Southern Africa Development Community," in A. Bös, A. D. Pisani, G. Erasmus, T. Hartzenberg and R. Sandrey (eds.), "Monitoring Regional Integration in Southern Africa," in *Yearbook*, vol. 10 (Tralac/Konrad Adenauer Stiftung, 2011) (available at www.tralac.org), p. 13.

[172] J. Buchanan and G. Tullock, *The Calculus of Consent: Logical Foundations of Constitutional Democracy* (Ann Arbor, MI: University of Michigan Press, 1962).

politics," which refers to the decisions (often taken by majority) in legislative assemblies. The upper level is "constitutional politics": the set of framework rules that establish the boundaries of what ordinary politics can and cannot do. In the opinion of Buchanan, majority rule in ordinary politics produces results which are both inefficient and unfair, but those rules (majority) are permissible for ordinary politics if there is consensus on the framework rule, the Constitution (whose functional equivalent under international law is a treaty).[173]

For Buchanan and Tullock, consensus means unanimity, which was thought both desirable and achievable: since constitutional rules will be stable in a wide temporal sequence comprising a large range of options and policies, individuals cannot identify (in this temporal and material range) concrete interests, nor can they calculate the effect of the functioning of the constitutional rules. Actors may be deemed to be in a situation akin to Rawls' "veil of ignorance." Hypothetically, if this is the case, the maximization of utility dictates that universal criteria such as fairness or justice guide the calculus of constitutional rules, rather than calculations based on net income or expected wealth. In their opinion, it was easier to reach an agreement on the rules rather than an agreement on possible alternatives which can be agreed with these rules.

Other authors within the constitutional economy approach argue robustly that the constitutional choice of decision rules should steer clear of the generalized adoption

[173] J. Buchanan, "Public Choice: The Origins and Development of a Research Program" (Center for Study of Public Choice, George Mason University, 2003) (available at www.gmu.edu).

of unanimity rules, given the paradox of unanimity voting: given the opportunity to receive side payments, each voter will have incentives to falsify their preferences, generating negative externalities for other voters. Hence the "unanimity paradox": even if all voters agree in principle to a policy proposal, they are likely to fail to reach unanimous consensus, if subjected to unanimity rule.[174]

1.7 Secondary norms and their incorporation into national orders (including compliance)

Treaty-based organizations can opt for establishing the content of obligations exclusively in primary legislation (that is, in the treaties themselves), or, alternatively, they can decide that specific organs within the integration scheme may create secondary legislation with the purpose of developing more general treaty provisions.[175]

The first option offers a large degree of precision and certainty of commitments entered into, but precisely because of this, it creates very rigid organizations. Moreover, the very idea of international organizations suggests that these entities are capable of performing acts. Creating an entity with a separate identity only makes sense if that entity can subsequently do certain things. In order to do these things, the organization must be able to adopt or create legal

[174] F. Parisi and J. Klick, "The Disunity of Unanimity," 14:2 *Constitutional Political Economy* 83–94 (2003).

[175] See Chapter 2 below.

instruments.[176] Thus, the second option appears as the natural one, even though it presents other kinds of problems, not least of which are questions related to the production of derived norms and their character. In any case, most integration organizations have adopted the second option, and this shows that States accept secondary legislation as consubstantial to integration agreements. According to Klabbers, the most solid theory to explain decision-making by international organizations is delegation of powers, meaning that when States consent to be bound by the constitution of an international organization, they are also logically consenting to be bound by the norms which the attributed law-making powers allow the organization to create.[177]

As a standard characteristic, regional organizations produce norms (it is a standard feature). The choice of legal instruments says something about the nature of the organization: the extent to which national authorities wish to be bound by formal instruments that they may not control. It also says something about the kind of institutional problems (compliance and legitimation) that the organization may face. Table 1.15 summarizes the typology of derived norms and their obligatory character in different organizations. The largest group of organizations encompasses those whose regulating treaties remain silent on the obligatory character of derived norms. However, a significant group of organizations do explicitly recognize the obligatory character of these

[176] J. Klabbers, *An Introduction to International Institutional Law* (Cambridge University Press, 2nd edn., 2009), p. 178.

[177] *Ibid.*, pp. 185 *et seq.*

Table 1.15 *Typology of derived norms and their obligatory character*

	General reach	Particular reach
Explicitly binding	AEC (Decisions and Regulations) Arab League (Decisions) CAN (regulated in the Treaty on the Andean Court) CARICOM (Decisions) COMESA (Regulations, Directives and Decisions) EAC (Regulations, Directives and Decisions) ECCAS (Decisions) ECOWAS (Regulations and Directives) EFTA (Decisions) EU (Regulations) MERCOSUR (Decisions, Resolutions and Directives) OECD (Decisions) OECS (Decisions Authority Heads of State) SADC (Decisions) SICA (Decisions, Resolutions, Regulations) UEMOA (Regulations) UNASUR (Decisions)	ECCAS (Directives addressed to institutions; Regulations addressed to specific States and/or institutions) ECOWAS (Decisions apply to Member States addressed) EU (Directives and Decisions) OECS (Decisions and Directives Council of Ministers of Foreign Affairs and Defense Committee: institutions) SICA (Agreements on the institutions addressed) UEMOA (Decisions addressed to specific States)
Implicitly binding	AAEU (Member States shall execute the resolutions adopted)	
Explicitly not binding	EFTA (Recommendations)	

Table 1.15 (*cont.*)

	General reach	Particular reach
No explicit mention	ACS, ASEAN, CEN-SAD, CIS, GCC, GUAM, ICES, IHO, ILO, IMF, IMO, IMSO, IOM, ITSO, KEDO, LAFTA, LAIA, OAU, SAARC, WAMZ, WIPO, WTO	

Source: Own elaboration

derived norms, and in a number of cases they have instruments which allow assigning a general or particular reach for obligations. In one case, the AAEU, the obligation may be implicitly deduced, whilst in another case (EFTA Recommendations), this binding character is explicitly rejected.

The nomenclature of derived "norms" (that is, those created by the organs of an international organization) is fairly reduced and not terribly consistent.[178] Treaties refer to "decisions," "regulations," "resolutions," "directives," "recommendations" and "agreements."[179] Among these, "decisions"

[178] Klabbers, *ibid.*, distinguishes (a) law-making norms; (b) acts applying the law; (c) acts on the internal functioning of the organization; (d) acts that aim at influencing the behavior but without creating the law.

[179] ASEAN refers to the use of "instruments," and the 2010 Protocol defines them as any instrument which is concluded by Member States, as ASEAN Member States, in written form, that give rise to their respective rights and obligations according to international law. The typology includes declarations, agreements, conventions, concords, treaties and other instruments. Article 52.1 ASEAN Charter refers to treaties, conventions, agreements, concords, declarations, protocols and other ASEAN

is the most common way to refer to derived norms, but no global consensus seems to exist on the meaning of the different terms. In a few cases, terms are associated with the different organs in charge of their production,[180] but this is not a general pattern. Nor does any *a priori* rationale seem to exist that assigns to each of these norms specific legal effects. These have to be identified either by explicit recognition, jurisprudential construction and/or scholarly interpretation.

Analysis of the legal structure underlying derived norms must take into account two important legal characteristics: their explicit binding character and whether they apply directly or instead require transposition into the domestic legal order. Tables 1.15 and 1.16 summarize the *status quo* on these two features.

As for obligation, some terms such as "recommendations,"[181] "opinions," "declarations" or "guidelines" seem *prima facie* to convey a non-obligatory character, whilst others, such as "resolutions," "regulations," "directives" and "decisions" seem *prima facie* to convey a stronger sense of obligation. In any case, it is necessary to interpret treaties in order to establish the obligatory nature of derived norms,

instruments. A large number of the 490 documents are not binding, and around 100 of these have "entering into force" provisions.

180 For instance, Article. 11 UNASUR South American Union of Nations Constitutive Treaty assigns Decisions to the Council of Heads of State, Resolutions to the Council of Ministers and Dispositions to the Council of Delegates.

181 For instance, MERCOSUR Recommendations have the objective of creating general orientations, plans for action or stimulating initiatives that contribute to the consolidation of the integration process.

regardless of their nomenclature. As Table 1.15 shows, quite a few integration organization treaties explicitly grant binding character to derived norms. In general, there is also a strong correlation between functional purpose organizations and lack of an explicit recognition of the binding character of derived norms (with ASEAN included in this group). In some cases, the obligatory nature of derived norms was disputed. Thus, in CAN, it was the later Treaty on the Andean Tribunal (TTA) which established that decisions oblige Member States from the moment they are approved either by the Andean Council or the Commission (Article 2 TTA). Beyond the treaty, jurisprudential interpretation may play a crucial role in establishing the obligatory character of secondary norms, even in the presence of explicit treaty provisions. For instance, MERCOSUR's Permanent Revision Tribunal ruled in 2008 that "MERCOSUR law is not domestic law of States Parties (or conventional international law). This is a new species distinct from them and which, despite its embryonic state, obliges States Parties to comply due to the free expression of their will reflected in the Treaty of Asunción and the Protocols of Ouro Preto and Olivos and additional rules under national law and internationally."[182] Some of the integration schemes have two types of derived norms that differentiate the reach of the obligation: apart from the ordinary general

[182] Resolución No. 1/2008 Resolución Plenaria del Tribunal Permanente de Revisión respecto del Planteo Procesal de Previo Pronunciamiento introducido por la República Argentina en el Marco Asunto No. 1/2008, "Divergencia sobre el Cumplimiento del Laudo No. 1/05 iniciada por la República Oriental del Uruguay (Article 30 del Protocolo de Olivos)."

reach (that is, obligation affects all States party),[183] derived norms may impose specific obligations on specific subjects, that is, specific States (ECOWAS and UEMOA Decisions), institutions (OECS Decisions and Directives of Council of Foreign Affairs Ministers and Defense Committee; ECCAS Directives and SICA Agreements) or particular States and institutions (Regulations ECCAS). The choice of whether to grant binding force to legal instruments is crucial and it moves between one end of the spectrum, in which national authorities remain totally unconstrained by commitments acquired within integration organizations, and the other end, in which these authorities are totally bound, not only by the initial commitments, but also by the derived instruments.

Besides obligation, a second key characteristic of secondary legislation refers to whether it applies immediately/directly (**direct applicability**) or, to the contrary, requires the intervention of national institutions to internalize derived norms within domestic law. Table 1.16 summarizes the two opposing options. Whenever no explicit mention is made, interpretation may be open. However, a safer bet seems to be that, in the absence of regulation on the application of derived norms, States expect that derived norms need to be explicitly internalized.

[183] In the case of CAN, according to S. Mejía and J. Luis, *El derecho administrativo en los procesos de integración: la Comunidad Andina* (Caracas: Fundación Estudios de Derecho Administrativo, 2005), p. 265, although no provision in the Cartagena Agreement establishes the characteristics of Decisions, the general understanding is that they have a general reach.

Table 1.16 *Secondary norms/derived norms: transposition or direct effect*

Direct applicability	AEC (Decisions and Regulations) CAN (Decisions of the Andean Council) COMESA (Regulations, Directives and Decisions) EAC (Regulations and Directives) ECCAS (Regulations, Directives and Decisions) ECOWAS (Decisions and Regulations) EU (Regulations, Directives, Decisions) UEMOA (Regulations)
Explicit transposition required	AAEU (Resolutions) Arab League (Decisions) CAN (Decisions Andean Council Foreign Affairs) CARICOM (Decisions) MERCOSUR (Decisions) UNASUR

Source: Own elaboration

Explicit recognition of direct applicability seems to be a prevalent characteristic of African integration schemes. For instance, ECOWAS has closely followed the EU model since 2012. Prior to that, only Decisions of the Authority were immediately applicable and binding on Member States, whilst those emanating from the Council of Ministers were only applicable and binding on the Community Institutions. In 2012, ECOWAS enacted a new regime for Community acts[184] which extends direct applicability to norms approved by the Council of Ministers. The new typology distinguishes between Supplementary Acts, Regulations, Directives, Decisions, Recommendations and Opinions. The most innovative additions

[184] See www.comm.ecowas.int/dept/stand.php?id=a__about&lang=en.

are Supplementary Acts that complete and/or supplement the Treaty. They substitute previous Protocols and Conventions supplementing the Treaty which required Parliamentary ratification processes. These delayed the entry into force of the legal texts, thereby paralyzing the integration process. Supplementary Acts are approved by the Authority of Heads of State and they are binding on Member States and the institutions of the Community. The Council of Ministers, in turn, enacts Regulations and Directives and makes Decisions and Recommendations. Regulations have general application and all their provisions are enforceable and directly applicable in Member States. They are enforceable in the institutions of the Community. Decisions are enforceable in Member States and for all the subjects designated therein. Directives and their objectives are binding on all Member States. The modalities for attaining such objectives are left to the discretion of States.

Outside Africa, only CAN (and the EU) contemplates such a principle (although Decisions of the Andean Council of Foreign Affairs are excluded and require transposition). In CAN, direct applicability evolved from the initially opposite position: before the approval of the TTA, Member States considered that Decisions should go through the incorporation procedures foreseen in domestic law and, in particular, legislative approval.[185] The creation of the Andean Tribunal provided an opportunity to spell out obligations clearly:

[185] S. Mejía and J. Luis, *El derecho administrativo en los procesos de integración: la Comunidad Andina* (Caracas: Fundación Estudios de Derecho Administrativo, 2005), p. 275.

Article 3 of the TTA established that CAN Decisions apply directly from the date of the publication in the Official Journal of CAN. Procedures for the reception and/or incorporation of treaties required by domestic law do not apply to decisions. The only exception is that a particular decision may establish explicitly the necessity to resort to these reception/incorporation mechanisms.[186] Decisions may require incorporation into domestic law through an express act, which will indicate the precise moment for entry into force in each State (Article 3, Treaty of the Andean Community). The only exception is the so-called "indispensable complement," that is, an indispensable piece of domestic legislation for the implementation of a Community norm. In Africa, the SADC Treaty currently has a similar complexity to the original situation in CAN, since it does not state if binding decisions of the summit have a direct effect on the territory of Member States.[187]

The obvious alternatives to an explicit recognition of direct applicability are cases in which treaties remain silent or refer explicitly to domestic organs and/or procedures for implementing a given derived norm from integration organizations. By default, it may be argued that silence fits more comfortably with assuming domestic transposition than with an implicit recognition of direct applicability, although

[186] *Ibid.*, p. 273.

[187] A. Afadameh-Adeyemi and E. Kalula, "Re-examining the Legal and Institutional Anatomy of the Southern Africa Development Community," in A. Bös, A. D. Pisani, G. Erasmus, T. Hartzenberg and R. Sandrey (eds.), "Monitoring Regional Integration in Southern Africa," in *Yearbook*, vol. 10 (Tralac/Konrad Adenauer Stiftung, 2011) (available at www.tralac.org), p. 12.

this depends on a case-by-case analysis. Table 1.16 contains a number of cases that require explicit transposition. This procedure grants States significant control over the efficacy of secondary legislation and, additionally, it may be regarded as a mechanism for increasing the democratic legitimacy of the law insofar as the involvement of national parliaments in transposition is to be expected. However, there are negative aspects to this: without guarantees as to when derived norms begin to exert legal effects on persons, the predictability of the process and the rule of law are weakened, directly affecting credibility. These problems have been illustrated by MERCOSUR.[188] Article 40 of the Ouro Preto Protocol establishes that the norms will enter into force once all Member States have incorporated them into their domestic orders. This means, plainly, that the less willing State determines when a norm will enter into force. Thus, a State can delay entry into force simply by delaying internalizing a given norm, and this adds a second veto option (on top of consensual decision-making) that may create additional lack of interest in the creation of derived norms.[189] Commenting on MERCOSUR secondary legislation, Torrent and Lavopa argue

[188] C. Pena and R. Rozemberg, *MERCOSUR: A Different Approach to Institutional Development* (The Canadian Foundation for the Americas (FOCAL), 2005) (available at www.focal.ca); R. Torrent and F. Lavopa, "La producción del derecho de la integración en América Latina: un talón de Aquiles del MERCOSUR reproducido en la Unión de Naciones Sudamericanas," in *Integración regional en América Latina: desafíos y oportunidades* (New York and Geneva: UNCTAD, 2010), pp. 100–115.

[189] Torrent and Lavopa, *ibid.*, pp. 112–113.

that the real problem with MERCOSUR derived norms is that they are not created in a really autonomous way, since the norm does not enter into force until they have been internalized (that is, transposed into the domestic order).[190] This compares unfavorably with either WTO or NAFTA law, which, in their opinion, probably works better for individuals (despite lacking any effect internally) than other integration laws with larger domestic effects but which do not work as well, creating obligations among States.[191] UNASUR has reproduced the same requirement for derived norms: its Treaty makes the obligatory nature of secondary norms dependent on their incorporation into the domestic order of *all* Member States.

Scholars have often criticized the shortcomings of the lack of direct applicability of derived norms, focusing on the discretion of national governments and authorities, the lack of efficiency and, lately, the lack of direct effect for individuals. These criticisms concur, irrespectively of whether they address African or Latin American schemes. Thus, Afadameh-Adeyemi and Kalula denounced the fact that implementation of SADC Summit Decisions remains at the discretion of Member States.[192] Pena and Rozemberg comment that

[190] *Ibid.*, p. 111. [191] *Ibid.*, p. 109.

[192] A. Afadameh-Adeyemi and E. Kalula, "Re-examining the Legal and Institutional Anatomy of the Southern Africa Development Community," in A. Bös, A. D. Pisani, G. Erasmus, T. Hartzenberg and R. Sandrey (eds.), "Monitoring Regional Integration in Southern Africa," in *Yearbook*, vol. 10 (Tralac/Konrad Adenauer Stiftung, 2011) (available at www.tralac.org), p. 12.

MERCOSUR lacks an agile and transparent mechanism to incorporate MERCOSUR norms and to make them operative, and it also lacks a system guaranteeing the hierarchy of these norms over national ones.[193] They additionally point to the potential for imperfect implementation following the idiosyncratic character of these norms.

Treating secondary norms as customary international norms that require transposition reproduces *ad infinitum* the potential for two-level games:[194] an agreement (decision, norm) reached in level 1 (decisions reached within the integration decision-making organs) can be vetoed or ratified in level 2 (that is, the domestic organs which need to transpose the decision into domestic legislation). This model of norm also transfers the effects of the "paradox of weakness": those actors who have a powerful and potential domestic veto may enhance their bargaining power. The chances of blockade increase in presidential constitutional structures in which the alignment between the executive and parliament (the organ, *prima facie*, responsible for transposition) is not secured (which is different to the position in parliamentary systems, in which majorities in the executive and in parliament normally coincide). In addition, the larger the organization, the greater the potential for transposition failures to emerge.

[193] C. Pena and R. Rozemberg, *MERCOSUR: A Different Approach to Institutional Development* (The Canadian Foundation for the Americas (FOCAL), 2005) (available at www.focal.ca).

[194] R. O. D. Putnam, "Diplomacy and Domestic Politics: The Logic of Two-level Game," 42:3 *International Organization* 427–460 (1988).

1.8 Models of regional integration

The foregoing sections have illustrated the kind of objectives and the toolkit of institutional devices available to international/integration organizations. This section integrates both objectives and institutional design to create "models of regional integration," whose differential characteristic is, precisely, the different combination of objectives and institutional design. The thesis of this study is that the objectives of a given organization require a certain structure of institutional commitments (organs, decision-making and the existence of derived norms) if States are serious about their willingness to achieve their objectives. Naturally, commitments may be purely formal and States may simply ignore them. As a rule of thumb, the quality of institutional commitments for a given organization is, *ceteris paribus*, as good as the quality of the rule of law in the State parties. Hence, implementation of less ambitious objectives may be as good as, or even better than, the most ambitious ones. This depends not only on the structure of international institutional commitments, but also on the domestic institutional structure which anchors these commitments.

Contemporary scholarship tends to adopt an unqualified view on regional organizations: *any* existing organization may be associated with regionalism and/or regional integration. Thus, Behr and Jokela argue that regionalism has taken many forms and shapes, varying from tiny associations that include no more than a few actors and focus on a single issue, to huge continental unions that address a multitude of common problems.[195] Whilst this position introduces a huge richness to the discussion, it also renders it difficult to reach substantive conclusions, and it renders futile any comparison between different integration schemes. Comparison, though, allows for mastering knowledge on the functioning of a given scheme in relation either to similar ones to or different ones.

Comparison, in turn, requires a prior classification that establishes similarity and dissimilarity among empirical cases. This section classifies regional integration organizations out of the data set constructed, which contains eighty-five cases of multilateral (that is, $n > 2$) international organizations. The classification applies the criteria discussed in Sections 1.3 to 1.7 above: the organization's objectives; the geographical requirement for membership; the institutional structure; the decision-making rule; and the kind of secondary legislation produced. Then, empirical cases from the data set are associated with each of the categories to illustrate them. Naturally, empirical cases may not fit perfectly within analytically induced categories. On the other hand, the boundaries between categories may be somehow blurred. Table 1.17 summarizes the results.

Following the criteria, the classification produces seven categories or types. What explains the variance in institutional design among organizations? Organizations with

[195] T. Behr and J. Jokela, *Regionalism and Global Governance: The Emerging Agenda*, Notre Europe Studies and Research No. 85 (2011) (available at www.notre-europe.eu/en/axes/europe-and-world-governance/works/publication/regionalism-global-governance), p. 39.

Table 1.17 *Models of regional integration*

Type	Geographic membership requirement	Objectives	Structure of delegation			Decision-making rule	Norms and their effect	Cases
			Decision-making organs	Parliaments	Delegation to agencies (executive/ judiciary)			
Integration								
Free trade area	Any	Free circulation of goods		No	No (arbitration panels and national systems)	Unanimity/ consensus	No	AFTA, ANZCER, CEFTA, EFTA, GAFTA, NAFTA
Customs union/ common market	Regional	Free circulation production factors	Intergovernmental/ presidentialism	Yes, but no powers	Courts	Unanimity/ consensus	Few. Effects according to public international law	AEC, CARICOM, COMESA, EAC, MERCOSUR, SADC, SICA (CACM)
Communities	Regional	Economic policies	Intergovernmental/ presidentialism	Yes, some powers	Courts and executive delegation plus some legislative delegation	Consensus	Direct effect, direct applicability, primacy	Andean Community, ECOWAS

Table 1.17 (*cont.*)

Type	Geographic membership requirement	Objectives	Structure of delegation			Decision-making rule	Norms and their effect	Cases
			Decision-making organs	Parliaments	Delegation to agencies (executive/ judiciary)			
Political unions	Regional	Political objectives	Decisional triangle: government/ agencies/ representative assembly	Yes, increased powers	Courts, legislative and executive delegation	Qualified majority	As above	EU
No integration								
Continental and cultural "framing" organizations	Continental	Identity, values, security		No (only CoE)	Limited/courts			CoE, OAS, OAU, ODECA, OIC, AU, UNASUR
Security organizations	Any	Defense	Intergovernmental		No. Military committees	Consensus	No	CENTO, NATO, OSCE, SEATO
Functional agencies	Any	Sector-specific	Technical	No	Yes. Strictly defined along functional lines	Majority		IHO, ILO, UPU

higher, wider, deeper and more ambitious objectives that spread across spheres in which different public goods and policies (security, economic, social, cultural, political and so on) are provided correlate, if drafters and agents take them seriously, with an institutional design that imposes stronger commitments on Member States. Commitment means accepting to be bound by the organization's rules and institutions, and these obviously restrict sovereignty. The fact that members simultaneously accept the same commitments makes them credible for all participating actors. The classification of integration organizations reflects this trade-off between objectives, on the one hand, and, on the other, the structure of credible commitments to attaining them which the institutional design creates.

1.8.1 Free trade areas

Scholars usually consider free trade areas within the loose universe of economic integration. These have a very clear and specific purpose – enabling goods to move freely across Member States – and they do not have any more ambitions beyond that. They have mushroomed in the last decades and one of the reasons may be related to membership: free trade areas do not require restricting membership to a given geographical area and/or contiguous Member States. Even though the more consolidated and old free trade areas remain in the neighborhood of "regions" (these are the cases of EFTA, NAFTA and so on), free trade areas among countries not sharing geographical contiguity have emerged powerfully in the last decades (for instance, APEC Forum). Generally speaking, free trade areas possess a very light (or indeed non-existent) institutionalization. In some cases (AFTA or GAFTA), no institutions are created, whilst more commonly technical agencies manage the working of the agreement (such as the Trade Commission and the Secretariat or the Working Groups in NAFTA). The most advanced cases (EFTA and LAFTA) also include intergovernmental bodies. The lack of decision-making bodies correlates with the absence of derived norms: in general, they do not exist, and when they do, as with the LAFTA recommendations, they are not binding. An exception to this pattern is the decisions of EFTA, which, adopted by the Council, are binding upon Member States (Article 43.4). Free trade areas rely either on a panel system and/or domestic courts for the settlement of disputes. Finally, the only decision-making procedure is unanimity consensus.

Free trade areas require a relatively low cession of sovereignty towards supra-State institutions (be these organs, secondary legislation or decision-making rules). Because of this and their flexible substantive content (which can be adapted to different participating partners with an infinite number of possibilities), and the growing belief in free trade as a source of economic growth and development, States have increasingly engaged in the negotiation of this kind of model of "integration."

Bela Balassa pointed to them as the first and original stage in the process of economic integration.[196] This

[196] B. Balassa, *The Theory of Economic Integration* (Homewood, IL: Richard D. Irwin, 1961).

evolutionary model has influenced much subsequent thinking, and hence, there is a theoretical case for including free trade as a model of integration. However, there is no empirical case in which free trade areas, defined in isolation and not as part of a bigger scheme, have evolved towards other kinds of integration types, such as common markets, let alone communities or political unions. In almost all cases, there exists a clear distinction between free trade areas and the three other forms of economic integration which do possess certain evolutionary potential.

1.8.2 Common markets

In the classical economic integration theory, customs unions and common markets have two different objectives. Empirically, few integration schemes limit themselves to the objective of creating a customs union, renouncing explicitly the creation of a common market. Even when the objective of a customs union is explicitly formulated, the tendency is for an evolution towards richer objectives. SACU is perhaps the best example of a customs union which lately aspires to larger objectives. One of the reasons for this may be that customs unions may imply external tariffs that may clash with WTO requirements. Common markets mean, first of all, free circulation of goods and production factors (capital and workforce). Nevertheless, in practice, States are more reluctant to implement the free circulation of the latter. As examples, SADC signed a 1995 Protocol on free movement of persons which has not been implemented; SICA has not advanced much in this dimension; MERCOSUR agreed only in December 2012 on implementing free circulation of workers; and CARICOM restricts free movement to skills (that is, certain categories of qualified workers). Given the implications of immigration (whether massive or not), allowing the free movement of persons seems to require from States a degree of commitment and a cession of sovereignty which most States are not prepared to accept. At this point, economic integration theory and political realism clash.

Common markets have a characteristic objective which differentiates them from free trade areas: the creation of regional public goods. These are associated with activities related to the regional market, and in this respect, transport is a good example: improving regional transportation networks is very effective in enhancing trade exchanges. In Latin America, the Initiative for Integrating South American Regional Infrastructure (IIRSA) related to UNASUR beats other domains of integration in terms of achievements.

States may find it more logical to create regional public goods rather than global ones, not only because of the reduced costs of coordination with a smaller number of States involved, but also because in some domains (for instance, physical infrastructure), "club goods" (which are a specific variety of regional public goods) make sense: members extract benefits for themselves from their own cooperation. Hence, one clear difference between, on the one hand, customs unions and common markets and, on the other, the category of free trade areas is that the former are always based on some form of territorial contiguity, and what can be called a *regional* dimension.

What marks a clear departure from free trade areas is the creation of a proper institutional structure tilted towards intergovernmentalism and, in particular, towards the dominance of heads of State (presidents). Two other institutions emerge within common markets: a (powerless) parliament and courts with recognized attributions but lacking respect from political actors. The procedure for adopting decisions is unanimity/consensus; the derived norms are scarce and their effects are those recognized under public international law (that is, transposition is required, generally speaking). MERCOSUR, SADC and SICA are the cases that may fit the ideal type.

1.8.3 Communities

Names are important: calling an organization "community" signals a commitment to provide public goods beyond trade. Intuitively, the notion of community associates with people and with attributes linked to them, such as identity or rights. This does not mean that the name automatically triggers a firm commitment; rather, it indicates preparedness to do so. The word "communities" has different meanings in different contexts. Thus, for instance, ASEAN targeted 2015 for the establishment of its own 'Community', but this meant something much shallower than the "homogeneous" community pursued by CAN. So the use of a term by itself does not mean automatic attribution to a category in the classification.

The dividing line between common markets and communities is a diffuse one in the sense that organizations may at the same time have properties of either of them. Both share the regional requirement for membership, the institutional emphasis on presidential intergovernmentalism and the consensus/unanimity procedure for decision-making. Communities, though, place themselves firmly within the domain of the provision of regional public goods and more clearly assert their character as "clubs." A constant feature of communities is their enrichment of the nature and number of objectives that they set for themselves. They enlarge the range of objectives to include economic goals beyond markets to affect economic policies, and other policies with an economic effect (such as regional and/or infrastructures). Moreover, they channel these objectives through common policies which transcend purely intergovernmental policies. By definition, common policies require a minimum common implementing institutional framework, and this explains why communities thicken the institutional structure of commitments: regional parliaments have some (limited) powers and courts play a more salient role. What is more important: communities generally establish a model of derived norms whose effects bypass international public law and which develops the characteristics of direct applicability and, in some cases, primacy. Communities are prevalent in Africa, although the first (historically) was the Andean Community.

Among the African schemes, EAC fits nicely into this category, whilst ECOWAS, COMESA and even the AEC fit more uneasily.

1.8.4 Political unions: n = 1

The EU remains a case apart, whose characteristics differentiate it from other types of regional organization related to "integration." Its objectives are much broader than any other existing organization, and its means and instruments often match these ambitions (regardless of shortcomings in a number of policy areas, such as foreign policy or monetary policy). The institutional structure consolidates a model of decision-making with three intervening organs, each of them representing different constituencies: the Council (representing States), the Parliament (representing the people) and the Commission (representing technical and general interests). Although leadership is also concentrated in the European Council, the organ of heads of State/government, the day-to-day working of the EU, as long as there is a treaty provision with clear attribution of competence, does not depend on this organ. Qualified majority secures a procedure which may bypass existing blockades, and decisions may be translated in a set of secondary legislation (Regulations, Directives and Decisions) which have the attributes of immediate applicability, direct effect and primacy totally unmatched as a set by any other integration organization. The EU has also passed through the preliminary stages of a common market and a community, and this evolutionary nature may explain why some may take it as a model for schemes in any of these categories.

1.9 Conclusion

The institutional design of international organizations presents some variance along seemingly constant features which we reviewed in this study. The thesis emerging at the end is that the ambition of the organization, as marked by the number, scope and intensity of their objectives, acts as a good predictor of the kind of institutional commitments that States accept as deriving from their accession to and membership of the organization. Thus, the larger, wider and deeper the objectives, the stronger will be the delegation of power in favor of supra-State organs. Organizations committed to large, deep and nonspecific objectives require a highly imperfect model of contract, that is, one which leaves great margin for its ulterior interpretation and development. The determination of more specific contents for the contract depends on the action of the organizations and procedures created for the implementation of the objectives. Ambitious objectives signal *a priori* the preparedness of States to commit to highly imperfect and open contracts. States in this situation signal *prima facie* their acceptance of the eventual unfolding of contractual obligations. Still, commitment to an incomplete contract does not predict well its actual completion: States may ignore their commitment with certain objectives and goals, which acquire in this way a highly rhetorical value. *Ceteris paribus*, it seems that institutional design by itself does totally overcome the domestic anchoring of institutions. What makes credible supra-State commitments work is that they are anchored into working and efficient domestic institutions. The existence of these institutions (for instance, the existence of effective domestic courts) may emerge as a useful and important predictor of the ability of an organization to attain its objectives.

Chapter 2

The development of international legal regimes

Models and instruments for legal integration beyond States

Lorenzo Casini*

2.1 Introduction

Having analyzed governance structure and processes in integration organizations,[1] this chapter focuses on the legal mechanisms and instruments that drive the development of international regimes, their institutional features and their functioning.[2]

Therefore, the aim of this chapter is twofold. First, it purports to outline and critically describe the typology of international organizations and their regimes, to identify common themes and illustrate the main legal techniques of governance.[3] To this end, the analysis will cover not only

* University of Rome "Sapienza"; IMT Lucca.

[1] See Chapter 1 above.

[2] See K. Raustiala and D. G. Victor, "The Regime Complex for Plant Genetic Resources," 58 *International Organization* 277 (2004). More recently, R. Mushkat, "The Dynamics of International Legal Regime Formation: The Sino-British Joint Declaration on the Question of Hong Kong Revisited," 22 *European Journal of International Law* 1119 (2011), the reply by K. Y. L. Tan, and the rejoinder by Mushkat.

[3] W. Mattli and N. Woods (eds.), *The Politics of Global Regulation* (Princeton University Press, 2009); also J. Pauwelyn, R. Wessel and

regional organizations, but other international institutions too, of both an intergovernmental (such as the World Trade Organization (WTO), the World Health Organization (WHO) or the International Labour Organization (ILO)) and a hybrid public–private nature (such as the International Organization for Standardization (ISO) and the Internet Corporation for Assigned Names and Numbers (ICANN)). Second, this chapter aims to provide a comparative toolbox of legal instruments that can assist determining which solutions may be more or less effective in processes of regional integration;[4] this will also enable verifying which legal technique is adopted more often, and why, in a given model of integration, amongst those outlined in Chapter 1.

Sharing the assumption that integration is a "formal process," the perspective adopted here is essentially a "managerial" one, which seeks to avoid bias connected to any given political objective. The latter may of course significantly influence the preference for one solution or another (for example, the establishment of an international parliament or court within a given regime, or of a requirement that each Member State within the entity create a

J. Wouters (eds.), *Informal International Lawmaking: Mapping the Action and Testing Concepts of Accountability and Effectiveness* (Oxford University Press, 2012).

[4] For a similar, but much broader, enterprise, see the seminal research conducted by M. Cappelletti, M. Seccombe and J. H. H. Weiler (eds.), *Integration Through Law: Europe and the American Federal Experience* (6 vols.) (Berlin and New York: Walter de Gruyter, 1985) (see especially vol. I, *Methods, Tools, and Institutions*).

domestic terminal entrusted with ensuring the implementation of the policies set by the international organization).

However, this chapter seeks to adopt a neutral approach, investigating the common threads in the development of international regimes by examining mainly how they work towards their objectives. International regimes have increasingly been using accountability mechanisms, but principally to ensure their own efficiency and effectiveness rather than to address any democratic gaps. In other words, the need to enhance the legitimacy and accountability of IOs has a functional reason; this is confirmed by the fact that all regimes tend to adopt similar mechanisms, regardless of the degree of "democracy" they may present. Furthermore, it is precisely the quest for democracy, or more traditional forms of legitimacy and accountability, that often produces negative effects and tends to decrease the effectiveness of IOs' decision-making processes: this is the case with certain principles, such as "participation," for instance, because the increasing involvement of private actors may either be merely formal, or entail the "freezing" of decision-making processes.[5] Another example is the conception of parliaments entertained by regional organizations; on their view, parliaments often act more like consultative bodies rather than actual "legislators" (see Section 2.5 below).

[5] B. Kingsbury and L. Casini, "Global Administrative Law Dimensions of International Organizations Law," in L. Boisson de Chazournes, L. Casini and B. Kingsbury (eds.), Symposium on "Global Administrative Law in the Operations of International Organizations," 6:2 *International Organizations Law Review* 319 (2009).

The analysis will therefore commence with a classification of different IOs (Section 2.2), to thereafter examine the common threads of the development of international regimes and their accountability mechanisms (Sections 2.3 to 2.6), and finally consider the main techniques of governance and models of legal integration beyond the State (Section 2.7).[6]

2.2 The context: the rise of international organizations, international regimes and … States

"International organizations (or IOs) – intergovernmental entities established by treaty, usually composed of permanent secretariats, plenary assemblies involving all Member States, and executive organs with more limited participation – are a twentieth-century phenomenon having little in common with earlier forms of institutionalized cooperation, including those in the ancient world."[7] In fact, although the proliferation and differentiation of IOs and their activities have been viewed as

[6] Due to the extremely high number of IOs and regimes, this chapter provides a conceptual framework that relies on the analytical data used in Chapter 1 above, and on the 100-odd cases examined in S. Cassese *et al.* (eds.), *Global Administrative Law: The Casebook* (Rome, New York and Edinburgh: IRPA-IILJ, 3rd edn., 2012). Other relevant sources of case studies include: A. Berman, S. Duquet, J. Pauwelyn, R. Wessel and J. Wouters (eds.), *Informal International Lawmaking: Case Studies* (The Hague: TOAE, 2012); and, though focused on global private regimes, F. Cafaggi (ed.), *Enforcement of Transnational Regulation. Ensuring Compliance in a Global World* (Cheltenham: Edward Elgar, 2012).

[7] J. E. Alvarez, "International Organizations: Then and Now," 100 *American Journal of International Law* 324 (2006).

a challenge (and opportunity) for international law since the 1860s or even earlier[8] – and the phenomenon of "unions" or "federations" of States is certainly not new,[9] it was only after the Second World War that IOs began to grow in number significantly, and that a field of international institutional law (or the law of international organizations) developed.[10] With the end of the Cold War and the rise of globalization, the growth of IOs accelerated even more (see Figure 2.1).

Consequently, legal scholars have engaged in examining different types of IOs, and have proposed classifications based on their structure, functions, and/or legal nature. The principal distinction remains that between IOs that have States as their members (intergovernmental organizations

[8] F. F. Martens, *Le droit international actuel des peuples civilisés* (Paris: Ed. A. Marescq Aine, 1883) (3 vols.); P. Kazansky, "Théorie de l'administration internationale," 9 *Revue Générale de Droit International Public* 353 (1902); P. Reinsch, "International Administrative Law and National Sovereignty," 3 *American Journal of International Law* 1 (1909); U. Borsi, "Carattere ed oggetto del diritto amministrativo internazionale," *Rivista di Diritto Internazionale* 384 (1912); S. Battini, *Amministrazioni senza stato. Profili di diritto internazionale* (Milan: Giuffrè, 2003); R. Wolfrum, "International Administrative Unions," in R. Bernhardt (ed.), *Encyclopaedia of Public International Law* (Amsterdam: North Holland, 1st edn., 1995), vol. 2, p. 1041 (and in the second edition edited by R. Wolfrum). See also R. Ago, "The State and International Organizations," in C. W. Jenks, R. Ago and O. Schachter (eds.), *International Law in a Changing World* (New York: Oceana Library on the United Nations, 1963), pp. 12 *et seq.*

[9] See A. Brunialti, "Unioni e combinazioni fra gli Stati. Gli Stati composti e lo Stato federale," in A. Brunialti (ed.), *Biblioteca di scienze politiche* (Turin: Utet, 1891).

[10] J. Klabbers, *An Introduction to International Institutional Law* (Cambridge University Press, 2nd edn., 2009).

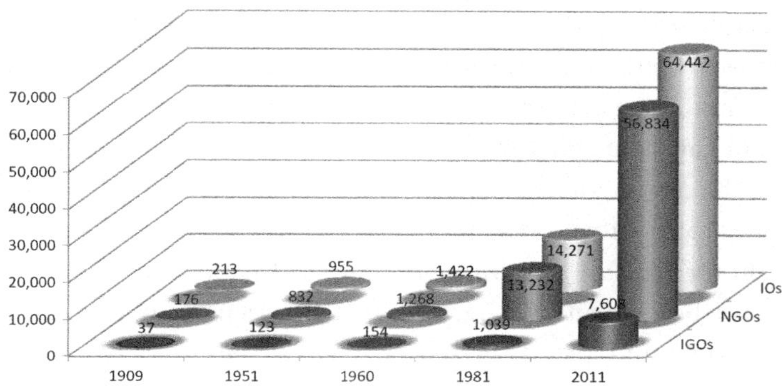

Figure 2.1 Historical overview of the number of international organizations
Source: Union of International Associations, *Yearbook of International Organizations* (Brussels: Union of International Associations, 48th edn., 2011); and S. Cassese, "Relations between International Organizations and National Administrations," in IISA, *Proceedings, XIXth International Congress of Administrative Sciences* (Berlin: IISA, 1983)

(IGOs)) and those that do not (non-governmental organizations (NGOs)); however, with over 60,000 bodies to consider, more nuance is required.[11] The diversity of the functions

[11] A more complex approach may be found, for example, in the classification adopted by the Union of International Associations (UIA) in its *Yearbook of International Organizations*: fifteen subtypes of IOs are identified, including federations of international organizations; universal membership organizations; intercontinental membership organizations; regionally defined membership organizations; organizations emanating from places, persons, proprietary products or other bodies; or organizations having a special form, including foundations and funds. Each subtype has additional further specifications (see www.uia.be/types-organization-type-i).

performed by IOs often implies differences in their structure, powers and relations with States. Thus, one of the most common criteria of classification is "functional" in nature, and can be divided further into three sub-criteria: the depth of the cooperation that the IO has the mission of engendering; the scope of this cooperation; and the means used to effect it.[12] On the basis of this criterion, other distinctions between IOs have been identified, such as that between regional, supranational and special or technical organizations.[13] Also, distinctions have been founded on differing conceptions of the role of international organizations (such as that based on a "management-oriented, functionalist and progressive understanding" of IOs on the one hand, and the idea of the international organization as a "classical agora" on the other).[14]

In addition, States and IOs themselves often create other specialized agencies or committees: an example is the International Agency for Research on Cancer, which was established in 1965 as an extension of the WHO, but has its own governing bodies; or the well-known Codex Alimentarius Commission. Also, within certain IOs, mechanisms or even specific entities to connect national administrative bodies have been created, such as the Organisation for Economic Co-operation and Development's (OECD) system of National Contact Points (NCPs), based on the Organization's

[12] M. Virally, "Definition and Classification: A Legal Approach," 29 *International Social Science Journal* 58 (1977).

[13] H. G. Schermers and N. M. Blokker, *International Institutional Law: Unity Within Diversity* (Leiden: Martinus Nijhoff, 5th edn., 2011).

[14] J. Klabbers, "Two Concepts of International Organizations," 2 *International Organizations Law Review* 277 (2005).

Guidelines for Multinational Enterprises. Finally, one may mention the increasing practice of IOs contracting with private entities and the establishment of public–private partnership mechanisms, which produce many more institutional models.[15]

The proliferation of IOs has been accompanied not only by an increased differentiation in their organizational structures, but also by growing complexity in many regimes.[16] Today, there are over 2,000 international regulatory regimes,[17]

15 J. E. Alvarez, "Governing the World: International Organizations as Law-Makers," 31 *Suffolk Transnational Law Review* 596 (2007–2008).

16 See J. G. Ruggie, "International Responses to Technology: Concepts and Trends," 29 *International Organization* 557 (1975), p. 570, who defined regimes as "set[s] of mutual expectations, rules and regulations, plans, organizational energies and financial commitments, which have been accepted by a group of States"; S. D. Krasner (ed.), *International Regimes* (London: Cornell University Press, 1983), particularly S. D. Krasner, "Structural Causes and Regime Consequences: Regimes as Intervening Variables," pp. 1 *et seq.*, and R. O. Keohane, "The Demand for International Regimes," pp. 141 *et seq.*; and B. Simma, "Self-Contained Regimes," 16 *Netherlands Yearbook* 111 (1985). See also B. Simma and D. Pulkowski, "Of Planets and the Universe: Self-Contained Regimes in International Law," 17 *European Journal of International Law* 483 (2006); K. Raustiala, "The Architecture of International Cooperation: Transgovernmental Networks and the Future of International Law," 43 *Vanderbilt Journal of International Law* 1 (2002); A. Hasenclever, P. Mayer and V. Rittberger, *Theories of International Regimes* (Cambridge University Press, 1997); and V. Rittberger (ed.), *Regime Theory and International Relations* (Oxford: Clarendon Press, 1993).

17 S. Cassese *et al.* (eds.), *Global Administrative Law: The Casebook* (Rome, New York and Edinburgh: IRPA-IILJ, 3rd edn., 2012); K. Raustiala, "The Architecture of International Cooperation: Transgovernmental Networks and the Future of International Law," 43 *Vanderbilt Journal of*

which are often interconnected. In this context, several legal phenomena may be observed: a greater amount of norms and scope of mandates; multifaceted relationships between different IOs, and between IOs and other actors; and an increase in the number of States participating in IOs (the WTO, for instance, currently has over 150 Member States; in the original GATT 1947, there were only 23). In some cases, networks of IOs acting together have gone beyond interagency coordination and cooperation to develop new institutional forms. The result of this inexorable rise is that the activities of IOs now cover almost all conceivable fields, from forest preservation and water regulation to sport and health.[18]

2.2.1 Four types of international organization

Within this framework, traditional mechanisms based on State consent as expressed through treaties or customs are simply no longer capable of accounting for all global activities. A new regulatory space is emerging, distinct from the space of inter-State relations and that transcends the spheres of influence of both international law and domestic administrative law: one that can be defined as the "global administrative space." IOs have become much more than instruments of the governments of their Member States; rather, they set

International Law 1 (2002); K. Jayasuriya, "Globalization, Law, and the Transformation of Sovereignty: The Emergence of Global Regulatory Governance," 6 *Indiana Journal of Global Legal Studies* 425 (1999).

[18] S. Cassese, *The Global Polity. Global Dimensions of Democracy and the Rule of Law* (Seville: Editorial Derecho Global/Global Law Press, 2012).

their own norms and regulate their own field(s) of activity; they generate and follow their own legal proceedings;[19] and they have the power to grant participatory rights to the (public and private) actors affected by their activities. Ultimately, therefore, they have emerged as genuine global public administrations.[20]

Unsurprisingly, therefore, recent attempts to classify IOs have been based on the notion of international administrative law[21] or on the approach of global administrative law.[22] Insights from administrative law and from public law more generally may provide some conceptual resources that could facilitate outlining the law and practice of international organizations.[23] For example, the functionalist approaches mentioned above overlap with national law theories insofar as the public function of administrative action (advancement of the public interest, as identified and regulated by law) justifies the application of public-regarding

19 R. W. Cox and H. K. Jakobson (eds.), *The Anatomy of Influence. Decision Making in International Organizations* (New Haven, CT: Yale University Press, 1973); J. von Bernstorff, "Procedures of Decision-Making and the Role of Law in International Organizations," 9 *German Law Journal* 1939 (2008).

20 B. Kingsbury and M. Donaldson, "Global Administrative Law," in *Max Planck Encyclopaedia of International Law* (Oxford University Press, 2011).

21 E. Kinney, "The Emerging Field of International Administrative Law: Its Contents and Potential," 54 *Administrative Law Review* 415 (2002).

22 B. Kingsbury, N. Krisch and R. B. Stewart, "The Emergence of Global Administrative Law," 68 *Law and Contemporary Problems* 15 (2005).

23 D. Sarooshi, "The Role of Domestic Public Law Analogies in the Law of International Organizations," 5 *International Organization* 237 (2008).

administrative law rules to the conduct of administrative actors.[24] It thus becomes possible to identify certain activities as "administration" in theoretical terms (this is the German *Begriff der Verwaltung*); but a unitary definition in practical terms remains both difficult to find and perhaps unnecessary. To conceive of administration as functionally oriented towards achieving a public goal leads to variability in the delimitation of the public sphere: therefore, there is not one sole definition, but rather a range of notions of what can constitute "public administration."[25]

Of the numerous attempts made to classify IOs and international regimes, those based on international administrative law and global administrative law appear to be very helpful in understanding the development of international regimes and the emergence of different models of legal integration. Thus, we will now illustrate four different types of

[24] M. Virally, "La notion de fonction dans la théorie de l'organisation internationale," in La communauté internationale, *Mélanges offerts à Charles Rousseau: La communauté internationale* (Paris: Pedone, 1974), p. 277.

[25] That many important activities of IOs can be regarded as administrative in nature does not suggest the existence of a general global public administration; there is no global government or global parliament, nor are there real global equivalents of the other structures within which national administrations are nested. Nevertheless, some normative demands and procedural principles are found sufficiently commonly across different IOs to suggest that a unified field may be discernible: transparency in rule-making; due process (in certain cases including notice-and-comment, hearings and reason-giving requirements) in decisions that directly affect private parties; review mechanisms to correct errors and ensure rationality and legality; and, in addition to review, a variety of other mechanisms to promote accountability.

international organizations, and how this system of classification can interact with that outlined in Chapter 1 for models of regional integration.

A first type of model is that of *formal intergovernmental organizations*. This is the model traditionally adopted by States when setting up international institutions. Examples are the United Nations, the WHO, the ILO, UNICEF and the World Intellectual Property Organization (WIPO). Although the institutional design of these IOs has been studied for many decades, the types of activities that have become common for these bodies in recent years display features similar to administrative action. For instance, consider the various forms of recommendations, guidelines, best practices, technical advice, findings, conclusions, committee rules and other normative products issued by IOs. Increasing demands for transparency, reason-giving, review and, in some cases, participation or accountability, have arisen in relation to these instruments; different agencies take very different approaches to these demands, and there is often uncertainty as to the exact legal framework applicable to these activities and what procedural standards are – or ought to be – required. This type of international organization is unavoidable when States wish to establish a more structured regime through their governments. However, while this choice may be satisfactory when expectations (in terms of legal integration) are low, it may not be sufficient for building more complex systems beyond the State. This is why IOs often and increasingly establish other bodies, or create new offices within their organizations.

A second type refers to *hybrid public–private organizations and private bodies exercising public functions*. Both

States and IOs increasingly create, and operate through, formalized partnerships with private commercial and civil society entities.[26] For example, the Global Fund has close links with the World Health Organization, but is, in formal legal terms, a Swiss foundation. Its Board comprises representatives of donor and recipient States and of groups affected by HIV and other infectious diseases that the Global Fund seeks to combat; it has a sophisticated independent review system, and ties to some very large funding sources such as the Gates Foundation. Other examples are the Internet Corporation for Assigned Names and Numbers (ICANN), the World Anti-Doping Agency (WADA), the private Stewardship Councils for forest products and marine products (which comprise industry and civil society members) and the International Organization for Standardization (ISO). This type of global administration, therefore, encompasses both hybrid public–private and fully private bodies that exercise public functions. These institutions constitute a very interesting example of how the use of private law instruments to fulfill public functions is widespread at the international level too. In terms of integration, this second type of IOs is, of course, less relevant for intergovernmental regimes. However, even more traditional institutions increasingly use private law mechanisms and establish new forms of public and private partnerships.

[26] B. Bull and D. McNeil, *Development Issues in Global Governance: Public–Private Partnerships and Market Multilateralism* (Abingdon: Routledge, 2007).

A third type is that of *transgovernmental and transnational networks*. These are less structured forms of governance in which the relationships between States, IOs and/or other actors are less formalized, although they can be even more effective than traditional IGOs. Examples of this kind of network are the G-20, the Basel Committee and the International Competition Network (ICN). "Transgovernmental networks" can be defined as "all the different ways that individual government institutions are interacting with their counterparts either abroad or above them, alongside more traditional state-to-state interactions." Therefore, a network is "a pattern of regular and purposive relations among like government units working across the borders that divide countries from one another and that demarcate the 'domestic' from the 'international' sphere."[27] Other examples are "harmonization networks," that is, "networks of public regulatory authorities (at times in collaboration with private partners) that are in the business of harmonising their domestic rules, setting standards or other norms."[28] It is thus easy to see that this type of "global administration" is crucial for strengthening all models of integration: from free trade and common markets to political unions, transgovernmental

[27] A.-M. Slaughter, *A New World Order* (Princeton University Press, 2004).

[28] A. Berman and R. A. Wessel, "The International Legal Form and Status of Informal International Lawmaking Bodies: Consequences for Accountability," in J. Pauwelyn, R. Wessel and J. Wouters (eds.), *Informal International Lawmaking: Mapping the Action and Testing Concepts of Accountability and Effectiveness* (Oxford University Press, 2012).

networks, often based on multilateral agreements, enable common objectives to be pursued with a lesser – at least (if not only) apparently – loss of sovereignty by the States involved.

A fourth – and final – type transcends the concepts of institution and network and includes more *complex forms of governance*, such as hybrid, multi-level or informal global regulatory regimes. These are characterized by composite mechanisms and procedures that involve several actors at international and domestic levels. Examples are global and national proceedings under the International Patent Cooperation Treaty; mutual recognition in the field of free movement of professionals; and the decision-making procedures in the governance of fisheries and forestry, in the World Heritage Convention and in the clean development mechanism, and emissions trading. This type of "global administration" is the most sophisticated: the fulfillment of public functions is ensured through the creation of a set of principles, rules and institutions operating both internationally and nationally.[29]

These four types may often overlap and combine with each other: an IGO can be part of a complex form of governance and/or of a network; likewise, a public–private institution can act as a key player in a transnational network. In addition, the borders between these categories (as with most,

[29] This fourth type therefore includes the hypothesis of "distributed administration," where "domestic regulatory agencies act as part of the global administrative space: they take decisions on issues of foreign or global concern" (B. Kingsbury, N. Krisch and R. B. Stewart, "The Emergence of Global Administrative Law," 68 *Law and Contemporary Problems* 15 (2005), p. 21).

if not all, such IO classifications) "are just as vague" because "practice is more multifarious than these distinctions may suggest."[30] ASEAN, for instance, falls into the first type insofar as it is a treaty-based IGO,[31] but it also displays elements of the third type – intergovernmental networks – if some specific sectors of its activity, such as international investment agreements, are considered.[32] In addition, there are often cases of overlap and competition between IOs' missions: this happens in regional integration organizations, such as the case of African institutions.[33] Therefore, considering the various models of integration outlined in Chapter 1, it emerges that the greater the complexity of the model, the greater is the tendency to present a combination of different types of IOs: while single-mission institutions can mostly fit into one category or another, Communities or Unions easily move to a mix of interlinked organizations, which fall into complex forms of governance.

[30] H. G. Schermers and N. M. Blokker, *International Institutional Law: Unity Within Diversity* (Leiden: Martinus Nijhoff, 5th edn., 2011).

[31] See M. Ewing-Chow and L. Bernard, "I. B.7. The ASEAN Charter: The Legalization of ASEAN," in S. Cassese *et al.* (eds.), *Global Administrative Law: The Casebook* (Rome, New York and Edinburgh: IRPA-IILJ, 3rd edn., 2012). See also S. Chesterman, "Does ASEAN Exist? The Association of Southeast Asian Nations as an International Legal Person," 12 *Singapore Yearbook of International Law* 199–211 (2008).

[32] M. Ewing-Chow and G. R. Fischer, "I. D.3 ASEAN International Investment Agreement: The Incorporation of Global Regulatory Governance," in S. Cassese *et al.* (eds.), *Global Administrative Law: The Casebook* (Rome, New York and Edinburgh: IRPA-IILJ, 3rd edn., 2012).

[33] See Chapter 1 above.

It is clear, therefore, that institutional differentiation is an important feature of contemporary IOs and, more generally, of contemporary global governance, on a wide range of issues. This phenomenon has both a horizontal dimension (the relations between IOs and other global actors) and a vertical one (the relations between IOs, States and national administrations). Most IOs can now be studied on the basis of these coordinates: in the WTO, for instance, we find both the vertical dimension of the relations between the WTO and its members' domestic administrations, and the horizontal dimension, exemplified by the WTO's recognition of regulatory standards set by other global regulatory bodies (under the TBT and SPS agreements). Furthermore, the proliferation and differentiation of IOs led to the multiplication, on the one hand, of IO field offices, and on the other, of new specialized domestic bodies (this often happens with hybrid public–private regimes such as the ISO, and Internet or sports governance). Nevertheless, from an organizational point of view, it appears possible to identify certain basic features that are common to all these different institutions: for example, their organizational structure usually comprises four organs (a collegial body or assembly; a smaller collegial body, usually called a council; an executive body, called a secretariat, which consists of regular employees of the organization; and committees, generally made up of functionaries of national administrations).[34] In addition, except in the cases of hybrid

[34] S. Cassese, "Administrative Law Without the State? The Challenge of Global Regulation," 37 *New York University Journal of International Law and Politics* 663 (2005).

public–private bodies, most IO organs are based on intergovernmental mechanisms: this is what happens in regional organizations, which are all structured in a similar way, featuring an organ of top executives, councils of ministers, a secretariat and some or several agencies; in some cases there may also be a parliament and a court.[35]

Lastly, the scope and differentiation of IOs and their activities are accompanied by a multiplicity of rules, principles, decisions, soft law and non-legal norms.[36] In some cases, this increase in normative functions led to the creation of complex sectoral legal orders, which often display distinctive features (Section 2.3 below). The activities of IOs and of the other actors in complex governance regimes, as well as those of national public bodies, must be managed not only by means of formal norms, but also with a dynamic process of regulation. Treaty law (like legislation at the national level) is not sufficient. The regulatory approach focuses on process, the direction of change and gradual improvement rather than instant results, and is dynamic rather than static. In regulatory processes, law does not take up the entire field; and it is generated through accretion, accumulation and shifting, resulting from dialogue between multiple regimes.[37]

[35] See Chapter 1 above.

[36] J. E. Alvarez, *International Organizations as Law-Makers* (Oxford University Press, 2005).

[37] S. Cassese, "Is There a Global Administrative Law?," in A. von Bogdandy, R. Wolfrum, J. von Bernstorff, P. Dann and M. Goldmann (eds.), *The Exercise of Public Authority by International Institutions: Advancing International Institutional Law* (Heidelberg: Springer, 2010).

In conclusion, the degree of complexity of a given model of regional integration is usually related to the number of types of IOs operating in that given regime. It would be difficult to establish a plausible political union if States and the relevant IOs did not develop transgovernmental networks and structure forms of public–private partnerships. Therefore, the more ambitious the objective, in terms of integration, the more numerous and diverse will be the IOs involved in pursuing it.

2.2.2 *States as key actors (still)*

The degree of legalization and institutionalization of the international context is increasing worldwide.[38] However, this cannot be taken to mean that States are losing their powers, or that the notion of State is experiencing a crisis. Quite to the contrary, there is much evidence that "State sovereignty is not withering away."[39]

First, since the end of the Second World War, the number of States has been rising: in 1945, there were fifty States; by 2010, there were approximately 200.[40] The cases of

[38] As for the Asian context, see J. E. Alvarez, "Institutionalised Legalization and The Asia–Pacific 'Region'," 6 *New Zealand Journal of Public International Law* 9 (2007); and more generally, M. Beeson, *Institutions of the Asia–Pacific: ASEAN, APEC and Beyond* (Abingdon: Routledge, 2009), pp. 92 *et seq.*

[39] J. E. Alvarez, "State Sovereignty Is Not Withering Away: A Few Lessons for the Future," in A. Cassese (ed.), *Realizing Utopia: The Future of International Law* (Oxford University Press, 2012), pp. 26 *et seq.*

[40] The phenomenon is illustrated by A. Alesina and E. Spolaore, *The Size of Nations* (Cambridge, MA and London: MIT Press, 2003).

Kosovo and Palestine demonstrate that the concept of State is still determinant at the international level: on the one hand, the concept still appears to be the only one that is capable of fulfilling national expectations of independence; on the other, from a more managerial point of view, States are the key actors within IOs and they are "reluctant" to relinquish sovereignty (unless they receive credible commitments):[41] as a matter of fact, the fewer States that are part of a given international regime, the more sophisticated and developed the latter will be (as in global private regimes like the Internet or sport).

Second, all of these international regimes – even those that are private (Internet, sports and so on) – need States if they are to develop. To establish a global network, almost all IOs and regimes require the creation of domestic "terminals," which are often public administration bodies regulated by the domestic law of the country in which they operate (Section 2.3.1 below). Moreover, international regimes grow and develop by adopting legal mechanisms (norms, institutions, procedures), which are mostly "inspired" by State legal systems (according to a "mimetic" process). However, such mechanisms often change once adopted, because States are both regulators and regulatees. The "Leviathan," therefore, still very much "hold[s] sway over international dealings."[42] Even in the most developed forms of legal integration, such as

[41] See Chapter 1 above.

[42] L. Condorelli and A. Cassese, "Is Leviathan Still Holding Sway over International Dealings?," in A. Cassese (ed.), *Realizing Utopia: The Future of International Law* (Oxford University Press, 2012).

the EU, supranational decision-making processes alternate with intergovernmental ones, as Member States defend their prerogatives.[43]

Nevertheless, recent episodes – such as the global financial crisis – prove that no State can face globalization without cooperating with other States and without establishing forms of international or regional legal integration. This is why scholars have attempted to define models and common elements in the structure and development of global regulatory regimes. The analysis of IOs and their regimes thus enables main threads in the development of legal apparatuses beyond the State to be identified. These threads – which were implicitly already seen in Chapter 1 – may resemble those that already exist in domestic contexts, although the presence of States as regulators and addressees leads to significant differences.

The first thread is the increasing differentiation and separation of functions (Section 2.3 below): "legislative" (norm-making); "judicial" (dispute settlement); executive-administrative. The second is the emergence of *intra-* and *inter-*IO institutional pluralism (Section 2.4 below) at both international and national levels (see the expansion of the domestic "terminals" of international regimes). The third thread relates to the growing degree of proceduralization (Section 2.5 below), in terms of both the number of procedures instituted and the adoption of procedural principles (participation,

[43] See the well-known ECOWAS decision by the ECJ, Case C-91/05, *Commission* v. *Council* (2008); on this, see D. Eisenhut "Delimitation of EU-Competences under the First and Second Pillar: A View Between ECOWAS and the Treaty of Lisbon," 10 *German Law Journal* 586 (2009).

transparency and so on). The fourth thread regards the need for multiple forms of legitimacy and the adoption of different mechanisms for accountability (Section 2.6 below).

2.3 The differentiation and separation of functions in international legal regimes

The first thread consists of the increasing differentiation and separation of functions within global regimes: further evidence of how these systems imitate domestic legal orders.[44] In particular, this differentiation relates to three aspects: the formation of a hierarchy of norms; the development of quasi-judicial dispute settlement mechanisms; and the growing importance of administrative tasks.[45] These aspects were

[44] However, the separation of powers is achieved by each State in different ways, as highlighted by B. Ackerman, "The New Separation of Powers," 113 *Harvard Law Review* 633 (2000); formerly, C. Schmitt, *Verfassungslehre* (1928); and H. Kelsen, "Die Lehre von der drei Gewalten oder Funktionen des Staates," in 17 *Archiv für Rechts-und Wirtschaftsphilosophie*, 374 (1923–1924). See also G. Silvestri, *La separazione di poteri* (2 vols.) (Milan: Giuffrè, 1979–1984).

[45] At the international level, this distinction has already been analyzed by G. Scelle, "Le phénomène juridique du dédoublement fonctionnel," in W. Scätzel and H.-J. Schlochauer (eds.), *Rechtsfragen der Internationalen Organisation – Festshrift für Hans Wehberg zu seinem 70. geburtstag* (Frankfurt am Main: Vittorio Klostermann, 1956), pp. 333 *et seq.*; and G. Scelle, "Le droit public et la théorie de l'État," in G. Scelle *et al.* (eds.), *Introduction à l'étude du droit*, vol. I (Paris: Arthur Rousseau, 1951), pp. 96 *et seq.* More recently, C. Möllers, *Gewaltengliederung: Legitimation und Dogmatik im nationalen und internationalen Rechtsvergleich* (Tübingen: Mohr Siebeck, 2005), where the cases of the ILO (pp. 287 *et seq.*) and of the WTO (pp. 311 *et seq.*) are also examined.

highlighted in Chapter 1, in the part discussing parliaments, secondary norms, executive bodies and courts in regional organizations. We will now focus on the activities of those bodies, and how they are related to the degree of legal integration of a given regime.

Of course, there are asymmetries between different regimes in terms of how this differentiation and separation of functions takes place. Some regimes have strong regulatory and administrative dimensions, but no court (such as the UNESCO World Heritage Convention System). Others rely on their regulatory functions and on a dispute settlement system, but are still weak when it comes to developing their own "administration" (this is the case of the WTO, for example). However, it emerges that norm production is always the principal activity. As a matter of fact, law-making was the first task to be delivered at the international level, and the proliferation of IOs entails the need to regulate their functions. In addition, it becomes crucial to institute norm-making mechanisms that are more flexible than traditional ones, and this development of procedural tools requires the adoption of principles such as transparency and participation. It is for this reason that even the oldest IOs, such as the International Telecommunication Union (ITU) established in 1865, designed as regulatory bodies from the very beginning, have used several administrative-law-type instruments. Moreover, the proliferation of norms often requires adequate enforcement mechanisms; therefore, oversight and reviewing bodies have also been increasing, although there may be differences in their type and degree of development according to legal traditions, politics and objectives.

2.3.1 *Towards a hierarchy of norms*

The main evidence of how international regimes tend to differentiate fundamental functions is the norm-making activity currently performed at the international level, an activity that is accelerating at an incredible pace.[46] As a matter of fact, the phrase "global regulatory regimes" highlights the regulatory nature of these systems.[47]

One significant example is the nuclear energy sector, where the International Atomic Energy Agency (IAEA) developed a complex framework based on standards and agreements to avoid such a sensitive field from being exposed to the arbitrary powers of States.[48] Similarly, in the health

46 J. E. Alvarez, *International Organizations as Law-Makers* (Oxford University Press, 2005); A. Boyle and C. Chinkin, *The Making of International Law* (Oxford University Press, 2007); see also D. Shelton (ed.), *Commitment and Compliance: The Role of Non-binding Norms in the International Legal System* (Oxford University Press, 2000); and B. Kingsbury, "The Concept of Compliance as a Function of Competing Conceptions of International Law," 19 *Michigan Journal of International Law* 345 (1998).

47 See B. Simma and D. Pulkowski, "Of Planets and the Universe: Self-Contained Regimes in International Law," 17 *European Journal of International Law* 483 (2006); M. Noortman, *Enforcing International Law. From Self-Help to Self-Contained Regimes* (Aldershot: Ashgate, 2005); and K. Jayasuriya, "Globalization, Law, and the Transformation of Sovereignty: The Emergence of Global Regulatory Governance," 6 *Indiana Journal of Global Legal Studies* 425 (1999).

48 W. Tonhauser, "IAEA Technical Standard Setting," paper presented at the Conference "Practical Legal Problems of International Organizations: A Global Administrative Law Perspective on Public/Private Partnerships, Accountability, and Human Rights" (Geneva, March 20–21, 2009) (available at www.iilj.org/GAL/GALGeneva.asp);

sector, a global legal order progressively emerged, constituted by the rules produced by the World Health Organization (WHO),[49] such as the International Health Regulations (IHR),[50] and connected to several norms created in other fields: environmental protection, food safety and so on.[51]

It is noteworthy that, beyond the State, the "constitutional" basis of a given regime is at the same time the statute or the bylaws governing the institution that oversees the regime itself: this is the case of the WTO, for example, but also of many private regimes, such as the Internet, the ISO

and H. Blix, "The Role of the IAEA in the Development of International Law," 58 *Nordic Journal of International Law* 231 (1989).

[49] Yet the WHO, although since its establishment in 1948 an IO with regulatory powers (Articles 19 and 21 of the WHO Constitution), has produced significantly fewer norms than other institutions (L. Gostin, "A Proposal for a Framework Convention on Global Health," 10 *Journal of International Economic Law* 989 (2007)). The role of the WHO as a "global administration" is examined by D. C. Esty, "Good Governance at the Supranational Scale: Globalizing Administrative Law," 115:7 *Yale Law Journal* 1550 (2006).

[50] D. P. Fidler, "From International Sanitary Conventions to Global Health Security: The New International Health Regulations," 4 *Chinese Journal of International Law* 325 (2005); and E. Mack, "The World Health Organization's New International Health Regulations: Incursions on State Sovereignty and Ill-Fated Response to Global Health Issues," 7 *Chicago Journal of International Law* 365 (2006).

[51] As in the case of the Codex Alimentarius: M. A. Livermore, "Authority and Legitimacy in Global Governance: Deliberation, Institutional Differentiation, and the Codex Alimentarius," 81 *New York University Law Review* 766 (2006); and M. Masson-Matthee, *The Codex Alimentarius Commission and its Standards* (The Hague: TMC Asser Press, 2007).

and ICANN. Moreover, the growth of norm-making activities has often coincided with the formation of a structured institutional system, in which IOs have been joined by other IOs, and regimes imposed the establishment of domestic legal terminals or a network organization.[52]

Thus, one of the main problems that arises in these contexts is the need to coordinate this mass of norms. It is for this reason that several instruments of coordination have been designed. These instruments may operate directly between norms, through mechanisms of cross-reference between treaties, conventions or other acts;[53] or they may act at the institutional level, through the establishment of a joint

[52] See the "National Contact Points" (NCPs) developed by the OECD under the Guidelines for Multinational Enterprises; see R. Chetrit, "Into GAL's Fragmentation and Unity Debate: Governance in Environmental Law," paper presented at the 4th Viterbo Global Administrative Law Seminar (2008).

[53] From this perspective, the WTO system – which includes, among others, the GATT, TBT, SPS and TRIPS agreements – is a clear example: there are often conflicts of norms (see J. Pauwelyn, *Conflict of Norms in Public International Law: How WTO Law Relates to Other Rules of International Law* (Cambridge University Press, 2003)); see also J. Pauwelyn, "Non-Traditional Patterns of Global Regulation," in C. Joerges and E.-U. Petersmann (eds.), *Constitutionalism, Multilevel Trade Governance and Social Regulation* (Oxford: Hart, 2006); R. Wolfrum, P.-T. Stoll and A. Seibert-Fohr (eds.), *WTO – Technical Barriers and SPS Measures* (Leiden and Boston: Brill, 2007). In addition, the WTO adopts guidelines, recommendations and best practices (see I. Feichtner, "The Administration of the Vocabulary of International Trade: The Adaptation of WTO Schedules to Changes in the Harmonized System," 9 *German Law Journal* 1481 (2008)).

organization (for example, the Codex Alimentarius Commission, created in 1963 by the FAO and WHO for the elaboration of food standards); the instruments may have a procedural dimension, such as when a joint action is provided by several different IOs and/or private actors (see the case of the environment[54]); or they may consist of dispute settlement mechanisms, with a regime borrowing the arbitration or quasi-judicial body of another: this happens with ICANN and the Internet, which both use the WIPO Arbitration System for the settlement of disputes concerning domain names.

Norm-makers have been multiplying. Today, IOs produce a large amount of norms, in many different forms.[55] The result is a great variety of names for these measures:

[54] This happens in climate change: R. B. Stewart, B. Kingsbury and B. Rudyk (eds.), *Climate Finance: Regulatory and Funding Strategies for Climate Change and Global Development* (New York University Press, 2009).

[55] See T. Franck, "Non-Treaty Law Making: When, Where, and How?," in R. Wolfrum and V. Röben (eds.), *Developments of International Law in Treaty Making* (Heidelberg: Springer, 2005), pp. 417 *et seq.*; comments by L. Boisson de Chazournes, "Treaty Law-Making and Non-Treaty Law-Making: The Evolving Structure of the International Legal Order," in R. Wolfrum and V. Röben (eds.), *Developments of International Law in Treaty Making* (Heidelberg: Springer, 2005), pp. 463 *et seq.*; M. Goldmann, "Inside Relative Normativity: From Sources to Standard Instruments for the Exercise of International Public Authority," 9 *German Law Journal* 1865 (2008); formerly, K. Nicolaïdis and J. L. Tong, "Diversity or Cacophony? The Continuing Debate Over New Sources of International Law," 24 *Michigan Journal of International Law* 1349 (2004); and A. Cassese, *International Law in a Divided World* (Oxford: Clarendon Press, 1986), pp. 169 *et seq.*

standards,[56] recommendations, guidelines, policies . . .[57] For example, the ILO was conceived and created for the very purpose of elaborating rules that would be more flexible than traditional treaties.[58] UNESCO adopts similar instruments

[56] "Standard setting" is probably one of the most ancient forms of norm-making at the international level: see the International Civil Aviation Organization (ICAO), on which, see T. Buergenthal, *Law-Making in the International Civil Aviation Organization* (New York: Syracuse University Press, 1969); and T. Fidalgo de Freitas, "From Participation Towards Compliance: The Role of Private Actors in the Making of SARPs by ICAO," paper presented at the 3rd Viterbo Global Administrative Law Seminar (2007). More generally, see H. C. Röhl, "Internationale Standardsetzung," in C. Mollers, A. Voßkuhle and C. Walter (eds.), *Internationales Verwaltungsrecht* (Tubingen: Mohr Siebeck, 2007), pp. 319 *et seq.*

[57] B. Kingsbury, "Operational Policies of International Institutions as Part of the Law-Making Process: The World Bank and Indigenous People," in G. S. Goodwin-Gill and S. Talmon (eds.), *The Reality of International Law: Essays in Honour of Ian Brownlie* (Oxford: Clarendon Press, 1999); and L. Boisson de Chazournes, "Policy Guidance and Compliance: The World Bank Operational Standards," in D. Shelton (ed.), *Commitment and Compliance: The Role of Non-binding Norms in the International Legal System* (Oxford University Press, 2000), pp. 281 *et seq.*

[58] See F. Maupain, "International Labour Organization: Recommendations and Similar Instruments," in D. Shelton (ed.), *Commitment and Compliance: The Role of Non-binding Norms in the International Legal System* (Oxford University Press, 2000), pp. 372 *et seq.*; A. C. L. Davies, "Global Administrative Law at the International Labour Organization: The Problem of Softer Standards" (paper presented at the New York University Law School Conference on "Global Administrative Law: National and International Accountability Mechanisms for Global Regulatory Governance," New York University, April 22–23, 2005) (available at www.iilj.org/GAL/documents/DaviesPaper.pdf); and L. R. Helfer, "Understanding Change in International Organizations:

too,[59] not to mention the many relevant examples of private regulatory regimes.[60] This major trend of international regimes naturally also affects – in some cases, to a very large extent – regional organizations. Indeed, the increase is both quantitative and qualitative: decisions, recommendations, guidelines, directives, policies and standards. Also, the number of secondary norms has been growing significantly: consider the African Union or the Arab League, to give just two examples.[61] In addition, some regional experiences allow scholars to identify new mechanisms of informal international law-making (for example, in the APEC).[62]

Globalization and Innovation in the ILO," 59 *Vanderbilt Law Review* 649 (2006).

59 See A. A. Yusuf (ed.), *Standard-Setting at UNESCO. Normative Action in Education, Science and Culture* (Leiden and Boston: Martinus Nijhoff, 2007).

60 H. Schepel, *The Constitution of Private Governance: Product Standards in the Regulation of Integrating Markets* (Oxford: Hart Publishing, 2005); more recently, K. W. Abbott and D. Snidal, "The Governance Triangle: Regulatory Standards Institutions and the Shadow of the State," in W. Mattli and N. Woods (eds.), *The Politics of Global Regulation* (Princeton University Press, 2009), pp. 44 *et seq.*; and H. Schepel, "Private Regulators in Law," in J. Pauwelyn, R. Wessel and J. Wouters (eds.), *Informal International Lawmaking: Mapping the Action and Testing Concepts of Accountability and Effectiveness* (Oxford University Press, 2012), pp. 356 *et seq.*

61 See Chapter 1 above.

62 T. Suami, "Informal International Lawmaking in Asia – An Examination of APEC," in A. Berman, S. Duquet, J. Pauwelyn, R. Wessel and J. Wouters (eds.), *Informal International Lawmaking: Case Studies* (The Hague: TOAE, 2012), pp. 55 *et seq.*

The proliferation of norms has led to the development of mechanisms for the resolution of conflicts; to reduce the fragmentation that characterizes such a multiplication,[63] forms of harmonization have also been developed, such as international standards.[64] Moreover, the need for harmonization could be perceived, by IOs themselves, as being more urgent in some sectors rather than in others.[65] From this point of view, instruments such as recommendations

[63] International Law Commission, *Fragmentation of International Law: Difficulties Arising from the Diversification and Expansion of International Law*, UN General Assembly, A/CN.4/L.682 (April 13, 2006); P.-M. Dupuy, "A Doctrinal Debate in the Globalisation Era: On the 'Fragmentation' of International Law," 1 *European Journal of Legal Studies* 1 (2007); B. Conforti, "Unité et fragmentation du droit international: glissez, mortels, n'appuyez pas!," 111:1 *Revue Générale du Droit International Public* 5 (2007); E. Benvenisti and G. W. Downs, "The Empire's New Clothes: Political Economy and the Fragmentation of International Law," 60 *Stanford Law Review* 595 (2007); and M. Koskenniemi and P. Leino, "Fragmentation of International Law? Postmodern Anxieties," 15 *Leiden Journal of International Law* 553 (2002).

[64] For example, in the WTO (S. Charnowitz, *International Standards and the WTO*, George Washington University Law School, Public Law and Legal Theory Working Paper 133), finance (S. Battini (ed.), *La regolazione globale dei mercati finanziari* (Milan: Giuffrè, 2007)) or environmental protection (D. Bodansky, "Is There an International Environmental Constitution?," 16 *Indiana Journal of Global Legal Studies* 565 (2009), who recognizes the existence of many orders, but not yet a constitutional one).

[65] V. Tafur-Domínguez, "International Environmental Harmonization – Emergence and Development of The Andean Community," 12 *Pace International Law Review* 283 (2000).

and directives should be capable of ensuring greater harmonization, especially among Member States' legal systems. Another solution typically deployed in regional organizations is "mutual recognition," adopted for instance in the EU, but also in ASEAN.[66]

However, the proliferation of norms and lawmakers also led IOs to establish a hierarchy, or more hierarchies, between norms:[67] as a consequence, a rule of "normative supremacy" has been affirmed.[68] This is why some scholars have claimed that a process of "constitutionalization" of specific sectors – such as the WTO[69] or of the UN more

[66] As testified by the many ASEAN framework agreements on mutual recognition arrangements (in the most diverse professions).

[67] D. Shelton, "Normative Hierarchy in International Law," 100 *American Journal of International Law* 291 (2006).

[68] The term "supremacy" is used by J. H. H. Weiler, "The Transformation of Europe," 100:8 *Yale Law Journal* 2403 (1991), to explain the relationships between the EC and States.

[69] See J. L. Dunoff, "The Politics of International Constitutions: The Curious Case of the World Trade Organization," in J. L. Dunoff and J. P. Trachtman (eds.), *Ruling the World? Constitutionalism, International Law, and Global Governance* (New York: Cambridge University Press, 2009), pp. 178–205; and C. Joerges and E.-U. Petersmann (eds.), *Constitutionalism, Multilevel Trade Governance and Social Regulation* (Oxford: Hart Publishing, 2006). The plurality of these systems is analyzed by N. Walker, "Beyond Boundary Disputes and Basic Grids: Mapping the Global Disorder of Normative Orders," 6 *International Journal of Constitutional Law* 373 (2008); and J. Klabbers, *Setting the Scene*, in J. Klabbers, A. Peters and G. Ulfstein, *The Constitutionalization of International Law* (Oxford University Press, 2009), pp. 1 *et seq.* (especially pp. 25 *et seq.*); and by P. Schiff Berman, "Global Legal Pluralism," 80 *Southern California Law Review* 1155 (2007).

generally – has been taking place.[70] In addition, individual "world orders" have emerged.[71] From this perspective, regional organizations present an interesting mechanism: the creation of parliaments. This option has the aim of endorsing the international regulatory body through democratic mechanisms. The name "parliament" usually implies that these bodies have sovereign power, as their national counterparts. But most of the time, this objective only results in a façade: in the EU, for example, while the Parliament may be important, norm-making power is in fact in the hands of the Council. With the exception of the EU,

[70] B. Fassbender, "The United Nations Charter as Constitution of the International Community," 36 *Columbia Journal of Transnational Law* 529 (1998); and E. De Wet, "The International Constitutional Order," 55 *International and Comparative Law Quarterly* 51 (2006). More recently, J. Arato, "Constitutionality and Constitutionalism Beyond the State: Two Perspectives on the Material Constitution of the United Nations," 10 *International Journal of Constitutional Law* 627 (2012). The most discussed constitutional process, however, is that of the EU: see J. H. H. Weiler, *The Constitution of Europe: Do the New Clothes Have an Emperor?, and Other Essays on European Integration* (Cambridge University Press, 1999); and, more recently, J. Habermas, "The Crisis of the European Union in the Light of a Constitutionalization of International Law," 23 *European Journal of International Law* 335 (2012).

[71] In the case of health, D. P. Fidler, "Constitutional Outlines of Public Health's 'New World Order'," 77 *Temple Law Review* 247 (2004); more generally, A.-M. Slaughter, *A New World Order* (Princeton University Press, 2004); and A. Hurrell, *On Global Order: Power, Values, and the Constitution of International Society* (Oxford University Press, 2007), pp. 239 *et seq.*

parliaments are in fact "weak" and "underdeveloped institution[s] in almost all integration schemes."[72]

All these issues lead to a broader question: what is the binding force of these norms? Are they law? The norms are generally labeled "soft law,"[73] but they also show a certain degree of "publicness."[74] For example, see the WTO Codes of

[72] See Table 1.13 above.

[73] A. Di Robilant, "Genealogies of Soft Law," 54 *American Journal of Comparative Law* 499 (2006); J. d'Aspremont, "Softness in International Law: A Self-Serving Quest for New Legal Materials," 19 *European Journal of International Law* 1075 (2008). See also P.-M. Dupuy, "Soft Law and the International Law of the Environment," 12 *Michigan Journal of International Law* 420 (1991); and K. W. Abbott and D. Snidal, "Hard and Soft Law in International Governance," 54 *International Organization* 421 (2000). As for the EU context, see S. Oana, "European Union Soft Law: New Developments Concerning the Divide Between Legally Binding Force and Legal Effects," 75 *Modern Law Review* 865 (2012).

[74] B. Kingsbury, "The Concept of 'Law' in Global Administrative Law," 20:1 *European Journal of International Law* 23 (2009), pp. 34 *et seq.*; and D. Dyzenhaus, *Accountability and the Concept of (Global) Administrative Law*, IILJ Working Paper 2008/7, Global Administrative Law Series, pp. 13–24, who examines respectively H. L. A. Hart, *The Concept of Law* (Oxford: Clarendon Law Series, 1961), and L. L. Fuller, *The Morality of Law* (New Haven, CT: Yale University Press, 1964); see also J. Waldron, "The Concept and the Rule of Law," 43 *Georgia Law Review* 1 (2008). Also, M. Goldmann, "Inside Relative Normativity: From Sources to Standard Instruments for the Exercise of International Public Authority," 9 *German Law Journal* 1865 (2008); M. Koskenniemi, *From Apology to Utopia: The Structure of International Legal Argument* (Cambridge University Press, 2006), pp. 303 *et seq.*; and L. Boisson de Chazournes, "Governance et regulation au 21ème siècle: quelques propos iconoclasts," in R. Mehdi and L. Boisson de Chazournes (eds.), *Une*

"Good Practice": although not binding, all international standard-setters comply with them in order to fall within the scope of the TBT Agreement.[75] In the nuclear sector, "a mixture of internationally binding and non-binding principles and norms"[76] has been created; in communications, the International Telecommunication Union (ITU) adopts hundreds of recommendations every year that, although not mandatory, are observed by States.[77]

Finally, the growing volume of norms has significant implications for domestic legal orders: on the one hand, conflicts between norms have become more numerous; on the other, instruments for coordination are adopted (for example, in the context of the EU, the mechanism for requesting preliminary rulings from the CJEU). The latter phenomenon is

société internationale en mutation: quels acteurs pour une nouvelle gouvernance? (Brussels: Bruylant, 2004), pp. 19 *et seq.*

75 B. Kingsbury, "The Concept of 'Law' in Global Administrative Law," 20:1 *European Journal of International Law* 23 (2009).

76 W. Tonhauser, "IAEA Technical Standard Setting," paper presented at the Conference "Practical Legal Problems of International Organizations: A Global Administrative Law Perspective on Public/Private Partnerships, Accountability, and Human Rights" (Geneva, March 20–21, 2009) (available at www.iilj.org/GAL/GALGeneva.asp). Indeed, the IAEA adopts recommendations which "take up where treaties leave off, filling in gaps by furnishing the elaborate detail of protective measures" (B. Kellman, "Protection of Nuclear Materials," in D. Shelton (ed.), *Commitment and Compliance: The Role of Non-Binding Norms in the International Legal System* (Oxford University Press, 2000), pp. 486 *et seq.*).

77 J. Hinricher, "The Law-Making of the International Telecommunication Union (ITU) – Providing a New Source of International Law," 64 *Zeitschrift für Ausländisches Recht und Völkerrecht* 489 (2004).

particularly significant in the case of regional organizations, which have been producing a great deal of secondary norms. To ensure the effectiveness of legal integration, the solution of according "direct applicability" to international norms in domestic legal contexts is often adopted: this happens in the EU, the CAN (for the decisions of the Andean Council) and ECOWAS, for example. But in other cases, it was chosen to require explicit transposition: this is the case of MERCOSUR, the Arab League and CARICOM.[78] The latter solution leaves many more discretionary powers to the State, which may have a serious adverse impact on the effectiveness of the international regime in question. This may explain why direct effect and direct applicability of international norms is usually present in more complex forms of regional integration, such as political unions or communities.

2.3.2 *The strategic role of (quasi-)judicial bodies*

Therefore, there is a connection between the increase in norms and administrative functions on the one hand, and the need for oversight and review mechanisms, on the other. The rising numbers of administrative tribunals within IOs is a clear example in point.[79] It is a matter

[78] See Chapter 1 above.

[79] O. Elias (ed.), *The Development and Effectiveness of International Administrative Law* (The Hague: Martinus Nijhoff, 2012); Katerina Papanikolaou, *International Administrative Tribunals in a Changing World* (New York: Esperia, 2007).

of fact that a greater body of rules requires more enforcement mechanisms.[80]

In international regimes, therefore, dispute settlement mechanisms are often used as reviewing bodies to control how IOs operate:[81] consider the ILO,[82] but also private regimes such as the Internet.[83] At the same time, the need to protect fundamental rights arises.[84] Indeed, international courts and tribunals appear to be more effective when they have more tools at their disposal, and if they can also perform different functions: dispute settlement, enforcement,

80 See J. H. H. Weiler, "The Geology of International Law – Governance, Democracy and Legitimacy," 64 *Zeitschrift für Ausländisches Recht und Völkerrecht* 547 (2004); T. Treves, "Judicial Lawmaking in an Era of 'Proliferation' of International Courts and Tribunals: Development or Fragmentation of International Law?," in R. Wolfrum and V. Röben (eds.), *Developments of International Law in Treaty Making* (Heidelberg: Springer, 2005), pp. 587 *et seq.* More generally, M. Cappelletti, *Dimensioni della giustizia nelle società contemporanee: Studi di diritto giudiziario comparato* (Bologna: Il Mulino, 1994), especially pp. 39 *et seq.*

81 J. Jowell, "The Universality of Administrative Justice?," in M. Ruffert (ed.), *The Transformation of Administrative Law in Europe/La mutation du droit administratif en Europe* (Munich: Sellier European Law Publishers, 2007), pp. 55 *et seq.*, especially pp. 62 *et seq.*; see also E. García de Enterría, *Democrazia, Jueces y Control de la Administración* (Madrid: Civitas, 2000).

82 ILO Constitution, Articles 26, 27, 28 and 33. See S. Charnovitz, "The International Labour Organization in Its Second Century," 4 *Max Planck Yearbook of United Nations Law* 147 (2000), especially pp. 175 *et seq.*

83 ICANN Bylaws, Article IV ("Accountability and Review").

84 M. Cappelletti, *Dimensioni della giustizia nelle società contemporanee: Studi di diritto giudiziario comparato* (Bologna: Il Mulino, 1994), pp. 39 *et seq.* See also M. Cappelletti, *Judicial Review in the Contemporary World* (New York: Bobbs-Merill, 1971), pp. 45 *et seq.*

administrative review and constitutional review. This happens when they do not only resemble one type of court, but rather deal with several issues (civil, administrative, constitutional, and even criminal). This mixed, hybrid nature of dispute settlement bodies appears to work extremely well, at least in those regimes where it is achieved.[85] In other cases, the solution is not found in courts but in faster alternative dispute resolution mechanisms such as arbitration (for example, investment law).[86] In addition, courts and tribunals play a crucial role in connecting different regimes:[87] this is the case of the WTO Dispute Settlement Body, when it is called upon to decide issues related to the TBT or SPS agreements.

The "judicial" function will continue to grow within international regimes.[88] This appears to happen very often in

[85] See the Dispute Settlement Body of the WTO (B. Marchetti, "Il sistema di risoluzione delle dispute del WTO: Amministrazione, corte o tertium genus?," 4 *Rivista Trimestrale Di Diritto Pubblico* 963–1001 (2009)). See also C. H. Koch, Jr., "Judicial Review and Global Federalism," 54 *Administrative Law Review* 491 (2002).

[86] G. Kaufmann-Kohler, "Mondialisation de la procédure arbitrale," in C. A. Morand (ed.), *Le droit saisi par la mondialisation* (Brussels: Bruylant, 2001), pp. 269 *et seq.*

[87] A.-M. Slaughter, "A Global Community of Courts," 44 *Harvard International Law Journal* 191 (2003); Y. Shany, *The Competing Jurisdictions of International Courts and Tribunals* (Oxford University Press, 2004); and Y. Shany, *Regulating Jurisdictional Relations Between National and International Courts* (Oxford University Press, 2007).

[88] See the Project on International Courts and Tribunals (available at www.pict-pcti.org), joint initiative of the New York University Center for International Cooperation and the London UCL Centre for International Courts and Tribunals.

regional organizations, if we consider the great number of institutions that have established a court: AEC, AU, CIS, CoE, COMESA, EAC, ECCAS, ECOWAS, EU, MERCOSUR, and ODECA.[89] The establishment of supranational judges seems to be more straightforward when a need to protect universal values or fundamental rights is felt (as was the case with the European Court of Human Rights, the Inter-American Court of Human Rights and the African Court of Human and Peoples' Rights), or when all parties call for a rapid dispute settlement system (for example, in relation to investments; this also explains why the majority of international "courts" belong – or belonged at least originally – to economic systems, such as the EU's CJEU, the Court of Justice of the ECOWAS, the WTO Dispute Settlement Body and the ASEAN Dispute settlement mechanisms). The latter type of body also displays the widest variety of functions, serving not only as mechanisms for dispute settlement (such as in ASEAN), but also for enforcement (MERCOSUR and the WTO, for instance) and review (as in the EU, CAN and COMESA). In some cases, the establishment of a supranational court is the direct result of a transplant from one regime into another (one of the most significant examples in point is the Andean Tribunal of Justice, which reproduces, at least on paper, the main features of the CJEU[90]).

[89] See Chapter 1 above.

[90] K. J. Alter and L. R. Helfer, "Legal Integration in the Andes: Lawmaking by the Andean Tribunal of Justice," 17 *European Journal of International Law* 701 (2011); and K. J. Alter and L. R. Helfer, "Nature or Nurture: Judicial Lawmaking in the European Court of Justice and the Andean Tribunal of Justice," 64 *International Organization* 563 (2010).

However, the effectiveness of these courts still very much depends on the role played by domestic judges. This is why it is important to involve these figures in the system. In the most sophisticated regimes, such as the EU, the judicial function is not only well-established (the CJEU also enjoyed a "benign neglect," which enabled it to contribute greatly to European integration),[91] but is also based on constant interaction with domestic judges, through the mechanism of preliminary ruling,[92] and this phenomenon can be framed as a case of "role-splitting."[93] As a matter of fact, when national courts are not integrated within an international "judiciary," they tend to react against international norms in favor of their domestic legal orders.[94] Moreover, international courts or

[91] E. Stein, "Lawyers, Judges and the Making of a Transnational Constitution," 75 *American Journal of International Law* 1 (1981), referring to the ECJ; see also K. J. Alter, *The European Court's Political Power* (Oxford University Press, 2009).

[92] M. Broberg and N. Fenger, *Preliminary References to the European Court of Justice* (Oxford University Press, 2010); C. O. Lenz, "The Role and Mechanism of The Preliminary Ruling Procedure," 18 *Fordham International Law Journal* 388 (1994–1995).

[93] P. De Sena and M. C. Vitucci, "The European Courts and the Security Council: Between Dédoublement Fonctionnel and Balancing of Values," 20 *European Journal of International Law* 193 (2009), and the reply by G. de Búrca.

[94] E. Benvenisti and G. W. Downs, *Will National Court Cooperation Promote Global Accountability? The Judicial Review of International Organizations* (2009) (available at www.iilj.org/courses/documents/Benvenisti-Downs.HC2009Oct7.pdf). Formerly, R. B. Ahdieh, "Between Dialogue and Decree: International Review of National Courts," 79 New York University Law Review 2029 (2004). More recently, A. Nollkaemper, *National Courts and the International Rule of Law*

tribunals play a key role in developing the regimes of which they are part: take the case of the WTO and its Dispute Settlement Body, which progressively launched a process of "constitutionalization" of international economic law;[95] or the promotion of the rule of law undertaken by dispute settlement systems in specific regional areas such as Latin America.[96] Finally, States may also be reluctant to use the dispute settlement body of a given institution, and opt to file their cases before a different body: ASEAN members, for example, often preferred to use the WTO system instead of the ASEAN dispute settlement mechanism. This confirms that overlapping and competition between IOs takes place at the infra-institutional level too.

It emerges, therefore, that the greater the variety in the functions of an international court, the greater the

(Oxford University Press, 2011), and A. Roberts, "Comparative International Law? The Role of National Courts in Creating and Enforcing International Law," 60 *International and Comparative Law Quarterly* 57 (2011).

95 D. Z. Cass, "The 'Constitutionalization' of International Trade Law: Judicial Norm-Generation as the Engine of Constitutional Development in International Trade," 12 *European Journal of International Law* 39 (2001); J. L. Goldstein and R. H. Steinberg, "Regulatory Shift: The Rise of Judicial Liberalization at the WTO," in W. Mattli and N. Woods (eds.), *The Politics of Global Regulation* (Princeton University Press, 2009), pp. 211 *et seq.*, who highlight the "emergence of Judicial Lawmaking" (pp. 227 *et seq.*).

96 See the empirical analysis by S. J. Powell and L. Mendoña Lopes Ribeiro, "Managing the Rule of Law in the Americas: An Empirical Portrait of the Effects of 15 Years of WTO, MERCOSUR, and NAFTA Dispute Resolution on Civil Society in Latin America," 42 *University of Miami Inter-American Law Review* 197 (2010–2011).

effectiveness of international norms, and the greater the degree of legal integration of the relevant regime.

2.3.3 The development of an international administration

The growth of both regulatory and "judicial" functions is connected to a dramatic increase in administrative tasks. The trend followed by the proliferation of IOs is indeed similar to that which can be seen in domestic administrations, that is, based on the need to pursue a public interest.[97] At the same time, relationships between IOs and domestic administrations have become more complex.[98]

There is a growing number of activities that are neither legislative nor judicial in nature.[99] This is also

[97] M. Virally, "La notion de fonction dans la théorie de l'organisation internationale," in *La communauté internationale, Mélanges offerts à Charles Rousseau: La communauté internationale* (Paris: Pedone, 1974), p. 277; and N. Blokker, "Comparing Apples and Oranges? Reinventing the Wheel? Schermers' Book and Challenges for the Future of International Institutional Law," 5:1 *International Organizations Law Review* 197 (2008), p. 201.

[98] S. Cassese, "Relations Between International Organizations and National Administrations," in International Institute of Administrative Sciences, *Proceedings of the XIXth International Congress of Administrative Sciences* (London: Kluwer Law and Taxation Publishers, 1983).

[99] N. Krisch and B. Kingsbury, "Introduction: Global Governance and Global Administrative Law in International Legal Order," 17 *European Journal of International Law* 1 (2006), p. 3, who refer to "recognizably administrative and regulatory functions" that, if "performed by State agenc[ies], there would be little doubt as to their administrative character."

enhanced by the role played by domestic administrations in the development of the regimes. The less that IOs engage in developing their own administration, the more they will rely on States and national administrations to operate.[100] At the same time, the more a global administration develops, the more likely it will be for IOs to require States to establish a domestic terminal entrusted with the delivery of a given function in that country. The EU has adopted this course of conduct almost since its foundation,[101] as have other entities among the most developed regimes too. However, this prevailing role of administrative functions raises several problems in terms of democracy,[102] legitimacy[103] and accountability.[104]

[100] D. Sarooshi, *International Organizations and Their Exercise of Sovereign Powers* (Oxford University Press, 2005), especially pp. 18 *et seq.*

[101] P. Craig and G. de Búrca (eds.), *The Evolution of EU Law* (Oxford University Press, 2nd edn., 2011).

[102] A. von Bogdandy, "Demokratie, Globalisierung, Zukunft des Völkerrechts – Eine Bestandsaufnahme," 63 *Zeitschrift für Ausländisches Recht und Völkerrecht* 853 (2003), and A. C. Aman, Jr., "Globalization, Democracy and the Need for a New Administrative Law," 10 *Indiana Journal of Global Legal Studies* 125 (2003).

[103] R. Wolfrum and V. Röben (eds.), *Legitimacy in International Law* (Berlin: Springer, 2008); M. Kumm, "The Legitimacy of International Law: A Constitutional Framework of Analysis," 15 *European Journal of International Law* 907 (2004); in political science, A. Buchanan and R. O. Keohane, "The Legitimacy of Global Governance Institutions," 20 *Ethics and International Affairs* 405 (2006). As for the concept of legitimacy in relation to IOs' regulatory functions, see T. Franck, *The Power of Legitimacy Among Nations* (New York: Oxford University Press, 1990).

[104] J. Ferejohn, *Accountability in a Global Context*, IILJ Working Paper 2007/5, Global Administrative Law Series; A. Reinisch, "Securing the Accountability of International Organization," 7 *Global Governance* 131

Data show that IOs are constantly adding new offices and employees. For example, in the last few decades, the number of field offices has been steadily growing.[105] As for regional organizations, the development of the administrative functions delivered at the supranational level may be examined from a dual perspective: the emergence of international administrations and the implementation of administrative decisions.

First, there is a tendency to establish an apparatus to support the IO in carrying out its primary task. In this connection, besides intergovernmental organs (such as Councils of Ministers), many regional organizations also have a Secretariat: this very name highlights its main function, that is, that of furthering the IO's mission. However, many regional organizations have progressively expanded the scope of their activity; in doing so, they also created several other bodies.

The example of the EU agencies is perhaps the most significant in this respect:[106] there are around thirty

(2001); R. B. Stewart, *Accountability, Participation, and the Problem of Disregard in Global Regulatory Governance*, Paper presented at New York University Law School, International Legal Theory Colloquium on Interpretation and Judgment in International Law (February 7, 2008); as for the UN system, S. Chesterman, "Globalization Rules: Accountability, Power, and the Prospects for Global Administrative Law," 14 *Global Governance* 39 (2008).

[105] See the case of Peacekeeping Operations, for instance (www.un.org/en/peacekeeping/resources/statistics/factsheet.shtml). A pioneering study was made by W. R. Sharp, *Field Administration in the United Nations System* (London: Stevens and Sons, 1961).

[106] See http://europa.eu/agencies.

decentralized agencies across Europe, independent legal entities with technical, scientific, operational and/or regulatory natures;[107] due to the great number of these bodies, the

[107] Agency for the Cooperation of Energy Regulators (ACER); Body of European Regulators for Electronic Communications (BEREC); Community Plant Variety Office (CPVO); European Agency for Safety and Health at Work (EU-OSHA); European Agency for the Management of Operational Cooperation at the External Borders (FRONTEX); European Agency for the Operational Management of large-scale IT Systems in the Area of Freedom, Security and Justice (eu-LISA); European Asylum Support Office (EASO) (at planning stage); European Aviation Safety Agency (EASA); European Banking Authority (EBA); European Centre for Disease Prevention and Control (ECDC); European Centre for the Development of Vocational Training (Cedefop); European Chemicals Agency (ECHA); European Environment Agency (EEA); European Fisheries Control Agency (EFCA); European Food Safety Authority (EFSA); European Foundation for the Improvement of Living and Working Conditions (EUROFOUND); European GNSS Agency (GSA); European Institute for Gender Equality (EIGE); European Insurance and Occupational Pensions Authority (EIOPA); European Maritime Safety Agency (EMSA); European Medicines Agency (EMA); European Monitoring Centre for Drugs and Drug Addiction (EMCDDA); European Network and Information Security Agency (ENISA); European Police College (CEPOL); European Police Office (EUROPOL); European Railway Agency – promoting safe and compatible rail systems (ERA); European Securities and Markets Authority (ESMA); European Training Foundation (ETF); European Union Agency for Fundamental Rights (FRA); Office for Harmonisation in the Internal Market (Trade Marks and Designs) (OHIM); The European Union's Judicial Cooperation Unit (EUROJUST); Translation Centre for the Bodies of the European Union (CdT). The three agencies under the Common Security and Defence Policy are the European Defence Agency (EDA); European Union Institute for Security Studies (EUISS); and European Union Satellite Centre (EUSC).

EU launched a Common Approach Program to harmonize the establishment and the functioning of decentralized agencies, which had been to date created on a case-by-case basis.[108] These agencies have greatly contributed to EU legal integration because they are distributed in different Member States (for example, the EFSA is in Italy, the EEA in Denmark, the ECHA in Finland, the EASA in Germany and so on) and they tend to require intense cooperation with domestic national administrations (such as in relation to the environment, health or food security, to mention but a few). In addition to these agencies, the EU also counts other bodies such as the executive agencies created under Council Regulation (EC) No. 58 of 2003: these bodies are established for a fixed period of time and are entrusted with tasks relating to the management of one or more Community programs (and are, therefore, located in Brussels or Luxembourg).[109]

The EU has therefore developed many institutions besides the three main governing bodies (Council, Commission and Parliament) and the CJEU: these "additional" institutions include the European Economic and Social Committee; the Committee of the Regions, which represents regional and local authorities; the European Investment Bank

[108] See http://europa.eu/agencies/regulatory_agencies_bodies/index_en.htm.

[109] They are currently: Education, Audiovisual, and Culture Executive Agency (EACEA); European Research Council Executive Agency (ERC Executive Agency); Executive Agency for Competitiveness and Innovation (EACI); Executive Agency for Health and Consumers (EAHC); Research Executive Agency (REA); and Trans-European Transport Network Executive Agency (TEN-T EA).

and the European Central Bank; the European Ombudsman; the European Data Protection Supervisor; the Publications Office; the European Personnel Selection Office; the European School of Administration; and the European External Action Service.

Other regional organizations have also established specialized agencies. For example, the ECOWAS (which has a Bank for Investment and Development and an Economic and Social Council (ECOSOC), which ensures the involvement of civil society) created a group of agencies including the West African Health Organization (WAHO), the West African Monetary Agency (WAMA), the West African Monetary Institute (WAMI) and the Water Resources Coordination Unit (WRCU). MERCOSUR developed a system based on working groups and technical committees rather than on independent legal entities. Other regional organizations, such as ASEAN, still maintain a "loose institutional structure."[110]

The second perspective is related to the forms of implementation. Of course, this issue is closely related to the previous one, as the more developed the administration is, the more decisions will be taken and thereafter implemented at the administrative level. From this point of view, the EU clearly demonstrates that so-called indirect administration, in which the regional organization rules and its States implement, cannot be the only form that is capable of ensuring legal integration, especially when the scope of activities

[110] See P. J. Davidson, "The Role of International Law in the Governance of International Economic Relations in ASEAN," 12 *Singapore Yearbook of International Law* 213–224 (2008).

delivered by the regime increases.[111] It is for this reason that the EU progressively adopted other forms of implementation, from direct administration to co-administration and distributed administration (through its thirty-odd agencies). This can explain why, since the 1990s, a specific field of EU administrative law has been developing.[112] There are no comparable cases in the context of regional organizations, in which the secretariat approach is still dominant. It is for this reason that, in such cases, which do not feature a developed international administration yet, much attention is paid to the implementation of regulatory policies and to the mechanisms of direct applicability available within domestic legal orders. Also, in many cases, the instrument for implementation is found in *ad hoc* dispute settlement bodies rather than in an international administration entity. However, even when regional integration has not led to the formation of an administration, IOs use coordination mechanisms based on committees or representation (such as in the case of ASEAN, where there is both a Committee of Permanent Representatives and a system

[111] See S. Krislov, C.-D. Ehlermann and J. H. H. Weiler, "Part I on European Community Policy Making and Implementation Processes," in M. Cappelletti, M. Seccombe and J. H. H. Weiler (eds.), *Integration Through Law: Europe and the American Federal Experience* (Berlin and New York: Walter de Gruyter, 1985), vol. I, Book 2, *Political Organs, Integration Techniques and Judicial Process*, pp. 3 *et seq.*, especially pp. 85 *et seq.* A political science perspective on policy implementation is given by D. S. Van Meter and C. E. Van Horn, "The Policy Implementation Process: A Conceptual Framework," 6 *Administration and Society* 445 (1975).

[112] P. P. Craig, *EU Administrative Law* (Oxford University Press, 2nd edn., 2012).

of national secretariats). In other cases, the intergovernmental organ may be entrusted with monitoring functions, to verify States' compliance with the IO's decisions (as happens in the AEC, ECAS and ECOWAS).[113]

2.4 Intra- and inter-IO institutional pluralism

The growth of IOs is dealt with above (Section 2.2). In the context of international regimes too, we are witnessing a proliferation of bodies and offices (secretariats, committees, councils and so on.) and of other international agencies.[114] As illustrated above, this phenomenon is particularly evident in regional organizations, since most of these include several bodies (such as the ACS, AU, CAN, CARICOM, CIS, COMESA, EAC, ECCAS, ECOWAS, EU, MERCOSUR, OAS and ODECA) (Section 2.3.3 above).

[113] See Chapter 1 above.

[114] Another significant example is that of "International Agencies," i.e. "international bodies that are not based on a treaty, nor on a bottom-up cooperation between national regulators, but on a decision by an international organization" (A. Berman and R. A. Wessel, "The International Legal Form and Status of Informal International Lawmaking Bodies: Consequences for Accountability," in J. Pauwelyn, R. Wessel and J. Wouters (eds.), *Informal International Lawmaking: Mapping the Action and Testing Concepts of Accountability and Effectiveness* (Oxford University Press, 2012)); see also E. Chiti and R. A. Wessel, "The Emergence of International Agencies in the Global Administrative Space: Autonomous Actors or State Servants?," in N. White and R. Collins (eds.), *International Organizations and the Idea of Autonomy* (London: Routledge, 2011).

Organizational links with domestic legal systems are also growing. Every regime, including networks, requires a "domestic terminal" to ensure its own effectiveness.[115] This triggers an expansion in the role of national administrations (see EU comitology[116] and global networks). Also, relationships with the private sector and civil society (NGOs, corporations) multiply.

The institutional dimension of international regimes is complex, and often consists of networks, shared functions and organs, and composite administrations.[117] New types of bodies are established, and innovative public–private forms of cooperation are designed. Institutional relations are diverse, and include autonomy, hierarchy and control. There is no longer only a vertical IOs–States dimension, but many more dimensions, both vertical and horizontal: there are both pyramids and networks.[118]

Furthermore, global public–private partnerships between States and IOs are increasing. These can take

[115] See J. S. T. Quah (ed.), *The Role of the Public Bureaucracy in Policy Implementation in Five ASEAN Countries* (Cambridge University Press, 2015).

[116] Recently, C. Dordi and A. Forganni, "The Comitology Reform in the EU: Potential Effects on Trade Defence Instruments," 47 *Journal of World Trade* 359 (2013).

[117] A. von Bogdandy and P. Dann, "International Composite Administration: Conceptualizing Multi-Level and Network Aspects in the Exercise of International Public Authority," 9 *German Law Journal* 2013 (2008).

[118] F. Ost and M. van de Kerchove, *De la piramide au réseau? Pour une théorie dialectique du droit* (Brussels: Publications des Facultés universitaires Saint-Louis, 2002), pp. 23 *et seq.*

institutional or procedural form, through Memoranda of Understanding. This hybrid public–private institutional design prompts several issues and questions. What kind of law regulates these hybrid bodies? Are they international organizations? What is the role, if any, of the national law of the States where their headquarters are located? These bodies often have field offices and lead several field operations: which legal regimes can be applied in these cases? More generally, what institutional devices can be adopted to balance public power and private actors? Under what conditions should international organizations engage in PPPs and related private law instruments? And how can "regulatory capture" be avoided?

It is clear that these problems are significantly similar to those habitually arising within domestic legal orders, especially since the development of "government by contract."[119] In particular, national administrative bodies' use of private law instruments, and the integration of private actors into national regulatory processes are among the characteristics of

[119] T. Daintith, "Regulation by Contract: The New Prerogative," 32:1 *Current Legal Problems* 41 (1979); I. Harden, *The Contracting State* (Buckingham: Open University Press, 1992); M. Freedland, "Government by Contract and Private Law," *Public Law* 86–104 (1994); J. P. Gaudin, *Gouvernement par contrat* (Paris: Sciences Po, 1999); J. Freeman, "The Private Role in Public Governance," 75 *New York University Law Review* 543 (2000), J. Freeman, "Private Parties, Public Functions and the New Administrative Law," 52 *Administrative Law Review* 8143 (2000); A. C. Aman, Jr., *Politics, Policy and Outsourcing in the United States: The Role of Administrative Law* (Oxford: Hart, 2008), pp. 205 *et seq.*

the "new public management" of national administrations that have acquired significance as techniques and, to some extent, ideologies, within international organizations too. The responses given to these phenomena in the realm of national administrative law may thus be of some relevance, even in the radically different contexts of international organizations.

In relation to legal integration, one highly significant implication of this institutional pluralism is the impact on domestic public administrations. The latter are key actors in implementing international or regional policies, and therefore, international regimes must ensure that national public bodies will comply with their objectives. There are two main mechanisms for doing so: the establishment of domestic terminals for international legal regimes; and the international regulation of national administrations.

2.4.1 *The domestic terminals of international legal regimes*

As mentioned above, IOs and, increasingly, hybrid public–private transnational networks, may regulate the form of their domestic terminals.[120] In particular, global networks constitute one of the most interesting cases of domestic authorities

[120] See L. Casini, "Domestic Public Authorities within Global Networks: Institutional and Procedural Design, Accountability, and Review," in J. Pauwelyn, R. Wessel and J. Wouters (eds.), *Informal International Lawmaking: Mapping the Action and Testing Concepts of Accountability and Effectiveness* (Oxford University Press, 2012), pp. 385 *et seq.*

operating beyond the State. Over the past few decades, States have adapted their legal orders either by redesigning existing bodies or creating new ones. These modifications originated in response to global networks or even IOs that required the presence of (usually not more than) one national "terminal."

As a consequence of the multiplication of global networks, we have domestic public bodies that act beyond the State, in accordance with norms produced through informal law-making mechanisms. In addition, the structure of these bodies can be established directly by the global networks themselves, which can require that specific criteria (such as independence or governmental endorsement) be met. Often, these bodies must be recognized or admitted for entry into the network by the international organization that heads the network itself (such as ICANN or the ISO).

Thus, global networks set forth rules on the participation of national actors in their own systems. However, the more structured the network at the global level, the more heavily regulated are the ways in which domestic bodies can participate or become members of the network. In other words, when the network is governed by formalized global institutions – other than traditional intergovernmental organizations of course – such as in ICANN, the ISO or the IOC, we can find specific rules on membership and affiliation. By contrast, the less formalized the institutional design of the network at the global level, the less regulated are the organizational issues of domestic bodies: this happens in the field of financial services, in which the Basel Committee has a peculiar informal mode of organization and does not have a statute or bylaws. Consequently, the Basel Committee does not establish the condition of having one sole authority for each country, because States may adopt different models of banking supervision: in the UK, for instance, there are both the Bank of England and the Financial Services Authority, and both participate in the Committee. The same goes for France and Germany, while Italy and Brazil are represented only by their Central Banks. The US, by contrast, numbers five representative authorities.[121]

In addition, the more public or governmental the network, the lower the level of its formality. Transgovernmental networks tend to refrain from regulating the conditions of membership, leaving these to individual States. This is partly due to the fact that this kind of network usually begins operating spontaneously, through cooperation between national public administrations (as happened with the Basel Committee or with the IOSCO, for instance). This element of "publicness" may have translated into a scarce necessity to regulate the way in which domestic authorities can become members of the network. By contrast, in hybrid public–private networks, the need to establish criteria and impose their observance on different countries becomes more impelling (and these criteria refer to legal capacity, independence and cooperation).

[121] The list of institutions represented on the Basel Committee on Banking Supervision is available at www.bis.org/bcbs/history.pdf. See D. S. Bieri, "Financial Stability, the Basel Process and the new Geography of Regulation," 2 *Cambridge Journal of Regions, Economy and Society* 303 (2009).

Although global networks do not require legal personality for their domestic terminals, they often establish principles to regulate their organization and functioning: in particular, they require that the domestic authorities that participate in the network be *independent*. This requirement is crucial for the very existence of global regulatory regimes; this in turn explains why both transgovernmental and hybrid public–private networks insist on this trait. The Basel Core Principles on Banking Supervision refer to the independence of supervisors, and IOSCO principles underscore the need for an independent regulator.[122]

Global networks set rules that regulate their domestic focal points and establish criteria and requirements. Nevertheless, States still retain ample discretionary powers in framing their own institutional model, which can interact with the network. The plurality of choices available to national orders emerges if the different domestic bodies of any given regime are compared.

Different institutional models can be found not only in hybrid public–private regimes, but also in transgovernmental networks. An example is that of financial networks,

[122] In the case of banking, however, States opted to design their central banks as independent and "distinct organizational structures" long ago: see M. Marcussen, "Central Banks on the Move," 12 *Journal of European Public Policy* 903 (2005). See also R. Bismuth, "The Independence of Domestic Financial Regulators: An Under Estimated Structural Issue in International Financial Governance," 2 *Goettingen Journal of International Law* 93 (2010).

in which States may adopt various alternatives.[123] The UK has been a relevant example in this sense.[124]

The case of global networks and how they build systems of national terminals may be extremely effective in the context of international or supranational legal integration. Indeed, on the one hand, the mechanism ensures the regime's development through the creation of a networked administration; on the other, it leaves wide discretionary powers to States as to the regulation of their bodies. What States do not appear capable of deciding is whether or not to establish a body, insofar as they must do so to be part of the regime. It is therefore a form of membership, that is materialized through a more or less formal association of several legal entities (as in the Basel Committee or the IOSCO, but also private regimes like the Internet or sport).

[123] See E. M. Cervellati and E. Fioriti, "Financial Supervision in EU Countries" (2003) (available at http://ssrn.com/abstract=873064); and K. Lannoo, "Supervising the European Financial System" (Centre for European Policy Studies Policy Brief No. 2, May 2002). In particular, E. Ferrari, "Understanding the New Institutional Architecture of EU Financial Market Supervision" (University of Cambridge Faculty of Law Research Paper, November 2010) (available at http://papers.ssrn.com/sol3/papers.cfm?abstract_id.=1701147), p. 10, notes that "the diversity that currently exists in national institutional arrangements for the oversight of financial markets indicates that there is no foundation of common transnational assumptions about what financial market supervisory architecture should look like on which to build an overarching pan-European federal structure from the bottom up."

[124] D. Singh, *Banking Regulation of UK and US Financial Markets* (Aldershot: Ashgate, 2009), pp. 14 *et seq*. See also E. Ferran, "The Break-up of the Financial Services Authority," 31 *Oxford Journal of Legal Studies* 455 (2011).

In relation to regional organizations, therefore, this instrument may be very useful to IOs seeking to implement their policies more effectively. The EU employs this option in regulating public utilities; it established groups of domestic regulators, requiring each Member State to have its own regulatory agency (and these groups thereafter became EU agencies). Adoption of this instrument may increase the regional organization's powers. By contrast, as long as the latter relies on genuinely intergovernmental mechanisms – such as the specialized Council of Ministers – States will retain greater control over the implementation of regional policy.

2.4.2 *The international regulation of national administrations*

The second perspective relates to cases in which the international regime chooses to regulate national administrations, which usually happens through the insertion of definitions in normative acts. This is mainly due to the need to harmonize States' behaviors and to ensure that the IO's policies are implemented. In this case, too, the EU's experience is one of the most significant examples.

To avoid the possibility of Member States influencing the effectiveness of public procurement regulation, EU law intervened to define "body governed by public law" as:

> any body:
>
> (a) established for the specific purpose of meeting needs in the general interest, not having an industrial or commercial character;

(b) having legal personality; and

(c)

- financed, for the most part, by the State, regional or local authorities, or other bodies governed by public law;
- or subject to management supervision by those bodies;
- or having an administrative, managerial or supervisory board, more than half of whose members are appointed by the State, regional or local authorities, or by other bodies governed by public law.[125]

In doing so, the EU provided a broad definition of public administration and managed to limit the chances of EU public procurement regulations being evaded. However, interpretation of the definition has been very difficult and the CJEU has often had to deal with this issue in its judgments, sometimes conflicting with national judges.

The CJEU has also had to intervene in other circumstances related to the definition of public administration. As for the free movement of workers within the EU, for example, the Court had to clarify the meaning of "employment in public service" as per Article 45 of the Treaty on the Functioning of the European Union. The Court limited the scope of the term to "posts involving direct or indirect participation in the exercise of powers conferred by public law and duties

[125] See Article 1, Para. 9, of Directive 2004/18/EC of the European Parliament and of the Council of March 31, 2004 on the coordination of procedures for the award of public works contracts, public supply contracts and public service contracts.

designed to safeguard the general interest of the State and of other public authorities."[126]

The example of free movement of workers and persons is crucial to regional integration. Therefore, in relation to ECOWAS, it was unsurprising that, during its first few years of existence and before its reform in 1993, the only Protocol that was approved thanks to the "good-will" of Member States was that on free movement of persons.[127] It is also noteworthy that the ECOWAS Supplementary Protocol on the implementation of the third phase (right of establishment) of the Protocol on free movement of persons, right of residence and establishment set forth that "[a]ctivities which, in a Member State, form part, even occasionally, of the exercise of public authority, shall be exempted from the provisions of this Protocol."[128] In this case, too, therefore, as in the EU, the regime carves out an exemption for public authorities.

Another example comes from the European Convention on Human Rights and the definition of public authorities given by its different Contracting States. The UK Human Rights Act 1998, for example, defines "public authorities" as "a court or tribunal, and any person certain of whose functions are functions of a public nature."[129] The House of Lords provided a broad and functional interpretation of this

[126] ECJ, Case C-473/93, *Commission of the EC* v. *Grand Duchy of Luxembourg* (July 2, 1996).

[127] S. Godwin, "Integrating Trade and Human Rights in West Africa: An Analysis of the Ecowas Experience," 32 *Windsor Review of Legal and Social Issues* 57 (2012).

[128] Article 4, Para. 6, of the ECOWAS Supplementary Protocol a/sp.2/5/90.

[129] Human Rights Act 1998, section 6(3).

definition, regardless of the formally public or private nature of the subjects considered.[130] In other words, the implementation of international regulation often requires States to redefine the notion of public administration, because these norms address, first of all, public authorities.

In conclusion, if international regimes aim to develop and reach a high level of integration, they will tend to regulate the borders of the public sphere in domestic legal orders. This will reduce the risk of States compromising the implementation of international or regional policies. However, it is crucial that such a top-down intervention on the definition of national administration take place following a case-by-case consideration, in accordance with the objectives pursued by the policy in question. Therefore, there may be more than one definition provided at the international level. This already happens in domestic legal contexts, where public administration may be defined differently in different sectors (employment, freedom of information, procurement, and so on). This is also what happens in the EU. The two cases illustrated above (public procurement and free movement of workers) indeed display two different and somewhat opposite techniques of regulating national administrations at the international level: on the one hand, the EU opted for a broad notion, that could include private bodies funded by States; on the other, the CJEU has interpreted the expression "public

[130] See the *Aston Cantlow* and *Marcis* cases, both from 2003. G. Jurgens and F. van Ommeren, "The Public–Private Divide in English and Dutch Law: A Multifunctional and Context Dependant Divide," 71:1 *Cambridge Law Journal* 172 (2012).

service" used in the Treaties very restrictively, to minimize exemptions from the general rule of free movement of workers.

2.5 The proceduralization of international legal regimes

The third thread in the development of international regimes is the growing degree of proceduralization. Procedures are, first of all, a device for governing complex organizations and their decision-making processes.[131] Data show that global regulatory regimes and global institutions have been increasingly engaged in developing procedures. Most of these can be likened to models adopted at the domestic level (such as procedures for granting licenses, permissions and grants), but the more complex legal framework of the global arena

[131] C. Lavagna, "Considerazioni sui caratteri degli ordinamenti democratici," 5 *Rivista trimestrale di diritto pubblico*. 392 (1956), p. 421, for example, highlighted the great number of procedural provisions established in the Civil Code that were aimed at regulating different forms of private actions in collective endeavors; similarly, E. Betti, *Teoria generale del negozio giuridico* (1st edn., 1943; 2nd edn., 1950) (Naples: Edizioni Scientifiche Italiane, reprint of 2nd edn., 2002), p. 300, observed that "le forme più complesse di procedimento s'incontrano nel campo del diritto pubblico, nelle figure del procedimento giurisdizionale e amministrativo; ma non mancano esempi nel campo del diritto privato." As for international organizations, see J. von Bernstorff, "Procedures of Decision-Making and the Role of Law in International Organizations," 9 *German Law Journal* 1939 (2008); and R. W. Cox and H. K. Jakobson (eds.), *The Anatomy of Influence: Decision Making in International Organizations* (New Haven, CT: Yale University Press, 1973).

enables other forms to be detected too, such as "policy-making" procedures;[132] the same is true of other supranational experiences (see the EU-related "composite" proceedings).

Examples of the rising number of procedures may be found in several sectors. The system built on the World Heritage Convention, for example, has progressively acquired a significant procedural dimension, which is regulated by the UNESCO Operational Guidelines for the Implementation of the World Heritage Convention:[133] there are new forms of cooperation between international institutions, States, domestic administrations and other actors. Other examples of the rise of proceduralization come from finance – where standard-setting procedures have become very complex – to sports, health and the environment. As a matter of fact, the reason for this growth lies in the above-mentioned links between delivery of functions and procedures: if procedure is, for an institution, a rational way of organizing its activities, the increase of the latter will directly entail the increase of the former.

[132] J. Barnes (ed.), *Transforming Administrative Procedure – La Transformación del Procedimiento Administrativo* (Seville: Global Law Press, 2009). See also G. della Cananea, "Beyond the State: the Europeanization and Globalization of Procedural Administrative Law," 9 *European Public Law* 563 (2003).

[133] See D. Zacharias, "The UNESCO Regime for the Protection of World Heritage as Prototype of an Autonomy-Gaining International Institution," 9 *German Law Journal* 1833 (2008); S. Battini, "The World Heritage Convention and the Procedural Side of Legal Globalization," 9 *International Journal of Constitutional Law* 340 (2011); and S. Battini, *Amministrazioni Nazionali e Controversie Globali* (Milan: Giuffrè, 2007), pp. 69 *et seq.*

Thus, proceduralization beyond the State features interactions between different levels of activity (national, regional and international), different bodies of law (public and private), and a plurality of actors (governments, administrations, international organizations, civil society).[134] Furthermore, once national borders have been transcended, the notion of proceduralization appears to lose neutrality and gains additional functions: it can enhance legitimacy[135] and democratic accountability, for example, or it can be an instrument to control power.[136] This can happen because procedures are also instruments for representing and negotiating interests, through participatory mechanisms.[137] However,

[134] S. Sassen, "The Participation of States and Citizens in Global Governance," 10 *Indiana Journal of Global Legal Studies* 5 (2003).

[135] N. Luhmann, *Legitimation durch Verfahren* (Neuwied: Luchterhand, 1969), where the concept of procedure is analyzed as a social system, an instrument capable of giving legitimacy to legislative, judicial and administrative functions. This theory, however, was criticized by J. Habermas, *Legitimationsprobleme im Spätkapitalismus* (Frankfurt am Main: Suhrkamp, 1973) (both positions are discussed by J. Přibáň, "Beyond Procedural Legitimation: Legality and Its 'Inflictions'," 24 *Journal of Law and Society* 331 (1997)).

[136] M. D. McCubbins, R. G. Noll and B. R. Weingast, "Administrative Procedures as Instruments of Political Control," 3 *Journal of Law, Economics, and Organization* 243 (1987); J. L. Mashaw, "Explaining Administrative Process: Normative, Positive and Critical Stories of Legal Development," 6 *Journal of Law, Economics, and Organization* 267 (1990).

[137] R. B. Stewart, "The Reformation of American Administrative Law," 88 *Harvard Law Review* 1670 (1975); and R. B. Stewart, "Administrative Law in the Twenty-First Century," 78 *New York University Law Review* 437 (2003).

these dynamics can be more or less evident, depending upon the type of institution and the model of regional integration in question: in cases such as ASEAN, the procedural dimension is not yet as pronounced as in complex forms of governance such as the EU system.

Global private regimes tend to develop and refine procedural tools such as participation, consultation and due process clauses. In doing so, they are often resonant of administrative law techniques (see, for example, the Internet or sports), for several reasons: governments and domestic administrations are part of the game; public and administrative law techniques are well-equipped to balance powers;[138] there is no democratic context; there is a need to guarantee procedural safeguards for addressees. On the other hand, international organizations often adopt private law instruments and PPPs. The increasing use of public procurement, for instance, triggers the adoption of procedural mechanisms that are capable of ensuring transparency and competition. Similarly, the need to involve civil society and the population affected in the establishment of public–private arrangements increases the use of participatory mechanisms.

The rise of proceduralization is also due to the creation of multi-level (international, regional and national) systems of governance.[139] Proceduralization becomes an

[138] S. Cassese, "New Paths for Administrative Law: A Manifesto," 10:3 *International Journal of Constitutional Law* 603 (2012); the point was already highlighted by H. Kelsen, *Reine Rechtslehre* (Vienna: Deuticke, 2nd edn., 1960), pp. 280–281.

[139] E. Schmidt-Aßmann, "Structures and Functions of Administrative Procedures in German, European and International Law," in J. Barnes

instrument for improving the effectiveness, accountability and legitimacy of these forms of public–private interactions. This means that, in this context, procedures transcend the neutral discourse of "more norms, more institutions, then more procedures" to represent a way to enhance the interactions between the public and private spheres: they can bring public powers into private regimes; they can introduce private actors into intergovernmental negotiations.

However, this is an optimistic view: IOs and States may often involve private interests and stakeholders to strengthen their powers or because they have been "captured" by stronger private powers; also, private actors can use public law tools – such as transparency, participation, review mechanisms – as "manifestos" or as merely formal requirements that do not actually affect the decision-making process, which will continue in its present state behind "closed doors." Some observers have already noticed, in relation to the EU system, that, among the problems caused by the emergence of transnational governance there is the problem "that maximizing transparency and participation for the interested minimizes transparency and participation for the disinterested."[140]

(ed.), *Transforming Administrative Procedure – La Transformación del Procedimiento Administrativo* (Seville: Global Law Press, 2009), pp. 47 *et seq.*

140 See M. Shapiro, "Administrative Law Unbounded: Reflections on Government and Governance," 8 *Indiana Journal of Global Legal Studies* 369 (2000), p. 373; and M. Shapiro, "'Deliberative', 'Independent' Technocracy v. Democratic Politics: Will the Globe Echo the EU?," 68 *Law and Contemporary Problems* 341 (2005).

In addition, the degree of proceduralization still varies significantly depending on the individual regime under consideration.[141] There are many asymmetries, which derive from the diversity of the functions delivered by different international organizations, but also from the level of involvement of public powers. Indeed, in almost all global regulatory regimes, procedural principles such as participation, due process and the duty to give reasons are first established in norms (for example, the Aarhus Convention on Access to Information, Public Participation in Decision-Making and Access to Justice in Environmental Matters for the environment, the WTO TBT Agreement, or the World Anti-Doping Code). When these principles are to be applied, the more public the supranational regime, the more their enforcement will be delegated to the States (as occurs with the Aarhus Convention). Instead, in private regimes, supranational bodies usually ensure observance of these principles directly, which enhances the degree of proceduralization of these very regimes.

2.6 The adoption of multiple mechanisms for legitimacy and accountability: a "managerial" perspective

A fourth thread refers to one of the most significant problems raised by the development of international regimes: the

[141] J. Mendes, "EU Law and Global Regulatory Regimes: Hollowing Out Procedural Standards?," 10 *International Journal of Constitutional Law* 988 (2012).

repeated outcry over their lack of legitimacy and accountability that affects almost all institutions, including the EU and other regional organizations.[142]

As for legitimacy,[143] IOs especially and intergovernmental regimes more generally cannot claim to possess the voluntary consensual mechanisms on which private law

142 See, for instance, L. O. Wauna Oluoch, "Legitimacy of the East African Community," 53 *Journal of African Law* 194 (2009).

143 Here, legitimacy can be broadly understood as a "generalized perception or assumption that the actions of an entity are desirable, proper, or appropriate within some socially constructed system of norms, values, beliefs, and definitions" (M. C. Suchman, "Managing Legitimacy: Strategic and Institutional Approaches," 20 *Academy of Management Review* 571 (1995)). See also A. Buchanan and R. O. Keohane, "The Legitimacy of Global Governance Institutions," 20:4 *Ethical and International Affairs* 405 (2006), p. 405, who distinguish between normative and sociological legitimacy. The first occurs when an authority "has *the right to rule* – where ruling includes promulgating rules and attempting to secure compliance with them by attaching costs to non-compliance and/or benefits to compliance"; in the second case, an authority "is widely *believed* to have the right to rule." See J. Delbrück, "Exercising Public Authority Beyond the State: Transnational Democracy and/or Alternative Legitimation Strategies?," 10 *Indiana Journal of Global Legal Studies* 29 (2003); particularly D. Bodanski, "The Concept of Legitimacy in International Law," in R. Wolfrum and V. Röben (eds.), *Developments of International Law in Treaty Making* (Heidelberg: Springer, 2005), pp. 309 *et seq.*; and L. H. Meyer (ed.), *Legitimacy, Justice and Public International Law* (Cambridge University Press, 2009). See also M.-S. Kuo, "Inter-Public Legality or Post-Public Legitimacy? Global Governance and the Curious Case of Global Administrative Law as a New Paradigm of Law," 10 *International Journal of Constitutional Law* 1050 (2010).

systems are usually based.[144] Legitimacy founded on the (political) authority of a given international institution,[145] enhanced by State consensus or at least non-opposition,[146] is more common. However, sometimes IOs base their legitimacy on ethical issues, so that it becomes extremely important to ensure their integrity.[147] In other cases, expertise and technocracy offer the reason for legitimating specific international regimes.[148]

144 See *lex mercatoria*, in F. Galgano, *Lex Mercatoria. Storia del diritto commerciale* (Bologna: il Mulino, 4th edn., 1993), F. Galgano, "Lex mercatoria e legittimazione," No. 2-3 *Sociologia del diritto* 179 (2005); and B. Druzin, "Law Without The State: The Theory of High Engagement and The Emergence of Spontaneous Legal Order Within Commercial Systems," 42 *Georgetown Journal of International Law* 559 (2010). In political science, A. Stone Sweet, "The New Lex Mercatoria and Transnational Governance," 13 *Journal of European Public Policy* 627 (2006).

145 D. Easton, *The Political System: An Inquiry into the State of Political Science* (New York: Alfred A. Knopf, 1953), p. 129: decision-making processes would be driven by "authoritative allocations of values."

146 A. Buchanan and R. O. Keohane, "The Legitimacy of Global Governance Institutions," 20:4 *Ethical and International Affairs* 405 (2006), p. 414.

147 Institutional integrity as an instrument of legitimacy is analyzed by A. Buchanan and R. O. Keohane, "The Legitimacy of Global Governance Institutions," 20:4 *Ethical and International Affairs* 405 (2006), pp. 422 *et seq.*, who mention the UN scandal of "Oil-for-Food."

148 Such as in the case of environmental protection: D. Bodansky, "The Legitimacy of International Governance: A Coming Challenge for International Environmental Law?," 93 *American Journal of International Law* 596 (1999), especially pp. 619 *et seq.* See also P. Trudel, "La lex electronica," in C. A. Morand (ed.), *Le droit saisi par la mondialisation* (Brussels: Bruylant, 2001), pp. 221 *et seq.* More generally on private "regulatory standard-setting," K. W. Abbott and D. Snidal,

However, the two main instruments of legitimacy at the international level are those based on procedure[149] and on the involvement of States. The first is often ensured through the participation of the affected parties in decision-making processes. This may materialize in different ways and through different mechanisms: notice and comment; request of advice; creation of consultative bodies or committees. The second type relies on the key role played by States within IOs and their organs. Concretely, this can consist in the involvement of governments (as usually happens) or domestic administrations (as in the case of transnational networks), or even of different levels of public authorities. The latter hypothesis occurs, for instance, in the Committee of the Regions of the EU, an advisory body that represents local and regional authorities and has almost 350 members. The Council and the Parliament are obliged to consult the Committee of the Regions before EU decisions are taken on matters concerning local and regional government (for example, on employment policy, the environment, education or public health).[150]

Furthermore, regional organizations appear to seek democratic and electoral forms of legitimacy.[151] This is also

The Governance Triangle: Regulatory Standards Institutions and the Shadow of the State, in W. Mattli and N. Woods (eds.), *The Politics of Global Regulation* (Princeton University Press, 2009), p. 44 *et seq.*

149 See Section 2.5 above.

150 See http://europa.eu/about-eu/institutions-bodies/cor/index_en.htm.

151 F. W. Scharpf, *Governing in Europe: Effective and Democratic?* (Oxford University Press, 1999), p. 6, who distinguishes between "input-oriented" and "output-oriented" "legitimizing beliefs," respectively related to "government *by the people*" and to "government *for the*

true of ASEAN, in which the last remaining authoritarian States have sought legitimacy by undertaking democratic and electoral forms: consider the latest democratic transition in Myanmar, largely due to "persuasion" exerted on Naypyidaw by Indonesia, the Philippines, Thailand, Malaysia and Singapore, and for which Myanmar was "rewarded" with the 2014 Chairmanship of ASEAN.

However, it is important to note that the main reason why international regimes have been increasingly using accountability mechanisms is to enhance their efficiency and effectiveness, rather than to fill a democratic gap. As a matter of fact, almost all regimes tend to adopt similar mechanisms, regardless of the degree of "democracy" they may present.[152]

The case of supranational parliaments within regional organizations appears to confirm this claim. Of forty-odd supranational parliaments, established by different

people"; and R. Goodin, *Reflective Democracy* (Oxford University Press, 2003), pp. 149 *et seq.*, who refers to "output" and "input" "democracy." See also P. Rosanvallon, *La légitimité démocratique. Impartialité, réflexivité, proximité* (Paris: Éditions du Seuil, 2008); R. O. Keohane, S. Macedo and A. Moravcsik, "Democracy-Enhancing Multilateralism," 63 *International Organization* 1 (2009); A. Peters, "Dual Democracy," in J. Klabbers, A. Peters and G. Ulfstein, *The Constitutionalization of International Law* (Oxford University Press, 2009), pp. 263 *et seq.*, especially pp. 338 *et seq.*, dedicated to the study of "complementary mechanisms of legitimacy and accountability."

152 See S. Wheatley, *The Democratic Legitimacy of International Law* (Oxford: Hart, 2010); S. Marks, "What Has Become of the Emerging Right to Democratic Governance?," 22 *European Journal of International Law* 507 (2011).

regional organizations, fewer than ten are formed through the direct election of their members (the organizations which fall into this latter category are CAN, EMMCA, EU, MERCOSUR, SICA and WAEMU; in the case of ECOWAS and ECCAS, this will happen in the future).[153] In all other cases, supranational parliaments are not elected directly by the population, but by the legislative assembly of their Member States. Moreover, regional parliaments have essentially consultative powers, while the actual legislative functions are firmly in the hands of the intergovernmental organs (this is true even in the EU). Basically, the creation of supranational parliaments often tends to result in a "manifesto," stopping short of replicating the dynamics of national parliaments: what appears to be an instrument of legitimacy gives way to the need for efficiency and effectiveness that requires fast decision-making processes. In addition, governments are reluctant to give powers to such organs.

This plurality of forms of legitimacy in international regimes has also determined the presence of at least four different mechanisms for accountability: supervisory, hierarchical, fiscal and legal[154] (although there may be

[153] See Table 1.13 above.

[154] R. W. Grant and R. O. Keohane, "Accountability and Abuses of Power in World Politics," 99 *American Political Science Review* 29 (2005); J. Ferejohn, *Accountability in a Global Context*, IILJ Working Paper 2007/5, Global Administrative Law Series; A. Reinisch, "Securing the Accountability of International Organization," 7 *Global Governance* 131 (2001); and R. B. Stewart, *Accountability, Participation, and the Problem of Disregard in Global Regulatory Governance*, Paper presented at New York University Law School, International Legal Theory Colloquium on

alternative forms based on the market or reputation, albeit less frequently).[155]

First, there is supervisory accountability, based on monitoring and oversight instruments. These functions can be attributed to specific bodies, such as the Court of Auditors in the EU; alternatively, one governing body can exercise them over another. When an international administration has developed, there may be specific monitoring bodies or an ombudsman. For example, the EU ombudsman investigates complaints against EU institutions, bodies, offices and agencies.[156] This type of body has also been applied

Interpretation and Judgment in International Law (February 7, 2008). In domestic legal contexts, J. L. Mashaw, "Structuring a 'Dense Complexity': Accountability and the Project of Administrative Law," in *Issues in Legal Scholarship: The Reformation of American Administrative Law* (Berkeley, CA: Berkeley Electronic Press, 2005, No. 4); and R. Mulgan, *Holding Power to Account: Accountability in Modern Democracy* (London: Palgrave MacMillan, 2003).

155 The reference is to market accountability and to public reputational accountability illustrated by R. W. Grant and R. O. Keohane, "Accountability and Abuses of Power in World Politics," 99 *American Political Science Review* 29 (2005), pp. 37 *et seq.* In the domestic context, J. L. Mashaw, "Accountability and Institutional Design: Some Thoughts on the Grammar of Governance," in M. Dowdle (ed.), *Public Accountability: Designs, Dilemmas and Experiences* (Cambridge University Press, 2006), pp. 122 *et seq.*, refers to market and social control over administrations.

156 Complaints from EU citizens, businesses and organizations may include cases of unfairness, discrimination, abuse of power, lack of or refusal to provide information, unnecessary delay and incorrect procedures. See M. Elisabeth de Leeuw, "The European Ombudsman's Role as a Developer of Norms of Good Administration," 17:2 *European Public Law* 349–368 (2011). In national legal contexts, T. Buck, R. Kirkham and

significantly in other fields, such as human rights[157] and development finance.[158]

Second, there is a hierarchical form of accountability whenever there are central bodies that direct field offices, for instance. This type of accountability is common in IOs and the UN systems, where there are many field offices. In regional organizations, instead, there are usually specialized agencies (such as in the case of EU distributed agencies that are independent from the Commission); otherwise, national implementation is ensured by domestic administration.

Third, there is fiscal accountability, often ensured through funding mechanisms (the UNESCO Palestine case exemplifies how important this issue could be for IOs, as the US withdrawal of funding from that specialized UN agency seriously affected its activity). However, regional organizations often use funding leverage to ensure States' commitment to supranational policies and objectives. First of all, several

B. Thompson, *The Ombudsman Enterprise and Administrative Justice* (Farnham: Ashgate, 2011).

[157] L. C. Reif, "Transplantation and Adaptation: The Evolution of The Human Rights Ombudsman," 31 *Boston College Third World Law Journal* 269 (2011).

[158] E. Mitzman, "The Proliferation of Independent Accountability Mechanisms in the Field of Development Finance," 62 *Rivista trimestrale di Diritto Pubblico* 93 (2012); and B. M. Saper, "The International Finance Corporation's Compliance Advisor/Ombudsman (CAO): An Examination of Accountability and Effectiveness from a Global Administrative Law Perspective," 44 *New York University Journal of International Law and Politics*. 1279 (2011–2012).

regional organizations have an investment bank (for example, the EU and ECOWAS). In addition, there may be instruments that are expressly devoted to fund development and supranational objectives of integration: this is the case for EU structural funds.

Fourth, there is legal accountability, which is essentially based on courts and tribunals. As illustrated above, this solution is increasingly common among international regimes. The number of courts is growing, and they are often entrusted with different tasks. As for regional organizations, legal accountability through courts, for instance, is widely adopted in African organizations.

It is crucial to understand that no international legal regime can survive and develop effectively unless it adopts multiple forms of legitimacy and accountability. This already happens at the national level, as States can no longer base their legal orders on a single type of legitimacy or accountability: take, for instance, the case of independent commissions, which are established by the law and granted rule-making powers, but act independently of the government. Moreover, the different environment in which IOs operate cannot replicate domestic dynamics and requires several different instruments to be adopted: the absence of a world government and world parliament cannot lead to an attempt to create either one of these two – which moreover appears far from being feasible. On the contrary, this premise should lead to a quest for more tools that are capable of simultaneously ensuring legitimacy, accountability and effectiveness. This is why international arbitration, for example, is becoming a very common instrument in settling disputes.

2.7 Techniques of governance and models of legal integration beyond the State

These common threads enable the main legal techniques of governance in international regimes to be identified: indirect rule; role-splitting; and normative supremacy. All these techniques can be productively adopted, at different levels, in the pursuit of legal integration.[159]

However, it should be clarified that several nuances may exist between different regimes. In addition, each of these techniques is adopted to reach a given objective consistent with the mission of a given regime or IO. To this end, the mechanisms outlined here, which can be found in the global administrative space, will also be analyzed, according to the models of regional integration illustrated in the previous chapter, that is, free trade areas, common markets, communities and political unions.[160]

2.7.1 "Indirect rule"

As illustrated above, most of the time international regimes are governed because an IO sets a principle and/or establishes

[159] For an overview of the different instruments for legal techniques of integration in the European Community, see the chapters by G. Gaia, P. Hay and R. Rotunda, in M. Cappelletti, M. Seccombe and J. H. H. Weiler (eds.), *Integration Through Law: Europe and the American Federal Experience* (Berlin and New York: Walter de Gruyter, 1985), vol. I, Book 2, *Political Organs, Integration Techniques and Judicial Process*, pp. 113 *et seq.*

[160] See Chapter 1 above.

a rule, which thereafter national actors may implement with wide discretion (e.g. the EU requires the creation of *ad hoc* national administrations in many fields, but States are free to decide how to regulate these bodies). This technique is based on "indirect rule."[161] According to this technique, international norms impose a given legal instrument (for example, the establishment of a national body or the adoption of a procedure), which is thereafter regulated in detail by States. At the same time, there are also forms of both "decentralization," that is, the creation of field offices, and instruments of "continuity," given the links between different institutions.[162]

[161] W. Wengler, "Die Rechtsformen der 'indirect rule' in den mittelafrikanischen Kolonien," 7 *Zeitschrift für ausländisches öffentliches Recht und Völkerrecht* 361 (1937); see also G. Scelle, "Le droit public et la théorie de l'État," in G. Scelle *et al.* (eds.), *Introduction à l'étude du droit* (Paris: Arthur Rousseau, 1951), p. 37. "Indirect rule" was used in the dominions of the British Empire: F. J. D. Lugard, *The Dual Mandate in British Tropical Africa* (Edinburgh and London: W. Blackstone and Sons, 1926); K. Heck, *Des Aufbau des britischen Reiches (der Verhandlungsbericht der Reichskonferenz von 1926)* (Leipzig: Walter de Gruyter, 1927); H. Speyer, *La constitution juridique de l'Empire colonial britannique* (Paris: Arthur Rousseau, 1906); and V. E. Orlando, "I presupposti giuridici di una federazione di stati," in O. Ranelletti (ed.), *Studi di diritto pubblico in onore di Oreste Ranelletti nel XXXV anno d'insegnamento vol. II* (Padua: A. Milani, 1931), pp. 149 *et seq.*, especially pp. 168 *et seq.*

[162] According to F. J. D. Lugard, *The Dual Mandate in British Tropical Africa* (Edinburgh and London: W. Blackstone and Sons, 1926), pp. 74 *et seq.*, "decentralization" and "continuity" were fundamental principles in ensuring "wise administration" in the British Empire. There was a "dual administration," based on the presence of British staff guiding and controlling "native rulers."

The EU offers many examples of these mechanisms, for example, whenever it mandates the creation of a national body that acts in compliance with EU law: this is the case of the national agencies for the protection of the environment, for example.[163] The principle of subsidiarity enshrined in the EU Treaty is also somewhat consistent with this technique, as it requires the EU to not take action (except in the areas that fall within its exclusive competence), unless it is more effective than the action that can be taken at the national, regional or local level.

Indirect rule is also used in the development of global private regimes such as the Internet and sport. However, it is a mechanism that can be usefully adopted once the regime seeks to build something more than a common regulatory space. This explains why this technique was adopted during the British Empire, and is now used mostly whenever a regime is based on significant administrative activity distributed throughout the world. However, this reference to colonial empires should be understood only in institutional-managerial terms and must be contextualized within the contemporary global context, for several reasons. First, the so-called "*laissez faire*" attitude adopted by the British Empire encountered exceptions, especially in Africa, and indirect rule also had the goal of favoring the construction of native institutions (such as local courts); in regional integration, this mechanism is used by IOs and States to reach a balance

[163] M. Busuioc, *European Agencies: Law and Practices of Accountability* (Oxford University Press, 2013); E. Chiti, *Le Agenzie Europee* (Padua: Cedam, 2003).

between regional objectives and the national discretionary powers to implement them.[164] Second, the analogy drawn with an instrument used in colonial empires does not claim that there is a similarity between that top-down approach and the contemporary bottom-up process of integration launched by States;[165] however, it is true that, once the regional organization has developed in all its aspects, new and less powerful Member States might also be subjected to the indirect-rule technique to enable them to create a domestic legal context that complies with the supranational system.

As a consequence, the technique is closely related to the international regulation of national public administrations (as in the case of EU public procurement directives) or to the establishment of global networks (such as when domestic terminals are required in order to create a global apparatus: this happens in the case of the IOSCO, but also in

[164] See the accurate analysis given by S. Humphreys, "Laboratories of Statehood: Legal Intervention in Colonial Africa and Today," 75 *Modern Law Review* 475 (2012). From a broader perspective, see also R. J. Daniels, M. J. Trebilcock and L. D. Carson, "The Legacy of Empire: The Common Law Inheritance and Commitments to Legality in Former British Colonies," 59 *American Journal of Comparative Law* 111 (2011), where the colonial experiences of eight formerly British-controlled territories – Barbados, Botswana, Burma, India, Jamaica, Kenya, Nigeria and Singapore – are examined to identify how the processes and policies of the colonial enterprise affected the respective contemporary outcomes in terms of the rule of law.

[165] An interesting study on the relationships between colonization and international law from the point of view of Marx's theory of capital is given by M. Neocleous, "International Law as Primitive Accumulation; Or, the Secret of Systematic Colonization," 23 *European Journal of International Law* 941 (2012).

sports). Therefore, in the context of models of regional integration, this technique can fruitfully operate in political unions (EU) and communities (ECOWAS), where the emergence of administrative tasks is more pronounced.

2.7.2 "Role-splitting"

It emerges, therefore, that national bodies play a dual role in international regimes, both as domestic actors and as instruments of these very regimes. This technique may be called "role-splitting" ("*dédoublement fonctionnel*").[166]

This kind of mechanism is among the most ancient in international law, because it was first conceptualized in relation to national civil servants working in IOs. Due to the high degree of institutional complexity that international regimes now present, this technique has acquired more facets: essentially, it expresses the situation in which a national body acts both for its domestic legal order and for the interest of the international one.

[166] G. Scelle, *Précis de droit des gens*, vol. I (Paris: Librairie du Recueil Sirey, 1932), pp. 43, 54 *et seq.*, and 217; G. Scelle, "Le phénomène juridique du dédoublement fonctionnel," in W. Scätzel and H.-J. Schlochauer (eds.), *Rechtsfragen der Internationalen Organisation – Festshrift für Hans Wehberg zu seinem 70. geburtstag* (Frankfurt am Main: Vittorio Klostermann, 1956), p. 324 *et seq.* On Scelle, H. Thierry, "The Thought of Georges Scelle," 1 *European Journal of International Law* 193 (1990); and A. Cassese, "Remarks on Scelle's Theory of 'Role Splitting' (Dédoublement Fonctionnel) in International Law," 1 *European Journal of International Law* 210 (1990); see also M. Koskenniemi, *The Gentle Civilizer of Nations. The Rise and Fall of International Law 1870–1960* (Cambridge University Press, 2001), pp. 327 *et seq.*

Apart from the traditional examples of IOs' intergovernmental organs, "role-splitting" can take place whenever a body with national representatives is established: this may happen in the case of ASEAN, for example, as well as in the EU with the Committee for the Regions. It can also happen when States establish public legal entities that operate both as national administrations and as agents of the international regimes: in the EU, for instance, domestic agencies play such a role in the agricultural sectors.

A significant case of role-splitting also takes place in the EU's judicial system,[167] in which national judges can act as part of the function of the EU too, when they refer questions to the CJEU for a preliminary ruling: this mechanism is extremely effective in ensuring the legal integration of regimes.[168] This is why the preliminary ruling instrument was also adopted in other courts (such as the EAC Court of Justice, the TJCA, the COMESA Court of Justice, the UEMOA Court of Justice and the CEMAC Court of Justice),[169] and was clearly viewed as a tool that

[167] Y. Shany, "Dédoublement Fonctionnel and the Mixed Loyalties of National and International Judges," in. F. Fontanelli, G. Martinico and P. Carrozza (eds.), *Shaping Rule of Law Through Dialogue: International and Supranational Experiences* (Groenigen: European Law Publishing, 2009), pp. 27 *et seq.*

[168] C. J. Carrubba and L. Murrah, "Legal Integration and Use of the Preliminary Ruling Process in the European Union," 59 *International Organization* 399–418 (2005).

[169] An overview is in R. Virzo, "The Preliminary Ruling Procedures at International Regional Courts and Tribunals," 10 *The Law and Practice of International Courts and Tribunals* 285 (2011). As for the MERCOSUR experience, see C. Espósito and L. Donadio,

could be imported into other regional contexts, as indeed happened in the case of ECOWAS: Article 22 of the 1991 Community Court of Justice Protocol establishes the exclusive competence of the Court, stating that "no dispute regarding interpretation or application of the Treaty may be referred to any other form of settlement except" for the Court itself; however, no form of referral or preliminary ruling involving domestic judges was provided.[170] Furthermore, application of this mechanism has also been called for in relation to international criminal courts.[171]

However, the effectiveness of the EU's judicial system in involving domestic judges should not be taken as a model that is easy to replicate. Indeed, the experience of the Andean Tribunal of Justice (ATJ) shows that "transplants" from supranational institutions do not necessarily translate into success. In this case, although the preliminary ruling procedure was emulated, no joint action by the ATJ and domestic courts in favor of Andean law took place, and national judges "declined to become the Tribunal's active

"Inter-Jurisdictional Co-operation in the MERCOSUR: The First Request for an Advisory Opinion of the MERCOSUR's Permanent Review Tribunal by Argentina's Supreme Court of Justice," 10 *The Law and Practice of International Courts and Tribunals* 261 (2011).

170 S. Godwin, "Integrating Trade and Human Rights in West Africa: An Analysis of the Ecowas Experience," 32 *Windsor Review of Legal and Social Issues* 57 (2012).

171 A. Cassese, *Realizing Utopia: The Future of International Law* (Oxford University Press, 2012). See also N. Carrillo-Santarelli and C. Espósito, "The Protection of Humanitarian Legal Goods by National Judges," 23 *European Journal of International Law* 67 (2012).

partners."[172] This picture is far from that painted by the CJEU for the EU system: the Court recently labeled Member States' judges as "guardians" and "ordinary courts" of EU law.[173]

Examining the models of regional integration, many institutions adopt role-splitting in its original form, that is, the presence of national officials and/or civil servants in the organs of the supranational institutions.[174] More complex forms of this technique, once again, are adopted in political unions and communities more than in free trade areas or common markets. But there are exceptions: the system of

[172] L. R. Helfer and K. J. Alter, "The Andean Tribunal of Justice and Its Interlocutors: Understanding the Preliminary Ruling Reference Patterns in the Andean Community," 42 *New York University Journal of International Law and Politics* 871 (2009), pp. 900–911; and, more generally, K. J. Alter, L. R. Helfer and O. Saldias, "Transplanting the European Court of Justice: The Experience of the Andean Tribunal of Justice," 60 *American Journal of Comparative Law* 629 (2012).

[173] R. Baratta, "National Courts as 'Guardians' and 'Ordinary Courts' of EU Law: Opinion 1/09 of the ECJ," 38:4 *Legal Issues of Economic Integration* 297–320 (2011). A similar claim was stated by the Central American Court of Justice (Decision in Case No. 10-23-09-2009, *Christy Airan Artero de Rodríguez* v. *El Salvador*, October 28, 2009).

[174] See G. Scelle, "Le phénomène juridique du dédoublement fonctionnel," in W. Scätzel and H.-J. Schlochauer (eds.), *Rechtsfragen der Internationalen Organisation – Festshrift für Hans Wehberg zu seinem 70. geburtstag* (Frankfurt am Main: Vittorio Klostermann, 1956), p. 331, who stated that "les agents dotés d'une compétence institutionnelle ou investis par un ordre juridique utilisent leur capacité 'fonctionnelle' telle qu'elle est organisée dans l'ordre juridique qui les institués, mais pour assurer l'efficacité des normes d'un autre ordre juridique privé des organes nécessaires à cette réalisation, ou n'en possédant que d'insuffisants."

working groups followed by MERCOSUR, for instance. Furthermore, the experience of supranational parliaments also represents an interesting case of role-splitting: this happens, and is most common, in cases where members of regional parliaments are not elected directly by the population but through the national assemblies. The latter therefore operate in function of regional integration.

In conclusion, it emerges that role-splitting can be a useful technique in ameliorating the degree of legal integration beyond the State. At the same time, due to the strategic role played by national actors, it may also be seen as a filter that allows States to retain more powers instead of ceding them to the supranational body.

2.7.3 "Normative supremacy"

The differentiation and separation of functions examined above brings the need to build a hierarchy of norms in international regimes, in accordance with the principle of "supremacy": domestic legal orders must comply with supranational norms.

Therefore, this third technique relies on the supremacy of international norms and the progressive formation of an international "higher law" which prevails over national law.[175] This happens in almost every regime, and especially in the most formalized ones such as the UN or

[175] On the "Higher Law Constitution," see A. Stone Sweet, "Constitutionalism, Legal Pluralism, and International Regimes," 16:2 *Indiana Journal of Global Legal Studies* 621–645 (2009), pp. 630 *et seq.*

the EU.[176] The presence of a hierarchy of norms and the supremacy of international law enhance the key role of courts in granting such supremacy;[177] and, of course, conflicts may arise.[178] Furthermore, regional organizations also appear to be moving towards more formalized means of integration, such as in the case of ASEAN.[179]

As mentioned above, norm-making is the first and most immediate activity delivered by IOs and international regimes; this explains why this activity is the most common at the international level. Unsurprisingly, therefore, the need for the law of regional organizations to prevail over States is met by many models of integration. A clear example of

[176] J. H. H. Weiler, *Il sistema comunitario europeo: struttura giuridica e processo politico* (Bologna: Il Mulino, 1985), pp. 55 *et seq.*; M. Cappelletti, M. Seccombe and J. H. H. Weiler (eds.), *Integration Through Law: Europe and the American Federal Experience* (Berlin and New York: Walter de Gruyter, 1985), pp. 315 *et seq.* As for the relationships between "general law" and "local law" in federal systems, see C. Nelson, "The Persistence of General Law," 106 *Columbia Law Review* 503 (2006).

[177] B. Kingsbury, "Weighing Global Regulatory Decisions in National Courts," *Acta Juridica* 90 (2009).

[178] ECJ, Cases C-415/05 and C-402/05, *Kadi* v. *Council and Commission*, discussed in G. de Búrca, "The EU, the European Court of Justice and the International Legal Order after Kadi," 51 *Harvard International Law Journal* 1 (2009); and P. Eeckhout and T. Tridimas, *Yearbook of European Law 2009* (Oxford University Press, 2010), pp. 533 *et seq.*

[179] D. A. Desierto, "ASEAN's Constitutionalization of International Law: Challenges to Evolution Under the New ASEAN Charter," 49 *Columbia Journal of Transnational Law* 268 (2010–2011); S. C. Tay Simon, "The ASEAN Charter: Between National Sovereignty and the Region's Constitutional Moment," 12 *Singapore Yearbook of International Law* 151 (2008), pp. 155–156.

how integration relies on the need to establish the primacy of IOs' norms may be found in the 1993 reform of ECOWAS. According to Article 5 of the 1993 Treaty, "Member States undertake to create favorable conditions for the attainment of the objectives of the Community, and particularly to take all necessary measures to harmonize their strategies and policies, and to refrain from any action that may hinder the attainment of the said objectives"; the pre-reform Article 3 of the 1975 Treaty stated instead that "Member States shall make every effort to plan and direct their policies with a view to creating favourable conditions for the achievement of the aims of the Community."[180] In addition, ECOWAS has progressively incremented the number of its sources of law[181] – as many other regional organizations have increased their production of secondary norms (Section 2.3.1).[182]

However, bare affirmation of the principle of supremacy may not be enough. In this connection, the main solutions are either a reduction of the discretion available to States in complying with supranational norms by introducing the direct applicability of the latter, or the establishment of

[180] See S. Godwin, "Integrating Trade and Human Rights in West Africa: An Analysis of the Ecowas Experience," 32 *Windsor Review of Legal and Social Issues* 57 (2012), p. 72; and E. Nwauche, "Enforcing ECOWAS Law in West African National Courts," 55 *Journal of African Law* 181 (2011).

[181] S. Babalola Ajulo, "Sources of the Law of the Economic Community of West African States (Ecowas)," 45 *Journal of African Law* 1 (2001), pp. 73–96; M. Forere, "Is Discussion of the 'United States of Africa' Premature? Analysis of ECOWAS and SADC Integration Efforts," 56 *Journal of African Law* 29 (2012).

[182] See Chapter 1 above.

(quasi-)judicial bodies that can enforce them. It emerges, therefore, that almost all models of regional integration follow the principle of normative supremacy and present either one or both of these mechanisms for implementation. Even free trade areas (for example, NAFTA), in which the supranational norms may not be directly applicable, have arbitration panels for the resolution of disputes in accordance with the higher law of the regional institution.[183] The higher the level of integration and the more ambitious the objectives pursued, the more structured will the principle of normative supremacy and its application appear.

2.8 Conclusion

This analysis has considered the main features of IOs and international regimes, attempting to illustrate their differing phenomenology.

In so doing, the common threads in the development of international legal regimes have been highlighted: the increasing differentiation and separation of functions – "legislative" (norm-making); "judicial" (dispute settlement); executive-administrative (Section 2.3); the emergence of intra- and inter-IO institutional pluralism (Section 2.4); the growing degree of proceduralization (Section 2.5); the need for multiple forms of legitimacy and the adoption of different mechanisms for accountability (Section 2.6). These threads may not all occur simultaneously in every regime, and there are

[183] P. J. Loyd, "What Is a Single Market? An Application to the Case of ASEAN," 22 *ASEAN Economic Bulletin* 251 (2005).

many asymmetries. Sometimes, one thread may be more common than another: this is the case of norm-making, for example; or the different ways in which the emergence of international administrations takes shape, being stronger in global private regimes or in political unions (such as the EU), but weaker in free trade areas. As a consequence, there may be some counterbalancing between these phenomena. For example, participation and other procedural principles for the consultation of States and affected parties may be very useful when there is no specialized agency that deals with a given issue (this is the case of the WTO, for instance, but also of MERCOSUR or ASEAN); at the same time, the proliferation of international agencies raises issues of legitimacy and accountability which can sometimes be solved through procedural mechanisms (as happens in the EU).

Moreover, the analysis of these common threads indicated the main techniques of governance that drive processes of legal integration beyond States: indirect rule; role-splitting; and normative supremacy.

These three techniques often interact with each other, of course. The principal result is a centralization of norm-making activities (through supremacy) and a decentralization of administrative functions (through "indirect rule" and "role-splitting").[184] In particular, two phenomena take place. First,

[184] G. Scelle, "Le droit public et la théorie de l'État," in G. Scelle *et al.* (eds.), *Introduction à l'étude du droit* (Paris: Arthur Rousseau, 1951), pp. 32 *et seq.*; and S. Cassese, "Le droit tout puissant et unique de la société. Paradossi del diritto amministrativo," *Rivista Trimestrale di Diritto Pubblico* No. 4 (2009), pp. 895 et seq. See also M. Kahler and D. A. Lake, "Economic Integration and Global Governance? Why So Little

there is the tendency to centralize regulatory functions, through the supremacy clause and compliance rules, together with efforts towards harmonization. Second, there is an increasing use of national administrations as terminals of more complex regimes and networks.[185] Such phenomena highlight the interaction between the different techniques: for example, the establishment of domestic bodies that operate in connection with IOs may be both an example of role-splitting and of indirect rule.

The reasons in favor of one or more of these techniques are diverse. They might focus on the different objectives and models of integration, as illustrated above. A free trade area, for instance, could insist only on supremacy and omit the adoption of instruments for indirect rule. A political union would rather engage with all three techniques in all their possible forms: from the most sophisticated, role-splitting (such as preliminary ruling by domestic judges) to the most effective, "higher law" clauses.

However, many other factors should be considered. The size of States and the geographical area can naturally be relevant. While in the case of universal organization this problem may be less relevant, for regional integration it can be crucial. There may also be issues related to socio-

Supranationalism?," in W. Mattli and N. Woods (eds.), *The Politics of Global Regulation* (Princeton University Press, 2009), pp. 242 *et seq*, who identify three scenarios: supranationalism, hierarchy and network.

185 G. Scelle, "Le droit public et la théorie de l'État," in G. Scelle *et al.* (eds.), *Introduction à l'étude du droit* (Paris: Arthur Rousseau, 1951), pp. 33 *et seq*.

economic and cultural bias, or to different legal traditions.[186] For example, there might be "Western bias" in conceiving some accountability mechanisms or procedures: the importance of participation and transparency can differ from one country to another (as the disputes between India and the World Bank in the procedure for approving infrastructure projects have shown). These aspects can explain in part the differences between Arab regional integration and that occurring in Central/Southern Africa, and why, for example, courts are so common in African institutions, presenting the danger of overlapping jurisdictions between continental judges[187] and competing ones between regional and international courts.[188] However, the problem of conflicting

[186] J. H. H. Weiler, "The Political and Legal Culture of European Integration: An Exploratory Essay," 9 *International Journal of Constitutional Law* 988 (2011).

[187] M. C. C. Mkandawire, "The SADC Tribunal Perspective on Enforcement of Judgments: State Support and Cooperation," 36 *Commonwealth Law Bulletin* 567 (2010); J. Ruhangisa, "Parallel Jurisdiction of Courts: The View from the EACJ," 36 *Commonwealth Law Bulletin* 575 (2010); and D. Kayihura, "Parallel Jurisdiction of Courts and Tribunals: The COMESA Court of Justice Perspective," 36 *Commonwealth Law Bulletin* 583 (2010).

[188] M. Oduor, "Resolving Trade Disputes in Africa: Choosing Between Multilateralism and Regionalism: The Case of COMESA and the WTO," 13 *Tulane Journal of International and Comparative Law* 177 (2005). As for Latin America, see N. Lavranos and N. Vielliard, "Competing Jurisdictions Between MERCOSUR and WTO," 7 *The Law and Practice of International Courts and Tribunals* 205 (2008). Regarding ASEAN, see M. Ewing-Chow, "Southeast Asia and Free Trade Agreements: WTO Plus Or Bust?," 8 *Singapore Yearbook of International Law* 193–206 (2004).

jurisdictions between courts appears unavoidable, due to the proliferation of IOs and regimes, as the CJEU has been experiencing too.[189]

In addition, different legal contexts may explain why processes of economic integration are connected with other objectives, such as the improvement of human rights: this happened in Africa, with the 1993 reform of ECOWAS;[190] but is also the case of the Arab League[191] and in Asia.[192] Similarly, more binding legal instruments can generate conflicts within institutions based on non-mandatory cooperation mechanisms such as ASEAN:[193] in this case, the divisions between

[189] See M. Parish, "International Courts and the European Legal Order," 23 *European Journal of International Law* 141 (2012).

[190] S. Godwin, "Integrating Trade and Human Rights in West Africa: An Analysis of the Ecowas Experience," 32 *Windsor Review of Legal and Social Issues* 57 (2012); S. T. Ebobrah, "Critical Issues in the Human Rights Mandate of the ECOWAS Court of Justice," 54 *Journal of African Law* 1 (2010).

[191] M. Rishmawi, "The Arab Charter on Human Rights and the League of Arab States: An Update," 10:1 *Human Rights Law Review* 169 (2010).

[192] Human Rights Centre, *Rule of Law for Human Rights in the ASEAN Region: A Base-Line Study* (Jakarta: Human Rights Centre, 2011).

[193] L. Chun Hung, "ASEAN Charter: Deeper Regional Integration under International Law?," 9 *Chinese Journal of International Law* 821 (2010); and L. Leviter, "The ASEAN Charter: ASEAN Failure Or Member Failure?," 43 *New York University Journal of International Law and Politics* 159 (2010–2011). Formerly, M. Ewing-Chow, "Culture Club or Chameleon: Should ASEAN Adopt Legalization for Economic Integration?," 12 *Singapore Yearbook of International Law* 225–237 (2008), and S. C. Tay Simon, "The ASEAN Charter: Between National Sovereignty and The Region's Constitutional Moment," 12 *Singapore Yearbook of International Law* 151–170 (2008).

the democratic Member States on the one hand, and the authoritarian ones on the other, ultimately produced an ASEAN Charter that prioritized the norms of sovereignty and consensus over those that would produce a more institutionalized and rule-based organization. Furthermore, States are still predominant; their political influence may hamper the process of regional integration regardless of the legal framework, as happened in the case of the Andean Community.[194]

It also emerges that there seems to be a "point" (a sort of "integration threshold") before which States do not accept ceding too many powers (when there are two or three States, the tendency is to prefer multilateral agreements), and after which they prefer playing a broad role (when an organization is global and States are numerous, there is greater formalization, but there is also greater difficulty in having powerful regimes: see the example of the UN).

What should always be kept in mind, however, is that any legal mechanism or technique adopted by international regimes will be based essentially on a mimetic process. These regimes tend to "*mirer sa vie dans celle d'autrui*";[195] and the

[194] This point is made by M. Baquero-Herrera, "The Andean Community: Finding Her Feet Within Changing and Challenging Multidimensional Conditions," 10 *Law and Business Review of the Americas* 577 (2004).

[195] M. E. de Montaigne (1533–1592), cited in E. Auerbach, *Mimesis. Dargestellte Wirklichkeit in der abendländischen Literatur* (1947) (the Italian translation of the German book was published in Turin by Einaudi in 1956, and the quote is taken from vol. II, p. 50, of the Italian translation).

"other" is basically the State.[196] But the latter too is part of the game and affects the regime's development: the State is not *just* a subject of international law; it is additionally both "a *source* and an *official* of international law."[197] These dynamics produce several implications, even when regional organizations attempt to imitate each other: while the mechanism may appear to be the same, the political and legal contexts are, however, different, and the actors change. Legal tools too have been changing, due to the links between international and national contexts and to horizontal imitative processes.[198] In addition, the conceptual model taken as a point of reference, that is, the State, is itself undergoing transformation, especially after the Cold War and due to globalization.[199] The

[196] A. Riles, "The Anti-Network: Private Global Governance, Legal Knowledge, and the Legitimacy of the State," 56 *American Journal of Comparative Law* 605 (2008), p. 629; and E. Meidinger, "Competitive Supragovernmental Regulation: How Could It Be Democratic?," 8 *Chicago Journal of International Law* 513 (2008), especially pp. 516 *et seq.*

[197] J. Waldron, "The Rule of International Law," 30 *Harvard Journal of Law and Public Policy* 16 (2006), p. 23.

[198] M. Kahler and D. A. Lake, "Economic Integration and Global Governance? Why So Little Supranationalism?," in W. Mattli and N. Woods (eds.), *The Politics of Global Regulation* (Princeton University Press, 2009), pp. 262 *et seq.*

[199] M. G. Kohen, "Internationalisme et mondialisation," in C. A. Morand (ed.), *Le droit saisi par la mondialisation* (Brussels: Bruylant, 2001), pp. 107 *et seq.*, especially pp. 112 *et seq.* (on the end of a "*monde bipolaire*") and pp. 119 *et seq.* (on the emergence of a "*nouveaux système juridique international*" linked to State sovereignty).

myth of the twentieth century is still alive;[200] but the financial crisis has demonstrated that there are no alternatives to cooperation.[201] This can open great opportunities for processes of legal integration beyond States.

Various objectives can be pursued, according to diverse models and through several legal instruments: these range from the differentiation of functions and international regulation of public administration to different techniques of governance. Such processes simultaneously take place in several regimes, which may overlap or compete with each other. To a certain extent, the phenomenon of regional institutions' overlap can also be explained with reference to the different techniques of governance adopted for reaching specific objectives: while single-mission forms of integration can often present a loose institutional structure, which can favor mutual competition between similar institutions, in more complex models – such as communities or unions – it is assumed that there are no competitors. This is why they tend to engage with all the legal techniques mentioned above. As a matter of fact, this mimetic process appears much stronger whenever the objectives pursued are more "ambitious." It is essential, however, to note that

[200] E. Cassirer, *The Myth of the State* (New Haven, CT: Yale University Press, 1961); M. van Creveld, *The Rise and the Decline of the State* (Cambridge University Press, 1999), especially pp. 336 *et seq.*

[201] See J. Black, "Paradoxes and Failures: 'New Governance' Techniques and the Financial Crisis," 75 *Modern Law Review* 1037 (2012); and G. Napolitano, "The Two Ways of Global Governance after the Financial Crisis: Multilateralism Versus Cooperation Among Governments," 9 *International Journal of Constitutional Law* 310 (2011).

no real legal integration can be attained without involving – directly or indirectly – both administrative systems of Member States[202] and their domestic courts.

[202] See J. S. T. Quah (ed.), *The Role of the Public Bureaucracy in Policy Implementation in Five ASEAN Countries* (Cambridge University Press, 2015).

Study

Lead, follow or get out of the way? International secretariats in comparative perspective

Omri Sender*

1 Introduction

Secretariats are the central organs of modern international organizations, so much so that they are often mistaken for the organizations themselves. At times referred to as "bureaus" or "commissions," they are in fact the permanent administrative bodies of such organizations, primarily responsible for coordinating their day-to-day work and executing much of

* Counsel, The World Bank; the findings, interpretations and conclusions expressed herein are mine, and do not represent the view of the World Bank, its Executive Directors or the countries they represent. I am grateful to Professor J. H. H. Weiler for inviting me to take part in the exciting project entitled "ASEAN Integration through Law," of which this contribution forms a part, and for his insightful guidance and support. I also wish to thank Patrick Tyler for his invaluable editorial comments; Alejandra Núñez and Geraldine Fischer for their assistance with translating some of the materials in Spanish; Daphne Livne-Sapir for her graphic design contributions; and the kind and helpful international civil servants working in the secretariats under review, for responding to innumerable queries and providing useful research material. I alone, of course, am responsible for any errors or omissions.

their will.[1] Although the international secretariat is, indeed, only one component of a broader institutional set-up created by the enabling agreement that is reached among the relevant parties (most often, States), it is "the organizational glue that holds the actors and parts of a treaty system together."[2] With multilateral responsibility as the principle underlying its work, the secretariat is ultimately a "guardian of the agenda" adopted by the founding or controlling State actors, providing the international organization with continuity and a consistent, recognizable profile in the global arena.[3] Traditionally,

[1] On secretariats in general, see H. G. Schermers and N. M. Blokker, *International Institutional Law: Unity Within Diversity* (Leiden: Martinus Nijhoff, 5th edn., 2011), pp. 320–397; P. Sands and P. Klein, *Bowett's Law of International Institutions* (London: Thomson Reuters, 6th edn., 2009), pp. 308–319; C. F. Amerasinghe, *Principles of the Institutional Law of International Organizations* (Cambridge University Press, 2nd edn., 2005), pp. 154–159; N. M. Blokker, "International Organizations or Institutions: Secretariats," in R. Wolfrum (ed.), *The Max Planck Encyclopedia of Public International Law* (Oxford University Press, 2008) (available at www.mpepil.com); A. L. Bennett and J. K. Oliver, *International Organizations: Principles and Issues* (Upper Saddle River, NJ: Prentice Hall, 7th edn., 2002), pp. 412–438.

[2] R. Sandford, "International Environmental Treaty Secretariats: Stage-Hands or Actors?," in H. O. Bergesen and G. Parmann (eds.), *Green Globe Yearbook of International Co-operation on Environment and Development* (Oxford University Press, 1994), p. 17. The architecture of international organizations commonly includes, apart from the secretariat, a main plenary body, a smaller executive organ and subsidiary entities responsible for specific mandates, all composed of representatives of the members.

[3] See T. G. Weiss, *International Bureaucracy* (Lexington, MA: Lexington Books, 1975), p. 33; R. A. Porrata-Doria, Jr., "MERCOSUR: The Common Market of the Twenty-First Century?," 32:1 *Georgia Journal of*

the role of secretariats has been limited to performing tasks of a technical-clerical nature, in particular facilitating the creation of the new international regime of which they form a part; mobilization of information; internal management; norm enforcement (through compliance monitoring); and direct service provision.[4] In the modern era, however, secretariats commonly perform policy-related functions as well, increasingly exerting influence and employing technocratic expertise. Rather than merely executing the agenda of the international regime that they serve, they are now often asked to take a substantive part in shaping it.

The gradual rise in the importance of secretariats within many international organizations has led to a greater focus on their role as "public nonstate actors" whose work is a form of "invisible governance."[5] After decades of being widely perceived as a minor feature of international cooperation and attracting only a marginal interest of scholars, secretariats are now of growing significance to international relations theory, international institutional law and political science at large, having won recognition as international actors in their own

International and Comparative Law 62 (2004); R. I. McLaren, *Civil Servants and Public Policy: A Comparative Study of International Secretariats* (Waterloo, ON: Wilfrid Laurier University Press, 1980), pp. 124–126.

[4] See also J. Mathiason, *Invisible Governance: International Secretariats in Global Affairs* (Bloomfield, CT: Kumarian Press, 2007), pp. 17–23.

[5] Terms used, respectively, in S. Bauer, "Does Bureaucracy Really Matter? The Authority of Intergovernmental Treaty Secretariats in Global Environmental Politics," 6:1 *Global Environmental Politics* 23 (2006), p. 28; and Mathiason, *ibid.*, p. xii.

right, who, "rather than acting like a concierge, are more like the managers of the hotel, still concerned with the comfort of guests but also with turning a profit."[6] Their sharper visibility has also prompted a debate on whether, and to what extent, secretariats are vital to the effective functioning of international regimes.[7] Some critics have asserted that secretariats are not only unnecessary in the quest for international cooperation, but might also prove counter-productive to it, emphasizing instead the usefulness of national bureaucracies collaborating directly. But others have shown that the most successful international regimes rely on empowered, well-staffed and energetic secretariats, which seem to fulfill the vision of the late British Prime Minister Harold Macmillan, who observed: "You cannot do anything without a Secretariat. In fact, the more you leave it to the Secretariat, the better it goes. It is only when the Government starts interfering that

[6] Mathiason, *ibid.*, p. 15. On the view of international bureaucracies as autonomous actors in the broader processes of global governance, see, for example, I. Venzke, "International Bureaucracies from a Political Science Perspective – Agency, Authority and International Institutional Law," in A. von Bogdany, R. Wolfrum, J. von Bernstorff, P. Dann and M. Goldman (eds.), *The Exercise of Public Authority by International Institutions: Advancing International Institutional Law* (Heidelberg: Springer, 2010), pp. 67–98; S. Bauer, P.-O. Busch and B. Siebenhüner, *Administering International Governance: What Role for Treaty Secretariats?*, Global Governance Working Paper 29, Amsterdam: The Global Governance Project, 2007 (available at www.glogov.org).

[7] See, for example, J. Ravenhill, *APEC and the Construction of Pacific Rim Regionalism* (Cambridge University Press, 2001), pp. 19, 167 and the references therein.

trouble comes."[8] While opinions on this matter may still vary, secretariats remain the prominent mechanism and instrument by which international organizations seek to realize their objectives. It has become clear that, in trying to understand the potential and constraints of institutionalized international cooperation, the role of secretariats must not be overlooked.

This study also sets out to take a close look at international secretariats, with the principle objective of providing distilled hard data on how secretariats are structured and what it is, precisely, that they do. In the following sections it constructs comprehensive profiles of six select secretariats, all serving regional organizations that, together, encompass the four corners of the earth: the Commission of the Economic Community of West African States (ECOWAS); the Technical Secretariat of the Common Market of the South (MERCOSUR); the Secretariat of the European Free Trade Association (EFTA); the Secretariat of the Asia–Pacific Economic Cooperation (APEC) forum; the Secretariat of the North American Free Trade Agreement (NAFTA); and the General Secretariat of the Organization of American States (OAS). These were chosen in the hope that their experiences would be most relevant to the *raison d'être* of the *ASEAN Integration through Law* book series. The first five have in common the service of regional integration schemes that, as their names imply, are or were originally marked by a single (economic) purpose; and, of

[8] British Prime Minister Harold Macmillan speaking in London on the occasion of the Economic Conference of the seven original EFTA Member States: see O. Long, *The European Free Trade Association* (Geneva: European Free Trade Association, 1961), p. 5.

them, the NAFTA Secretariat was chosen as a "control" owing to its unusual disaggregated structure. The sixth secretariat, of the OAS, was added to the list in light of its being the oldest international secretariat in the service of a regional organization (having an originally multi-purpose mandate). Each secretariat is put under the microscope for a close examination of its history and evolution, its mandate, organizational structure, financial underpinning, day-to-day functions and human resources. Such a formal inventory of secretariats in a comparative template will, it is hoped, illuminate the possibilities for institutional design (and their possible consequences in terms of actor quality), and serve as a toolbox for those contemplating the establishment of a new secretariat or reforming an existing one.

Surveying the secretariats in serial fashion also creates an opportunity to develop fresh insights from which to draw some broad conclusions, tentative as they may be given the limited array of case studies. These observations are presented in the closing section. In essence, they indicate that the analytical dichotomy that separates facilitative ("administrative") secretariats on the one hand and policy-shaping secretariats on the other, does not easily connect to the actual universe in which international secretariats operate. Using a more realistic frame of reference, secretariats can be best understood by a more nuanced classification that places them across a spectrum whose metrics measure the varying degrees of autonomy or involvement in the policy processes of the international organization that they serve. In each case, the secretariat's mandate reflects a decision by Member States that is first and foremost a political one, made in a distinct set of circumstances. The closing section then lists the general situations in which the facilitative secretariat model and the policy-shaping secretariat model are most likely to be adopted, and alludes to the implications of such a choice. It also suggests that, whatever role a secretariat is called upon to perform, several conditions – chief among them the political support of the sovereign masters – are essential to its effective functioning. The importance of each of these conditions is highlighted, along with practical advice on how to promote their formation or observe them in an operational context. Finally, it is conceded that international secretariats do tend to grow over time, acquiring a greater range of responsibility and action than those prescribed for them under a founding mandate and original structure. But this evolution, it is argued, is generally not pathological (in the Frankensteinian sense), but rather is the result of a conscious decision by Member States who wish for their organization to achieve greater and more rewarding results.

Drawing on official sources and direct inquiries to officials, this study produces a current snapshot of the selected secretariats. Being organizations that, as the following sections make clear, most often evolve over time, it should be borne in mind that the data presented herein are subject to change. As a predominantly descriptive account, the following text is, perhaps, more of a "dry biscuit" than a "rich plum pudding," to borrow the metaphor of the historian A. J. P. Taylor. Yet it is the elaboration which affords us a comprehensive view of each secretariat, and it is through this detailed examination that the greater comparative picture emerges. It is hoped that, just as even the most administrative work of secretariats can prove essential to the substantive functioning of international organizations, so can this largely illustrative text make a contribution not only to the theory of regional integration, but also to its application.

II The European Free Trade Association (EFTA) Secretariat

The European Free Trade Association was founded in 1960 as an intergovernmental organization dedicated to the promotion of free trade and economic integration to the benefit of its original seven Member States, who sought an economic counterbalance to the more politically motivated European Economic Community. With several countries acceding to EFTA in the decades that followed, or seceding from it to join the European Community (EC), EFTA Member States are currently four: Iceland, Lichtenstein, Norway and Switzerland.[9]

The EFTA Secretariat is only incidentally referred to in the 1960 Convention that gave rise to the Association, a choice of drafting that has been attributed to its framers "never intend[ing] to build a large bureaucracy, let alone one with executive powers comparable to the Commission of the European Communities."[10] According to the

9 On the origins of EFTA and its present form and operations, see K. Bryn and G. Einarsson (eds.), *EFTA 1960–2010: Elements of 50 Years of European History* (Geneva: EFTA Secretariat, 2010). Iceland has been negotiating accession to the European Union since 2009, but the negotiations were put on hold in June 2013.

10 "In the Service of EFTA," *EFTA Bulletin*, XXX-3 (July–September 1989), p. 12.

Convention's Institutional Provisions, the EFTA Council, which is the Association's governing body composed of representatives from each Member State, is to decide, *inter alia*, on "arrangements for the secretariat services required by the Association." It is this modest authorization in Article 34(b) (now Article 44(b)) that served as the legal basis for establishing the EFTA Secretariat, and which leaves it entirely to the Council to determine which administrative arrangements are to meet the practical needs of the Association. Numerous amendments to the Convention in the five decades of EFTA's existence, including the adoption of a revised Convention in 2001, have left this laconic language unchanged.

With the adoption of Staff Regulations by the EFTA Council in July 1960, a permanent EFTA Secretariat was established in Geneva, building on a small staff of some fifteen seconded civil servants who had assisted the EFTA Preparatory Committee in the preceding months.[11] These Staff Regulations, which set out the terms and conditions of service of the members of the Secretariat, were accompanied by salary scales based, in principle, on those of other international organizations in Geneva, and by a manning table which provided for a total staff of thirty-nine.[12] The Secretariat was soon said to be serving as the Council's "support and

[11] Creating the permanent secretariat was the first action taken by the Council. The 1960 proposal by the Preparatory Committee for setting up the Secretariat and the Council decisions which adopted it are, according to the Secretariat, "all confidential, as they deal with salaries, taxation and other sensitive issues."

[12] "Progress Report: May–September 1960," *EFTA Bulletin*, I-2 (November 1960), p. 9.

inspiration," with the two organs "collaborat[ing] very closely . . . [as] the two mainstays of the organization."[13] By the end of 1966, the number of Secretariat staff had risen to ninety-nine, but the secession of the United Kingdom and Denmark from EFTA in 1973 led to a reduction in personnel, which then numbered seventy people. At the end of the 1980s, the number was again close to 100, in light of increasing EFTA–EC relations and a shift within that framework from purely trade-related work to new areas of cooperation, such as education, environment, tourism, and research and development.

The EFTA Secretariat had originally comprised four departments: General and Legal, Trade Policy, Information and Press (including an office in Washington), and Administration and Finance. An Economic Affairs department was formed shortly thereafter, as was a Coordination and Development department. It was not long before the Secretariat took pride in the fact that "its service and advisory functions have not only been growing over the years, but have made an increasingly important contribution to the solution of a number of internal problems."[14] By the mid-1970s, a Council Secretariat department was established within the Secretariat as well, while the Legal Affairs unit was made independent of the Secretary General's Office, and the department of Coordination and Development was dismantled. A department for

[13] O. Long, *The European Free Trade Association* (Geneva: European Free Trade Association, 1961), p. 5.

[14] *Building EFTA: A Free Trade Area in Europe* (Geneva: EFTA Secretariat, 1966), p. 42.

Specific Integration Affairs was set up in the following decade, designated to deal with EFTA–EC cooperation in the internal market, as well as in other fields as mentioned above.

In April 1988, the Secretariat opened an office in Brussels, which was to provide logistic support to the growing intensity of EFTA's dealings with the EC while substantive work remained in Geneva.[15] The EFTA Bulletin of the following year made it known that "while the Secretariat remains basically, as in the past, a service organization at the disposal of the EFTA Council and the Association's member countries, its tasks go far beyond administrative and logistic matters. Its services include the preparation and servicing of all EFTA and EFTA–EC meetings through appropriate research and analysis of all questions dealt with by the Association as well as the preparation of documents, reporting on meetings and, more generally, ensuring the continuity of EFTA's work."[16] At that time, the Secretariat was also administering a number of reciprocal recognition schemes and conventions that were independent of EFTA but originally worked out in the Association, such as the Pharmaceutical Inspection Convention and the Hallmarking Convention. A third duty station of the Secretariat was set up in 1991 with the establishment of the EFTA Statistical Office in Luxembourg, created in order to contribute to the development of a broad and integrated European statistical system.

[15] See also "Interview with Georg Reisch, EFTA's Secretary-General," *EFTA Bulletin*, XXIX-2 (April–June 1988), p. 7.

[16] "In the Service of EFTA," *EFTA Bulletin*, XXX-3 (July–September 1989), p. 12.

With the entry into force of the EFTA–EC European Economic Area (EEA) Agreement in 1994,[17] and the subsequent withdrawal of Austria, Finland and Sweden from the EFTA Convention in 1995 to join the European Union as well, a dramatic change in the scope and orientation of EFTA's work inevitably followed: adapting to a new political and economic reality, the EFTA Secretariat soon underwent substantial reorganization and downsizing.

11.i Role and functions

EFTA's Secretariat plays an instrumental role in the Association's operations, not only performing administrative functions and executing the programmatic agenda, but also exercising some influence over policy-making by routinely counseling the EFTA Council (and Standing Committee). It employs approximately ninety staff members, of whom around one-third are based in Geneva, two-thirds in Brussels, and a small team in Luxembourg. It is headed by a Secretary General, who is assisted by two Deputy Secretaries General (one based in Geneva and the other in Brussels) and an Assistant Secretary General (based in Brussels as well). As will be explored in further detail below, the headquarters in Geneva services the EFTA Council and its committee

[17] The Agreement on the European Economic Area (EEA), which entered into force on January 1, 1994, brings together the twenty-eight European Union (EU) Member States and three of the EFTA States – Iceland, Liechtenstein and Norway – in a single market, referred to as the "Internal Market." Switzerland is not part of the EEA Agreement, but has a bilateral agreement with the EU.

structure,[18] and provides support to Member States in the negotiation and implementation of free trade agreements with non-EU countries. It occupies one floor in a seven-storey building, which until 1995 was fully inhabited by EFTA, with two storage rooms in the basement housing the EFTA archive.[19] Retaining the EFTA headquarters in Geneva after 1995, despite the significant shift in EFTA's focus towards Brussels, was the result of Swiss insistence, accompanied by willingness to pay for the Brussels office, even though Switzerland has only an observer status in most of its operations. Indeed, EFTA's Brussels office no longer merely provides logistical assistance to EFTA–EC relations; it now supports the management of the EEA Agreement, including by servicing committees and working groups established by the EEA Agreement or as a result of it. The EFTA Statistical Office in Luxembourg coordinates EFTA's participation in the work of the statistical office of the European Union (Eurostat), and provides statistical support for various other EFTA purposes. Overall, the Secretariat's activities thus center on the management and monitoring of (1) the relationship between the EFTA States on the basis of the EFTA Convention; (2) the worldwide network of free trade and partnership agreements between EFTA States and non-EU countries; and (3) the EEA Agreement.[20] It prepares all background

[18] In 2010, the Council met a total of eleven times, two of which were at ministerial level; all meetings took place in Geneva except the Summer Ministerial Meeting, which took place in Reykjavik.

[19] Since 2004, all documents have been stored only electronically. EFTA's Secretariat also has meeting rooms that are located on a separate floor.

[20] This description largely draws on EFTA's annual financial reports.

materials and decisions for the Council and the EEA Standing Committee and follows up on such decisions, carrying out any preparatory work, where appropriate, in consultation or cooperation with the national experts of the Member States.[21] The Secretariat moreover carries out administrative functions for the Financial Mechanism Office, which is affiliated to EFTA's Brussels operations and administers an extensive grants system set up by the EEA Agreement, as agreed upon in a separate Service Sharing Arrangement.

Despite the fact that (or, perhaps, because) it is not the native tongue in any EFTA Member State, English is the Secretariat's working language. Official documents and publications are all published in English, with the exception of EU legal texts that are relevant to the EEA Agreement, which are also translated into Norwegian and Icelandic and published on a weekly basis in the EEA Supplement to the Official Journal of the European Union. The *EFTA Bulletin*, which was published monthly from 1960 in English, French and German editions (and for some time in Norwegian and Swedish editions as well), has since 1999 generally been published once or twice a year, in English alone. In its new format, it surveys in depth

[21] For a detailed description of the Secretariat's "informal function" in the Free Trade Agreements context as "a 'think tank' providing the EFTA States with concrete input for their decision-making process," see R. Gschwend and P. Poretti, "The Role of the European Free Trade Association Secretariat and Select Legal Aspects of EFTA Free Trade Agreements," in A. H. Qureshi and X. Gao, *International Economic Organizations and Law: The Perspective and Role of the Legal Counsel* (Alphen aan den Rijn, The Netherlands: Kluwer Law International, 2012), pp. 351–375.

various themes relating to EFTA's work, such as the "EFTA Participation in EU Programs" or "Growth and Jobs: The Lisbon Strategy and European Economic Area." Other publications by the Secretariat include EFTA Factsheets and the EFTA Annual Reports, which provide information on EFTA's activities, achievements and institutional framework. The Secretariat further prepares commemorative publications, celebrating EFTA's decade anniversaries. All recent publications are posted on the EFTA website (www.efta.int), and the majority of them can be obtained in hard copy upon request, free of charge. Alongside the elaborate EFTA website, which also contains an extranet for distribution of restricted documents to members of EFTA's various committees, the Secretariat maintains a Twitter account that is updated regularly and has over 620 followers as of September 2014 (http://twitter.com/#!/EFTAsecretariat). In addition, the Secretariat supports an intranet site for internal communication.

As part of its information activities, the Secretariat also organizes seminars on EFTA-related topics, such as a biannual seminar on the EEA Agreement at the EFTA offices and elsewhere in Europe. Relevant information kits, distributed during these events, are produced by the Secretariat as well. The Secretariat further funds and/or arranges training, workshops and study visits associated with EFTA's technical cooperation programs, through which the Association seeks to assist its member and partner countries in harmonizing their respective statutory frameworks and implementing regulations for the purpose of facilitating trade. Additionally, it gives presentations at the EFTA offices in Geneva and Brussels to dozens of visiting groups each year, mostly consisting of high-school and university students, or public servants in governmental, regional or local administrations in the EFTA countries. The Secretariat also represents EFTA in various conventions and events relating to EFTA, such as meetings of the Standing Committee of the Lugano Convention of 1988, which deals with jurisdiction and enforcement of judgments in civil and commercial matters.

11.ii Organizational structure

As demonstrated in Figure s.1, EFTA's Secretary General has an office in both Geneva and Brussels, under which, respectively, the EFTA Legal Advisor and Information Officer operate. The Secretary General's Office also employs, *inter alios*, a Director, a Senior Economic Officer, a Council Affairs Officer and a personal assistant to the Secretary General at each of the two stations. The Office is in charge of: preparing Council meetings (monthly at the ambassadorial level and biannually at the ministerial level); supporting the activities of the Council's substructures; producing trade statistics and economic analysis relating to the Association; and handling information and communications. It further keeps a public register of documents drawn up by the Secretariat, and maintains the EFTA archive to which it may grant access after assessing such requests and consulting with the EFTA Member States. An Administration Department, located mostly in the Brussels office and comprising twenty staff members, is headed by a Director of Administration and supports the Secretariat management and staff in matters of human resources, finance, information technology and infrastructure.

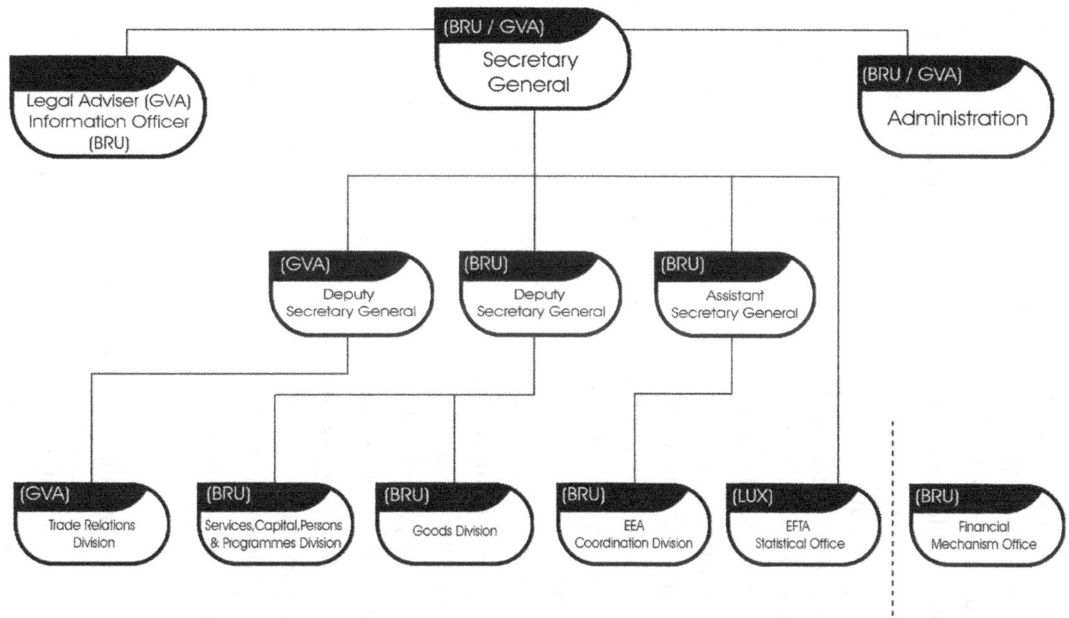

Figure s.1 EFTA Secretariat organizational structure

The Secretariat further comprises four specialized divisions, which reflect the different fields of EFTA's activities. The Trade Relations Division, located at the Geneva headquarters and headed by one of the Deputy Secretaries General, employs eight officers, two assistants and a trainee. It is entrusted with negotiating and preparing preferential trade agreements with non-EU countries, and with implementing some thirty such existing free trade agreements and Declarations on Cooperation. It also handles EFTA's abovementioned technical cooperation programs. Each of the Department's officers is assigned to one or more general issues of trade (for example, rules of origin, intellectual property rights, investment), as well as to several specific free trade agreements concluded between EFTA and other countries.

The Brussels-based EEA Coordination Division supports the execution of the EEA Agreement. Its director also holds the title of Assistant Secretary General,[22] and manages eight officers, a copy editor, three assistants and two trainees. Engaged in "decision-shaping," the Division takes part in monitoring and analyzing EU policy developments that are relevant to the EEA Agreement; supports Member States in preparing legislation for integration into the EEA Agreement; prepares the agendas, speaking notes and protocols of the

[22] The title of Assistant Secretary General was created in 2012 when Lichtenstein proposed for the first time in EFTA's history a national of its own as candidate for one of the top three management positions, which until then were traditionally staffed only by nationals of the three other (larger) Member States.

EEA Council, the EEA Joint Committee and the EFTA Standing Committee on the EEA; assists in drafting the decisions made by the EEA Joint Committee; and provides secretarial services to the EFTA Parliamentary and Consultative Committees. Two of the Division's officers handle legal matters, three are assigned to the various aforementioned auxiliary sub-organs created by the EEA Agreement, and three others (of which one is coordinator of EFTA publications) translate EEA-related legal texts into Norwegian and Icelandic.

The EEA Coordination Division is assisted by the two other secretariat divisions (which correspond to the Internal Market's Four Freedoms): the Goods Division, and the Services, Capital, Persons and Programs Division, both working out of the Brussels station as well. These are in charge of identifying and integrating relevant legal acts adopted by the European Council and Parliament into the EEA Agreement; assisting Member States in assessing the impact of such changes; initiating decision-making processes within EFTA regarding proposed EU legislation and policies in order to attempt to shape such proposals; and supporting EFTA experts and Member States in facilitating trade with the EU. The Goods Division employs a director, nine officers, an assistant and a trainee; the Services, Capital, Persons and Programs Division employs a director, eight officers, two assistants and a trainee. Each Division has a legal officer, while the other officers are each assigned to specific policy areas or sectors of trade.

The EFTA Statistical Office (ESO) in Luxembourg, created as a liaison office between the statistical office of the European Union (Eurostat) and the EFTA national statistical institutes, has a staff of five, which consists of the Head of

ESO, a Deputy, two assistants and a trainee. Its main objective is to sustain the integration of the EFTA States in the evolving European Statistical System, and thus to provide harmonized and comparable statistics on trade and economy supporting the general cooperation process between EFTA and the EU.

Since the restructuring process of 1994, the EFTA Secretariat no longer has a separate legal affairs department, but rather, as specified above, a Senior Legal Advisor working at the Geneva headquarters under the Secretary General, and five legal officers who are employed in the different substance divisions. This seems sensible to EFTA in light of the topical specialization required within each Division. The responsibilities of the Senior Legal Advisor lie with organizational and administrative matters as well as legal issues relating to the EFTA Council. He or she further maintains contact with the EFTA Court and the EFTA Surveillance Authority – two separate institutions that are not served by the EFTA Secretariat – in order to ensure that the administrative rules and regulations of the three EFTA bodies are harmonized.

II.iii The Secretary General

As head of the EFTA Secretariat, the Secretary General coordinates the Association's activities and the management of its resources. Responsible to the EFTA Council in the exercise of his functions and in respect of the way he exercises his authority, the Secretary General divides his time between the EFTA headquarters in Geneva and the Brussels duty station, and is assisted, as noted above, by two Deputy Secretaries General and an Assistant Secretary General.

The Secretary General's post was initially titled Executive Secretary, but was renamed soon thereafter.

Remarkably, the EFTA Convention makes no mention of the position of a Secretary General. It has been suggested that the establishment of this central post by the Council "should be understood to rest on the far-reaching powers conferred upon [it] by Articles 1(4) and 32(3) of the Convention 'to set up such organs ... as it considers necessary to assist it in accomplishing its tasks', rather than on the sparsely articulated authority of Article 34 'to make arrangements for the Secretariat services required by the Association'."[23] In any case, the position of the Secretary General indeed owes its existence to a decision of the Council and thus "has no guaranteed constitutional status, neither as an office nor in terms of its powers, responsibilities or functions."[24] Nevertheless, the appointment of highly qualified senior government officials from the ranks of Member States to the position of Secretary General, right from the very first days of EFTA, has been said to be "indicative of the conception of the office of the Secretary-General, by the Member States, as a key institutional tool for the operation of the Association."[25]

The Secretary General, Deputy Secretaries General and Assistant Secretary General are officially appointed, for three-year terms (renewable once), by means of a Letter of Appointment signed by the Chairman of the Council

[23] J. H. Lambrinidis, *The Structure, Function, and Law of a Free Trade Area: The European Free Trade Association* (New York: Praeger, 1965), p. 22.

[24] *Ibid.*, p. 56. [25] *Ibid.*, p. 21.

on behalf of the Association.[26] Member States nominate candidates for these posts and decide on the appointments by consensus at a ministerial meeting of the Council. Liechtenstein, EFTA's smallest Member State, has only recently put forward a nominee for the first time.[27] While the four posts are generally divided between the Member States, the decisions on appointment remain political and discrete, and there is no clear mechanism of rotation (although a Swiss national usually holds one of the two top posts at the Geneva headquarters). It might also happen that the Secretary General and one of his Deputy Secretaries General would be of the same nationality. A Council decision also establishes the emoluments of the Secretary General, the Deputy Secretaries General and Assistant Secretary General.[28]

EFTA's first Secretary General, Mr. Frank Figgures of the United Kingdom, was described by the Secretariat as holding a "triple role of top daily administrator, counselor of the EFTA member countries and executor of the EFTA Council's decisions."[29] Then as now, all staff members are subject to the Secretary General's authority and direction and are responsible to him in the exercise of their functions. It is the Secretary General who is formally in charge of recruiting and appointing

[26] EFTA Staff Regulations 14(2).

[27] See n. 22 above. Even at the EFTA Court, where each Member State is entitled to representation on the bench, Lichtenstein had preferred not to introduce its own judge, but to be represented by the Swiss one.

[28] The Secretary General and his Deputies and Assistant are also entitled to higher daily subsistence allowance rates than other employees.

[29] "EFTA Head to Resign," *EFTA Reporter* (May 31, 1965), p. 120.

staff, and who signs the employment contracts on behalf of the Association. He may also assign a staff member additional or new duties, temporarily or for the duration of his or her contract. Moreover, while it is the Council that established and holds the authority to amend the Staff Regulations, the Secretary General may propose regulations and amendments as he deems necessary, and is empowered to issue and enforce Rules that are consistent with the Staff Regulations (such rules should then be communicated to the Council). The Secretary General is responsible for the implementation of the Staff Regulations and Rules (although he may delegate this task to officials acting under him), and is authorized to exercise discretion in enumerated exceptional cases under them. Other duties of the Secretary General include depositing the texts of Council decisions with the EFTA Depositary, and notifying the Secretariat General of the EC of the adoption of EFTA Council decisions that are of relevance to them. The Secretary General participates in all meetings of the Council, as well as in the meetings of the EEA Council, the EEA Joint Committee and the EFTA Standing Committee. He reports to the EFTA Council biannually: a mid-year report is to be submitted by June 30 of each year, and an annual report is to be submitted by March 31 of the following year.

As noted above, the Secretary General further holds a key role in the management of the Association's financial resources. EFTA's Financial Regulations stipulate that, for each financial year (beginning on January 1), it is the responsibility of the Secretary General to present the Council with an annual budget proposal and a draft performance plan. These should be submitted no later than three months before the beginning of each financial year; and they are, in turn, referred by the

Council to its Budget Committee for examination. The latter is to consult with the Secretary General as that body deems necessary before making its recommendation to the Council. Once a budget has been adopted, the Secretary General is authorized "to incur commitments and make payments for the purposes for which the appropriations were voted and up to the amounts so voted," yet he or she is expected to verify the availability of funds prior to entering into any commitment.[30] Commitments for future financial years require the specific authorization of the Council, as does the transfer of money among budgets approved for Secretariat services on the one hand and cooperation programs on the other.[31] Reserve funds for these budgets, to which contributions are made by surpluses for income and expenditure, are under the responsibility of the Secretary General as well. The Financial Regulations further stipulate that the Secretary General is to designate the bank or banks in which the Association's funds are held, and that he or she may make "non-speculative short-term investments of moneys not needed for immediate requirements."[32]

The Secretary General is also responsible for the preparation of EFTA's final accounts at the end of each financial year; these are to be submitted to the Council for auditing "as soon as practicable ... and no later than three months after the end of the financial year."[33] Pertinent

[30] EFTA Financial Regulations 9(1) and 9(3).

[31] EFTA Financial Regulations 9(4) and 9(5).

[32] EFTA Financial Regulations 12(1) and 12(2).

[33] EFTA Financial Regulations 10 and 14(1).

documentation should include a statement of the Association's inventory, to which a depreciation schedule established by the Secretary General has been applied, and a statement concerning losses of cash, supplies, equipment and other assets authorized by the Secretary General to be written off, after full investigation on his behalf (the Secretary General is not authorized, however, to order the writing-off of arrears of contributions by Member States). In addition, the Secretary General is to provide the auditors of the final reports with "every facility necessary for the accomplishment of [their] tasks and in particular submit on demand any document which is relevant," including written explanations relating to issues for which the auditors did not find his verbal explanation satisfactory.[34] Although the auditors are required to submit their draft report to the Secretary General, publish his comments, and duly take them into account, they remain "the sole judge[s] as to acceptance in whole or in part of certifications and representations by the Secretary-General."[35]

As head of the Secretariat, the Secretary General is responsible to the Council for the implementation of the Financial Regulations, but may delegate decision-making pursuant to such regulations to officials acting under him. Moreover, while the Council is the organ which establishes and may amend the Financial Regulations, the Secretary General is authorized to issue and enforce rules that are consistent with these as he sees necessary. He or she is further entrusted with establishing procedures for effective financial

[34] EFTA Financial Regulations 15(2) and 15(3).

[35] EFTA Financial Regulations 15(4), 15(5) and 16(3).

administration and consistency in financial reporting; and with maintaining a comprehensive internal financial control.

The Secretary General was originally assisted by a Deputy Secretary General and an Assistant Secretary General (a position added subsequently), but since 1966 two Deputy Secretaries General serve in EFTA, and in 2012 the position of Assistant Secretary General was reintroduced. To date, the Deputy Secretary General in Brussels assists the Secretary General in coordinating the Association's activities in Brussels, providing support to the management of the European Economic Area, while the Deputy Secretary General in Geneva assists the Secretary General in managing the Association's activities regarding the negotiations and management of EFTA's free trade agreements. The Assistant Secretary General, serving in Brussels, fills the function of Director of the EEA Coordination Division. The Secretary General holds a weekly conference call ("*tour de table*") with his deputies and EFTA Directors.

In 2012, the Secretary General's services cost a total of CHF1,964,000 (the same as in the preceding year), out of a total annual budget of CHF22,066,000.[36] This figure relates to expenses incurred by the Secretary General's Office.

11.iv Staff

EFTA's stated general preference is to recruit and appoint nationals of Member States for all Secretariat positions of the

[36] P. Grønningsæter (ed.), *This Is EFTA 2012* (Geneva: European Free Trade Association, 2012), p. 26.

Table 5.1 *The distribution of nationalities among EFTA Secretariat staff members (March 2012)*

Norwegian	34
Swiss	14
Icelandic	12
British	8
Belgian	6
French	4
Lichtenstein	2
Irish	2
German	1
Finnish	1
American	1
Spanish	1
Swedish	1

Professional category A; for the General Services category B, the preference is to recruit locally.[37] In the event that the Secretariat wishes to recruit non-EFTA nationals for category A positions due to a lack of suitable candidates from EFTA States, the Council is to be consulted, and its approval is required. The recruitment process aims to obtain staff "of the highest standard of competence, efficiency and integrity," while the Secretary General is to pay due regard to "the desirability of recruiting staff as far as possible from all Member States" as

[37] Since EFTA's working language is English, which is not spoken in any of the Member States, the Secretariat attempts to recruit for the General Services category native English speakers who reside in the vicinity of duty stations.

well.[38] Candidates must also present certification attesting to their being in good health before they can be appointed as staff members,[39] and the first six months of an initial fixed-term position are regarded as a probationary period.

Originally, professional staff members of the Secretariat were effectively on loan from their respective national governments. EFTA defended this practice of seconding civil servants as serving a double purpose: "first to avoid creating a new international bureaucracy, secondly to ensure a constant influx of new blood into the central administration of the Member countries and the international Secretariat of the organization," in the hope that a growing understanding between the national administrations and the international organization would thus be promoted.[40] Today, however, while some professional staff members are on leave from their respective national administrations, the vast majority are recruited through competition (open to nationals of EFTA Member States). In any case, a rule introduced in 1995 mandates that staff members may not serve the Association for more than six consecutive years: the preliminary "first-time" appointment is normally granted for three years, and can be renewed only once, for an additional period of up to three years. Staff members have no entitlement to such renewal, which is dependent solely on the "interest of the Association."[41] They

[38] EFTA Staff Regulations 11(1) and 11(2).

[39] EFTA Staff Regulations 12; the expenses incurred in the medical examination "will not be met by the Secretariat."

[40] O. Long, *The European Free Trade Association* (Geneva: European Free Trade Association, 1961), p. 6.

[41] EFTA Staff Regulations 13(a)(iv) and 13(a)(v).

can, however, and often do, return to work in EFTA after a "break," during which they go home to serve their national government. Nevertheless, the Staff Regulations make clear that, once appointed, a staff member "is a servant of the Association" alone, and that "his responsibilities are not national": he "pledges himself to discharge his functions with the interests of the Association only," and "shall neither seek nor accept instructions from any government or from any body or person external to the Association."[42] Staff members may not accept any honor, decoration, favor, gift or remuneration from any government or any other source external to the Association, without the prior approval of the Secretary General.

The terms and conditions of service of the staff members of the Secretariat are set out in the Staff Regulations and in the accompanying Staff Rules. These are applicable to all staff members unless and to the extent that their letter of appointment provides otherwise. The Staff Regulations, which have been amended by the Council from time to time, deal with the obligations and conduct of staff members, their recruitment and appointment, their salaries and related allowances, social benefits and compensation arrangements, travel and removal expenses, working conditions, leave and discipline. As they stipulate, staff members are required to work a total of forty hours (excluding meal breaks) per five-day working week, although the Secretary General could call on the service of a staff member beyond this scope if the need arises.[43] Staff

[42] EFTA Financial Regulations 4 and 6.

[43] EFTA Staff Regulations 38; the Secretariat had indicated in the past that, due to the nature of the work carried out in its divisions, a time

members are eligible to receive thirty days of annual leave (on full emoluments), in addition to public holidays, as well as paid sick leave; a staff member appointed for periods exceeding one year is also entitled to paid maternity or paternity leave for six months or four weeks, respectively. Special leave on full, partial or without emoluments, including for "compassionate reasons," may be granted at the discretion of the Secretary General.

Staff members are also eligible to receive, *inter alia*, dependency benefits for their dependants; half the premium costs of health insurance schemes for them and their dependants; allowances for the education of dependent children; rent allowance in case a staff member pays rent exceeding 20 percent of his salary; and an accommodation loan. Non-locally recruited or transferred staff members may be awarded an installation allowance as well as removal expenses. In the event that a staff member and his spouse are both gainfully employed, EFTA would seek to verify that such benefits are claimed from only one of the employers. EFTA further provides its staff members with death and disability compensation and with unemployment benefits (for a maximum of six months); detachment allowance is paid to staff members during their temporary detachment to another duty station, and resettlement allowance to non-locally recruited staff members and

registration system "would inject an undesirable element of rigidity into the work environment and would not bring any economic benefits for the Member States," and the idea was abandoned as the Council shared this view (see letter from the Chairman of the Council to Mr. Engeseth of the EFTA Board of Auditors dated November 18, 2008, Ref. 21802).

their dependants in the event of separation from service after two or more continuous years of work. Moreover, a staff Savings Fund, open to all employees, was set up in order to protect staff members and their families "from the economic consequences of old age." Contributions to the fund, which is held in the name of the Association, are made each month by staff members who elect to join it (rather than take out a comparable insurance elsewhere) at a sum equal to 9.5 percent of their basic salary, as well as by the Association at a sum which equals 19 percent of that salary.[44] Staff members are permitted to spread their savings over several schemes in different banks and in different currencies, while the Secretariat monitors the performance and risk situation of each scheme. Those who elect to contribute to the Savings Fund receive the sum accrued in their name upon their separation from service.

The salaries of staff members are specified in basic salary scales that are drawn up in accordance with the recommendations of the Coordinating Committee on Remuneration of the "Coordinated Organizations."[45] The Council keeps this remuneration system under review in order to

[44] EFTA Financial Regulations 31(3), 31(4) and 31(5); the Association will contribute at the same rate to an insurance program if such an option is preferred by a staff member. Contributions can be made in four currencies (euros, Swiss francs, Norwegian krone or Icelandic krona) with either the investment bank Nordea, the Swiss National Bank or Banca Monte Paschi in Brussels.

[45] The term "Coordinated Organizations" (CO) refers to six independent intergovernmental organizations, which have a coordinated remuneration system (see www.sio-ios.org/public/public.php?irub=3).

maintain competitive employment conditions, as well as to ensure comparable purchasing power conditions in EFTA's three duty stations, and the Secretary General is authorized to formulate proposals in this regard. Salaries are not taxed by the States hosting the EFTA duty stations or by EFTA States, but all staff members are liable to an "internal tax" on salaries and other payments made to them by EFTA, for the benefit of the Association: this is mainly to cover staff contributions to the social security and pension arrangements mentioned above. The Staff Regulations further stipulate that, in case of "exceptional budgetary difficulties," the Council may decide not to award annual salary adjustments, although such a decision must be made openly in consultation with the Staff Committee that represents the interests of the Secretariat staff.

Employment at EFTA may be on a part-time basis as well (eight such posts currently exist); and staff could also be appointed for temporary positions for particular assignments, on either a full- or part-time basis, for positions that must not exceed twelve months in duration. A staff member is considered non-locally recruited when, prior to his or her appointment, his place of residence was more than fifty kilometers from his EFTA duty station; or when he was considered a non-locally recruited staff member at another public international organization or a diplomatic service; or if he had moved to the area of the duty station for professional or educational reasons no more than three or five years, respectively, prior to the appointment. The Secretary General is authorized to waive any of these requirements if it is deemed appropriate under exceptional circumstances. In addition, a locally recruited staff member who is transferred to another duty station would be deemed non-locally recruited at the new duty station, for the period of time that she would serve there. Non-locally recruited staff members are entitled to home leave in their home country for the purpose of spending there a substantial period of their annual leave, with EFTA paying for the travel expenses of the staff member as well as his or her dependants. The Secretary General may require a staff member to accept a transfer, or a detachment limited in time, to another duty station, if it is "necessary for the good functioning of the secretariat." While the Secretary General must pay due regard to the staff member's personal circumstances, the latter may not refuse such a transfer or detachment without reasonable grounds.

EFTA further offers traineeships, ten months in duration, to approximately ten nationals of the EFTA Member States each year.[46] Trainees are assigned to a specific division of the Secretariat or the Financial Mechanism Office according to their academic field of specialization, personal preferences and career objectives. The program aims to "provide junior civil servants and other qualified applicants with opportunities for training and familiarization with the work and functions of the EFTA Secretariat."[47] They receive a flat monthly allowance (net of taxes) of CHF2,394 if stationed in Geneva, and €1,397 if stationed in Brussels; accommodation in individual flats is provided by EFTA as well.

46 Traineeships at the Financial Mechanism Office are also open to nationals of the EU Member States.

47 See "Traineeship at EFTA" on the EFTA website (available at www.efta.int/about-efta/job-opportunities/traineeship.aspx).

Staff members must not exploit the privileges and immunities that attach to the Secretariat according to the Protocol on the Legal Capacity, Privileges and Immunities, drawn up by the Member States in 1961 as instructed by the EFTA Convention. In the event where a staff member fails to perform his or her private obligations or observe laws and police regulations, the Secretary General may decide to what extent privileges and immunities may be waived if such a question arises in particular cases. Staff members who are found guilty of professional misconduct or whose work is deemed unsatisfactory may be subjected to sanctions, including summary dismissal, in accordance with the disciplinary rules laid down by the Secretary General. A staff member may appeal the decision of the Secretary General to the Administrative Tribunal of the International Labour Organization.

The Secretary General may terminate the appointment of a staff member not only for reasons of unsatisfactory services or misconduct, but also due to "the abolition of [a] post or a reduction or reorganization of the manning table of the Secretariat affecting that post," unreasonable refusal of a staff member to accept a transfer or a detachment, or incapacity of a staff member to perform his duties due to illness or an accident. Three months' written notice (or one month during the probation period) is required, yet the Secretary General may decide to relieve a staff member from the duty to work during such period;[48] similarly, resignation

[48] EFTA Financial Regulations 19(1), 19(2) and 19(3). The Regulations further stipulate that a staff member's contract may not be terminated during sick leave or maternity leave (Regulation 19(4)).

by a staff member requires giving the Secretary General three months' written notice, though he may accept a shorter period of time. A staff member whose appointment has been terminated by the Secretary General may be eligible to receive a termination indemnity, in accordance with the conditions of the Staff Regulations.

The Staff Regulations explicitly recognize the right of association of the Secretariat staff, as well as the right of each staff member to join the EFTA Staff Association. An elected committee of the Staff Association represents the interests of the staff before the Secretary General, and must be consulted with regard to any proposed actions related to staff welfare and administration (except for instructions to meet emergency situations). If such consultations do not result in agreement, the matter may be referred to an Advisory Board composed of three members designated by the committee of the Staff Association, two members representing the Secretary General, and two representatives from the Member States that hold the Chairmanship and Vice Chairmanship of the Council (acting in their personal capacity). If the Advisory Board fails to transmit its opinion or proposals for settlement within sixty days, an appeal may be made to the Administrative Tribunal of the International Labour Organization.

An online recruitment system was introduced in 2004 on the EFTA website, making it possible to post, respond to and manage the Secretariat's job offers more easily and efficiently. The Secretariat maintains job descriptions for all positions, which include duties, and knowledge and experience requirements; these are harmonized in terms of structure and classification of information.

11.v Budget

EFTA's annual budget is prepared in two currencies – Swiss francs and euros – using a budgeting method based on the principle of framework budgeting, introduced in 2004 in order to increase awareness of budgetary spending at all levels and as established in public administrations of the Member States. According to this method, the budget is accompanied by a performance plan where the Secretariat's activities are divided into projects.

Norway is the largest contributor to the EFTA budget (currently funding 55.85 percent of it), followed by Switzerland (40.15 percent), Iceland (3.07 percent) and Lichtenstein (0.93 percent). The 2013 budget totaled CHF22,298,000, of which CHF3,924,000 was allocated to administration and management costs.

Table s.2 *EFTA Secretariat annual budget 2004–2013 (in CHF million)*

2004	21.5
2005	22.2
2006	23.1
2007	24.0
2008	25.3
2009	24.4
2010	25.0
2011	23.6
2012	22.0
2013	22.2

III The Asia-Pacific Economic Cooperation (APEC) Secretariat

The Asia-Pacific Economic Cooperation (APEC) forum was established in 1989 as an informal consultative body, seeking to promote economic integration of Asia-Pacific economies through trade and investment liberalization, business facilitation, and economic and technical cooperation. In the absence of an international agreement establishing APEC, there are no treaty obligations required of its now twenty-one Member Economies; decisions are reached by consensus, and commitments are undertaken on a voluntary basis.[49] APEC's policy is directed by the Leaders of Member Economies who gather annually in a summit meeting, and guided further by APEC Ministers, a Business Advisory Council and Senior Officials of Member Economies, who take part in APEC's four working-level core committees. Subcommittees, Experts' Groups, Working Groups and Task Forces, headed by Lead Shepherds elected by consensus among the Member Economies, then carry out the activities prescribed by the core committees. Within this framework, APEC currently funds over one hundred projects on average per annum, which are implemented normally within two financial years.[50] Each year, one of the

[49] The twenty-one Member Economies are referred to as such (as opposed to "Member States") due to the special status of Hong Kong and Taiwan ("Chinese Taipei"). On APEC more generally, see, for example, R. Garnaut, "APEC Ideas and Reality," in I. Yamazawa (ed.), *Asia Pacific Economic Cooperation: Challenges and Tasks for the Twenty-First Century* (Florence, KY: Routledge, 2000), pp. 1–16.

[50] The amount of funding available for projects varies each year, depending on the financial contributions by Member Economies (both mandated

Member Economies is designated as host of the APEC meetings and serves as the APEC Chair.

In the Bangkok Declaration that concluded the 1992 APEC Ministerial Meeting held in Thailand, representatives of Member Economies recognized that "the rapidly growing activities of APEC since its inception have increased the need for an effective support mechanism to facilitate and coordinate APEC activities in order to strengthen APEC's role and enhance its efficiency in promoting regional economic cooperation."[51] They announced that a permanent APEC Secretariat was thus to be established, "as a support mechanism to facilitate and coordinate APEC activities, provide logistical and technical services as well as administer APEC financial affairs under the direction of the APEC Senior Officials' Meeting (APEC SOM)."[52] The Declaration further stipulated that the Secretariat "will be composed of three elements: an Executive Director, Professional Staff and Support Staff"; and that it "will be empowered to act on behalf of APEC Members under the direction of Ministers as communicated through the APEC SOM," to which it was to report directly.[53] A consolidated report prepared earlier that year

and voluntary). In 2010–2011, approximately US$23 million was committed by APEC to projects.

51 Bangkok Declaration on Asia-Pacific Economic Cooperation (APEC), made by APEC Ministers in conclusion of their meeting in Bangkok on September 10–11, 1992.

52 Bangkok Declaration on APEC, Article A(1)(1). An APEC Fund was to be established as well (see Section 3.3.5 below).

53 Bangkok Declaration on APEC, Articles A(1)(2) and A(2). The Declaration also provided that, for the purpose of better coordination,

by APEC Senior Officials, which described in greater detail the functions of the proposed Secretariat, means for selecting its personnel, and its funding arrangements, was endorsed by the Ministerial Meeting in Bangkok as well. Committed to the principles of voluntarism and consensus that stood at the heart of APEC's form, the Ministers agreed in Bangkok to set up a secretariat that would effectively "be limited to a logistics role and would not be given the authority, resources, or staff to carry out an agenda that might infringe upon members' sovereignty."[54] Envisioned as "small in size, simple in structure, and flexible enough to meet APEC's evolving needs,"[55] its function was to "co-ordinate and assist APEC's work projects, facilitate communications between APEC members, and provide a point of contact for the public, other organizations, and the business community."[56]

Based in Singapore, the Secretariat became operational in February 1993. Its original personnel plan provided for eight professional positions (out of a total of thirteen staff members), and the annual budget for its administrative and

"direct and regular communications" were to be established "between the APEC Secretariat and APEC Members, Shepherds of Work Projects and Heads and other APEC committees and groups" (Article A(3)).

[54] R. Feinberg, "Book Review: J. Ravenhill, *APEC and the Construction of Pacific Rim Regionalism*," 77 *The Business History Review* 200 (2003), p. 201.

[55] *Future Steps on APEC: Consolidated Report of the APEC Senior Officials to the 4th APEC Ministerial Meeting*, endorsed by APEC Ministers in their 1992 Bangkok meeting.

[56] H. Soesastro, "The Institutional Framework for APEC: An ASEAN Perspective," in S. Y. Chia (ed.), *APEC: Challenges and Opportunities* (Singapore: Institute of Southeast Asian Studies, 1994), p. 36.

operational costs was set at US$800,000. By 1997, the Secretariat's total staff had increased to thirty-three, and a decade later it had grown to twenty-four professional staff members working alongside twenty-six support staff members, all operating under an annual budget of US$2.3 million. Having moved in 2003 from its temporary office premises to a rent-free, designated, seven-storey office building provided by the host government, the Secretariat presently employs approximately sixty professional and support staff members, who all come from APEC's Member Economies, with its annual operational budget totaling approximately US$4.7 million.

Indeed, APEC's expanding agenda and growing number of projects led early on to an increased workload and greater expectations of some Member Economies, and by the beginning of the millennium it became increasingly clear that "members so restricted the Secretariat's resources and autonomy that it was incapable even of playing the limited support role intended for it, let alone serving as a coordinator or innovator."[57] In 2002, APEC Ministers meeting in Los

[57] J. Ravenhill, *APEC and the Construction of Pacific Rim Regionalism* (Cambridge University Press, 2001), p. 132. See also S. Goodings, "The APEC Secretariat: A Management Perspective," in R. E. Feinberg (ed.), *APEC as an Institution: Multilateral Governance in the Asia–Pacific* (Singapore: Institute of Southeast Asian Studies, 2003), pp. 67–72; A. Oaxley, "APEC – The Next 10 Years" (Australian APEC Study Centre Issues Paper 16, May 1999) (available at www.apec.org.au/docs/iss16.htm); A. Gyngell and M. Cook, *How To Save APEC* (Sydney: Lowy Institute for International Policy, 2005); R. Feinberg and J. Lawrence, *Improving APEC's Coherence* (2006) (available at http://irps.ucsd.edu/assets/009/5861.pdf); D. MacDuff, "APEC After Shanghai: Which Path Forward?," 57 *International Journal* 439 (2002), p. 442; M. Beeson, *Institutions of the Asia Pacific: ASEAN, APEC and Beyond*

Cabos, Mexico, supported the implementation of recommendations made in a "Report on Improving the Functioning of the APEC Secretariat," which drew upon earlier reports of the Task Force for the Review of the APEC Secretariat (1995) and Task Force on Management Issues (1996, 1997).[58] An *ad hoc* Group on APEC Secretariat Reform was established in 2005 as well, and in the following year APEC Ministers agreed in the Vietnamese capital, Hanoi, that APEC's contemporary demands require that the Secretariat be provided with greater resources. In what has been called "the creeping institutionalism" of APEC,[59] several institutional reforms have since then been gradually pursued in order to strengthen the Secretariat's capabilities. A Chief Operating Officer was recruited in 2007 to oversee corporate management, and a Project Management Unit was formed in the same year to enhance project management processes; in 2008, a Policy Support Unit was established in order to enable APEC to carry out independent policy research and analysis, and recommendations on strengthening the budgetary position of the Secretariat were adopted in 2009. Member economies also

(Florence, KY: Routledge, 2008), p. 43; C. F. Bergsten, "Open Regionalism," in C. F. Bergsten (ed.), *Whither APEC? The Progress to Date and Agenda for the Future* (Washington, DC: Institute for International Economics, 1997), p. 16; SOM Chair's Report on *Management Review: The Next Steps*, APEC Document No. 1999/AMM/017, p. 1 ("[b]asic questions need to be asked . . . about whether the current structure is still appropriate for APEC's objectives and whether it is the best design to ensure that APEC achieves its goals").

58 These documents are not publicly available.

59 C. E. Morrison, "APEC: The Evolution of an Institution," in V. K. Aggarwal and C. E. Morrison (eds.), *Asia-Pacific Crossroads: Regime Creation and the Future of APEC* (New York: St. Martin's Press, 1998), p. 7.

agreed on substantially increasing their annual contributions to help strengthen the Secretariat. In 2011, APEC Ministers meeting in Hawaii's capital, Honolulu, welcomed the "continued efforts to strengthen the operational and institutional capabilities of the APEC Secretariat";[60] a year later, at their meeting in Vladivostok, Russia, they expressed their resolve to "continue to strengthen the operational and institutional capabilities of the APEC Secretariat."[61]

III.i Role and functions

Dedicated to operating as the core support mechanism for the APEC process, as called for in the Bangkok Declaration, the Secretariat plays primarily an administrative and project-management role. As described in further detail below, it provides coordination, technical and advisory support to APEC's many fora and initiatives, as well as information management, communications and public outreach services. It also administers APEC's annual budget. Having no power of initiative, the Secretariat has traditionally thought of its role in terms of customer service, as symbolized by its sustained efforts to obtain, in 2002, the ISO 9001 Quality Management Certification, "as a tool to enhance its efficiency in providing services to stakeholders." In line with its proclaimed goal of "provid[ing] professional support services that add value to

[60] Statement on the 23rd APEC Ministers' Meeting in Honolulu, Hawaii, November 11, 2011, p. 9.

[61] Joint Statement on the 2012 APEC Ministerial Meeting, Vladivostok, Russia, September 5–6, 2012.

the APEC process," the Secretariat's three-year strategic plan of 2010 identifies five "strategic priorities that feed into the Secretariat's role and APEC's vision":

> (1) Providing high quality and consistent advisory, operational, and logistical/technical services to member economies and APEC fora to coordinate and facilitate the business of the forum;
> (2) aligning projects to APEC's strategic goals and maximizing their effectiveness and efficiency, by advising and assisting APEC members in preparing, implementing and improving APEC funded projects and processes;
> (3) enhancing awareness, understanding and support of APEC's role, agenda and achievements through a range of communications, outreach and media activities targeted at key stakeholders;
> (4) providing research and analysis support to fora and members so that policy development is evidence-based, internal capacities are enhanced and implementation of policy measures can be evaluated; and
> (5) managing its internal resources effectively and cost-efficiently as well as strengthening processes to ensure their alignment with business needs.[62]

The Secretariat reports on all administrative, financial and project management issues to APEC's Budget and Management Committee (BMC), which in turn reports to SOM. Since 1999, it works in accordance with an annual operational plan. The Secretariat has no legal department, mainly due to the

[62] *The APEC Secretariat Three-Year Strategic Plan (2011–2013)*, APEC Document No. 2010/SOM1/006, p. 3.

construction and perception of APEC as lacking any binding force. Most legal work, such as employment-related matters, is outsourced to a local law firm; templates of legal documents are used as well.

Although its role "varies across fora, depending on the level of support required by the forum concerned, which is in turn dependent on the level of in-house support available to the forum by way of the existence of its own secretariat,"[63] the Secretariat is generally responsible for representing APEC fora at meetings of the BMC; for providing each forum with guidance on APEC policies and procedures, as well as information on relevant activities of other APEC fora; for producing generic information and promotional material on APEC and serving as media liaison; and for responding to fora requests for assistance. With regard to APEC projects in particular, the Secretariat shares the responsibility with APEC fora, Member Economies and the Project Overseers (POs) designated for each project. Initially, it plays a limited role in the selection of projects for APEC funding, by undertaking a compliance check of preliminary project proposals ("concept notes") and presenting these to the relevant APEC committees for ranking and prioritization. It then determines which proposals could be recommended for funding based on institutional prioritization, and identifies the source of funding. Next, Secretariat staff work with project proponents on developing full project proposals, assess their quality, and make a recommendation for BMC approval.

[63] *Division of Responsibilities between APEC Fora and the Secretariat*, APEC Document No. 2002/SOM1/JF/008, p. 2.

The Secretariat remains involved in the execution and monitoring of approved projects, which are undertaken in accordance with APEC project guidelines (and the APEC Project Guidebook). It administers and allocates related allowable expenses, negotiates and prepares contracts for APEC-funded work and, in accordance with APEC policy guidelines on procurement, may veto a proposed contract when it determines that a conflict of interest might exist or appear to exist. Secretariat staff members may attend all APEC working group meetings (in part to help maintain full documentation and provide guidance on policies and procedures), and are responsible for presenting periodical fora reports to the SOM. They also hold authorities relating to reprogramming or extending projects. Given that it has the best overview of all activities underway in APEC, the Secretariat is expected to ensure that instances of duplication of effort between fora are drawn to the attention of the core committees, and, as noted above, to take a proactive role in drawing the attention of fora to the possibilities for complementary actions and added value in each other's activities. Project Overseers are expected to maintain regular and frequent communication with the relevant Program Director (PD) and Program Executive (PE) working in the Secretariat to ensure effective project administration, and are asked to contact the Secretariat at least once every two months throughout a project's duration.[64]

[64] *Guidebook on APEC Projects* (7th edn.), Articles 2.1 and 2.10; 2008 APEC Secretariat Report on *APEC Developments*, APEC Document No. 2008/SMEWG26/038, p. 4.

A significant contribution of the Secretariat as APEC's central administrative organ has been its effort to harmonize practices across APEC fora and Member Economies. With the oversight and approval of related APEC bodies, the Secretariat has written and published an extensive set of detailed policies and procedures relating to APEC's processes and products. These include the APEC Project Guidebook; Guidelines for Lead Shepherds and Chairs of Working Groups and Task Forces; Guidelines for Hosting APEC Meetings; APEC Website Guidelines; Guidelines on Managing Cooperation with Non-Members; and Guidelines on Division of Responsibilities Between APEC Fora and the Secretariat. The Secretariat further promotes consistency and uniformity among APEC fora by offering presentation modules and document templates, and through its Publication Guidelines and Guidelines on Using the APEC Logo, as well as its intellectual property policy.

Throughout each year, the Secretariat further assists the hosting Member Economy in preparing meetings. It coordinates their execution and produces summary records (the secretarial work for ministerial working meetings and their supporting groups, however, is mainly carried out by government agencies of Member Economies). As the collective memory for APEC, the Secretariat moreover archives photos as well as all documents and presentations tabled at APEC events. It also operates the APEC Library, maintains information on all APEC contact points, and regularly updates a calendar of APEC events that is publicly available on APEC's website.

The prime communication tool within the Secretariat and in its contact with Member Economies and APEC fora is email. Such contact is also maintained through the APEC database system, for which APEC community members may receive a username and password which allow them access to restricted documents and to intra-APEC officials' communications. English is the working language of the Secretariat; APEC Members or fora may translate APEC publications into their own languages at their own expense, and pending Secretariat approval of any translation.

III.ii Organizational structure

Headed by an Executive Director appointed for a fixed term of three years, the Secretariat has an organizational structure characterized by a fairly flat hierarchy. The majority of its professional staff is composed of approximately twenty Program Directors, who are responsible for the "direct and regular communications ... between the APEC Secretariat and APEC Members, Shepherds of Work Projects and Heads and other APEC committees and groups," as mandated by the Bangkok Declaration.[65] These generalists, seconded from Member Economies' foreign or trade ministries on two- to three-year postings, are each assigned usually to three or four APEC issue areas, for which they provide support and coordination. Specifically, they serve as secretaries to APEC committees and sub-fora, assisting these with general inquiries and administration; offering guidance on the development of project proposals; advising on APEC project guidelines, timelines and tools; coordinating requests to amend or

[65] Bangkok Declaration on APEC, Article A(3).

extend projects; and reviewing and finalizing project reports, including monitoring and completion reports. The Secretariat's publication on *Best Practices Guidelines for APEC Program Directors* serves as a reference point for their work,[66] and they are further supported by locally hired Program Executives.

The Secretariat's Project Management Unit (PMU) provides advisory support for the development and implementation of APEC projects. Established in 2007 with the aim of improving the quality of APEC projects and the coordination of project activities, the PMU attempts to implement a professionalized approach in project management within the Secretariat and the wider APEC community. It provides advice and capacity-building assistance in the design and delivery of projects to both Secretariat staff and Project Overseers, and is responsible, *inter alia*, for instituting policies and processes to improve the overall quality and impact of APEC projects, and for integrating knowledge and experience from a range of areas within the APEC Secretariat. It has also been given the mandate to assess the quality of projects and to make project funding recommendations to APEC's Budget and Management Committee. Headed by a Director, the Unit employs two officers, one of them solely dedicated to assisting Member Economies to develop higher quality projects through providing advice, feedback and guidance on writing project proposals. The Unit is further

[66] See also *Revised Guidelines for Lead Shepherd/Chair and Deputy Lead Shepherd/Chair of APEC Working Groups and SOM Task Forces*, APEC Document No. 2012/SOM1/SCE-COW/004, p. 4.

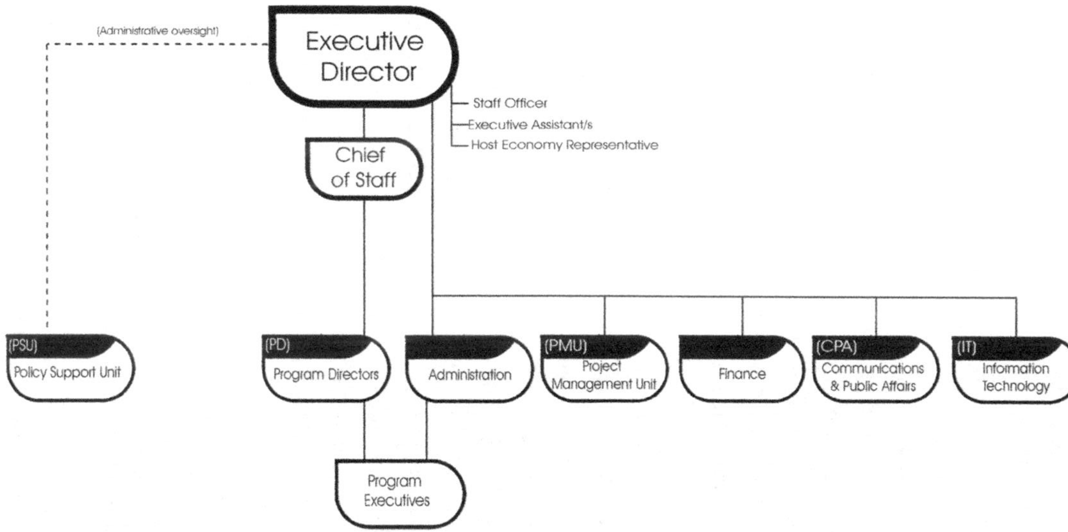

Figure s.2 APEC Secretariat organizational structure

assisted by several of the Program Directors, who serve as its team members as well.

Support for APEC's external communications and outreach efforts is provided by the Secretariat's Communications and Public Affairs Unit (CPAU). The Unit produces general information resources on APEC, among them an annual bulletin and a quarterly newsletter;[67] issues news releases for APEC events; assists APEC fora in drafting articles relating to their work and provides advice on APEC documentation requirements; gives presentations to business, government and student visiting groups, and receives visiting delegations; manages APEC's publishing program; approves project publications for printing, as well as contracts with book agents and distributors for the sale of APEC publications, and monitors sales patterns; maintains the online APEC Projects Database, the APEC library and other records; and provides public affairs and media support to the host economy of any given year. The Unit also operates the APEC website (www.apec.org), along with an APEC Facebook page, a YouTube channel and a Twitter account (https://twitter.com/APEC), which, as of September 2014, had approximately four thousand followers.[68] Headed by a Director, the Unit

[67] According to the Secretariat, its quarterly e-newsletter is sent to a subscription database of just over two thousand journalists, business people, government officials and academics, and more than twice this number access the e-newsletter directly through the APEC website.

[68] The Unit also released a mobile version of the APEC website for smartphones, as well as an APEC Glossary mobile application that serves as a reference tool for looking up unfamiliar terms related to APEC's work.

employs a Media Manager, an Information Manager, a Publishing and Corporate Affairs Manager, a Web Manager and a Communications and Outreach Officer.

An Information Technology Unit is responsible for the architecture, hardware, software and networking of APEC's computers and communication systems. Headed by a Director, the Unit further hosts an IT Manager, a Portal Manager and an IT Administrator, all locally recruited. Currently focusing on enabling data sharing as well as facilitation of corporate learning and knowledge management within the wider APEC community, the Unit supports the APEC Information Management Portal (IMP), the APEC Collaboration System (ACS), the Meeting Document Database (MDDB), the Project Data Base (PDB) and other internal IT systems.

A Finance Unit, headed by a Director, manages the financial systems of the Secretariat in line with established policies, guidelines and objectives approved by APEC's Budget and Management Committee. It administers day-to-day payments under APEC's Administrative Account, as well as project disbursements under the Operational Account, the Trade and Investment Liberalization and Facilitation (TILF) Special Account, the APEC Support Fund and other *ad hoc* arrangements under designated funds. Moreover, it advises Program Directors, APEC fora and Project Overseers on the interpretation and application of APEC financial guidelines, as well as the cost control of projects. Employing an Accountant, a Deputy Accountant and three Assistant Accountants, the Unit also prepares, on an annual basis, a rolling three-year budget proposal for APEC.

The Administration Unit is responsible for the Secretariat's general day-to-day operations as well as human resource management, including both recruitment and development of staff. It is also responsible for property maintenance and the meeting facilities at the APEC Secretariat. The Unit is headed by a Director, who is assisted by a Program Executive, and, in addition, employs a Manager (Administration) and an Office Assistant.

The Secretariat's Chief of Staff is in charge of assisting the Executive Director with overseeing the operational work of the Secretariat, in particular by liaising with and helping to extend the work of the Program Directors. The post replaced the position of Chief Operating Officer, introduced in 2007 to replace the position of Deputy Executive Director, which, until then, was held on an annually rotating basis by an official from the Member Economy that had been designated to host the following year's annual APEC Summit.

A Staff Officer assists the Executive Director in all coordination matters, providing the latter with policy inputs to facilitate his or her decision-making. Core responsibilities attached to this locally recruited position include assisting and advising the Executive Office on day-to-day management and planning issues; drafting and arranging internal meeting agendas; drafting and compiling the Executive Director's reports to Ministerial and Senior Officials' meetings, including gathering policy inputs from Program Directors; and coordinating and collaborating with the Host Economy Representative – a position reserved annually for the next APEC host – on substantive and logistical hosting matters.

The Policy Support Unit (PSU) is APEC's research, policy advice and analysis arm. It produces reports and statistics on issues relating to APEC's mission and initiatives, and assists in designing and implementing capacity-building programs for APEC's trade, investment, economic and technical cooperation agenda. It is meant, chiefly, to undertake analytical work or to otherwise outsource research for consideration by APEC committees; prepare policy dialogue papers for APEC committees; design and implement capacity-building programs; evaluate progress in the implementation of policy measures; and identify high-level policy principles and best practices. The Unit regularly collaborates with external researchers and with international organizations such as the World Bank, the World Trade Organization (WTO), the Asian Development Bank and the Organisation for Economic Co-operation and Development (OECD). Its core clients are APEC's SOM, Committee on Trade and Investment and Economic Committee, yet it serves other APEC fora as well. Headed by a Director, it employs a policy advisor, five analysts, two researchers and an administrative executive: these are nationals of Member Economies, hired according to merit (with no applicable quota system in terms of nationality), at internationally competitive rates for fixed terms, under professional employment contracts.

Remarkably, while the Policy Support Unit is identified as part of APEC's architecture, it is not a wholly integral part of the Secretariat; rather, it is managed under separate Governance Arrangements, and funded by voluntary contributions. APEC's Executive Director exercises only administrative oversight over the PSU, with management of its workload, activities, staff and budget entrusted to its Director, and its annual work program set and approved by a designated Board.[69] Furthermore, the Unit has its own internal policies regarding procurement and human resource management, submits an independent annual report to SOM, and relies on administrative assistance of the Secretariat in accordance with an agreement signed between the two. This peculiar institutional design owes to the fact that, initially, only a small number of Member Economies showed willingness to contribute to establishing and funding the PSU, and to the interest in assuring that its research is independent and objective.[70] Observing that the PSU "continues to be a valuable and integral part of APEC," APEC Ministers agreed in 2011 to "continue to explore [its] functional integration . . . into the APEC Secretariat, recognizing that it must maintain a degree of autonomy in its governance to maintain its professional integrity."[71] A review of the operation of the Unit, upon

[69] APEC PSU Governance Arrangements, Clauses 12, 13, 14, 17, 38 and 39. The PSU Director is to report regularly to the Executive Director of the Secretariat, and, while he/she is accountable to the Board for his/her performance in carrying out the work program, he/she is accountable to the Executive Director of the Secretariat on administrative and day-to-day issues.

[70] Until the establishment of the PSU in 2008, APEC had no significant analytical capacity within it, but relied instead on the Pacific Economic Cooperation Council (PECC) and national APEC Study Centres. The PSU was finally established, despite the reluctance of some Member Economies, as well as previous recommendations by a 1996 Task Force on Management Issues that the Secretariat should *not* develop a comprehensive research and analysis section of its own.

[71] Statement on the 23rd APEC Ministers Meeting in Honolulu, Hawaii, November 11, 2011, p. 9.

which a decision will be made whether to extend its mandate or dissolve it, was due to be undertaken in 2013.

Alongside the Secretariat operates the United States-funded APEC Technical Assistance and Training Facility (TATF), which works to help strengthen APEC operations by providing training and technical assistance to the Secretariat and to APEC Member Economies, and by supporting the design and implementation of APEC projects. In helping the Secretariat become an increasingly customer-driven institution, it has thus far contributed, *inter alia*, to improving APEC's IT infrastructure (for example, upgrading the project database), digitizing APEC products and structuring the strategic planning processes in APEC sub-fora. The APEC TAFT is not an official part of the Secretariat, and its staff members – five in Singapore and three in Washington, all working under a Chief of Party – are paid for their services by the United States Department of State and the United States Agency for International Development (USAID). The United States has recently indicated that it is willing to extend the TATF term beyond its current period of four and a half years.

III.iii The Executive Director

The position of APEC's Executive Director was originally held on an annually rotating basis by an officer of ambassadorial rank from the Member Economy that hosted the annual APEC Summit (usually after serving for the previous year as Deputy Executive Director). In 2007, however, a Leaders' Meeting decision provided that, from 2010 onwards, Executive Directors would be appointed for a three-year term of office, with the position open to professional candidates from all Member Economies. This, too, was part of the effort to strengthen the Secretariat's capabilities, as it became widely acknowledged at the time that the short tenures of Executive Directors and their Deputies made them ill-suited to lead any significant processes and initiatives, let alone develop any deep attachment to the regional process.[72]

The 1992 Bangkok Declaration, which established the office of the Executive Director as one of the three elements composing the APEC Secretariat (the other two being the professional and support staff), did not stipulate the role and responsibilities of the Executive Director. The United States had assigned a senior diplomat to the position of APEC's first Executive Director, whose successors also held the title of Ambassador. The Executive Director traditionally participates in SOM and attends the APEC Leaders' meetings, focusing his or her efforts toward "advanc[ing] APEC's agenda by effectively executing APEC's work programmes as mandated by Leaders and Ministers who meet annually."[73] As head of the Secretariat, he or she chairs weekly management meetings and, since 1999, submits to the APEC Ministerial Meeting each year a report that is his or her "annual performance accountability statement." The Executive Director travels often to Member Economies for purposes of outreach and to deliver speeches, gives interviews to the international media, and publishes

[72] See also J. Ravenhill, *APEC and the Construction of Pacific Rim Regionalism* (Cambridge University Press, 2001), p. 131.

[73] See "Executive Director" on APEC's official website (available at www.apec.org/About-Us/APEC-Secretariat/Executive-Director.aspx).

op-eds in various newspapers of Member Economies. In the past, the Executive Director was assisted by a locally recruited Executive Assistant and by one Program Director, who served as a Special Assistant to the Executive Director; as described above, however, this role now belongs to the Staff Officer. A suggestion by APEC's first Executive Director that the top Secretariat position be elevated to a Director General's post has yet to be acted upon by the Member Economies.

III.iv *Staff*

The APEC Secretariat has two categories of staff: the first is Professional Staff Members (PSMs), who are seconded from governments of Member Economies for two- or three-year terms; and the second is Support Staff Members (SSMs), employed through fixed-term contracts and fulfilling specialist and support functions, who are recruited in Singapore by an open competitive process, with no overarching requirement for geographic distribution. While the salaries and accommodation of nearly all Professional Staff Members are paid directly by their governments, the salaries of the locally hired Chief of Staff and Support Staff Members are paid by the Secretariat, based on local salaries for similar positions. The latter may also receive annual bonuses for outstanding performance upon the decision of a Personnel Board, and the Secretariat further makes contributions in their name to the Central Provident Fund (CPF) scheme in Singapore, a defined contribution pension scheme. The positions of receptionist, cleaners and security staff at the Secretariat are outsourced.

APEC's first Executive Director, Mr. William Bodde, Jr., asked Member Economies "to send me workers, not diplomats!," and later wrote that "[t]his brought a chuckle, but they got the message."[74] Member Economies are expected to consult with the Executive Director on the skills and timing of seconding professional staff to the Secretariat, yet the final say on these matters remains their own, and it is not uncommon that Program Directors do not possess technical expertise in the particular subject areas of the fora to which they are assigned. More often than not, they see themselves as representing the Member Economy from which they are seconded as opposed to the organization. Recommendations that the Secretariat be given permanent staff have thus far been ignored, despite the fact that (or perhaps precisely because) "[t]he constant rotation of officials makes the development of a sense of organizational identity, institutional modus operandi, or institutional memory difficult."[75] Openings for Support Staff positions are advertised to the general public on APEC's website and other Internet job search websites, as well as in the Singaporean press; for the positions of managers or specialists, Member Economies are asked to advertise the positions as well.

[74] W. Bodde, Jr., *View from the 19th Floor: Reflections of the First APEC Executive Director* (Singapore: Institute of Southeast Asian Studies, 1994), p. 10.

[75] I. Yamazawa, P. Drysdale and H. Soesastro, "Summary and Recommendations," in I. Yamazawa (ed.), *Asia Pacific Economic Cooperation: Challenges and Tasks for the Twenty-First Century* (Florence, KY: Routledge, 2000), pp. 303 and 315.

The Secretariat also accepts two interns per year through the APEC Secretariat Internship Framework (ASIF), open since 2005 to students who are nationals or permanent residents of APEC Member Economies. Candidates "must possess an undergraduate degree and may be enrolled, or planning to enroll, in a full-time graduate study program," and would ideally have "a strong interest in the work of international organizations, and, in particular, international affairs and international economics."[76] Depending on the needs of the Secretariat for the year, interns could be placed in any one of its units or take part in project/research work. They are provided by the Secretariat with a small allowance.

New staff members receive focused briefings and training sessions on their work, and professional staff are also assigned a mentor for three months, to help them settle into their position.[77] An annual training program is conducted for all Secretariat staff, in accordance with the APEC Guidelines on Manpower Development; the Secretariat's three-year strategic plan of 2011 attaches much importance to developing the Secretariat's human capital in order to improve the Secretariat's performance. In 2008, the Secretariat adopted four "CORE" values – Community, Open, Respect and Excellence – that are meant to serve as a foundation on which staff members work and conduct themselves, together with staff rules and

[76] See "Internship" on APEC's official website (available at www.apec.org/About-Us/APEC-Secretariat/Internship.aspx).

[77] Support for professional staff in terms of relocation to Singapore and settling in there is mostly offered through the embassy of the seconding Member Economy, not by the Secretariat.

Table s.3 *The distribution of APEC Secretariat staff from different Member Economies (July 2012)*

Australia	3
Canada	2
Chile	1
China	2
Hong Kong, China	1
Indonesia	3
Japan	2
Korea	2
Malaysia	2
Mexico	2
New Zealand	1
Peru	2
Philippines	4
Russia	2
Singapore	25
Chinese Taipei	1
Thailand	1
US	4
Vietnam	1

regulations of conduct that are found in the Secretariat's staff manual.[78] Performance appraisal takes place on a biannual basis for all staff members, who are assessed on key performance indicators set out by their immediate supervisors.

Professional Staff Members (apart from those of Singaporean nationality or permanent residency) enjoy privileges and immunities in accordance with an agreement between the Government of Singapore and the Secretariat,

[78] The staff manual is not publicly available, "since it was not written by lawyers," in the words of a Secretariat official.

and the Singaporean Presidential Declaration of February 1993 establishing the APEC Secretariat under Singapore law.

III.v Budget

The 1992 Bangkok Declaration stipulated that the Secretariat "will, under the direction of the APEC SOM, establish and administer a fund to cover APEC administrative and operational costs."[79] Control of the APEC Administrative Account indeed lies mostly with the Secretariat, while management of the other accounts comprising the APEC Central Fund – the Operational Account, the Trade and Investment Liberalization and Facilitation Special Account, and the APEC Support Fund Account – is carried out by APEC's Budget and Management Committee (BMC). The latter instructs the Secretariat on how to administer payments and allocations derived from these accounts, and lays out the guidelines and procedures for doing so.

Each year, the Secretariat's Finance Unit prepares a rolling three-year budget for the BMC's consideration. The budget for the succeeding year requires the approval of the BMC, which then submits it for approval by APEC Senior Officials and, subsequently, by the APEC Ministerial Meeting. Unlike the other APEC accounts, the budget for the Administrative Account is quoted (since 2011) in Singapore dollars rather than United States dollars. The APEC accounts are audited annually by an external auditor, with the Secretariat

[79] Bangkok Declaration on APEC, Article B(5).

Table s.4 *APEC Administrative Account budget 2005–2013 (in US dollars/Singapore dollars millions)*

2005	US$ 3.3
2006	US$ 2.3
2007	US$ 2.9
2008	US$ 3.5
2009	US$ 3.1
2010	US$ 3.9
2011	S$ 6.2
2012	S$ 6.1
2013	S$ 5.6[a]

Note

[a] The reduction as compared to the budget in 2012 is mainly due to the lower travel costs for Secretariat officials in view of the APEC hosting location for 2013, which was close to Singapore.

responsible for preparing and presenting financial statements in accordance with the Singapore Financial Reporting Standards.

IV The Organization of American States (OAS) General Secretariat

Serving the world's oldest regional organization, the General Secretariat of the Organization of American States (OAS) is a complex structure endowed with a long institutional memory. Its roots date back to the founding, in 1890, of the International Union of American Republics, whose permanent offices in Washington were later named the "Pan American Union";[80]

[80] The name "Pan American Union" was adopted in the Fourth International Conference of American States (1910); prior to that, the

these continued to serve the inter-American system through a reorganization that led to the establishment in 1948 of the OAS and, following a Charter amendment in 1967, became known as the General Secretariat of the new organization.[81]

Carrying out myriad functions, as detailed below, the General Secretariat works under a mandate to support and carry out the actions and policies adopted by the General Assembly of the OAS, and to implement the decisions of its Permanent Council. The General Assembly is the Organization's supreme organ, which convenes annually in the

permanent offices of the International Union of American Republics were named the Commercial Bureau of the American Republics (1890–1902), and later the International Bureau of the American Republics (1902–1910). From 1890 to 1910, the offices effectively operated as a branch of, and were based in, the US Department of State. See O. C. Stoetzer, *The Organization of American States: An Introduction* (New York: Frederick A. Praeger, 1965), pp. 39–40.

[81] Latin American States "wanted to eradicate any romantic notion that might be linked to the name" Pan American Union and its idealistic ring, and to "prevent any possible political misunderstanding connected" with it: see O. C. Stoetzer, *The Organization of American States* (Westport, CT: Praeger Publishers, 2nd edn., 1993), pp. 3–4, 67 and 70–73. For a detailed history of the institutional evolution of pan-Americanism, see also C. M. Shaw, *Cooperation, Conflict, and Consensus in the Organization of American States* (New York: Palgrave Macmillan, 2004), pp. 39–58; J. L. Kunz, "The Bogota Charter of the Organization of American States," 42 *American Journal of International Law* 568 (1948); M. Herz, *Organization of American States (OAS): Global Governance Away From the Media* (Florence, KY: Routledge, 2011); F. V. Garcia-Amador, *The Inter-American System: Treaties, Conventions and Other Documents*, vol. I, Part I (New York: Oceana Publications, 1983); A. Van Wynen Thomas and A. J. Thomas, Jr., *The Organization of American States* (Dallas: Southern Methodist University Press, 1963), pp. 128–131.

territory of one of the Member States in order to "decide on the general action and policy of the Organization, determine the structure and functions of its organs, and consider any matter relating to friendly relations among the American States."[82] It is further empowered, *inter alia*, to "approve the program budget of the Organization and determine the quotas of the Member States," as well as "adopt general standards to govern the operations of the General Secretariat."[83] The Permanent Council, comprising permanent representatives of ambassadorial rank from each Member State, meets twice monthly (or more frequently if so decided) at the Washington headquarters of the Organization and directs the ongoing actions of the OAS. It is responsible, *inter alia*, for daily administrative policy and for supervising the work of the General Secretariat. To this end, it is authorized to "adopt provisions of a regulatory nature that enable the General Secretariat to carry out its administrative functions" when the General Assembly is not in session.[84]

IV.i *Role and functions*

The OAS Charter – an international treaty embodying the obligations of the Organization's thirty-five Western hemisphere Member States to "achieve an order of peace and

[82] OAS Charter, Article 54(a). The General Assembly is usually made up of the foreign ministers of Member States or, in their place, their permanent representatives to the Organization.

[83] OAS Charter, Articles 54(e) and 54(g).

[84] OAS Charter, Article 91(b).

justice, to promote their solidarity, to strengthen their collaboration, and to defend their sovereignty, their territorial integrity, and their independence"[85] – refers to the General Secretariat as the "central and permanent organ" of the Organization.[86] As such, it is responsible for performing "the functions assigned to it in the Charter, in other inter-American treaties and agreements, and by the General Assembly" of the OAS, and for carrying out "the duties entrusted to it" by the Organization's superior political organs.[87] These functions and duties are far from merely administrative; indeed, the central responsibility of the General Secretariat is to "promote economic, social, juridical, educational, scientific, and cultural relations among all the Member States of the Organization, with special emphasis on

[85] OAS Charter, Article 1. All countries of North, Central and South America have signed the OAS Charter and are members of the Organization; Cuba was a suspended member between the years 1962–2009, and has not yet been restored as a full participating member as not all conditions enumerated in the relevant OAS General Assembly Resolution have been satisfied. The Charter, with its 22 chapters and 146 articles, is divided into three distinct parts: Part One, dealing with the Organization's nature, purposes and principles, and the fundamental rights and duties of its Member States; Part Two, detailing the structure of the Organization and the mandate of each of its organs; and Part Three, enshrining the supremacy of the UN and containing other miscellaneous provisions. The original 1948 Charter has been modified, via Protocols of Amendment, on four occasions: Buenos Aires, 1967; Cartagena de Indias, 1985; Washington, 1992; and Managua, 1993. For a detailed summary on the general structure of the OAS, see W. M. Berenson, *The Structure of the Organization of American States: A Summary* (2002), available at the General Secretariat.

[86] OAS Charter, Article 107.

[87] OAS Charter, Article 107.

cooperation for the elimination of extreme poverty."[88] In addition to implementing the programs and policies of the OAS as directed by the General Assembly and the Permanent Council, the General Secretariat performs the administrative and clerical functions enumerated in the Charter as well. These include transmitting to the Member States notice of the convocation of various OAS meetings; giving advice to other organs in the preparation of agenda and rules of procedure; serving as custodian of the documents and archives, and as the depository and archive of inter-American treaties and agreements; providing "adequate secretariat services" for the General Assembly and other organs and meetings of the Organization; and preparing the proposed program budget of the Organization.[89] The General Secretariat is also in charge of establishing cooperative relations with intergovernmental organizations that are established by multilateral agreements and have specific functions with respect to technical matters of common interest to the American States ("Specialized Organizations"), as well as with other national and international organizations. In light of developments unforeseen by the framers of the Charter, the General Secretariat moreover serves various ministerial meetings of the Americas; and implements mandates that are delegated to it by the Heads of

[88] OAS Charter, Article 111.

[89] OAS Charter, Article 112, and the General Standards, Article 5. See also, for example, Rules of Procedure of the General Assembly (Part IV), and the detailed list of functions of the General Secretariat in the Rules of Procedure of the Permanent Council (Part X). The General Secretariat also provides administrative support to certain specialized organizations of the OAS.

State and Government of the Western Hemisphere through the declarations and plans of action of the Summits of the Americas (for which it serves as secretariat as well).[90]

Such a broad mission and multiple mandates have meant for the General Secretariat a branched organizational structure comprising numerous departments, divisions and sections, which correspond to its many diverse roles.[91] Employing at present approximately 665 staff members, the General Secretariat works under considerable financial strain to promote over 1,500 mandates, "addressing nearly every issue facing the nations of the hemisphere."[92] While it has limited capacity in controlling the agenda of the OAS, it is very much relied upon for its execution.

The operations of the General Secretariat are governed by several legal instruments: the OAS Charter;

[90] On the relationship between the OAS and the Summits of the Americas, see R. L. Rosenberg, "The OAS and the Summits of the Americas: Coexistence, or Integration of Forces for Multilateralism?," 43 *Latin American Politics and Society* 80–101 (2001).

[91] One author suggested that designing a General Secretariat originally composed of a great number of units "whose norms were often drafted in vague terms and which overlapped in their functions and were restricted in their activities" was also motivated by the fear of Member States of vesting too much authority in the General Secretariat: see O. C. Stoetzer, *The Organization of American States* (Westport, CT: Praeger Publishers, 2nd edn., 1993), p. 78.

[92] See *Multilateralism in the Americas: Let's Start by Fixing the OAS*, a Report to the Committee on Foreign Relations of the United States Senate, 111th Congress, Second Session, January 26, 2010, p. 4; the Report (like the OAS Board of External Auditors) urged a comprehensive review of all mandates and prioritization among competing goals in the face of limited resources.

General Standards to Govern the Operations of the General Secretariat, adopted by the General Assembly in 1973 and amended from time to time since then; executive orders, administrative memoranda, and directives, all from the desk of the Secretary General; staff rules; budgetary and financial rules; and other administrative instruments and regulations, such as personnel circulars issued by the Department of Human Resources. These are all made available on the OAS website, and staff members of the General Secretariat are obligated to remain informed of and comply with them.

Containing ten chapters and over 140 articles, the General Standards to Govern the Operations of the General Secretariat incorporate the relevant provisions of the OAS Charter and expand on them. Accordingly, they detail the functions of the General Secretariat and of the Secretary General, the procedures of recruiting personnel and the terms of employment, and the requirements for preparing, executing and supervising the program budget. The Permanent Council is empowered to "[w]atch over the observance of the standards ... and, when the General Assembly is not in session, adopt provisions of a regulatory nature that enable the General Secretariat to carry out its administrative functions."[93] General Standards relating to personnel matters, however, may be amended only by the General Assembly.[94]

[93] OAS Charter, Article 91(b).

[94] General Standards, Article 70. Nonetheless, on several occasions, the General Assembly has expressly authorized the Permanent Council to amend certain chapters or adopt new standards to cover issues of concern.

The General Standards serve, in turn, as a foundation for the more specific and elaborate regulatory instruments mentioned above.

Other relevant instruments include the General Secretariat's Code of Ethics, which summarizes "in concise, non-legalistic words the general ethical principles contained in our Internal Law that most commonly arise . . . in daily activities"; and its Access to Information Policy, which recognizes that "access to information is a fundamental human right and an essential condition for all democratic societies," and follows the standards of other multilateral organizations in "reaffirming [the General Secretariat's] commitment to transparency in its operations while striking an appropriate balance with its obligation to respect privacy in its relations with the Member States of the Organization of American States (OAS), staff, independent contractors, and others."[95] A Projects Evaluation Committee, chaired by the Secretary General, regularly evaluates "the appropriateness and importance of projects under way and of proposed projects submitted for execution using funds administered by the [General Secretariat]," as a mechanism for overall planning, control and internal control.[96] As required by the General Standards, the General Secretariat further maintains a database of its current mandates that includes information on the origin of the mandate, its program area and the organ responsible for its execution.[97]

[95] Executive Order No. 12-02 (May 3, 2012), (para. 1).

[96] Executive Order No. 05-11 Rev.1 (January 12, 2006).

[97] General Standards, Article 88; the database is meant to facilitate the formulation of the program budget proposals by the General Secretariat.

Communication within the General Secretariat is carried out mainly through email. Although there are four official working languages of the OAS – Spanish, English, Portuguese and French – most of the documents produced by the General Secretariat are available in English and Spanish alone, due to budgetary constraints. The exception lies with documents prepared for the General Assembly and the Permanent Council, which are made available in all official languages. A Board of Publications exercises general jurisdiction over all publications produced by the General Secretariat, and is in charge of overseeing and coordinating the implementation of the general publications policy.

The OAS website (www.oas.org), maintained by the Press and Communications Department within the Secretariat for External Relations, is a central tool of the General Secretariat for disseminating information on the Organization and its operations. It contains a wealth of data that is updated regularly, including a guide to the OAS missions and structure, a calendar of events, important documents and links to other reference materials. An online Media Center makes available to the public live webcasts of meetings of various OAS fora, including the General Assembly and the Permanent Council. Press releases, speeches by OAS officials, periodic newsletters of the Secretariats, and other OAS brochures and publications (among them an annual review of the Organization and its work) are uploaded to the Media Center as well. The General Secretariat keeps very active in the Internet-based social media: it maintains an OAS page on Facebook (www.facebook.com/OASofficial), and a Twitter account (http://twitter.com/oas_official) that has over 13,200 followers as of September 2014; and, moreover, shares pictures and video clips of OAS activities on Flickr (www.flickr.com/photos/oasoea) and Vimeo (http://vimeo.com/oastv), respectively.

IV.ii Organizational structure

Reforms to the Organization's machinery and objectives have, over the years, inevitably resulted in corresponding adjustments to the structure of the General Secretariat. At times, however, the General Secretariat itself was the focus of such reforms. This was the case, for example, when in 1968 an *ad hoc* committee was charged with advising on reforms to the public administration and finance of the OAS; its recommendations led to a broad restructuring of the entire General Secretariat.[98] The year 2004 saw yet another major reorganization of the General Secretariat, following the findings of a study of its operations undertaken by a private consulting firm.[99] In its current orientation, whose complexity can be appreciated by examining Figure S.3, the General Secretariat comprises six Secretariats (formerly known as "sub-Secretariats"), each of which executes numerous programs and each of which is headed by a Secretary. The Secretaries are appointed by the Secretary General as a position of trust;

[98] C. R. Thomas, *The OAS in Its 50th Year: Overview of Regional Commitment* (Washington, DC: OAS General Secretariat, 1998), p. 61.

[99] See the 2003 Deloitte and Touche Management Study of the Operations of the General Secretariat of the OAS; its operative result was Executive Order No. 04-01 (September 2004).

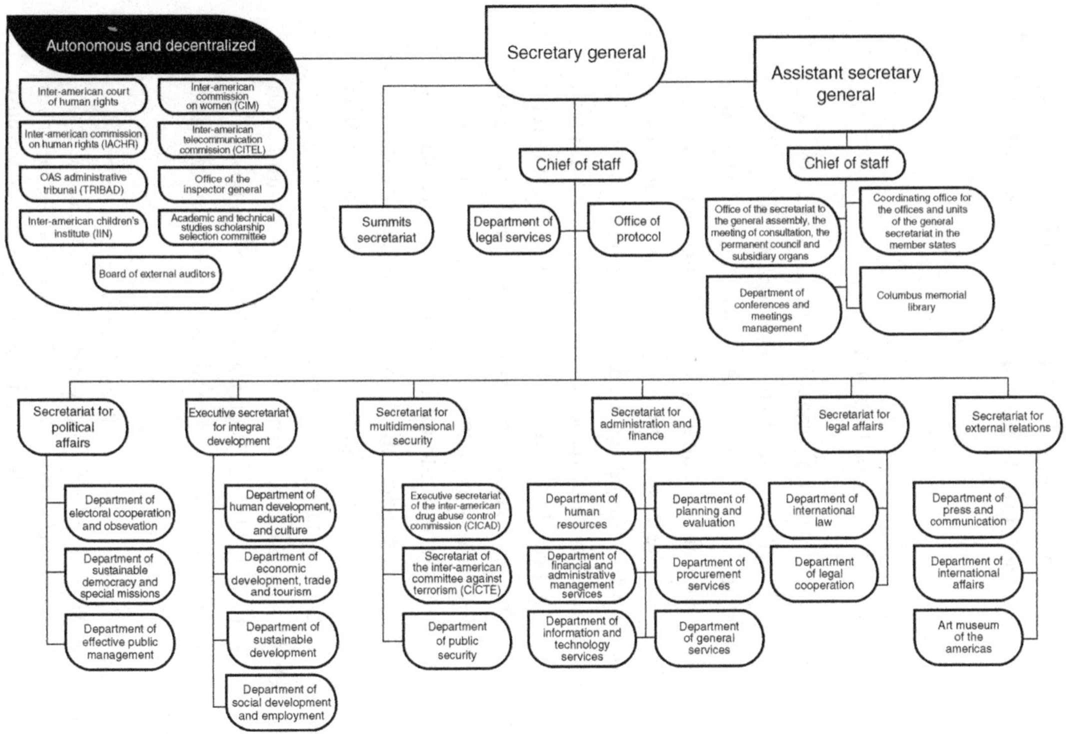

Figure s.3 OAS General Secretariat organizational structure

candidates may either come from within the ranks of the General Secretariat or be hired externally. Accordingly, the hierarchy of the dependencies of the General Secretariat, in descending order, is as follows: the Secretary General; the Assistant Secretary General; the Chief of Staff of the Secretary General; the six Secretaries; the Chief of Staff of the Assistant Secretary General; the department directors; the office directors; and the section chiefs.[100]

The Secretariat for Political Affairs (SPA) aims to help strengthen political processes in the Member States, in particular to support democracy as the best option for ensuring peace, security and development. It focuses on strengthening the role of the OAS as the primary political forum in the inter-American system and on actively helping to maintain democracy in the Member States.[101] In addition to the Executive Office of the Secretary for Political Affairs, whose structure is divided principally between an Administrative Support Section and a Democracy Program Unit, the SPA is composed of three dependencies: the Department for Electoral Cooperation and Observation, the Department of Democratic Sustainability and Special Missions, and the Department for Effective Public Management.

The Secretariat for Multidimensional Security (SMS) was created in 2005 to reflect the objectives and principles

[100] Executive Order No. 08-01 Rev. 5 (April 2012) ("Structure of the General Secretariat"), Article 1(b); Executive Order No. 11-01 (November 2011) placed the Chief of Staff ahead of the six Secretaries.

[101] The description of the Secretariats borrows from the OAS website (see www.oas.org/en/about/organizational_list.asp), which contains further information on the work of the various departments.

embodied in the "Declaration on Security in the Americas," adopted by the Member States during the OAS Special Conference on Security in 2003. It works to coordinate cooperation among the Member States to fight threats to national and citizen security, and to mitigate the harmful effects of such threats on the health and well-being of citizens and societies in the Member States. The Secretariat further aims to prevent the abuse of drugs, crime and violence; and engages for that purpose in capacity-building, legal and legislative assistance, and the promotion of health and education. The Executive Office of the Secretary for Multidimensional Security hosts an Administrative Support Section and an Inter-American Defense Board Liaison Section, and the Secretariat further includes a Department for Public Security and two sub-secretariats: one is the Executive Secretariat of the Inter-American Drug Abuse Control Commission (CICAD), and the other is the Secretariat of the Inter-American Committee against Terrorism (CICTE), both of which are at the department level.

The Executive Secretariat for Integral Development[102] assists the Member States with their efforts to reduce

[102] The name "Executive Secretariat," rather than "Secretariat," as the other five Secretariats are referred to, owes to specific language of the OAS Charter (Articles 98 and 117). There are no significant differences between the Secretariats and the Executive Secretariat, apart from the fact that the Executive Secretary of the Executive Secretariat for Integral Development can only be appointed by the Secretary General with the approval of the Inter-American Council for Integral Development, while the appointment of the other Secretaries by the Secretary General requires no further approval by the political bodies.

poverty and achieve greater economic and social development. It does this by implementing programs, projects and activities in partnership, and by supporting dialogue at the highest levels to define policies and set priorities in nine areas of action: social development and the creation of productive employment; education; economic diversification and integration; trade liberalization and market access; scientific development and exchange and transfer of technology; strengthening of democratic institutions; sustainable development of tourism; sustainable development and environment; and culture. Apart from an Administrative Support Section, the Executive Office of the Executive Secretary for Integral Development also contains the Secretariat of the Inter-American Committee on Ports (CIP), and a Policies and Programs Section. Additionally, four departments operate under the Executive Secretary: the Department of Human Development, Education, and Culture; the Department of Economic Development, Trade, and Tourism; the Department of Sustainable Development; and the Department of Social Development and Employment. These, in turn, contain topical sections and offices.

The Secretariat for External Relations (SER) works to strengthen the OAS institutional image and to publicize its role as the institution for promoting democratic governance, sustainable development, multidimensional security and respect for human rights in the hemisphere. The Executive Office of its Secretary contains an Administrative Support Section, under which there are two operative departments: the Press and Communications Department; and the Department of International Affairs (managing relations with Permanent Observers, other institutions and civil society, and serving as a public liaison). The Secretariat is also in charge of the Art Museum of the Americas, which operates on the campus of the Secretariat's main building and draws on the arts to showcase a constructive vision of the future of the Americas via local and hemispheric cultural exchange.

The Secretariat for Administration and Finance (SAF) is responsible for providing leadership and guidance on administrative support activities. It comprises the Executive Office of the Secretary for Administration and Finance, and six departments operating under it, each headed by a director: the Department of Human Resources; the Department of Financial and Administrative Management Services; the Department of Information and Technology Services; the Department of Planning and Evaluation; the Department of Procurement; and the Department of General Services (in charge of maintenance, inventory, transportation, mail and security).

The Secretariat for Legal Affairs (SLA) develops, promotes and implements the Inter-American Program for the Development of International Law; provides advisory services concerning international law and the development and codification of inter-American law; supports the follow-up mechanisms for certain inter-American conventions; serves as a depository and source of information on more than 200 international treaties and 6,000 bilateral cooperation agreements; disseminates information on the legal instruments of the OAS and its legal programs; and provides other services related to inter-American legal cooperation.

The Secretariat is composed of the Executive Office of the Secretary for Legal Affairs (containing an Administrative Support Section) and its two dependencies: the Department of International Law (DIL); and the Department of Legal Cooperation (DLC, a technical secretariat for legal cooperation mechanisms).[103] The former currently employs a Director, an assistant to the Director, four attorneys, one to four interns and several external consultants; the latter employs a Director, an assistant to the Director and six attorneys. An additional dependency, the Department of Special Legal Programs (DSLP), was recently dismantled.[104] Apart from its staff members working in the Washington headquarters, the Secretariat for Legal Affairs has staff members in Rio de Janeiro who serve the Inter-American Juridical Committee. In the past, the Secretariat for Legal Affairs also included the Secretariat for the OAS Administrative Tribunal, which now operates autonomously.

The Secretariat for Legal Affairs is not to be confused with the Department of Legal Services (DLS), which operates within the office of the Secretary General and

[103] These were created in 1996 as specialized departments, replacing the old Department of Development and Codification of International Law. The latter was working alongside the Department of General Legal Services, which was placed under the Office of the Secretary General as part of the restructuring. See C. R. Thomas, *The OAS in its 50th Year: Overview of Regional Commitment* (Washington, DC: OAS General Secretariat, 1998), pp. 66–67.

[104] The necessity of the department and its contribution were criticized in the above-mentioned report to the US Senate (see n. 92 above), and this subsequently led to its elimination.

whose Director is the legal advisor to the Secretary General. Reporting to the Chief of Staff of the Secretary General, the DLS attends principally to the operational legal work of the General Secretariat, providing legal advice to the OAS political bodies, to the Secretary General and the General Secretariat as a whole, and to the other organs, agencies and entities of the OAS. Its functions, enumerated in an executive order of the Secretary General, include the interpretation of normative instruments; counseling on administrative, budgetary and personnel matters, internal regulations, and the application of national laws relating to taxation, labor relations and privileges and immunities; and negotiating contracts and treaties, including cooperation and electoral agreements. In addition, the DLS serves as the Secretary General's representative in litigation, arbitration and mediation. Employing a director and five attorneys, in 2010 the DLS received more than 2,250 requests for opinions, issued approximately 3,000 legal opinions (in writing and orally), and provided advisory services at approximately 500 meetings. It moreover maintains its own legal archives. The DLS had relocated several times between the Secretariat for Legal Affairs and the Office of the Secretary General until, for political and professional reasons, it was once again put under the Secretary General's Office in 2005.[105]

[105] Several attempts to put the DLS under the Secretariat for Administration and Finance (traditionally headed by a US national) have thus far failed.

Three buildings in Washington, in close proximity to one another, house the General Secretariat: the Main building (over a hundred years old, where the Permanent Council convenes as well); the General Secretariat building (where the majority of staff members work); and the Administration building (a historical name that no longer corresponds necessarily to the actual occupants of this building).[106] Each of the six Secretariats pays the General Secretariat rent for the space it uses (in addition to telecommunications expenses) out of the budget appropriated to it. Regular working hours at the headquarters are from 9:00 am to 5:30 pm, Monday through Friday, with one hour dedicated for lunch. The Secretary General may make exceptions to this as the needs of service require.

The General Secretariat further maintains offices in a majority of the Member States, the first of which were established in 1954. The offices originally carried out modest representational functions, such as dissemination of information and liaison with national authorities, but significantly expanded their operations in the years that followed – mainly as external instruments for promoting technical cooperation.[107] Budgetary constraints forced the Organization in subsequent years to consider closing these field offices, yet

[106] The OAS headquarters in Washington further comprises the Art Museum of the Americas and the Casita (used as administrative offices for the Museum), as well as the "*Casa del Soldado*" (also known as the "Pink Palace"), a building located a mile away from the headquarters and housing the Inter-American Defense Board.

[107] See O. C. Stoetzer, *The Organization of American States* (Westport, CT: Praeger Publishers, 2nd edn., 1993), pp. 79–81.

most Member States (the Caribbean and Central American countries being most insistent on this issue) decided to retain the offices in their respective countries.[108] Still, the financial situation has led to reduced staffing of the offices of the General Secretariat in the Member States, which greatly limits their effectiveness and capabilities. They nevertheless remain responsible for executing organizational mandates in Member States, and for monitoring projects in direct coordination with local executing agencies and the respective Secretariat or Department at headquarters.

A number of "autonomous and decentralized" organs and institutions of the OAS also maintain close relations with the General Secretariat. These include the Inter-American Human Rights Court, the Inter-American Human Rights Commission, the Six Specialized Organizations that existed prior to 1948 and were incorporated into the Organization under the Charter, and a number of other specialized entities created over the years by the General Assembly. Most of these are staffed by personnel of the General Secretariat that are appointed by the Secretary General, financed under the Organization's annual Regular Fund Program Budget, and subject to the personnel, budgetary and financial rules of the Secretariat.[109] In addition, there are basic cooperation

[108] See C. R. Thomas, *The OAS in its 50th Year: Overview of Regional Commitment* (Washington, DC: OAS General Secretariat, 1998), pp. 76–77.

[109] The Inter-American Court of Human Rights is kind of a hybrid: its Executive Secretary is appointed by the Secretary General but is not a Secretariat Staff Member, and the rest of the staff are appointed by the Court and, similarly, are not General Secretariat staff. Nonetheless, the Court receives most of its financing under the OAS Regular Fund

agreements between the Six Specialized Organizations and the OAS, and, for those Specialized Organizations that rely on financing and staffing from the General Secretariat, there are special provisions in the agreements covering those issues. The Chiefs of Staff of the Secretary General or Assistant Secretary General act as liaisons to these organs and entities.

IV.iii The Secretary General and the Assistant Secretary General

The OAS Charter confers upon the Secretary General the authority to direct the General Secretariat, to serve as its legal representative, and to participate "with voice but without

Budget. The Specialized Organizations and entities which rely on the General Secretariat for staffing and the OAS Regular Fund Budget almost entirely are: the Inter-American Children's Institute in Uruguay; the Inter-American Commission on Women; the Inter-American Telecommunications Commission; the Inter-American Drug Abuse Control Commission; the Administrative Tribunal; the Inter-American Human Rights Commission; the OAS Retirement and Pension Fund Committee; the Inter-American Juridical Committee; the Inter-American Drug Abuse Control Commission; and the Inter-American Committee against Terrorism. The entities that are most autonomous have their own staff, their own financing mechanisms and budget, and their own regulations and rules. They include the Inter-American Defense Board; the Pan American Health Organization, which is also the regional agency of the World Health Organization in the Americas; the Inter-American Institute for Cooperation in Agriculture in Costa Rica; the Inter-American Institute in Mexico City; and the Pan-American Institute of Geography and History in Mexico City.

vote" in all meetings of the Organization.[110] The Secretary General is further empowered to "bring to the attention of the General Assembly or the Permanent Council any matter which in his opinion might threaten the peace and security of the Hemisphere or the development of the Member States,"[111] and holds additional autonomous diplomatic responsibilities that are provided for in other OAS instruments, such as the Inter-American Democratic Charter.[112] Presenting the annual proposed program budget for consideration by the pertinent political organs, and managing the General Secretariat's funds also fall within the mandate of the Secretary General.

The Charter further stipulates that, in accordance with the regulatory and budgetary framework established by

[110] OAS Charter, Articles 109 and 110. The Secretary General serves as the legal representative of the General Secretariat – not of the Organization as a whole.

[111] OAS Charter, Article 110; it is further stipulated that this authority "shall be exercised in accordance with the present Charter." Secretaries General have used it broadly over the years.

[112] According to the Inter-American Democratic Charter, the government of a Member State may request the assistance of the Secretary General or Permanent Council when it "considers that its democratic institutional process or its legitimate exercise of power is at risk" (Article 17); in addition, "the Secretary General or the Permanent Council may, with the consent of the government concerned, arrange for visits or other actions to analyze the situation," and "adopt decisions for the preservation and strengthening of the democratic system" (Article 18). Similarly, General Assembly Resolution 1080 of 1991 instructs the Secretary General to convoke the Permanent Council or the General Assembly in the event of an interruption of democratic governance among the Member States.

the General Assembly, the Secretary General is authorized to "[e]stablish such offices of the General Secretariat as are necessary to accomplish its purposes," as well as "[d]etermine the number of officers and employees of the General Secretariat, appoint them, regulate their powers and duties, and fix their remuneration."[113] Secretaries General have frequently utilized this power and the wide discretion associated with it to reorganize the General Secretariat or influence the division of labor within it, at times motivated not only by professional considerations, but also by political patronage or the desire to grant personal favors.[114] They have also made wide usage of their ability to appoint advisors as trust personnel, whose employment may last as long as the Secretary General is in office. It is under this authority that the Secretariat Staff Rules, and other regulatory provisions regarding the formulation and execution of the budget, have been issued.

The Secretary General is elected by the General Assembly, to whom he or she is responsible for the proper

[113] OAS Charter, Article 113; see also General Standards, Article 12. According to Article 4 of the General Standards, however, "The Secretary General must obtain the express approval of the General Assembly to establish new secretaries or other dependencies with similar attributes and of similar importance, or to abolish already existing ones."

[114] Organizational changes in the General Secretariat are implemented through executive orders, administrative memoranda and directives of the Secretary General. It is not uncommon that the General Assembly interferes with this authority of the Secretary General by determining itself the powers and duties of a unit within the General Secretariat, in resolutions which assign specific units various tasks.

fulfillment of the obligations and functions of the General Secretariat.[115] The term of office is five years, and the Secretary General may not be reelected more than once (prior to the 1967 amendment to the Charter, the Secretary General was elected by the Permanent Council for a ten-year period and could not be reelected).[116] The General Assembly may also remove the Secretary General from office (as well as the Assistant Secretary General, or both) "whenever the proper functioning of the Organization so demands,"[117] by a two-thirds vote of the Member States. In the event that the office of Secretary General becomes vacant, the Assistant Secretary General is meant to assume his or her duties until the General Assembly elects a new Secretary General for a full term. The Charter mandates that the Secretary General and the Assistant Secretary General would not be succeeded by a person of the same nationality as their own, and that these two top officials "shall be of different nationalities."[118] Accordingly, the position of the Secretary General has in recent decades been unofficially reserved for one of the large Latin-American States, and the position of Assistant Secretary General for a smaller Caribbean or Central American State – although there have been exceptions owing to particular political

[115] OAS Charter, Article 109. During his or her term of office, the Secretary General is given an official residence in the District of Columbia, in a house owned by the OAS.

[116] OAS Charter, Article 108. The amendment has been seen as strengthening the General Secretariat: see F. V. Garcia-Amador, *The Inter-American System: Treaties, Conventions and Other Documents*, vol. I, Part I (New York: Oceana Publications, 1983), p. 186.

[117] OAS Charter, Article 116.

[118] OAS Charter, Article 115.

circumstances.[119] The position of Secretary General has traditionally been held by distinguished diplomats and senior politicians of the Member States (among them former presidents), while the position of Assistant Secretary General mainly attracts former ambassadors. Both officials enjoy "the privileges and immunities corresponding to their positions and necessary for the independent performance of their duties,"[120] and have the rank equivalent to that of ambassador in all protocolary acts that they attend in performance of their official duties.

The Secretary General chairs the Executive Committee of the General Secretariat, which further comprises the Assistant Secretary General, the five Secretaries and the Executive Secretary for Integral Development, the Chiefs of Staff of the Secretary General and the Assistant Secretary General, the Executive Secretaries of the Inter-American Commission on Human Rights and Inter-American Commission

[119] The United States consents to this tradition, in return for a silent understanding that a US national will head the Secretariat for Administration and Finance and have a seat on the Board of External Auditors.

[120] OAS Charter, Article 134; Chapter III of the Multilateral Agreement on Privileges and Immunities of the Organization of American States (1949) further stipulates that "The Secretary General and the Assistant Secretary General of the Organization, their spouses and minor children, shall be granted the privileges and immunities, exemptions and facilities granted to diplomatic envoys"; only thirteen OAS Member States have ratified this agreement, while the other Member States have subscribed to bilateral agreements with the OAS General Secretariat extending functional immunity to the Organization, the General Secretariat and its rank-and-file staff.

of Women, and such other staff as the Secretary General may appoint. Convening at the instance of the Secretary General, the Executive Committee serves to assist the Secretary General with supervising, coordinating and directing the work and activities of the General Secretariat. Each year, the Secretary General submits to the General Assembly an annual report, which serves as a factual account of what most organs of the Organization – not only the General Secretariat – have done during the year, and details the OAS's financial condition.[121] The Secretary General spends several weeks each year away from headquarters when traveling on various missions of the General Secretariat, meeting with the heads of the Member States, and participating in ministerial and other international conferences and events.

The Office of the Secretary General, coordinated by a Chief of Staff, assists with the Secretary General's high-level executive functions associated with implementing the programs and policies of the OAS, and serves as liaison with the permanent missions, government agencies and civil society.[122] It hosts the Department of Legal Services and the Office of Protocol (both reporting to the Secretary General's Chief of Staff), as well as the Summits of the Americas Secretariat (at a

[121] The Permanent Council considers the report and presents to the General Assembly any observations and recommendations it deems necessary; see OAS Charter, Article 91(f).

[122] On the distribution of functions in the Secretary General's cabinet, see the Secretary General's Memorandum of November 11, 2011, entitled "Distribución de funciones en el Gabinete de la Oficina del Secretario General."

department level) and independent advisors. While some Secretaries General choose to have their office at the General Secretariat building – where the majority of staff members work – most of them, including the current Secretary General, prefer to have it located at the Main building, where the political organs meet.

The Assistant Secretary General, also elected by the General Assembly for a five-year term renewable once, is called upon by the Charter to serve as advisory officer to the Secretary General and to act as his delegate in all matters which the latter may entrust to him. During a temporary absence or disability of the Secretary General, the Assistant Secretary General is authorized to perform his functions. The Charter furthermore designates the Assistant Secretary General to serve as the Secretary of the Permanent Council, and in this capacity the office of the Assistant Secretary General works with the permanent representatives of the Member States and the permanent observers to prepare and hold regular, special and protocolary meetings of the Permanent Council. An Executive Order has made the Assistant Secretary General responsible for providing secretarial services to the General Assembly, the Meeting of Consultation and Subsidiary Organs as well; and, moreover, has put him in charge of the Secretariat's Department of Conferences and Meetings Management, the Coordinating Office for the Offices and Units of the General Secretariat in the Member States, the Columbus Memorial Library and the Secretariat of the Inter-American Committee on Ports. In the event that the office of Assistant Secretary General becomes vacant, the Permanent Council is to elect a substitute to hold that office until the General Assembly elects a new Assistant Secretary General for a full term.

Aware of "the concern of Member States that those who serve as Secretary General and Assistant Secretary General of the Organization should commit to fulfilling the purposes proclaimed in the OAS Charter and diligently performing the functions established in said Charter, in other inter-American treaties and agreements, and by the General Assembly," the General Assembly resolved in 2005 that the Permanent Council will invite the candidates for these posts "to give a public presentation to this Organization prior to the elections, in order to describe in greater detail their proposals and the initiatives they would undertake should they be elected."[123] The Resolution did not, however, "impair the authority of Member States ... to present candidates for the positions of Secretary General and Assistant Secretary General until the [very] day of the corresponding election."[124] An additional concern has been that having the Assistant Secretary General owing his or her appointment not to the Secretary General but to the Member States "introduces the

[123] Resolution AG/RES. 2103 (XXXV-O/05), adopted at the fourth plenary session, held on June 7, 2005. The Resolution further provides: "An opportunity shall also be provided for a separate dialogue between the candidates and representatives of civil society organizations duly accredited to the Organization; such participation shall be governed by the guidelines for the participation of civil society organizations in the OAS."

[124] Elections for the two posts of Secretary General and Assistant Secretary General have been held in different years since 1984, the year when Secretary General Alejandro Orfila resigned prior to the expected end of his term.

possibility of institutional rivalry between the two posts,"[125] a possibility that has occasionally become a reality. As this could undermine the efficiency of administering the General Secretariat, a suggestion has been made that the Charter be amended to allow the Secretary General to appoint his own assistant or assistants.

Upon appointment or re-election and at the end of their terms of office, both the Secretary General and the Assistant Secretary General are required to submit to the Permanent Council a sworn statement containing information on their creditors and business connections as well as their net worth, to prevent financial conflicts of interest. In the event that the Permanent Council considers that a specific matter could give rise to a conflict of interest, the Secretary General or the Assistant Secretary General, as the case may be and at their choice, can either disqualify themselves from working on any related matter or divest themselves of the interest.[126]

IV.iv *Staff*

The number of staff members working for the General Secretariat has changed dramatically over the years, expanding in correlation to periods of increased political importance and

[125] See W. M. Berenson, *The Structure of the Organization of American States: A Summary* (2002), available at the General Secretariat, p. 21.

[126] General Standards, Articles 132–136.

robust organizational budget, and declining during periods of diminished relevance and dwindling resources. While the General Secretariat at one point employed over 1,200 staff members, it currently has a staff of approximately 655.[127] Showing a real inter-American character, staff members of the General Secretariat are chosen from among nationals of the Member States, "except in cases where the needs of the service require the appointment of nationals of other States."[128] As a general rule, selection is to be carried out by competition, "with the advice of the Advisory Committee on Selection and Promotion appointed by the Secretary General."[129] The OAS Charter mandates that the first consideration in selecting staff will be given to efficiency, competence and integrity, but that "at the same time, in the recruitment of personnel of all ranks, importance shall be given to the necessity of obtaining as wide a geographic representation as possible" as well.[130] As a condition for appointment, candidates are required to undergo medical examination (usually paid for by the General Secretariat) that will prove them physically competent to perform their duties. The first six

[127] This figure excludes the many independent contractors who provide services to the General Secretariat as well.

[128] General Standards, Article 42. According to Staff Rule 104.15, the General Secretariat recognizes only one nationality for each staff member.

[129] General Standards, Article 44, which further mandates that the President of the Staff Association will be a member of that Committee and all its subcommittees. The Article also details the exceptions to the rule.

[130] OAS Charter, Article 120; see also General Standards, Article 41.

months of an appointment for a period longer than one year are considered a probationary period.[131]

Upon appointment, staff members sign – together with the Secretary General or his or her authorized representative – a document which states the nature and conditions of employment. They are further required to sign a declaration relating to potential conflicts of interest and a statement of loyalty in which they undertake to perform their duties in accordance with the provisions of the OAS Charter, the General Standards "and other pertinent provisions."[132] General Secretariat posts are classified into fourteen grades within two categories – Professional and General Services.[133] Within this framework, seven types of employment exist within the General Secretariat, each carrying with it its own terms and status: (1) career service personnel, who were appointed prior to 1994 (this category is now permanently closed and is being phased out by attrition); (2) personnel on continuing contracts; (3) personnel on fixed-term contracts; (4) trust

[131] General Standards, Article 46; this period may be extended by the Secretary General to a maximum of one year from the day of reporting for duty.

[132] General Standards, Articles 25 and 36; Staff Rule 101.7. The declaration relating to conflicts of interest is to be updated annually or when circumstances so require. Further details and statements are required from those holding positions of trust or that are directly subordinate to a member of the management or substantially involved in transactions of the General Secretariat.

[133] Staff Rule 102.2. This is done in accordance with Classification Standards and pertinent resolutions of the General Assembly; the positions of Secretary General, Assistant Secretary General and Secretaries are unclassified posts.

personnel, appointed at the discretion of the Secretary General for the duration of his or her term; (5) local professional personnel; (6) temporary support personnel; and (7) associate personnel, who are retained under an agreement with institutions participating in programs of common interest.[134] The General Secretariat submits to the Member States each quarter an updated register of all staff members and their performance ranks (as well as statistics relating to their geographic distribution); and every four or six years at least one audit of the classification of all posts must be carried out and presented to the Permanent Council.[135]

All staff members of the General Secretariat are subject to the authority of the Secretary General with respect to the performance of their duties. As international civil servants, they are prohibited from seeking or receiving instructions from any government or any authority outside the OAS, and must refrain from "any action that may be incompatible with their position as international officers responsible only to the Organization."[136] They enjoy privileges and immunities that are necessary for the performance of their duties, as

[134] General Standards, Chapter III, Subchapter A (Articles 17–24).

[135] General Standards, Articles 38 and 47; the statistics presented to Member States also include the distribution of staff members by their source of funding (within the organizational budget), their grade and their gender.

[136] OAS Charter, Article 118; the Charter further obligates Member States "to respect the exclusively international character of the responsibilities of the Secretary General and the personnel of the General Secretariat, and not to seek to influence them in the discharge of their duties" (Article 119). See also General Standards, Articles 27–36.

determined by a multilateral agreement among some Member States and bilateral agreements between the General Secretariat and other Member States.[137] The Secretary General may, however, waive the immunity "of any staff member in any case" where he or she is of the opinion that the immunity "would impede the course of justice and can be waived without prejudice to the interests of the Organization."[138] Pursuant to the General Standards, the performance of each staff member is evaluated at least once a year by his/her superior, according to guidelines established by the Department of Human Resources. Staff members whose annual performance has been particularly outstanding may be awarded cash incentive awards, according to guidelines established by the Secretary General.

Remuneration of staff members of the General Secretariat is based on the United Nations' salary scale, to which a post adjustment and rent allowance may be added. Salary scales are to be published by the Secretary General at least once a year, and include periodic within-grade increases for staff members whose performance has been satisfactory. Staff

[137] See OAS Charter, Article 135; and General Standards, Article 37. Indeed, while the OAS Charter granted the Secretary General and the Assistant Secretary General functional privileges and immunities, it left the elaboration of the specific immunities to be enjoyed by the staff of the General Secretariat to further agreement among the Member States. For more information on these agreements, see W. M. Berenson, "Immunity for International Organizations? Squaring the Concept of Immunity with the Fundamental Right to a Fair Trial: The Case of the OAS" (2010) (available at the General Secretariat), pp. 5–6.

[138] Staff Rule 101.9(a).

members who pay income taxes on their salary to a Member State (or a State or local government within the Member State) may receive reimbursement for those taxes, provided that the Member State where such taxes are paid funds the full amount of the reimbursement. Contributions to the OAS Retirement and Pension Fund are deducted from each salary, as are health insurance payments. The General Secretariat also pays travel, installation/mobilization and repatriation expenses for relevant staff members and their dependants; language allowance and education grants for dependent children may also be available to some staff members. Annual leave varies between twenty-one and thirty days, depending on length of service at the General Secretariat.[139] Permanent staff members are further eligible to take part in a social insurance system that is maintained by the General Secretariat, and which includes provisions for health protection, sick leave and maternity/paternity leave, retirement and pension savings, and compensation in the event of illness, accident or death resulting from the performance of official duties. Retirement age for staff of the General Secretariat is sixty-five.

The elaborate Staff Rules further detail, *inter alia*, the procedures for promotion, disciplinary action and separation from service; guidelines relating to official travel of staff members; and the definition of staff members who are to be regarded as locally recruited. They also establish a prohibition against workplace and sexual harassment, as well as protection for whistleblowers, informants and witnesses;

[139] General Standards, Article 48; the Secretary General may authorize special leave in exceptional circumstances.

define illegitimate relations of staff members with Member States and delegations; and regulate the involvement of staff members in the election of the Secretary General and Assistant Secretary General. The Secretary General may amend the Staff Rules by an Executive Order, provided that such amendments are consistent with the General Standards. Any modification of the Staff Rules that entails budgetary implications must first be approved by the Permanent Council.[140]

In order to maintain strong collegial relations among staff members and the Secretary General, the General Standards establish a Staff Association, made up of all staff members of the General Secretariat and headed by a Staff Committee.[141] The Staff Association is empowered to make proposals "on all matters that are of common interest to the staff members or that affect their well-being," and to discuss them with the Secretary General. As such, it aims to support, promote and defend employee compensation and benefits, career development, working conditions and the general welfare of staff members and their families. The Staff Committee traditionally comments on the proposed program budget prior to its

[140] Staff Rule 113.4. One suggestion that is currently pending is the suggestion to recognize same-sex and domestic partners within the meaning of "family members" (such recognition is already awarded in practice).

[141] General Standards, Article 53; Staff Rule, Chapter IX ("Relations with the Staff"). Any person occupying a position in the OAS on a permanent appointment or temporary appointment for six months or more, and who has signed the Statement of Loyalty, may join the Staff Association (and pay monthly dues). The Staff Association has its own website (see http://staff.oas.org/english/default.asp).

deliberation by the OAS Committee on Administrative and Budgetary Affairs, especially when it includes recommendations to eliminate posts due to budgetary constraints.

Disputes between the General Secretariat and its staff members are heard by an Administrative Tribunal whose six judges are elected by the General Assembly. The judges must all be lawyers who are nationals of different Member States, and cannot hold positions within the Organization or the delegations of Member States. Pursuant to the Statute of the Administrative Tribunal, the internal legislation of the OAS shall take precedence over general principles of labor law and the laws of any Member State in any dispute entertained by the Tribunal. Access to the Tribunal is available to all staff members and others claiming entitlement to the rights of staff members, once they have exhausted the corresponding internal grievance procedures. Current staff members are not required to pay any filing fees, while all others are required to post a bond to cover possible attorneys fees and costs, in the event that the Reconsideration Committee, which considers each case before it goes to the Tribunal, does not find in the complainant's favor. The Reconsideration Committee, which also advises the Secretary General on the disposition of employment-related grievances, is made up of a representative of the Staff Association, a representative of the Secretary General, and a Chair appointed by both of them.[142]

[142] For more details, see W. M. Berenson, "Immunity for International Organizations? Squaring the Concept of Immunity with the Fundamental Right to a Fair Trial: The Case of the OAS" (2010) (available at the General Secretariat), p. 7.

Internships at the General Secretariat headquarters are offered three times a year (winter/spring, summer and fall), with fixed start and end dates for each session. Approximately seventy interns are selected annually and placed in the various General Secretariat departments, working either full-time (forty hours per week) or part-time (twenty hours per week). Alongside the projects assigned to them, interns are required to participate in a weekly orientation program coordinated by the Department of Human Resources, and may take part in a Model OAS exercise that simulates the work of the Permanent Council. Internships are unpaid, and interns are not considered staff members of the General Secretariat. A performance evaluation is done for each intern at the end of the internship, allowing all interns to have a complete file in the Department of Human Resources of the OAS for future references. Internships are also available at the General Secretariat's national offices and in some special programs located in the Member States, where the duration of the internships is a minimum of ten weeks and a maximum of six months. The length of the internship, and its start and end dates, vary from one office to another.

IV.V Budget

The OAS budget draws upon three primary sources, chief among them the Regular Fund, which supports General Secretariat operations through Member State quota contributions.[143]

[143] The quotas are calculated based on gross national income, with adjustments for debt burden and low per capita income. See General Standards, Chapter IV ("General Provisions of a Financial and Budgetary Nature").

The Regular Fund is divided in turn into two sub-funds: the Operations Sub-Fund and the Reserve Sub-Fund, with the latter designated to hold 30 percent of the annual quotas and to be used only on a temporary basis to cover liquidity shortages.[144] A second significant source of funding is found in the specific funds for special programs of the General Secretariat, which derive from voluntary contributions from various countries and private entities, and are meant to complement the Regular Fund. Finally, OAS operations are also supported through the Special Multilateral Fund of the Inter-American Council for Integral Development (also known as the Voluntary Fund), through which countries can contribute to financing national and multilateral development programs. Within this framework, some OAS projects are funded by States that are not members of the OAS, primarily Spain (which, as a Permanent Observer to the OAS and its main external contributor, has a permanent office in one of the General Secretariat's buildings). The OAS derives additional miscellaneous income from renting out office space or the Hall of the Americas for private events, and from copyrights attached to its various publications.[145]

[144] See General Standards, Article 72. Despite a payback provision relating to use of the funds of the Reserve Sub-Fund, the General Secretariat has in recent years increased its expenditures by relying on the sub-fund without a commitment by Member States to increase their quota contributions. The sub-fund has now been depleted, causing further concern for the financial stability of the OAS.

[145] Revenues from the OAS gift shop go to support the General Secretariat's Staff Association. On the insufficient budgeting of the OAS, in general, see G. Mace and D. Migneault, "Hemispheric Regionalism in the

Struggling to "do a great deal more with significantly fewer resources,"[146] the General Secretariat has been forced in recent years to deal with severe budgetary limitations and weak financial solvency. These have been aggravated by the ongoing increase in the cost-of-living adjustment (COLA) component of staff salaries, coupled with the freeze imposed on the Regular Fund budget. The financial situation is directly linked to the level of political support for the Organization in the capitals of the Member States (and, in particular, to the relationship between the Secretary General and influential Member States).

The program budget of the OAS is annual, with the fiscal period running from January 1 through December 31. It is meant to reflect all the activities that are designated to be financed through the Regular Fund and the Voluntary Fund, with activities funded through other sources included only to the extent feasible. The General Secretariat had recently indicated a desire to move towards a results-based budget that will emphasize outputs and outcomes,[147] yet to date no concrete steps have been taken in this regard. The overall Regular Fund program budget of the OAS for the fiscal year

Americas," in T. M. Shaw, J. A. Grant and S. Cornelissen (eds.), *The Ashgate Research Companion to Regionalisms* (Farnham: Ashgate, 2011), pp. 159, 167–168.

146 C. Gaviria (former Secretary General of the OAS), *The OAS in Transition: 1994–2004* (Washington, DC: Organization of American States, 2004), p. 293.

147 *Multilateralism in the Americas: Let's Start by Fixing the OAS*, a Report to the Committee on Foreign Relations of the United States Senate, 111th Congress, Second Session, January 26, 2010, p. 5.

Table s.5 *OAS Regular Fund expenses and obligations per chapter (in US$ thousands) (2013)*

Secretary General	4,029.2
Assistant Secretary General	3,676.7
Secretariat for Legal Affairs	2,342.2
Secretariat for Multidimensional Security	4,124.3
Secretariat for Political Affairs	4,112.0
Executive Secretariat for Integral Development	14,361.9
Secretariat for External Relations	3,183.6
Secretariat for Administration and Finance	9,904.0
Basic Infrastructure and Common Costs	12,798.4
Conferences and Meetings Management	5,160.1
Offices and Units in the Member States	6,597.4
Compliance Oversight Management Bodies	1,404.4

2013 appropriated US$83,870,507, with special contributions for that period estimated at an additional US$67,590,400. Regular Fund appropriations in 2013 for the various General Secretariat units are shown in Table s.5.

The proposed program budget as prepared by the General Secretariat contains three general activity categories: (1) support services for the organs, agencies and entities of the Organization; (2) partnerships for development services; and (3) general support services. These are divided into subcategories, and present the objects of expenditure in accordance with guidelines established by the General Assembly through the General Standards.[148] The Secretary General is responsible for presenting the proposed program budget at

[148] General Standards, Chapter V ("Preparation of the Program Budget").

least ninety days prior to the opening date of the General Assembly session, and for providing any related information requested by the Permanent Council in its capacity as Preparatory Committee of the General Assembly; once the latter approves the program budget, the Secretary General may execute it, submitting administrative and financial management reports to the Council on a quarterly basis.[149] He or she is further in charge of designating the banking institutions in which the funds of the Organization shall be deposited, and may invest the funds that are not essential to meet immediate disbursement needs.[150] The General Secretariat's functional currency is the US dollar.[151]

v The Economic Community of West African States (ECOWAS) Commission

The Economic Community of West African States (ECOWAS) was established in 1975 with the aim of promoting in the sub-region "cooperation and development in all fields of economic activity."[152] Its fifteen Member States had originally

[149] General Standards, Chapter VI ("Discussion and Approval of the Program Budget") and Chapter VII ("Budget Execution"); Annex to General Assembly Resolution AG/RES.1 (XLIII-E/12) on the Program Budget of the Organization for 2013, adopted on November 15, 2012.

[150] General Standards, Articles 78 and 79.

[151] General Standards, Articles 76 and 77; these provide, however, that the "accounts of offices away from headquarters and those of the applicable parts of the multilateral, specific, and trust funds may be kept initially in such currency as the Secretary General determines."

[152] Article 2(1) of the 1975 Treaty establishing ECOWAS, signed in Lagos, Nigeria, on May 28, 1975. The fourteen countries that signed the Treaty

envisaged it as an economic community operating as a unified trade bloc, but faced with external and internal pressures endemic to the region, they soon realized that "[y]ou need an environment that is peaceful, stable and secure enough to constitute the foundations on which you can build an economic integration super-structure."[153] Having gradually widened the scope of its activities, the organization today conducts not only economic, social and cultural activities

were Benin, Burkina Faso, Gambia, Ghana, Guinea, Ivory Coast, Liberia, Mali, Mauritania, Niger, Nigeria, Senegal, Sierra Leone and Togo. Guinea-Bissau acceded to the treaty later in 1975, and Cape Verde joined in 1976; Mauritania left the organization in 2002.

153 Words of Dr. Abass Bundu, Executive Secretary of ECOWAS, in an interview on the occasion of the Community's 15th summit: see P. Idowu, "Revitalising ECOWAS: Interview with Dr. Abass Bundu, Executive Secretary, Economic Community of West African States," 3906 *West Africa* 1253–1254 (UK, 1992). On the history leading up to the establishment of ECOWAS, see A. Adedeji, "ECOWAS: A Retrospective Journey," in A. Adebajo and I. Rashid (eds.), *West Africa's Security Challenges: Building Peace in a Troubled Region* (Boulder, CO: Lynne Rienner Publishers, 2004), pp. 21–49; E. Kessie, "Trade Liberalisation Under ECOWAS: Prospects, Challenges and WTO Compatibility," 7 *African Yearbook of International Law* 31 (1999); B. Zagaris, "The Economic Community of West African States (ECOWAS): An Analysis and Prospects," 10 *Case Western Reserve Journal of International Law* 93 (1978), pp. 98–101; O. Anukpe Ovrawah, "Harmonisation of Laws within the Economic Community of West African States (ECOWAS)," 6 *African Journal of International and Comparative Law* 76–78 (1994); and J. E. Okolo, "ECOWAS Regional Cooperation Regime," 32 *German Yearbook of International Law* 111 (1989). The major objective of the Community remains the establishment of a West African common market and monetary union.

within the Community, but also political tasks such as conflict resolution, mediation and prevention.

The 1975 Treaty of Lagos that gave rise to ECOWAS created five "Institutions of the Community" to realize the objectives of the organization. First among these was the Authority, a policy-making body comprising the Heads of State and Government of Member States, who were to meet at least annually as the principal governing institution of the Community. Next in the hierarchical order, a Council of Ministers was to monitor the functioning and development of the Community, make recommendations to the Authority on relevant matters of policy, and direct all subordinate institutions of the Community.[154] A third institution was the Executive Secretariat of the Community, headed by an Executive Secretary in charge of the day-to-day administration of the Community and all its institutions, and responsible for "concerting the spirit of solidarity proclaimed by the political authorities."[155] The Treaty stipulated that the Executive Secretariat would service and assist all other Community Institutions in the performance of their functions, as well as keep track of the functioning of the Community overall and report on the matter to the Council of Ministers. A Tribunal of the Community was established as the fourth institution, to "ensure the observance of law and justice in the interpretation

[154] 1975 ECOWAS Treaty, Article 6; the Council is to comprise the Ministers in charge of ECOWAS affairs, Ministers of Finance and Ministers of Foreign Affairs.

[155] "ECOWAS: Ninth Anniversary of Foundation Treaty," 5329 *West Africa* 2327 (UK, 1984), p. 2328.

of the provisions of this treaty" and to settle related disputes between the Member States. Finally, the Treaty had set up "Technical and Specialized Commissions," four in number, which were to draw up integration programs in their respective fields of expertise and make recommendations as to their implementation.

By 1989, however, ECOWAS Member States had acknowledged the poor record of regional programs and progress, and determined that the institutional framework of the Community was insufficient: "a new impetus was needed to put the process of regional integration in West Africa back on track."[156] A Committee of Eminent Persons was set up to undertake a review of the 1975 Treaty and propose amendments to it, with a view to strengthening ECOWAS and ensuring it could indeed achieve its goals. The result was a 1993 revised treaty "that [brought] out more sharply what

[156] E. Kessie, "Trade Liberalisation Under ECOWAS: Prospects, Challenges and WTO Compatibility," 7 *African Yearbook of International Law* 31 (1999), p. 40. See also E. Momoh, "West Africa Responds to Europe 1992," 11 *Africa Economic Digest* 3–4 (1990); S. K. B. Asante, "ECOWAS, the EEC and the Lomé Convention," in D. Mazzeo (ed.), *African Regional Organizations* (Cambridge University Press, 1984), pp. 171–195; and the study carried out at ECOWAS's request by the Economic Commission for Africa (and presented at the Authority's 1984 summit meeting), which found that despite a twenty-five-year effort, no real progress was made towards economic integration and proposed fundamental changes in the framework for cooperation in the subregion (copy available at the Commission). A reform was also seen as necessary in light of international and regional developments, in particular the creation of the European Community and African Economic Community.

needs to be done to accelerate the integration process,"[157] and "highlight[ed] the political side of Community co-operation,"[158] in which ECOWAS Heads of State and Government accepted "the need to establish Community Institutions vested with relevant and adequate powers."[159] Accordingly, the revised treaty introduced not only a new set of policy objectives, but also a new legal regime of a fundamentally supranational nature: decisions of the Authority – the "supreme institute of the Community ... responsible for the general direction and control of the Community" – were now binding not only on all institutions of the Community, but also on its Member States. The Council of Ministers, meeting at least twice in a year at ordinary session and acting through Regulations that are binding on the institutions under its authority, remained in charge of the functioning and

[157] The anticipatory words of ECOWAS Executive Secretary Dr. Abass Bundu, as quoted in P. Da Costa, "A New Role for ECOWAS," 36 *Africa Report* 37–40 (1991). The recommendations of the Committee of Eminent Persons for the Review of the ECOWAS Treaty (chaired by former Nigerian head of State and ECOWAS founder, General Yakubu Gowon) are found in its Draft Report, ECW/CEP/TREV/VI/2 (Lagos, 1992); see also K. O. Kufuor, "Law, Power, Politics and Economics: Critical Issues Arising Out of the New ECOWAS Treaty," 6 *African Journal of International and Comparative Law* 429–442 (1994).

[158] Words of General Yakubu Gowon, former Nigerian President and Chairman of the Group of Eminent Persons charged with reviewing the ECOWAS Treaty of 1975, in an interview on the occasion of the Community's 15th summit: see P. Idowu, "'Change Is Necessary': Interview with Gen. Yakubu Gowon, Chairman of the Group of Eminent Persons Charged with Reviewing the ECOWAS Treaty of 1975," 3906 *West Africa* 1256 (UK, 1992), p. 1257.

[159] Preamble to the revised ECOWAS Treaty (1993).

development of the Community. The new treaty further established an ECOWAS Parliament, an Economic and Social Council, four more Technical Commissions, and a Community Court of Justice. The Community's Fund for Cooperation, Compensation and Development, established under the 1975 Treaty as the financial instrument of the Community, received the status of "Institute of the Community" as well.

Greater detail was provided in the revised treaty as regards the Executive Secretariat, which the Member States now formally recognized in its strengthened configuration and took it upon themselves to cooperate with.[160] Relocated in 1993 from an old government building in Lagos to a large headquarters in Abuja, the Executive Secretariat was now charged with the overarching responsibility of "harmonising and co-ordinating all activities and programmes of the

160 Revised ECOWAS Treaty, Article 20(3). One author had commented prior to the adoption of the revised treaty that "ECOWAS integration could also be impeded by the present inability of the secretariat to implement effectively decisions and Protocols agreed upon by the Authority of Heads of State and Government": see Y. Omorogbe, "The Legal Framework for Economic Integration in the ECOWAS Region," 5 *African Journal of International and Comparative Law* 355 (1993), p. 367. See also O. B. J. Ojo, "Integration in ECOWAS: Successes and Difficulties," in D. C. Bach (ed.), *Regionalisation in Africa: Integration and Disintegration* (Oxford: James Currey Ltd, 1999), pp. 119 and 120 ("The Secretariat's sensitisation missions to the Member States, its campaign for a deepening of the integration process instead of a broadening into new areas, and its relentless push for an enabling environment, all paved the way for the revision of the ECOWAS treaty adopted by the Heads of State and Governments summit of July 1993 in Cotonou").

institutions of the Community within the context of regional integration."[161] While most provisions relating to the Executive Secretariat in the revised treaty centered on the role and responsibilities of the Executive Secretary, the enumerated duties attached to that office illustrate, effectively, the functions of the Executive Secretariat as a whole. These include publishing and executing the Decisions taken by the Authority and applying the Regulations of the Council; convening meetings of sectoral Ministers; preparing draft budgets and programs of activity for the Community and supervising their execution once approved by the Council; submitting reports on Community activities in all meetings of the Authority and the Council, and preparing such high-level meetings and others; initiating draft texts for adoption by the Authority or the Council; and preparing studies and proposals that "may assist in the efficient and harmonious functioning and development of the Community."[162]

The Executive Secretariat underwent several restructuring exercises in the years that followed until, in 2006, Heads of State and Government, emphasizing the importance of it having "a structure that will be efficient and effective in achieving the objectives of ECOWAS," announced its transformation into a Commission.[163] This dramatic organizational

[161] Revised ECOWAS Treaty, Article 80.

[162] Revised ECOWAS Treaty, Articles 9(5), 19(3)(a)–(f), (h) and (i).

[163] ECOWAS Press Release 5/2006; Authority Decision A/DEC.16/01/06 of January 12, 2006 on Transforming the Executive Secretariat into a Commission (and contemplating additional institutional reforms). The representation of Member States within the Commission's new management team was fixed "for the initial take-off of that Institution"

change was to enable the new high-level body to assist ECOWAS to "focus better on the discharge of its core functions"[164] and promote "the deepening and acceleration of the [regional] integration process";[165] it was seen, moreover, as essential in order to adapt the Executive Secretariat to the international environment of rising regionalism, with the European model of integration serving as a particular source of inspiration. Given a more muscular mandate with managerial backbone, the Commission, led by a President, Vice President and seven other Commissioners, was designated to take the lead in designing Community policies and formulating them for adoption by the political bodies, as well as to serve as one of the two central Community Institutions entrusted with their implementation.[166] An enhancement

by an Authority decision, allocating the statutory Commissioner positions and the position of the Financial Controller to specified Member States (Authority Decision A/DEC.1/6/06 of June 14, 2006).

164 ECOWAS Press Release 5/2006.

165 ECOWAS Press Release 67/2006. ECOWAS Heads of State and Government further decided that the nine Member States whose nationals would occupy the Commission's management positions by rotation would be Burkina Faso, Ghana, Ivory Coast, Mali, Niger, Nigeria, Senegal, Sierra Leone and Togo. According to the Rules of Procedure of the ECOWAS Commission, the President of the Commission, the Vice President and the Commissioners "shall neither solicit nor accept instructions from any government or external body, and Member States shall respect their independence" (Rule 4(2)).

166 The other institution being the ECOWAS Bank for Investment and Development, formerly the Fund for Cooperation, Compensation and Development, headquartered in Lomé, Togo. On the initial development of the Fund into an institution of ECOWAS, including its tense relations with the Executive Secretariat at that time, see

of ECOWAS's supranational powers, giving a greater force to all Community Acts, was put in place to make it all feasible. In essence, the Supplementary Acts and Directives of the Authority, as well as the Regulations, Directives and Decisions of the Council of Ministers, were now directly binding on the Member States and all institutions of the Community – as were the subsequent Enabling Rules adopted by the Commission in order to implement such Acts (the Commission can also formulate recommendations, but these are not binding).[167] ECOWAS's Executive Secretary at that time hailed the institutional renewal, predicting that "it will make the organization more dynamic and effective."[168]

J. E. Okolo, "ECOWAS Regional Cooperation Regime," 32 *German Yearbook of International Law* 111 (1989), pp. 122–123. The Fund was transformed in 1999 into a regional holding company, and the Bank in its current form was established by Article 21 of the revised ECOWAS Treaty, as amended by the Additional Act A/SA.9/01/07 of January 19, 2007.

[167] See Supplementary Act A/SA/3/01/10 amending new Article 9 of the ECOWAS Treaty as amended by Supplementary Protocol A/SP1/06/06 (February 16, 2010); Authority Decision A/DEC.1/6/06 of June 14, 2006, Article 7. The institutional change itself was declared and implemented through a Supplementary Act of the Authority, seen as completing the ECOWAS Treaty, in order to avoid lengthy national processes of ratification of ECOWAS conventions and protocols – a dynamic that was seen as paralyzing the regional integration process. Future amendments to the ECOWAS Treaty were carried out in similar fashion, so at present, no consolidated text guides ECOWAS as an institution; rather, the revised Treaty now stands alongside the Supplementary Acts.

[168] ECOWAS Press Release 10/2006.

v.i Role and functions

Launched in January 2007, the Commission referred to its transformation as a "difference [that] goes beyond a name change and an increase in the number of officers at the management level," appearing confident that receiving greater authority "and having its Commissioners in charge of smaller and clearly defined sectors" will guarantee that it has more impact and make it more visible in the Member States.[169] A strategic four-year plan for the Commission, published in 2007 with the financial support of the German Federal Ministry for Economic Cooperation and Development, identified the central responsibility of the Commission as "implementing the ECOWAS mandate and vision through policy definition and action," and suggested that "[t]he Commission must play a central role to ensure that the Community institution is solidly rooted in the realities of the region."[170]

The Commission is, indeed, ECOWAS's central institution. Charged with developing regional policy and then initiating and monitoring its implementation, it is predominantly occupied with translating the decisions of the Community's political bodies into planned and implementable programs, and then works with the Member States to launch such programs (while usually leaving with the States the responsibility for sustained implementation). In its advisory capacity, the Commission makes "all necessary recommendations to enable the

[169] ECOWAS website (see www.ecowas.int/dept/index.php?id=p_p1_commission&lang=en).

[170] *ECOWAS Commission Strategic Plan 2007–2010* (2007), p. 14.

[governing bodies of ECOWAS] to decide on the main policy thrusts as well as any other recommendation that [it] may deem necessary for the promotion and development of the Community."[171] In its implementing and monitoring capacity, it works with the national ECOWAS ministries of Member States, in particular with their ECOWAS National Units; convenes and facilitates meetings, including emergency regional consultative meetings; produces project documents; organizes regional capacity-building workshops and international conferences on regional issues; sends support and supervision missions to Member States; collects data on domestic policies, particularly economic and financial; maintains dialogues with development partners and potential investors, as well as other international organizations; communicates ECOWAS activities to stakeholders; and serves as repository for Community documents, including the original signed Community Acts. As the Community's executive arm and front office, it is expected to exercise its powers "to ensure the smooth functioning of the Community and protect [its] overall interest."[172]

The Commission's work is based on the priorities set by the Authority and the Council, as well as a general stated vision of being "the pace-setter in regional integration management." Its operations and planning are further guided

[171] Council Regulation C/REG.13/06/10 of June 2, 2010 ("Approving the Rules of Procedure of the Commission of the Economic Community of West African States (ECOWAS)"), citing Authority Decision A/DEC.1/06/06 of June 14, 2006.

[172] Supplementary Protocol A/SP.1/06/06 Amending the Revised ECOWAS Treaty, p. 6 (the New Article 19(4)).

by the Community's "Strategic Pillars," drawn from the Fundamental Principles elaborated in the revised ECOWAS treaty and anchored in the multi-year Regional Strategic Plan (2011–2015) prepared by the Commission. These include Peace, Security and Good Governance; Cooperation and Development; Competition and Equity; Socio-Economic and Monetary Integration; Institutional Capacity; and Global Relevance. The Commission's work and organization are also governed by the revised ECOWAS treaty (as amended), and by the Rules of Procedure adopted by the Council of Ministers in 2010 in order to improve the performance of the Commission.[173] The latter stipulate, *inter alia*, the functions of the Commission overall and of each of its Commissioners; how the latter are to cooperate in managing the Commission; and the position of the Commission *vis-à-vis* other Community Institutions. Finally, a set of six "core values" has been developed by the Commission following an internal consultative process, to guide all actions of the Commission as well: teamwork, respect, service, commitment, loyalty and integrity.

As the Community's central organ, the Commission is to be consulted on any draft text that other Community Institutions may wish to submit to the governing bodies of the Community, and receives from them activity reports that are incorporated into the Commission's annual report on

[173] Council Regulation C/REG.13/06/10 of June 2, 2010. The Rules may be amended or revised by the Council "at the instance of the President of the Commission" (Rule 18).

the activities of the Community. Its service units, such as the directorates for Communications, Human Resources, External Relations or Legal Affairs, serve all of the institutions and agencies of the Community. The Commission is authorized to suggest amendments to the ECOWAS Treaty, and to receive such suggestions from Member States in order to pass these on to the Authority. In consultation with the ECOWAS National Units of the Member States, it may request from national institutions any information that may be useful to it in the accomplishment of its mission. The Commission also works within a greater African framework, where ECOWAS is the African Union's "strategic and operational relay in West Africa," and with other external partners, in particular the European Union and the United Nations.

The Commission's official languages are "all West African languages so designated by the Authority as well as English, French and Portuguese," while its working languages are English, French and Portuguese.[174] Most documents of the Commission, however, are prepared either in English or in French alone,[175] creating difficulties in the dissemination of information, as the majority of ECOWAS staff members (and other stakeholders) are not bilingual. The biannual *Official Journal of the Community*, containing all Community Acts adopted in the preceding respective six months, is currently

[174] Revised ECOWAS Treaty, Article 87(1).

[175] One example is the ECOWAS weekly bulletin, *Echoes of ECOWAS*, published since the beginning of 2012 by the Directorate of Communication.

published by the Commission in English and French alone, with the capacity for doing so in Portuguese still being developed. The ECOWAS website (www.ecowas.int), maintained by the Commission's Community Computer Centre (CCC) in collaboration with the Communication Directorate as a gateway to information about the Community at large, is not fully available in the three languages either. Internal communication is, to a large extent, paper-based, due to presently inadequate information communication infrastructure; when Commission officials make use of email, many of them often rely on their personal accounts in public Internet domains, such as Yahoo or Gmail, rather than on the formal organizational domain (ecowas.int).[176]

Organizational productivity and the capacity for effective staff work remain an ongoing challenge for the Commission, whose current institutional capabilities have been described in its present Strategic Plan (2011–2015) as "weak."[177] The Plan further identified in the Commission "an absence of institutional culture to drive efficiencies," as well as a lack of clearly defined structures, job descriptions, processes, roles and responsibilities; an absence of an integrated planning system; inadequate monitoring and performance evaluation; a poor working environment; insufficient

[176] A new system, ECOWAS Mail, is currently being deployed. At present, there is no functioning intranet system.

[177] The Plan was prepared by the Commission with the assistance of a team of private consultants, and covers a situational analysis for the Commission, core strategies for the above-mentioned period and associated risk factors.

cooperation between staff members, who are often inadequately skilled and trained; and administrative processes that are "manual, slow and tedious."[178] A program to enhance institutional capacity currently focuses on developing a larger and more qualified staff, increased technology and administrative support, and improved internal structures and procedures. Such efforts rely to a large extent on support programs funded by external donors and development partners, such as the World Bank, the European Union and the African Capacity Building Foundation. While the significant contribution of external consultants has been firmly acknowledged in ECOWAS, there is also awareness that "the pervasive use of consultants undermines the productivity and capacity of staff": outside consultants "are often

[178] *ECOWAS Commission Strategic Plan (2011–2015)*, pp. 13, 17 and 31. The *ECOWAS Regional Strategic Plan (2011–2015): A Proactive Mechanism for Change, The Reader Friendly Version* (Abuja: ECOWAS Commission, 2010) makes similar observations, among them that "[w]ithin the Commission, work methods and processes of both technical and support departments, including the use of [information communication technology], have not improved significantly. A planning and programming system is yet to be instituted and the budgetary programme is not aimed at a results-based management system" (at p. 16); that "[t]here appear to be poor linkages within and between the ECOWAS institutions" (at p. 31); and that "[p]oor implementation of policies, priorities and agreements, both at individual and organizational levels [exist and] have consequences for staff morale and productivity . . . fundamentally, vertical and horizontal communications suffer from defects in the Commission, thus giving way to grapevine information, with all its destructive tendencies" (at p. 37).

undertaking tasks that more properly were the responsibility of management or are doing work that should have been done by staff."[179]

v.ii *Organizational structure*

The transformation of ECOWAS's Executive Secretariat into a Commission was accompanied by a comprehensive reorganization that gave rise to twenty-six directorates (up from sixteen prior to 2007), subdivided in turn into divisions and sections, which were all established in accordance with a Council Regulation that approved the organizational structure of the Commission.[180] Several other business units were set up in the period that followed, bringing to thirty-three the total number of operational offices operating under the oversight of the President of the Commission, the Vice President and the seven other Commissioners. The Commission's Strategic Plan for 2011–2015 has labeled the current organizational structure as "dysfunctional, with overlaps of functions at different levels,"[181] and it is therefore likely that

179 *ECOWAS Regional Strategic Plan (2011–2015): A Proactive Mechanism for Change, The Reader Friendly Version* (Abuja: ECOWAS Commission, 2010), p. 37.

180 See Regulation C/REG.7/06/07 of June 2007, correcting errors identified in a previously adopted organogram and intended to finalize the organogram "for the continued and efficient functioning of the Commission."

181 *ECOWAS Commission Strategic Plan (2011–2015)*, p. 31. ECOWAS's *Regional Strategic Plan (2011–2015)*, p. 9, has called for a "review of not only the treaty [of 1993] but also the institutional arrangements as a matter of urgency."

the President of the Commission will soon recommend to the Council of Ministers a reorganization of the Commission, as he or she is empowered to do.

ECOWAS's seven Commissioners are responsible for smaller and more clearly defined sectors, as compared to past management positions of the Executive Secretariat, and enjoy an expanded political profile in supervising the implementation of their Departmental mandates.[182] Serving under the authority of the President of the Commission and reporting to him through the Vice President, their offices' responsibilities correspond to areas of regional cooperation that are expressly stated in the ECOWAS Treaty and other Community instruments (apart from that of the Commissioner responsible for Administration and Finance).[183] They are all required to operate "in the spirit of collegiality, cohesion and broad consensus."[184] In 2012, a recommendation to increase the number of Commissioners from nine to twelve, "to give Community Member States a

182 The Commissioners may, *inter alia* and in consultation with the President of the Commission and the Vice President, enter into relations related to their respective competence (particularly relations of a technical nature) with the Commission's external partners, "namely, the United Nations, the African Union, international financial institutions and development partners": see Rules of Procedure of the ECOWAS Commission, Rule 12 ("General Functions of the Commissioners").

183 On the general functions of the Commissioners, see Rules of Procedure of the ECOWAS Commission, Rule 12 ("General Functions of the Commissioners").

184 Rules of Procedure of the ECOWAS Commission, Rule 9 ("Collegial Character of the Commission").

sense of belonging,"[185] was endorsed by the Heads of State and Government, who moreover instructed the Council to "urgently finalise the modalities for the implementation of this decision," and "continue its reflection on the feasibility of a 15-member Commission."[186] Such enlarged membership of the Commission was indeed decided upon in 2013, and will probably entail future reorganization within the Commission.

While the vast majority of the Commission's business units operate at the Abuja headquarters, the Commission structure further comprises the Gender Development Centre, located in Dakar, Senegal; the Coordination Centre for Water Conservation, and the Youth and Sports Development Centre, both operating in Ouagadougou, Burkina Faso; and four Observation and Monitoring bureaus, set up as part of the Community's Early Warning System for conflict prevention and operating in Banjul (The Gambia), Cotonou (Benin), Monrovia (Liberia) and Ouagadougou. The Commission also maintains a liaison office in Lagos, Nigeria, responsible for protocolary tasks such as receiving delegates and travel arrangements; and a small ECOWAS office in Brussels, headed by a staff member of ambassadorial rank, in charge

[185] ECOWAS Press Release 163/2012 of June 13, 2012 ("Council of Ministers Recommends Expansion of ECOWAS Commission").

[186] ECOWAS Press Release 180/2012: Final Communiqué following the Forty-First Ordinary Session of the ECOWAS Authority Heads of State and Government. The Authority of Heads of State and Government may modify the number of Commissioners if it deems it necessary (Authority Decision A/DEC.1/6/06, Article 1(3)).

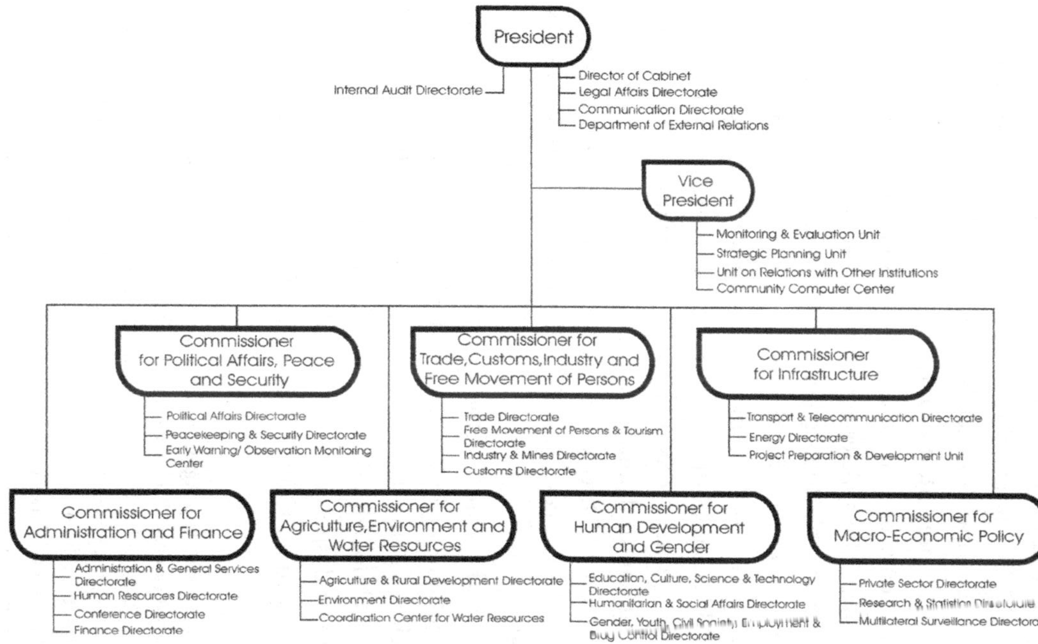

Figure 6.4 ECOWAS Commission organizational structure

of ECOWAS economic cooperation with the European Union (in particular, monitoring the Community's interests under the ACP–EU partnership[187] and facilitating the negotiations for an Economic Partnership Agreement).

At present, the Office of the Commissioner for Agriculture, Environment and Water Resources works to ensure, in line with the policies and objectives adopted by the Authority, "sustainable food security and rational management of natural resources in member countries, a living wage to agricultural workers, and the expansion of trade on a sustainable basis, both within the sub-region and with the rest of the world." It comprises three technical Directorates: the Agricultural and Rural Development Directorate, the Environment Directorate, and the Coordination Centre for Water Resources. Staff members of this office number twenty-seven.

The Office of the Commissioner for Human Development and Gender is entrusted with promoting Community policies relating to education and training, health, science and new technologies, gender, social and humanitarian affairs, youth and sports, and arts and culture. It is composed of an Education, Culture, Science and Technology Directorate;

[187] The Partnership Agreement between the members of the African, Caribbean and Pacific Group of States, and the European Community and its Member States was signed in June 2000 in Cotonou, Benin, to promote the objective of reducing and eventually eradicating poverty, as well as the objectives of sustainable development and the gradual integration of the ACP countries into the world economy. It was concluded for a twenty-year period from March 2000 to February 2020, entering into force in April 2003.

a Gender, Youth, Civil Society, Employment and Drug Control Directorate; and a Humanitarian and Social Affairs Directorate. These replaced the Human Development Department of the former Executive Secretariat and have assumed broad mandates in these fields, arising from the ECOWAS Treaty and various other Community Acts. The office employs fifty-six staff members.

The Office of the Commissioner for Infrastructure, charged with coordinating and monitoring Community policies in the transportation, energy and telecommunication sectors, is responsible for facilitating the development of infrastructure that would enable a competitive business environment and encourage investment in the sub-region. It comprises two Directorates: the Transport and Telecommunication Directorate, which seeks to promote regional connectivity through upgraded infrastructure; and the Energy Directorate, which works to coordinate and harmonize the policies and programs of Member States in the field of energy. It currently employs twenty-two staff members.

The Office of the Commissioner for Macro-Economic Policy supervises the work of a Private Sector Directorate, a Multilateral Surveillance Directorate, and a Research and Statistics Directorate, employing thirty-nine staff members in total. These are expected to work together to promote the ECOWAS vision of a competitive, dynamic and diversified regional economy. In particular, they are entrusted with designing Community policies on monetary cooperation, economic management and multilateral surveillance, as well as macroeconomic stability and convergence among the Member States, with the Directorate for Research and Statistics expected to serve as "the economic policy design and analysis centre of the ECOWAS Commission."

The Office of the Commissioner for Political Affairs, Peace and Security, with 124 staff members, is entrusted with facilitating the achievement of good governance in the Member States and with strengthening the Community's conflict prevention, management and resolution mechanisms. As such, it is in charge of implementing the 1999 ECOWAS Protocol Relating to the Mechanism for Conflict Prevention, Management, Resolution, Peacekeeping and Security, as well as other relevant protocols relating to peace and security, such as the 2001 Protocol on Democracy and Good Governance and the 2008 ECOWAS Conflict Prevention Framework.[188] The office oversees the functioning of three directorates, of which the first is the Political Affairs Directorate, comprising a Political Affairs and International Cooperation Division, a Democracy and Good Governance Division, an Electoral Assistance Division, and a Mediation and Facilitation Division. Next is a Peacekeeping and Regional Security Directorate, which oversees the ECOWAS peacekeeping operations and is further responsible for mobilizing resources and policies for promoting peace, justice and security as a basis for sustainable development. The Commissioner stays abreast of potential crises and rapid developments through an Early

[188] See also Rules of Procedure of the ECOWAS Commission, Rule 13(6) ("Specific Functions of the Commissioners"). On ECOWAS's Protocol Relating to the Mechanism for Conflict Prevention, Management, Resolution, Peacekeeping, and Security, see A. Abass, "The New Collective Security Mechanism of ECOWAS: Innovations and Problems," 5 *Journal of Conflict and Security Law* 211–229 (2000).

Warning Directorate, which is responsible for observing and monitoring sub-regional peace and security indicators, including humanitarian, political and other human security issues within the framework of conflict prevention. The staff of an Observation and Monitoring Centre at the Commission headquarters, whose monitoring work is supplemented by input from the four Observation and Monitoring Bureaus mentioned above, regularly report on the security situation within the Community.

The Office of the Commissioner for Trade, Customs, Industry and Free Movement works to deepen the economic and monetary integration in the sub-region. It operates through a Trade Directorate, a Free Movement of Persons and Tourism Directorate, an Industry and Mines Directorate, and a Customs Directorate, all of which aim to promote Community policies in the fields under its overall purview, at the national, Community and international levels (including through trade agreements with third States and international organizations). It currently employs thirty-two staff members.

The Office of the Commissioner for Administration and Finance, charged with formulating and administering "a system and procedures based on internationally recognized standards and best practices" in order to support the Commission's operations, underwent a significant transformation during the restructuring process discussed above. It currently supervises four directorates: the General Administration Directorate, the Human Resources Directorate, the Conference and Protocol Directorate, and the Finance Directorate. The latter employs two principal accountants (one for financial reporting and the other for budget and external funds), three accountants, a treasurer and an IT support officer, all working under a Director. In total, the office has 257 staff members.

v.iii The President and Vice President of the Commission

v.iii.a The President

Appointed by the Authority of Heads of State and Government for a non-renewable four-year term, the President of the Commission serves as Chief Executive Officer of the Commission, and as the Principal Officer of the Community at large. In this latter role, the President is responsible for preparing and implementing the Decisions of the Authority and the Regulations handed down by the Council of Ministers, and for the overall political and economic integration in the sub-region. He is also responsible for strategic planning and policy analysis, as well as for coordinating the activities of all of the Community's Institutions. The President convenes, where necessary, meetings of sector Ministers and of representatives of other high institutions of the Member States to enhance the attainment of Community objectives, and formulates the draft activity program as well as the budget of the Community, supervising their execution once approved by the Council. He participates in the meetings of the Authority and the Council, wherein he presents an interim or annual report on the activities of the Community and delivers a "State of the Community" address at the annual summit of the Heads of State and Government. The President regularly engages in regional and international diplomacy, and is vested with broad political authority to initiate actions for conflict prevention, management and resolution, as well as for peacekeeping and security operations in the sub-region, including fact-finding, mediation, facilitation, negotiation and reconciliation among the parties to any conflict.[189] The President is entrusted, moreover, with managing the relations with ECOWAS's external partners, "particularly the United Nations, the African Union, international financial Institutions and friendly powers,"[190] and, as the legal representative of the Community, signs all of its major cooperation agreements. He or she regularly collaborates with the other Community Institutions, particularly the ECOWAS Parliament (that currently has a solely consultative role).

[189] See Article 15 of the 1999 ECOWAS Protocol Relating to the Mechanism for Conflict Prevention, Management, Resolution, Peacekeeping, and Security ("Role and Functions of the Executive Secretary"). Recent examples of the use of this authority include the appointment of the Special Representative of the President to Mali (2012), and the dispatching on the President's order of fact-finding missions to Ghana, Sierra Leone and Senegal, with regard to election monitoring in those countries (2012). See also H. Didigu, "Developing a Common Agenda for Subregional Organizations for Peace, Security and Conflict Prevention in Africa: A View from ECOWAS," in *Proceedings of the UNESCO-ISS Expert Meeting on Peace, Human Security and Conflict Prevention in Africa held in Pretoria, 23–24 July 2001* (available at the ECOWAS Commission).

[190] Rules of Procedure of the ECOWAS Commission, Rule 10(3) ("Functions of the President of the Commission"). The President also receives letters of credence from foreign envoys who serve as permanent representatives to the regional organization.

In his capacity as Chief Executive Officer of the Commission, the President is responsible for directing and coordinating the operations of the Commission's various units, for authorizing the Commission's budget expenditures, and for appointing, in accordance with the Staff Rules and Regulations, all of the Commission's staff (except for the other Commissioners) and exercising authority over them. He may, "for the sake of efficiency," delegate part of these duties to one or several of the other Commissioners, and usually does so where those duties fall within the specific or technical purview of a Commissioner. The President convenes and chairs bimonthly meetings with the Vice President and other Commissioners ("departmental meetings," where five Commissioners represent a quorum), which are held in closed sessions and whose deliberations are classified as confidential.[191] Assistance in preparing such meetings, including setting their agenda, is provided by the Director of the Cabinet of the President, who attends as an observer.

While in ECOWAS's early years the Executive Secretary was appointed following an unofficial understanding reached between the Member States, the post of President of the Commission is currently allocated to Member States "in line with an established rotational system based on alphabetical order in which Member States' names are listed," to ensure

[191] Rules of Procedure of the ECOWAS Commission, Rule 6 ("Deliberations of the Commission"); decisions may also be taken by the Commissioners by written procedure when circumstances so dictate, Rule 7 ("Decisions by Written Procedure").

transparency, fairness and predictability.[192] All Member States have a right to occupy the post of President of the Commission except for the State that hosts the headquarters of the Commission. A State will not be allocated the post, however, if one of its nationals is serving at that time as the head of another Community Institution; and, furthermore, will automatically lose its turn if a *coup d'état* or a taking of power by other unconstitutional means occurs in it within the period of consideration, or if its government attempts to remain in power indefinitely or does not comply with "convergence criteria on democracy." Failure to pay the Community Levy (see below) would lead to denial of the right to occupy the post of President of the Commission as well. The President must be a national of the Member State that nominates him or her to the post, and is required to be "a person of proven competence and integrity with a global vision of political and economic issues and regional integration." The Heads of State and Government meet the candidate nominated by the relevant Member State during their annual summit preceding the vacancy of the post, and then deliberate on the appointment in a closed-door session. Support by an absolute majority of the Member States represented at the session is required for appointing the candidate as President of the Commission; if the candidate does not receive the necessary votes or is

[192] Supplementary Act A/SP.14/02/12 of the Authority of Heads of State and Government ("Modalities of Allocation of the Position of the President, Vice President and Other Commissioners of the Commission, and Other Statutory Appointees of ECOWAS Institutions"), February 17, 2012, Preamble and Article 14 ("Method for Allocating the Posts").

rejected by a simple majority, the nominating Member State is to immediately recommend the appointment of an alternate, who should be named ahead of time.[193] The President is officially sworn in at the next ordinary session of the Authority of ECOWAS Heads of State and Government (sometimes months after actually assuming office), with the oath of office administered by the President of the Community Court of Justice.

As the highest-paid official of the Community, the President receives an annual salary currently set at 72,333 ECOWAS Units of Account (approximately US$111,170, as fixed by the Council of Ministers), and is further entitled to free furnished accommodation (including all utilities); a "responsibility allowance" equal to 10 percent of the basic salary; a spouse allowance equivalent to 5 percent of his or her basic salary; a settlement grant to cover household appliances and soft furnishing, in the amount equal to 15,000 ECOWAS Units of Account (approximately US$23,055); an unlimited communications allowance; an official car and a driver; and an annual home leave, including for eligible dependants.

[193] Supplementary Act A/SP.14/02/12 of the Authority of Heads of State and Government, Article 24 ("Voting for the Election of the President of the Commission"), Article 12 ("Disqualification of a candidate for the office of President of the Commission"); the Heads of State and Government "may not provide justification" for their decision to reject a candidate. In the past, a Member State to whom the post of Executive Secretary was allocated was required to present the Authority with a choice of three candidates, in order to appoint the most qualified of them.

The Office of the President has several dependencies: the Office of the Cabinet of the President, a Communication Directorate, a Department for External Relations, an Internal Audit Directorate and a Legal Affairs Directorate. The latter, which serves as the "Legal Advisor to the Community" since the Executive Secretariat's first days of operation, significantly grew in importance following the creation of the Commission, in light of the Community's expanded ambitions and, in particular, the supranational legal regime it adopted.[194] In this capacity, it is responsible for giving advice on all legal and judicial matters, as mandated by the Commission's Rules of Procedure;[195] formulates draft Community texts for the governing bodies of ECOWAS; assists in the interpretation of Community texts and contributes to decision-making relating to them; and plays the role of the custodian of Community Acts. The Directorate, moreover, takes part in the negotiation and conclusion of agreements that ECOWAS may enter into, and in all dispute settlement procedures relating to the Community. Finally, it initiates and assists in

[194] The *ECOWAS Commission Strategic Plan 2007–2010*, p. 55, provided that "[t]he management of Legal Affairs and mitigation of the institutional risks therein constitute a fundamental question which is becoming serious owing to the institutional transformation that has been carried out within ECOWAS. The importance of Legal Affairs in the organizational chain of the Community cannot be overemphasized given its cross-cutting nature."

[195] The Commission's Rules of Procedure mandate that the Legal Directorate be consulted with "on all draft Legal Acts and all documents that could have legal or judicial implications"; see Rules of Procedure of the ECOWAS Commission, Rule 15(3) ("Cooperation Among Departments of the Commission").

the implementation of Community-wide legal and judicial programs and policies, such as the efforts to harmonize national laws in Member States in selected topics ranging from commerce to human rights, and promotes mutual assistance relating to crime prevention and criminal justice. Headed by a Director, the Directorate of Legal Affairs further employs four legal officers (one of them on a short-term contract basis), as well as support staff comprising a clerk, two secretaries and a messenger. A "Strategic Vision of the Directorate of Legal Affairs" dated 2010 recommended that eight more lawyers be recruited to deal with the growing volume of work, and proposed a new organogram in which the Directorate would be divided into two main divisions – a Legal Advice and Drafting Division (divided in turn into a legal advice section and a drafting section), and a Programs and Legal and Judicial Cooperation Division (comprising a programs section, and a legal and judicial cooperation section) – working alongside a Documentation Section. At present, the Directorate remains understaffed, and seeks donor contributions in order to finance additional staff positions.

The Director of Legal Affairs plays a consultative role (with no voting privileges) in the Management Succession Committee that approves all appointments and promotions to senior managerial positions in Community Institutions and reviews long-term plans for management development within them. He or she is also a member of the Commission's Advisory Committee on Appointments and Promotions of Professional Staff, and of the Joint Disciplinary Board of the Community, and moreover attends meetings of the Committee of the Legal and Judicial Affairs of the ECOWAS Parliament.

As for the other units operating under the Office of the President of the Commission, the Office of the Cabinet of the President is headed by a Director, who acts as a principal advisor to the President. He or she assists the President in monitoring and follow-up activities, carries out any other tasks as assigned by the President, reviews documents and organizes working sessions between the President, staff and various visitors to the Commission, and acts as secretary for the departmental meetings The Communication Directorate, operating under the Office of the President as well, is designated to facilitate the "enlightenment of the West African citizens about their Organization." As such, it devises publicity programs to enhance the profile and image of ECOWAS among the citizenry of Member States (coordinating such strategies with other ECOWAS Institutions as well), and plays the role of spokesperson and public relations advisor for the Community. The Directorate serves as both publisher and archivist for all texts and Community Acts issued by ECOWAS. The Internal Audit Directorate is headed by the Community's Chief Internal Auditor, reporting to the Council of Ministers through its Audit Committee, and executing an annual audit plan for the Community that focuses on risk and control assessment, and policy and procedure development. A Department of External Relations is entrusted with sustaining cooperation with Member States through ongoing consultations and coordination with the ECOWAS national units, permanent representations in Abuja and Special Representatives of the President.

v.iii.b The Vice President and other Commissioners

The original ECOWAS Treaty provided that the Executive Secretary would be assisted by two Deputy Executive Secretaries appointed by the Council of Ministers. This was indeed the case during ECOWAS's first two decades, with one Deputy responsible for administrative matters and the other for economic matters. The revised treaty of 1975 removed the quantitative limitation on the number of Deputy Executive Secretaries, establishing instead that the Executive Secretary would be "assisted by Deputy Executive Secretaries and such other staff as may be required for the smooth functioning of the Community."[196] Thereafter, with the establishment of the Commission, the posts of Vice President and seven more Commissioners were created, with the former designated to play "a pivotal role in the definition and establishment of [the Commission's] orientation,"[197] and in ensuring the organizational continuity of the Community in the absence of the President. The Vice President is expected, in particular, to assist and support the President in the discharge of his or her duties, and to assume any other responsibilities that are delegated to him/her by the President. Moreover, he or she is expected, at the direction of the President, to coordinate, monitor and evaluate all regional programs, as well as the relations between the Commission and other ECOWAS institutions and partners. The Vice President is further entrusted

[196] Revised ECOWAS Treaty, Article 17(2).

[197] Rules of Procedure of the ECOWAS Commission, Rule 11(2)(c). The same applies to all Commissioners except the President, who follows a different procedure, as detailed above.

with identifying and effectively managing "national, regional and international developments and trends likely to impact on ECOWAS."[198] Accordingly, three Units operate under the Office of the Vice President, forming his or her cabinet: the Monitoring-Evaluation Unit, the Unit on Relations with other Institutions and the Strategic Planning Unit. The latter, established in 2008, aims to "facilitate the development of a regional strategy for structural and institutional transformation as well as interface all the programs and plans of ECOWAS Institutions and align them with the overall vision of the region,"[199] and has taken the lead, with support from international actors and private consultants, in preparing the Community's Strategic Plans. The Vice President also supervises the Community Computer Centre, which supports the information and communication technologies of the Community.

Like the President of the Commission, the Vice President and the other Commissioners are elected for a non-renewable four-year term in accordance with the rotational mechanism for allocating statutory posts among all Member States. Nigeria, as the host of the Commission, is entitled to, on an exceptional basis, a permanent seat among the Commissioners, although it may not encumber any particular position permanently. The Vice President and the other Commissioners must be nationals of the Member State that nominates them to the post, and be "persons of proven

[198] Rules of Procedure of the ECOWAS Commission, Rule 11 ("Functions of the Vice President").

[199] "Message from the Vice President" (available at www.spu.ecowas.int).

competence and integrity in their field of work . . . [who also] have a global vision of regional integration issues."[200] The Member State that is allocated one of these posts is required to nominate three candidates, who are then interviewed by a Ministerial Committee for Selection and Evaluation of Statutory Appointees that convenes in closed session at the call of the President of the Commission and ranks the candidates for each of the positions by order of merit. Those recommended for appointment by an absolute majority of Member States represented on the Committee may then be appointed for the posts of Vice President or Commissioner by the Council of Ministers, so long as the Council votes as an absolute majority on the nomination. The President and Vice President of the Commission must not be nationals of the same Member State (as no State shall be allocated more than one statutory post in any Community Institution), and must not be nationals of Member States "belonging to the same language group." Upon taking office, the Vice President and all other Commissioners appear at a session of the Council to take an oath to discharge their duties independently and honestly.

v.iv *Staff*

Under the previous Executive Secretariat model, fewer than 300 staff members carried out the duties of the institution, but

[200] Supplementary Act A/SP.14/02/12 of the Authority of Heads of State and Government, Article 10(2) ("Criteria of Integrity and Competence").

today the ECOWAS Commission employs over 700 staff members, representing – in varying proportions – all fifteen Member States. The Council of Ministers imposed a freeze on recruitment in 2009, citing the need for improvement in staffing, training and the balancing of costs between administrative and programmatic activities, but this ban has been partially lifted following a comprehensive staff audit mandated by the Council, as part of an effort to improve the efficiency of the Commission and develop within it a team spirit that had been judged to be lacking.[201]

Staff members of the Commission are considered international civil servants whose responsibilities are exclusively international in nature. The revised ECOWAS treaty stipulates that, in the discharge of their duties, all staff members of the Commission owe their loyalty entirely to the Community: they are to neither "seek nor accept instructions from any government or any national or international authority external to the Community," and are to "refrain from any activity or any conduct incompatible with their status as international civil servants."[202] Staff Regulations,

[201] *ECOWAS Regional Strategic Plan (2011–2015)*, p. 77. The staff audit, launched in March 2012, was introduced to staff members by the Commission's Vice President as part of the management's strategy "to engage with the staff and ensure full participation and joint ownership of corporate decisions towards achieving common goals for the good of Community citizens": ECOWAS Press Release 53/2012.

[202] Revised ECOWAS Treaty, Article 20(1). The Member States are under a corresponding obligation "to respect the international character of the office of the Executive Secretary, the Deputy Executive Secretaries, and other staff of the Community and . . . not to seek to influence them in the performance of their duties": see Article 20(2). The Rules of

issued in 1983 and updated from time to time since to reflect "the principles applicable in other similar international organizations,"[203] forbid staff members of the Commission to accept "any honour, decoration, remuneration or other sort of favour incompatible with their obligations and duties towards the Community" from any source external to ECOWAS; and moreover stipulate that they may not engage in any political activity "which is inconsistent with the independence and impartiality required by their status as staff members of an international organization or which is in any way detrimental to ECOWAS."[204] Following concerns about "disloyalty to the Community," a requirement for all staff members to take an oath of secrecy was extended in 1990, with Professional staff obligated to take an oath of office as well.[205] The Staff Regulations also stipulate that all staff members are obligated to maintain the confidentiality of

Procedure of the ECOWAS Commission also mandate that the Commissioners "shall act independently in the exercise of their functions, and in the overall interest of the Community" (Rule 4, "Status of Members of the Commission"), and they are required to take an oath of office containing such obligation. See also Principles of Staff Employment of the Economic Community of West African States (ECOWAS) (2005), Article 3.1 ("General Obligations").

203 The Regulations apply to employees of all ECOWAS Community Institutions, as a supplement to the Principles of Staff Employment of the Economic Community of West African States (ECOWAS) (2005).

204 ECOWAS Staff Regulations, Articles 4(f) and 4(g) ("Duties and Obligations"). The Regulations do recognize that staff members "may discharge their civic duties."

205 *Annual Report of the ECOWAS Executive Secretary, 1989–1990.*

information made known to them in their professional capacity (including for a period of five years after the end of their service), and that intellectual property rights emanating from work officially performed at the Commission are the sole property of ECOWAS.

Alongside the Staff Regulations, the employment of Commission staff members is governed in general by the ECOWAS Treaty; the Community's Principles of Staff Employment; and the ECOWAS Schemes of Service Framework, adopted in 1991 and revised in 2007, which describes the foundations of the career development program for all Community Institutions. All staff members are explicitly required to show diligence in discharging their duties, be regularly present at their duty stations, and "scrupulously abide by the working hours" established by the President of the Commission; they must not accept any other employment without prior authorization from the President.

The Commission's staff are divided among five categories: (1) Statutory Appointees, who are those appointed as Commissioners according to the specific procedure set out in the revised ECOWAS treaty, as amended; (2) Professional Staff, those "involved in the execution of the duties" assigned to the Commission; (3) General Service Staff, who are recruited locally as "qualified administrative official[s]," primarily involved in executing day-to-day administrative tasks; (4) Auxiliary Staff, who are "semi-skilled and non-technical personnel" recruited locally as well; and (5) Domestic Staff, who are those "living in housing officially provided to Statutory Appointees and providing domestic services to these

Appointees."[206] Appointments to the Commission may be permanent (for an indefinite period, with one year's probation); for a fixed term (not to exceed three years, but renewable once for another such period, with six months' probation); per contract; or on a temporary basis (not to exceed six months, but renewable up to three times for periods not exceeding six months each).[207] Statutory appointees and Professional Staff are entitled to "the same privileges and immunities as are accorded to diplomatic envoys," while all other staff members are entitled, in the territory of all Member States, to the immunities provided in the General Convention on the Privileges and Immunities of ECOWAS, the Headquarters Agreement, and any agreements that are concluded between ECOWAS and host countries of its duty

[206] ECOWAS Staff Regulations, Article 3 ("Definitions"). The Regulations further stipulate that "[t]he Council of Ministers shall be responsible for the classification of posts, based on the nature of the duties and responsibilities attached thereto" (Article 11). The Professional Staff category for senior managerial, managerial and professional technical or administrative positions, is divided into the following salary grades and steps: (1) Grade D1, comprising ten steps intended for the senior Director cadre; Grades P1 to P5, each comprising ten steps; and (3) P6 level, "intended for unique circumstances" of employing a "recognized expert." The General Service category is divided into Grades G1 to G7, each comprising eleven steps (Step 11 being a longevity step for staff serving ECOWAS for at least twenty years). The Auxiliary Staff category is made up of Grades M1 to M7, each comprising seven steps (Article 10, "Grades and Steps").

[207] ECOWAS Staff Regulations, Article 15 ("Nature of Appointment") and Article 19 ("Probation and Confirmation"); staff members are those who hold a permanent or a temporary appointment and are paid on a monthly basis (as distinguished from consultants).

stations. The President informs the Ministry of Foreign Affairs of the host country of staff members who enjoy privileges and immunities, and is required to update such lists from time to time; it is only the President who may waive the immunities and privileges.[208]

As a general rule, recruitment for staff positions at the Commission is done through a competitive process. Applicants for Professional Staff positions, who must be nationals of a Member State holding a university degree "or equivalent professional qualification," and may not be older than fifty years of age, are interviewed by the Commission's Advisory Committee on Appointments and Promotions of Professional Staff, chaired by the Commissioner for Administration and Finance. Due regard is to be given by the Committee – "subject to ensuring the highest standards of efficiency and technical competence" – to the maintenance of "equitable geographical distribution of posts among nationals of all Member States."[209] For locally recruited General Service and

[208] See Principles of Staff Employment of the Economic Community of West African States (ECOWAS) (2005), Article 3.3 ("Privileges and Immunities"); ECOWAS Staff Regulations, Article 8 ("Privileges and Immunities"); General Convention on Privileges and Immunities of the Economic Community of West African States (1978); Headquarters Agreement between the Economic Community of West African States and the Government of the Federal Republic of Nigeria (1984).

[209] ECOWAS Staff Regulations, Article 12 ("Professional Staff") and Article 63 ("Advisory Committee on Appointments and Promotions of Professional Staff"). Any vacant permanent Professional Staff post must be advertised, with the application deadline being sixty days from the date of publication of the vacancy. The Regulations make clear that "[i]n selecting between equally qualified applicants, preference shall

Auxiliary Staff, candidates "shall normally [but do not have to] be recruited from nationals of Member States"; and the Commission's designated Advisory Committee on Appointments and Promotions of Locally Recruited Staff, chaired by the Commissioner for Administration and Finance as well, is to be guided by the primary consideration of "ensuring the highest standards of efficiency and technical competence."[210] The Commission, like other Community Institutions, is also required to give "due regard" to gender balance in recruiting for staff positions.[211] It is the President of the Commission who decides, on the recommendation of the Advisory Committees, to appoint (or promote) staff, and he or she is required to communicate such decisions (and the adopted reports of the Committees) to Member States. Appointments to senior management posts in the Commission other than those of Statutory Appointees have a separate procedure: these (like senior management posts in other Community Institutions) are considered by a Community-wide Joint Management Succession Committee comprising the heads of all ECOWAS Institutions and their deputies,

be given to nationals of Member States which have the lowest representation of staff in the organization."

210 ECOWAS Staff Regulations, Article 13 ("General and Auxiliary Service Staff") and Article 65 ("Advisory Committee on Appointments and Promotions of Locally Recruited Staff").

211 Principles of Staff Employment of the Economic Community of West African States (ECOWAS) (2005), Article 4.1 ("Recruitment"). The Commission has recently been criticized for not fulfilling "its outspoken aim of gender mainstreaming in all its frameworks and initiatives" (see http://makeeverywomancount.org), and has been conscious of the need to improve in that regard.

for which the Commissioner for Administration and Finance serves as secretary. The Committee is guided by an ECOWAS Career Development Policy, which aims, among other things, to predict future vacancies, track promising staff members for such positions, and provide them with targeted relevant training and development.

Existing staff members are given priority in filling vacant positions at the Commission, and furthermore have the option of being seconded to other ECOWAS institutions or select international organizations for a maximum period of two years, while retaining a lien on their original post and grade level, for the purpose of professional development. Recruitment of immediate family members of a staff member is forbidden, "[e]xcept in cases where no comparable alternative is possible."[212] Open positions are advertised in various publications circulating within the Member States, as well as on the Community's Careers website, which is user-friendly, fully available in the three working languages of the Community, and connected with a designated Twitter account announcing vacancies; the Community's human resources portal provides staff members with information on their rights and obligations, relevant procedures and other related matters.

Upon appointment, a staff member must provide the personal information required to determine his or her status in accordance with the Staff Principles and Regulations, and,

[212] ECOWAS Staff Regulations, Article 14 ("Recruitment of Personnel Related to Staff Members"). In the event that staff members get married, "the contractual basis of their employment remains unchanged, but their rights and benefits shall be modified accordingly."

if holding a financial interest in any enterprise, disclose its nature and extent, and pledge in writing that he or she will not be actively involved in the management of such enterprise.[213] Professional Staff are entitled to an installation allowance in the amount of one month's salary upon arrival at their duty station, and to a housing allowance.[214] If they are internationally recruited, the Commission bears the expenses related to their travel and shipment of personal and household goods.[215] General Service or Auxiliary Staff are eligible to receive a compensatory housing allowance as well. Domestic Staff members, with the exception of security guards, are appointed for the time of tenure of the staff member for whom they work.

213 ECOWAS Staff Regulations, Article 4(d) ("Duties and Obligations"). Such disclosure is also required of those acquiring such interest while working for the Commission, within five working days of the date of acquiring the interest.

214 ECOWAS Staff Regulations, Article 35(a) ("Installation and Resettlement Allowances") and Article 32(a) ("Housing Allowance"). Many staff members were formerly provided residential accommodation by ECOWAS for which they contributed 5 percent of their net annual salary, to be deducted at source, but this ended in 2007. The amount of the housing allowance is to be determined by the Council of Ministers, "on the recommendation of the Administration and Finance Commission taking into account considerations such as the actual situation in each duty station."

215 ECOWAS Staff Regulations, Article 55 ("Travel on Initial Appointment"), Article 56 ("Travel on Separation from Service") and Article 57 ("Shipment of Personal and Household Effects"). Travel expenses are borne only for those whose appointment is for over one year, and cover eligible dependants as well.

The three main staff categories, those of Professional, General Service and Auxiliary Staff, are each divided into specified salary grades and steps. The salary scale for all categories of staff is determined by the Council of Ministers (and reviewed at least every five years to ensure its "fairness and competitiveness"), with the salaries offered at the African Union for equivalent positions serving as the primary reference point in establishing and adjusting the salary scales for Statutory Appointees and Professional Staff, and the salaries offered by the United Nations agencies in Abuja for equivalent positions serving as the primary reference point with regard to salary scales for General Service and Auxiliary Staff. The salary of each staff member within an approved scale is determined according to his or her assigned grade, upon the recommendation of an advisory committee. Post adjustment, to ensure equivalent purchase power in all duty stations, is provided to ECOWAS staff working outside Abuja, and based on the indices published by the United Nations International Civil Service Commission.

In addition, staff members who are not provided with vehicles are paid a monthly transport allowance. Dependency allowance is paid for "legally married" spouses who are unemployed, and for unmarried children under the age of eighteen (or twenty-four, if the child is in full-time attendance at an educational institution).[216] Staff members are further

[216] ECOWAS Staff Regulations, Article 33 ("Dependency Allowance") and Article 3 ("Definitions"). Staff members must show that they do not receive a similar allowance from other sources in respect of the said spouse. A spouse may still qualify as "Dependent Spouse" when

entitled to education grants ("reasonable assistance") for their dependent children.[217] General Service or Auxiliary Staff "who are called upon to discharge extra responsibilities on a continuing basis or who are subject to special constraints because of the nature of their appointment," are entitled to Special Overtime Allowance,[218] and those who are required to work "in excess of the normal working week [only] on an occasional basis" are eligible to receive payment of overtime. If staff members are called upon temporarily to discharge the duties and responsibilities of a post higher than their own, and do so satisfactorily and for at least sixty uninterrupted days, they are entitled to Acting Allowance in addition to their regular salary. Furthermore, staff members may request salary advances and loan guarantees, to be granted upon the authorization of the President. The salaries of internationally recruited Professional Staff members are exempt from taxation.

working for a salary not exceeding an amount fixed by the President of the Commission for that purpose (approximately equivalent to the salary scale of the lowest entry level at ECOWAS). The amount of dependency allowances "shall from time to time be reviewed by the Council of Ministers on the recommendation of the Administration and Finance Commission." Dependency allowance for children is limited to a maximum of four children.

217 ECOWAS Staff Regulations, Article 41 ("Education Benefits"). This allowance, payable in respect of an academic year at a recognized primary, secondary or higher education institution, is limited to a maximum of four children as well.

218 ECOWAS Staff Regulations, Article 36(a) ("Other Official Allowances"). The Council of Ministers, upon the recommendation of the President of the Commission, approves the list of such eligible staff and determines "the conditions and modalities of payment for each category of staff." Those granted such payments are not entitled to other overtime pay.

Staff members holding a Statutory, permanent or fixed-term appointment receive thirty days of paid leave per year of active service, and as a general rule must take a minimum of twenty days of annual leave each year.[219] ECOWAS Day (May 28) and official public holidays observed in the host country are official holidays as well; and nationals of a Member State may be granted one paid day off on the national day of their Member State. Internationally recruited staff members (and their eligible dependants), from the second calendar year following their assumption of duty, are entitled to home leave every two years in lieu of their accrued annual leave; locally recruited staff (and their dependants) are entitled to transport allowance when proceeding on annual leave.[220] A special leave may be authorized by the President of the Commission with full or partial pay, or without pay, for personal reasons such as marriage, death of a family member or any other compelling reason. Maternity leave of fourteen weeks on full salary is provided to female staff members (and may be extended without pay), and paid paternity leave for their male colleagues is set at three working days. All staff

219 ECOWAS Staff Regulations, Article 38(a), (b) and (c) ("Annual Leave"). A staff member may be granted up to twenty days of advance annual leave (not yet accrued) "for exceptional and urgent reasons," provided that it is anticipated that he or she will remain in service long enough to accrue them. In addition, a maximum of ninety working days of unused annual leave may be carried over from one leave-year to the next.

220 ECOWAS Staff Regulations, Article 39 ("Home Leave"). The Regulations stipulate that home leave shall be granted "only when it is expected that the service of the staff member shall continue at least six months beyond the date of his return from home leave and outside the home country."

members (and their dependants) may join a comprehensive medical insurance plan provided by ECOWAS, and are subscribed to a group accident and life insurance. Sick leave on full salary, and medical evacuation if necessary, are available to staff members as well.[221] Staff members serving for one year or more may be enrolled in one of the three ECOWAS Pension Plans, contributing each month 6 percent of their base salary while the Commission contributes an additional 14 percent.[222] Contracted staff receive a salary equal to the scale used for the corresponding category of ECOWAS staff, plus a 10 percent addition in lieu of social benefits. The Commission also offers unpaid internship positions that are advertised and filled on a needs basis.

A written assessment of performance is to be held annually for each staff member, in accordance with the manual on "Policies and Procedures for Planning and Evaluation of Individual Performance (PEIP) in ECOWAS Institutions" issued by the Commission. Satisfactory performance

[221] ECOWAS Staff Regulations, Article 42 ("Sick Leave"). Staff members holding a permanent appointment may be granted sick leave each year on full salary for up to three months, and on half-salary for an additional three months; staff members holding a fixed-term contract for one year or longer may be granted sick leave each year on full salary for up to two months, and on half-salary for an additional two months.

[222] ECOWAS Staff Regulations, Article 47 ("Pension"). One plan is open to internationally recruited staff members, another for locally recruited staff members, and a third for all categories of staff in the Community. These are not available to Statutory Appointees and officers holding contract appointments receiving 10 percent payment in lieu of benefits. Staff members may also contribute to the Staff Provident Fund.

provides for an automatic advancement of one salary step within the relevant grade of the position, and such increment may be withheld in cases of unsatisfactory performance or for disciplinary reasons. In order to develop skills that are relevant to their function, as identified in the PEIP exercise, staff members may be sent on officially sanctioned training programs or granted special leave for advanced studies in the interest of the Community.[223]

Commission staff members must generally retire when turning sixty years old, or once they have served in the Community continuously for thirty-five years (the Commission may nevertheless retain such staff members, "if their services are deemed essential," for another maximum period of five years). Early retirement is available for staff members who have reached the age of fifty-five or have served in the Community for at least thirty years. The President of the Commission may also terminate the appointment of a staff member, by advance written notice, for a number of reasons enumerated in the Staff Regulations, relating either to the staff member's performance or to the redundancy of his or her post.[224] Those terminated

[223] Such leave may be for a period not exceeding one year, renewable once, and may or may not be paid; see ECOWAS Staff Regulations, Article 25 ("Skills Development") and Article 26 ("Study and Training").

[224] ECOWAS Staff Regulations, Article 59 ("Termination of Appointment"). Three months' notice is required if the staff member holds a permanent appointment, and one month's notice if he or she holds a confirmed fixed-term appointment. The President may authorize payment in lieu of notice "when deemed in the interest of the Institution."

because of redundant employment, following the withdrawal of their country of nationality from ECOWAS, or as a consequence of medical reasons, are entitled to severance pay; such pay is generally not awarded to those terminated for reasons of unsatisfactory performance. Upon separation from service, staff members are further entitled to one month's salary for every year of service rendered to the Community (up to a maximum of twelve years).[225] Professional Staff receive an additional resettlement allowance of three months' salary on their separation from the Commission, provided they were not summarily dismissed, did not resign and had served the organization for at least four years.

ECOWAS's Principles of Staff Employment mandate that the President of the Commission set up "appropriate mechanisms allowing for consultations with the duly elected staff representatives when policies on human resources, conditions of service, and general staff welfare, are put in place or changed, and when [the] Principles, and Staff Regulations are introduced, amended or revoked."[226] Moreover, staff members are represented, for each of the three main staff categories, on the appointment and

[225] ECOWAS Staff Regulations, Article 35(d) ("Installation and Resettlement Allowances"); this refers to all staff except Statutory Appointees, who are in turn entitled to a gratuity for each year of service, at a rate to be determined by the Council of Ministers.

[226] Principles of Staff Employment of the Economic Community of West African States (ECOWAS) (2005), Article 10 ("Consultations with Staff").

disciplinary committees of the Commission. The latter, comprising two managers appointed by the President and one staff representative, consider any infractions by staff members punishable under first- and second-degree sanctions as defined in the Staff Regulations. A Joint Disciplinary Advisory Board, established by the President for the whole Community, handles the most serious infractions, punishable under third-degree sanctions. Staff Regulations differentiate offenses punishable by these first-, second- and third-degree sanctions: they begin with a warning and reprimand by a superior officer in the case of first-degree sanctions; they escalate to censure, suspension of biennial increments, surcharge, suspension, termination or demotion in the second degree, and for those offenses punishable by third-degree sanctions, a staff member faces summary dismissal with or without pension. The President may also suspend (with full pay) staff members charged with a serious criminal offense until the investigation is concluded, if maintaining them at their post "may be prejudicial to the interests of the Community or the investigations." If accused or charged in court, staff members are to be suspended with half-pay; and, if convicted and sentenced, they automatically forfeit their employment at the Commission. The President must provide reasons for a decision to apply sanctions, and may make it public. As with any other decision concerning their career, staff members have a right to appeal against sanctions imposed on them, first to the Council of Ministers, and then, if rejected, to the Community Court of Justice that has a jurisdiction over disputes between Institutions of the Community and their officials.

v.v *Budget*

Funding has been a chronic problem for ECOWAS since its inception, and the Commission – much like the erstwhile Executive Secretariat – has been plagued by enduring financial constraints. Community operations were originally funded by annual budgetary contributions from Member States, assessed according to a contribution arrangement requiring that the largest Member States pay the greatest quota share. Arrears in such payments, which became "a whiskery old ECOWAS chestnut,"[227] had compelled the Executive Secretariat to often cancel or suspend activities, as well as resort to short-term borrowing (mainly from the ECOWAS Fund, the Nigerian government and even commercial banks) in order to maintain operations. Wishing to avoid such difficulties, the revised ECOWAS Treaty of 1993 introduced a new autonomous mechanism (that is, outside national budgets) to provide the funding for regional integration: a special Community Levy, imposed on the "total value of [a Member State's] import duty derivable from goods imported into the Community from third [non-ECOWAS] countries."[228] The four main financing

[227] K. Whiteman, "Dreams and Dangers: 15th ECOWAS Summit opens in Dakar," 3907 *West Africa* 1312 (UK, 1992).

[228] Revised ECOWAS Treaty, Article 72 ("Community Levy"). The level of the Levy is determined by the Council of Ministers, and is currently set at 0.5 percent; the Commission maintains accounts in the central banks of the Member States, into which their contributions are to be deposited. "Recently, the implementation of the Community levy regime has been faced with challenges mainly related to the interpretation of the goods covered by the levy": ECOWAS Press Release 314/2013.

sources for ECOWAS at present are the Community Levy (as a principal source), arrears clearance by Member States (of contributions and Community Levy proceeds), donor/development partners' contributions, and special contributions by Member States. Securing funding for operations and programs remains a challenge for the Commission, whose weak cash-flow position owes most to the continued arrears in remittances of Member States, and unforeseen costs of emergency peacekeeping and security interventions in the Community.

The responsibility for preparing a draft consolidated annual budget (for the following financial year) for all ECOWAS Institutions lies with the President of the Commission, who is required to submit the draft to the Council of Ministers for consideration and approval no later than two months prior to the end of the financial year. The draft is to be accompanied, *inter alia*, by a work program for the year, as well as data pertaining to the budget implementation level for the previous and current year and to outstanding commitments. The budget is established in Units of Account (UA), equal to the Special Drawing Rights mechanism employed by the International Monetary Fund, and once approved by the Council it is published by the Commission in the ECOWAS Official Journal. Requests for supplementary budgets to meet extra-budgetary expenditures of the Community during the financial year, usually relating to security and humanitarian interventions, are considered by the Council on the recommendation of its Administration and Finance Committee. All financial management and oversight are to be carried out in accordance with ECOWAS's Financial Regulations and Manual of Accounting Procedures of the Community.

The Commission's annual budget has not seen substantial increases in recent years, and in 2013 was set at UA 136,859,600 (US$210.3 million), out of a total Community Institutions budget of UA 192,223,052 (US$295.4 million).[229] The defunct Executive Secretariat, for the sake of comparison, in 1995, had a budget of approximately US$7 million. A significant portion of the budget is allocated to staff expenditures.

The President of the Commission is also the Principal Authorizing Officer of the Community for managing income and expenditure (but may, and does, delegate this power), and he or she may, as such, be personally financially liable if he or she, intentionally or through gross negligence, causes prejudice to the Community by not following its financial rules. The ECOWAS Financial Regulations insist on a clear separation of the functions of authorizing officer, accounting officer, imprest holder and financial controller within each Community Institute, and stipulate a detailed liability regime for mismanagement of funds.[230] At the Commission, the Commissioner for Administration and Finance serves as

[229] The total figure includes the funding allocated to the Commission, the West African Health Organization (WAHO), the Inter-Governmental Action Group against Money Laundering in West Africa (GIABA), the ECOWAS Parliament and the ECOWAS Court of Justice. The total ECOWAS budget for 2013, including the financing allocated for "statutory obligations, interventions in Member States and peace and security," is UA 495,889,568 (US$762.1 million).

[230] See Financial Regulations of the Institutions of the Economic Community of West African States (ECOWAS), Chapter V ("Financial Actors: Principle of Separation of Functions"), Chapter VI ("Liability of Financial Officers"). The Regulations entered into force in January 2010 (see Council Regulation C/REG.5/05/09 of May 27, 2009).

Table s.6 *The ECOWAS Commission's annual budget, 2007–2013 (in US$ million)*

2007	105.7[a]
2008	145.5[a]
2009	190.0[a]
2010	176.7[a]
2011	204.8
2012	180.7
2013	210.3

Note

[a] A figure excluding the budgets for the Commission's Gender Center, Water Resources Center, Youth and Sports Center, liaison office in Brussels, and the offices of the Financial Controller and Chief Internal Auditor.

the Accounting Officer, in charge of managing the Commission's funds and reviewing the accounts of other Community Institutions. Further checks are applied through the offices of the Community's Chief Internal Auditor and Financial Controller, with the latter reporting directly to the Council of Ministers.[231] The consolidated accounts of the ECOWAS Institutions, moreover, are audited annually by external

[231] See Council Regulation C/REG.27/12/06 of December 2006, Articles 2 and 3, relating to the reorganization of the Office of the Financial Controller of the Community Institutions. All internal auditors at ECOWAS are bound by a code of conduct adopted by the Council, as well as by the ECOWAS Internal Audit Charter: see Council Regulation C/REG.22/12/06 of December 2006, Article 1 ("Adoption of a Code of Conduct for Internal Auditors of Community Institutions"); Council Regulation C/REG.15/12/06 of December 2006 ("Adoption of an ECOWAS Internal Audit Charter").

auditors appointed by the Heads of State and Government on the recommendation of the Council for a period of two years, renewable for a maximum of two terms of two years each.

Efforts are under way at ECOWAS to adopt a budgetary program that supports a result-based management system, as the current process of financial management "remains especially weak in the areas of budgeting and accounting systems, and auditing, owing to insufficient and inappropriate systems (including computer systems)."[232] Program budgeting is also considered necessary in light of the difficulties encountered over the years, due to the fact that the budget is prepared for one year, irrespective of project duration.

VI The Common Market of the South (MERCOSUR) Technical Secretariat

The Common Market of the South (*El Mercado Común del Sur*, MERCOSUR) was established in 1991 with the signing of the Treaty of Asunción, bringing Argentina, Brazil, Paraguay and Uruguay into a regional economic integration scheme.[233]

[232] *ECOWAS Commission Strategic Plan (2011–2015)*, pp. 35–36.

[233] On the historical evolution of MERCOSUR (also known as MERCOSUL, the Portuguese equivalent of the Spanish acronym), see G. L. Gardini, "MERCOSUR: What You See Is Not (Always) What You Get," 17 *European Law Journal* 683 (2011), pp. 685–689; A. D. De Klor, "The Legal-Institutional Structure of MERCOSUR," in M. T. F. Filho, L. Lixinski and M. B. O. Giupponi (eds.), *The Law of MERCOSUR* (Oxford: Hart Publishing, 2010), pp. 29–30; J. Guira, *MERCOSUR: Trade and Investment Amid Financial Crisis* (The Hague: Kluwer Law

Wishing to expand their domestic markets "for accelerating the processes of economic development with social justice," and respond to the global "trend towards formation of large economic areas,"[234] the States Parties decided that their common market would become effective by the end of 1994, and for the transition period entrusted two bodies with the implementation and management of the process. First, the Common Market Council, comprising the Ministers of Foreign Affairs and Ministers of Economy of the States Parties, was designated as the highest organ of MERCOSUR, and charged with providing for "the Common Market's political leadership and for decision-making aimed at ensuring compliance with the goals of and time limits set for the full implementation" of the Treaty.[235] Second, a Common Market Group, composed of four members and four alternates for each State Party (representing the Ministry of Foreign Affairs, the Ministry of the Economy and the Central Bank), was to

International, 2003), pp. 15–24; J. M. Quijano, "Mercosur: Balance y Perspectivas," 92 *Revista Mexicana de Política Exterior* 57–95 (2011); L. V. Pereira, "Toward the Common Market of the South: Mercosur's Origins, Evolution, and Challenges," in R. Roett (ed.), *MERCOSUR: Regional Integration, World Markets* (Boulder, CO: Lynne Rienner Publishers, 1999), p. 20; M. Schelhase, "The Changing Context of Regionalism and Regionalisation in the Americas: Mercosur and Beyond," in T. M. Shaw *et al.* (eds.), *The Ashgate Research Companion to Regionalisms* (Farnham: Ashgate, 2011), pp. 175–184. Venezuela signed a membership agreement in 2006, and became a full member in 2012; Bolivia, Chile, Colombia, Ecuador, Peru and Guyana currently have Associate Member status.

[234] Preamble to the Treaty of Asunción.

[235] Treaty of Asunción, Articles 10 and 11.

serve as the executive body of MERCOSUR, with a mandate to monitor compliance with the Treaty, initiate measures to realize its objectives, and enforce the decisions adopted by the Council.[236] The Treaty further stipulated that the Common Market Group would be assisted in the interim period by an Administrative Secretariat based in Montevideo, Uruguay, "whose main functions shall be to keep Group documents and to report on Group activities."[237]

According to schedule, MERCOSUR was given a permanent institutional structure and an international legal personality four years later, with the signing of the more elaborate 1994 Protocol of Ouro Preto. The Protocol designated three intergovernmental organs as the bloc's decision-making bodies: the Common Market Council (CMC), meeting at least biannually (in tandem with MERCOSUR's presidential summits) to direct the integration process through Decisions adopted by consensus to be binding on the States Parties; the Common Market Group (GMC), the executive organ of MERCOSUR, empowered to hold ordinary or extraordinary meetings as often as necessary, and to issue Resolutions that would be binding on the States Parties as well; and the MERCOSUR Trade Commission, created to assist the GMC by meeting at least once a month to oversee the implementation of the common trade policy instruments agreed upon by the States Parties (the Commission was also charged with ruling on questions submitted by the States Parties, and with reviewing various related issues, under its authority to

[236] Treaty of Asunción, Articles 13 and 14.
[237] Treaty of Asunción, Article 15.

issue binding Directives and make non-binding Proposals). The Protocol moreover established a Joint Parliamentary Commission representing the Parliaments of the States Parties, to assist in internalizing MERCOSUR norms into the domestic legal systems and harmonizing relevant legislation; and an Economic and Social Consultative Forum representing the economic and social sectors within the bloc, with the responsibility to make recommendations to the GMC on economic and social issues of interest. All organs were to consist of an equal number of representatives from each State Party.[238]

The Protocol of Ouro Preto also established a permanent Administrative Secretariat of MERCOSUR (*Secretaría Administrativa del MERCOSUR*) "to provide operational support" to the other MERCOSUR bodies.[239] Overseen by the GMC and led by a Director, this small structure was charged with carrying out purely administrative tasks, namely: maintaining MERCOSUR's official archives; publishing and circulating the decisions adopted within the Common Market; providing logistical support to meetings; informing the State Parties on a regular basis about measures taken by each State to incorporate MERCOSUR decisions into the respective domestic legal regime; and facilitating MERCOSUR's

[238] The Protocol enumerates the specific composition, duties and powers of each of these organs, and the States Parties reserved the right to create auxiliary bodies as necessary; see Protocol of Ouro Preto: Additional Protocol to the Treaty of Asunción on the Organizational Structure of the MERCOSUR, Articles 1–30.

[239] Protocol of Ouro Preto, Article 31.

dispute settlement mechanism.[240] Housed in a former luxury hotel building in Montevideo,[241] the Administrative Secretariat was initially divided into four departments: Administration; Norms; Documents and Communications; and Information Technology. As the only MERCOSUR organ to be funded through a community budget and comprise a permanent staff of officials not directly appointed by the national governments, the Administrative Secretariat was given neither substantive functional responsibilities nor power of initiative; it was to serve as the administrative arm of a regional bloc that opted to create no supranational actors and no autonomous regional bureaucracy. Instead, the States Parties adopted an "exclusively inter-governmental decision-making structure."[242] Put differently, "the Member States of MERCOSUR have clearly sought to ensure that control of the integration process remains in the hands of

[240] Protocol of Ouro Preto, Article 32; the Administrative Secretariat was further mandated with performing other tasks requested by the Common Market Council, the Common Market Group and the MERCOSUR Trade Commission. On MERCOSUR's dispute settlement system, see the two other key documents relating to the Common Market's legal and institutional foundation: the Brasilia Protocol on the Resolution of Controversies (1991) and the Olivos Protocol for the Resolution of Controversies (2002).

[241] Pursuant to a Headquarters Agreement signed between MERCOSUR and Uruguay in 1996, the headquarters building is owned by the city of Montevideo, and is maintained by a Uruguayan superintendent.

[242] M. Doctor, "Prospects for Deepening MERCOSUR Integration: Economic Asymmetry and Institutional Deficits," 20 *Review of International Political Economy* 515 (2013), p. 518.

the Member States and not in a group of independent international civil servants."[243]

Yet in less than a decade and after significant initial achievements, the treaty's integration process was at a standstill; with the dawn of the new millennium, the onset of financial crises in the region, and the ascent of center-leftist governments who saw the regional enterprise not only as a trade bloc, but also as "a catalyst of values, traditions and a shared future,"[244] MERCOSUR's neo-liberal orientation and minimalist institutional design were under pressure to change. A "relaunch" of the Common Market was proclaimed in 2000 in an effort to enhance the credibility of the organization, confront external challenges and accommodate an expansion of the regional agenda. As a result, significant

[243] R. A. Porrata-Doria, Jr., "MERCOSUR: The Common Market of the Twenty-First Century?," 32:1 *Georgia Journal of International and Comparative Law* 62 (2004), p. 18. See also A. Crawely, *MERCOSUR: In Search of an Agenda – Rapporteur's Report* (Institute for the Integration of Latin America and the Caribbean, 2004), p. 7: "attitudes to MERCOSUR's institutional dimensions have been conditioned by a desire to avoid the perceived risks inherent in introducing the issue of supranationality to an agreement whose largest member clearly seems to favor strictly inter-governmental mechanisms"; R. Bouzas, *The Politics and Economics of Mercosur: Old Challenges, New Approaches* (University of San Andres, 2008), p. 4, suggesting, instead, that the decision to have no autonomous bureaucracy separate from national administrations was driven by the desire to "prevent the isolation of decision making layers from the national agencies responsible for enforcement."

[244] Statement of MERCOSUR leaders, quoted in the European Commission's *Regional Strategy Paper for MERCOSUR 2007–2013*, E/2007/1640 (2007), p. 6.

institutional revisions and reinforcements were put in place in the period that followed, to realize these goals. In 2002, the States Parties set up a Permanent Review Tribunal as part of a wider reform in MERCOSUR's dispute settlement procedure; the following year, 2003, they also created a Commission of Permanent Representatives, composed of a Permanent Representative from each State Party and a President, to assist the CMC and the State Party serving as MERCOSUR's President *pro tempore*. Soon after, an Administrative-Labor Tribunal to resolve disputes between MERCOSUR and its staff was set up as well, and in 2004, a Center for Promotion of the Rule of Law was established. The Joint Parliamentary Commission established under the Protocol of Ouro Preto was transformed in 2005 into a MERCOSUR Parliament (PARLASUR), comprising eighteen representatives from each country and serving as a forum for regional deliberation (without any legislative or control authority); and a Democracy Observatory was established in 2007. Additional organs were formed as well, joining the wide array of dozens of specialized committees and working groups operating under the decision-making bodies.

The institutional restructuring did not pass over the Administrative Secretariat. In response to criticisms which suggested that "[t]he lack of an independent technical body is, undoubtedly, one of MERCOSUR's clearest institutional deficits," and recommendations that the Secretariat be given "human, technical and financial resources to enable it to become a body that devotes itself to the *regional* project,"[245]

[245] To borrow, respectively, the words of C. Pena and R. Rozemberg, *MERCOSUR: A Different Approach to Institutional Development*

the States Parties resolved in 2002 to transform the Administrative Secretariat into a Technical one (*Secretaría Técnica*).[246] A central element of the transformation process was the establishment within the Secretariat of a Technical Advisory Department, created as a "common space for reflection on the development and consolidation of the integration process,"[247] to provide legal and economic advice to MERCOSUR decision-makers. The Department was to be staffed by four "technical advisors" (one from each State Party at that time), two of them experts in international law and two of them expert international economists, who were to be recruited through a competitive process and appointed for a renewable

(The Canadian Foundation for the Americas (FOCAL), 2005) (available at www.focal.ca/pdf/mercosur_Pena-Rozemberg_different%20approach%20institutional%20development_March%202005_FPP-05-06_e.pdf), p. 11, and A. Crawely, *MERCOSUR: In Search of an Agenda – Rapporteur's Report* (Institute for the Integration of Latin America and the Caribbean, 2004), p. 9. See also, for example, W. Baer, T. Cavalcanti and P. Silva, "Economic Integration without Policy Coordination: The Case of MERCOSUR," 3 *Emerging Markets Review* 269–291 (2002).

246 CMC Resolution 30/02 of December 6, 2002 ("Transformation of the Administrative Secretariat of MERCOSUR into a Technical Secretariat"). The Resolution recognized that "the current needs of the integration process require institutional reforms that will enable the creation of a technical advisory entity that could act from a common perspective and contribute to the consolidation of MERCOSUR," and that "the creation of an entity with ample operational capacity capable of generating an effective space for reflection on the integration process should take place in a gradual manner in light of the evolution of that process and the human and material resources available."

247 CMC Resolution 30/02 of December 6, 2002, Annex 1 ("Competence of the Technical Advisory Department").

three-year term.[248] The Secretariat was now authorized to operate under the name "Secretariat of MERCOSUR" (albeit for information dissemination purposes only, without legal effect).[249] A new organizational structure for the Secretariat was adopted soon after, with the CMC defining in great detail the updated roles of each department and the number and functions of the positions allocated to its staff. Yet another reorganization, to "enable the Secretariat to better perform the tasks assigned to it" and "give it greater technical and operational capacity,"[250] was carried out in 2007, and in this context, two new units were created within the Secretariat: a Technical Unit on MERCOSUR External Trade Statistics; and a Technical Unit for administering the Structural Convergence Fund for MERCOSUR (FOCEM), set up to finance projects that benefit the small MERCOSUR economies in an effort to address structural asymmetries within the bloc. By 2010, the Secretariat had grown to encompass a staff of forty, up from twenty-five in 2000. The European Union was invited to assist in reinforcing the Secretariat's role and institutional capacity, mostly by training officials, and through the provision of technical assistance and training in best practices.[251]

[248] CMC Resolution 30/02 of December 6, 2002, Annex 2 ("Rules for Selecting and Appointing Technical Consultants").

[249] CMC Resolution 30/02 of December 6, 2002, Article 6.

[250] See, respectively, CMC Decision 07/07 of January 18, 2007 ("Structure and Functions of the Secretariat of MERCOSUR"); "La Secretaría del MERCOSUR" (a description of the Secretariat provided on the MERCOSUR website, www.mercosur.int).

[251] The European Commission's *Regional Strategy Paper for MERCOSUR 2007–2013*, E/2007/1640 (2007), pp. 31–32.

VI.i *Role and functions*

The Secretariat's transformation, however, soon proved to be not much more than a name change. Much like its predecessor, MERCOSUR's Technical Secretariat is an essentially administrative body, one that "enjoys neither steering autonomy nor political leverage."[252] With the States Parties keen on having the Secretariat support them as such rather than the regional project, the role envisioned for the Technical Advisory Department as the bloc's first organ of supranational nature was soon "disfigured by restrictive regulations,"[253] among them the classification of the Department's semi-annual reports on the integration process as confidential.[254]

[252] A. Malamud, "The Internal Agenda of MERCOSUR: Interdependence, Leadership and Institutionalization," in G. Jaramillo (ed.), *Los nuevos enfoques de la integración: más allá del regionalismo* (Quito: FLACSO, 2008), pp. 115 and 125.

[253] D. Ventura, "The Role of Academia in Regional Governance," in M. Botto (ed.), *Research and International Trade Policy Negotiations: Knowledge and Power in Latin America* (New York: Routledge, 2010), pp. 41 and 44: "MERCOSUR's institutional system has so violently rejected the first supranational, technical advisory body in its history . . . the Secretariat's Technical Advisory Sector (SAT) was created by Council Decision 30/02 as an 'arena for joint reflection on the development and consolidation of the integration process'. The functions foreseen in that decision, however, were later disfigured by restrictive regulations that were incompatible with the spirit of the decision itself." See also A. D. De Klor, "The Legal-Institutional Structure of MERCOSUR," in M. T. F. Filho, L. Lixinski and M. B. O. Giupponi (eds.), *The Law of MERCOSUR* (Oxford: Hart Publishing, 2010), pp. 29 and 53.

[254] GMC Resolution 16/04 (2004) ("Procedure for Application for Technical Support from the MERCOSUR Secretariat") made it clear,

Proposals to award the Secretariat (and its Director) a greater profile by having it report directly to the CMC, or by authorizing it to represent MERCOSUR in international fora and submit initiatives relating to the integration process, were all rejected due to a lack of consensus among the States Parties.[255] Newly established MERCOSUR organs, such as the Forum for Consultation and Policy Formation, the MERCOSUR Training Institute and the Labor Market Observatory, were all set up outside the Secretariat, subordinated instead to the decision-making bodies and evidencing a consistent determination to limit the Secretariat's mandate and refrain from making its Director a significant regional figure. This became most clear with the creation in 2010 of the post of High Representative General of MERCOSUR, a position that was to be held by a renowned politician, who would operate directly under the CMC and serve as its representative and advisor on regional policies.[256]

moreover, that the topics handled by the Technical Advisory Department must be approved by the decision-making bodies, and "cannot be a matter that is controversial among the States Parties."

255 See CMC Decision 56/08 of December 15, 2008, of which the suggestions to upgrade the Secretariat were ultimately rejected, and the powers contemplated with regard to such upgrade were eventually assigned to the new post of MERCOSUR's High Representative General. An earlier CMC Decision 56/07 of 2007 instructed the high-level *ad hoc* group that was formed in 2005 to propose institutional reforms in MERCOSUR to contemplate, with regard to the Secretariat, only budgetary requirements (and not a change in substantive roles and work methods).

256 CMC Decision 63/10 of July 16, 2010 ("High Representative-General of MERCOSUR"). The High Representative General is authorized to

With national bureaucracies of the States Parties maintaining absolute control of the regional process, MERCOSUR "has never developed any kind of autonomous regional bureaucracy."[257] Its Secretariat, lacking any substantive decision-making power and confined by a restrictive procedural framework carefully set up by the CMC and GMC, thus serves as the administrative offices of the bloc and performs predominantly clerical functions. As further elaborated below, these functions mostly include provision of logistical support to meetings of other MERCOSUR bodies; dissemination of information on the Common Market's activities; translation of documents and administering communications with the States Parties; monitoring and reporting on the implementation of MERCOSUR rules by the States Parties; and gathering other information as requested. Moreover, the Secretariat garnered only an administrative role in the bloc's dispute settlement procedure, established by the States Parties to resolve any dispute arising between them with regard to the interpretation, application or breach of MERCOSUR agreements and norms. The Secretariat has no

request the Secretariat's Technical Advisory Department to prepare studies, reports and other working documents relating to her functions. He or she is appointed by the CMC for a term of three years that may be renewed once; the GMC is authorized to propose to the CMC an appointment of other High Representatives of MERCOSUR, for topics that are of particular interest to the bloc.

[257] A. Malamud, "The Internal Agenda of MERCOSUR: Interdependence, Leadership and Institutionalization," in G. Jaramillo (ed.), *Los nuevos enfoques de la integración: más allá del regionalismo* (Quito: FLACSO, 2008), p. 127.

significant legal capacity of its own (the CMC serving as MERCOSUR's legal representative), and, in general, turns to outside lawyers for handling legal matters as they may arise. As with all other MERCOSUR entities that report to the decision-making bodies, it is required to submit each year an annual program of work, which is to be deliberated on and approved by the GMC.[258]

The Secretariat operates on a standard eight-hour work day, although staff may be required by the Director to work overtime, particularly when support for meetings of the MERCOSUR organs is necessary. All staff members apart from the Director must record their hours of work on a regular basis. While Spanish and Portuguese are the two official languages of MERCOSUR, and Secretariat staff members are generally required to speak both languages at a working level,[259] communication within the Secretariat is mostly in Spanish, "and the deal is to speak slowly," in the words of a former Secretariat official.

VI.ii Organizational structure

MERCOSUR's Technical Secretariat is composed of four departments (referred to in Spanish as "sectors") and the technical units for statistics and for international cooperation,

[258] CMC Decision 36/10 of 2010 ("Programs of Work").

[259] Protocol of Ouro Preto, Article 46; suggestions to award the status of MERCOSUR official (third) language to Guaraní, one of the two official languages of Paraguay (alongside Spanish), have not yet been considered.

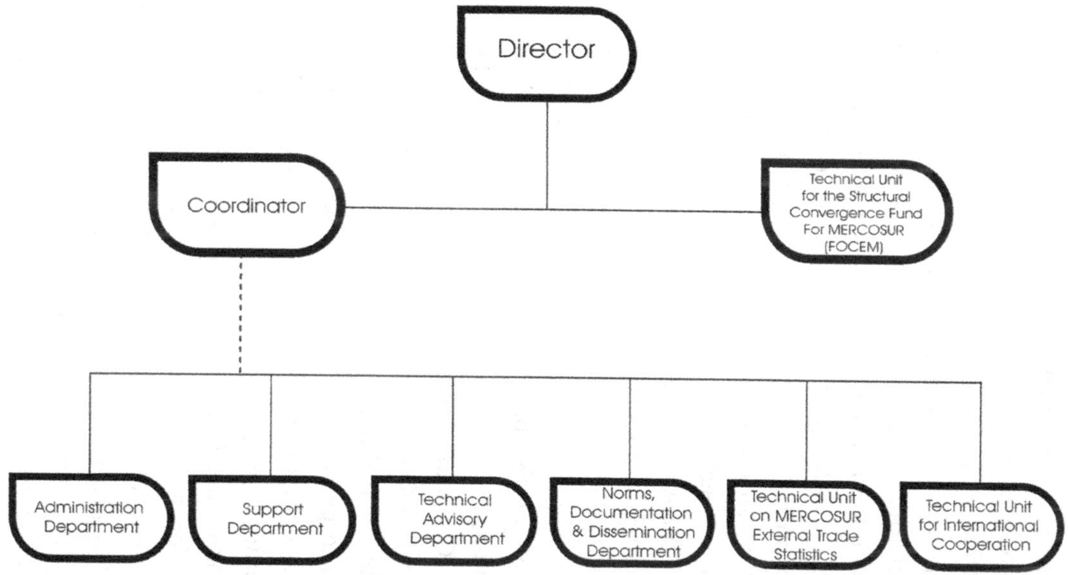

Figure s.5 MERCOSUR Technical Secretariat organizational structure

which are all overseen by a Coordinator operating under the Director. The Coordinator serves as the Director's deputy, and is responsible for facilitating the day-to-day work of the Secretariat by supervising the fulfillment of the tasks assigned to the various departments and compliance with the Staff Rules. The Secretariat further comprises the technical unit for managing the Structural Convergence Fund for MERCOSUR (FOCEM), operating directly under the Director in light of the substantial funds under its purview (as well as an ongoing delay in finding a coordinator dedicated to managing it).

The Administration Department is responsible for all activities related to financial, asset and human resource management in the Secretariat. As such, it is charged with preparing the Secretariat's budget proposal and supporting the execution of the budget once approved; maintaining the accounting records, which are to be approved annually by the GMC; planning and executing the annual plans of procurement; and serving as custodian of the Secretariat's assets, including by maintaining an updated inventory. The Department also prepares the documentation required for recruitment of staff, and plans and implements training programs in coordination with the other departments. It assists the Director of the Secretariat in execution of the disciplinary regime for staff, ensures adequate recording of attendance and absence of staff members, and supervises maintenance and safety issues at the headquarters premises.

The Support Department is entrusted with handling information systems, translation and other general services required for the day-to-day work of the Secretariat. More specifically, it provides IT and communication services to the Secretariat and to meetings of MERCOSUR fora that are held at headquarters; maintains the MERCOSUR website, as well as the Secretariat's computer networks and databases; and advises the Director of the Secretariat on any related issues. Department staff further translate (into Spanish and Portuguese) all draft and final MERCOSUR rules (in cooperation with the States Parties and the Department for Norms, Documentation and Dissemination), administer the Secretariat's correspondences, provide assistance in protocol matters and perform photocopying tasks.

The Technical Advisory Department is charged with providing advice and technical assistance to MERCOSUR's governing organs with regard to the development of the integration process. Comprising four high-level academics, of whom two are experts in international law and two are experts in international economics, with four assistants, it carries out a monitoring and analysis role to evaluate obstacles to integration and possible courses of action to address them. The Department undertakes studies in accordance with an annual program of work approved by the CMC; according to procedure, a topic that is controversial among the States Parties will not be eligible for consideration by the Department. Output of the Department includes various "technical documents," among them biannual reports on the evolution of the integration process and any other working documents requested by the decision-making bodies. Yet another task of the Department is to examine draft MERCOSUR rules and comment on their possible implications,[260] as well as supervise the legal consistency of all such acts in general. In performing its tasks, the Department may cooperate with other international organizations or academic institutions, provided that express authorization for doing so has been granted by the GMC.[261]

The Norms, Documentation and Dissemination Department has, as its name implies, several functions. First, it supports the processes of preparing MERCOSUR rules by the technical fora and the implementation of such rules by the States Parties. This includes proposing changes to the form (rather than substance) of draft norms and ensuring their equivalent content in the two official language versions, as well as recording notifications by States Parties on the incorporation of norms into the domestic legal systems and communicating such information to other States Parties. Second, the Department manages the official MERCOSUR archive and library, and maintains and updates the MERCOSUR database, including by collating records of minutes and making corrections in electronic versions if these differ from handwritten ones. Third, it provides support services for negotiations and meetings of MERCOSUR organs by preparing detailed documents on the activities of MERCOSUR bodies and legal dossiers on any given topic. Fourth, the

[260] It has been made clear, however, that the absence of such analysis by the Department is not an obstacle to the consideration or adoption of any such act or draft rule by the decision-making bodies of MERCOSUR; see CMC Resolution 30/02 of December 6, 2002, Annex 1 ("Powers of the Technical Advisory Sector"), Article 2(d).

[261] To date, such cooperation is not known to have taken place.

Department assists the dispute resolution proceedings of MERCOSUR in accordance with applicable rules and agreements, and maintains a list of arbitrators and experts that may be contacted with regard to such proceedings. Finally, it serves as the communication center for MERCOSUR by disseminating documentation and information, publishing the official gazette of MERCOSUR, responding to outside inquiries, managing the content of the MERCOSUR website, and maintaining a directory of corresponding authorities in States Parties.

The Technical Unit on MERCOSUR External Trade Statistics is responsible for designing, constructing and maintaining a database of detailed trade statistics relating to the exports and imports among MERCOSUR's States Parties, in order to provide periodical studies of trade performance and analysis thereof.

The Technical Unit for the Structural Convergence Fund for MERCOSUR (FOCEM) administers operations carried out under the Structural Convergence Fund for MERCOSUR, set up in 2004 to finance programs proposed by the States Parties, or by other MERCOSUR organs, in order to reduce asymmetries in the bloc, promote competitiveness and social cohesion, and strengthen the integration process. The Unit takes part in the selection process for programs by reviewing proposals and verifying that they meet the eligibility criteria, and then assesses and monitors the implementation of programs that were selected to receive funding; it has not hesitated to propose projects as well, among them the project for the "Jurisprudential Data Base of MERCOSUR," and the project for "Institutional Strengthening of the MERCOSUR Secretariat for the Information System of the Common Market Tariff."

The Unit currently consists of eight officials, of whom four are Senior Technicians and four are Assistant Technicians.

Following the approval in 2012 of MERCOSUR's new policy on international cooperation,[262] a *Technical Unit for International Cooperation* is currently being set up. Reporting to MERCOSUR's International Cooperation Group (a forum comprising representatives of States Parties), the Unit's principal functions are to assist the International Cooperation Group in promoting technical cooperation projects; to advise MERCOSUR fora and other administrative agencies, at the request of the International Cooperation Group, on planning, executing, monitoring and evaluating such projects; and to maintain information relating to MERCOSUR's international cooperation, in particular administrative and financial data.

VI.iii The Director

The Director of the Secretariat, who must be a national of one of MERCOSUR's States Parties, is elected on a rotating basis by the GMC following consultation between the States Parties, and then appointed by the CMC for a non-renewable two-year term.[263] The unusual separation of election and appointment procedures is, reportedly, a compromise between the position of Uruguay, whose government "wished to enhance the standing of the Director and the Secretariat, by

[262] CMC Decision 11/12 of June 29, 2012 (and Annex).

[263] Protocol of Ouro Preto, Article 33. The MERCOSUR Parliament is empowered to issue a non-binding opinion on the appointment of an individual to the position.

having the former designated by the Council," and the insistence of the other States Parties, whose leaders preferred a mechanism under which the Common Market Group, as the executive body most often served by the Secretariat, would be responsible for naming the Director.[264] Candidates for the position must, as a minimum, hold a university degree and have a deep knowledge of MERCOSUR, as well as proven experience in relevant work; the GMC may add additional criteria if deemed appropriate.

Serving as the highest authority within the Secretariat, the Director is a chief administrative officer. He or she has no role in setting policy for the bloc and no power of initiative. All attempts by holders of the office of Director – including those who had previously served as senior politicians in the States Parties – to introduce a minimal political element to the job have failed. The Director only participates in the meetings of the decision-making bodies if invited to do so by the State Party which holds the interim presidency of MERCOSUR, and has no power to influence the agenda of such meetings. His or her decision-making authority, even within the limited mandate in which he or she operates as top administrator, is often conditional, requiring the consent of the GMC.

As the States Parties would have it, the Director is responsible for the overall performance of the Secretariat and for managing the tasks assigned to it. In particular, he or she is charged with directing and supervising the work carried out by the Secretariat's departments; for defining, in consultation

[264] L. O. Baptista, "MERCOSUR, Its Institutions and Juridical Structure" (available at http://ctrc.sice.oas.org/geograph/south/mstit2_e.pdf), p. 85.

with the GMC, the priorities and terms of the Secretariat's work; for supervising the preparation of the Secretariat's annual budget proposal and the administration of its accounts; for preparing an annual report on the work of the Secretariat, to be considered by the GMC; and for coordinating the relations between the Secretariat and other MERCOSUR organs, regularly providing such entities with reports and information. He or she signs all staff employment contracts on behalf of the Secretariat, and may issue internal Service Instructions for the proper functioning of the Secretariat. He or she may also designate, after consulting with the States Parties, the staff members who would head the Administration Department and the Norms, Documentation and Dissemination Department (chosen from within the ranks of staff working for those Departments); any delegation of his or her power of coordination to designated personnel similarly requires prior approval of the GMC. The Director's most significant task is overseeing the Structural Convergence Fund for MERCOSUR (FOCEM), and this is carried out via the Director's authority over the above-mentioned Technical Unit for the Structural Convergence Fund. Financed by annual contributions of the States Parties,[265] FOCEM

[265] Brazil is responsible for providing 70 percent of FOCEM's budget; Argentina for 27 percent; Uruguay for 2 percent; and Paraguay for 1 percent. The Fund can also receive contributions from third countries, institutions and international organizations. For more information, see F. De Andrade Correa, "A Legal/Institutional Analysis of FOCEM, the MERCOSUR Fund for Structural Convergence," in M. T. F. Filho, L. Lixinski and M. B. O. Giupponi (eds.), *The Law of MERCOSUR* (Oxford: Hart Publishing, 2010), pp. 395–403.

presently supports a portfolio of projects valued at US$1 billion, and the Director's power obtains from his authority to sign checks and oversee the day-to-day management and support for each of the projects.

In his or her absence, the Director's duties are assumed by the Coordinator, who is appointed by the GMC from within the ranks of the States Parties on a rotating basis, and whose nationality must be different to that of the Director. The Coordinator's two-year term must begin or end no less than six months from the corresponding date of the Director's term of office. If the Director resigns, dies while in office, becomes incapacitated in the performance of his duties, or is absent for more than six months, he or she is to be replaced by a person of the same nationality as the Director if the remaining term of office is more than six months.

The Director enjoys a "Chief of Mission" diplomatic status, and his or her monthly salary, as set by the GMC, is currently approximately US$7,500. If he or she relocates to Montevideo from outside Uruguay, he or she may receive, upon the approval of the States Parties, a relocation grant in the sum of one month's salary, both when taking office and at the end of his or her term.

VI.iv Staff

The Secretariat's staff comprises the Director, the Coordinator, technical advisors, technicians, technical assistants and support staff, who must all be nationals of the MERCOSUR States Parties. Contracted consultants and advisors, who may only work for the Secretariat on a short-term basis, do not count as staff, and their employment is governed by the terms of their contracts alone.[266] With the exception of the Director and the Coordinator, all staff members are recruited in accordance with the overarching principle of equal representation, which mandates that the Secretariat will have an equal number of nationals of each State Party, not only overall, but also in practically all levels and positions; thus the imperative to maintain an equilibrium of nationals is an ever-present factor in the recruitment procedures followed to employ personnel.[267] In these circumstances (and given the modest number of staff) the nationality of each staff member does not go unnoticed, and, although staff members do identify with their regional responsibilities, they generally feel more comfortable with their fellow nationals, and normally maintain a relationship with the embassies of their home countries.

Staff members, who all work under the authority of the Director, are required to perform their roles loyally and faithfully, avoiding any public or private activities that are incompatible with their work at the Secretariat. They are to remain discreet with regard to the work of the Secretariat, respect the confidentiality of the information they have access to, and avoid making any statements related to the

[266] The framework for hiring consultants/advisors on "exceptional and transitory circumstances, for performing tasks that cannot be carried out by the Secretariat's staff," including a model employment contract, is provided in GMC Resolution 07/04 of June 25, 2004 ("Regime for Staff Hired on Short-Term Contracts for Specific Works or Services"). Such hiring by the Director requires prior notification to the GMC.

[267] CMC Decision 05/09 of July 24, 2009 ("Procedures for Competitive Recruitment of MERCOSUR Staff"), Article 1.

Secretariat without the prior authorization of the Director. Under no circumstances are they to speak on behalf of MERCOSUR. They may not solicit or receive instructions from any government or other national or international entity, and must abstain from any activity that might affect the reputation of the Secretariat or intervene "actively or publicly" in the internal affairs of a State Party. Privileges and immunities are granted to staff members in their professional capacity and only with respect to the interests of the Secretariat.[268]

Recruitment to all staff positions must be carried out through competition "on the basis of exams, merit and qualifications,"[269] with vacancies announced by the Secretariat to all States Parties, along with a specification as to which nationals may apply to the position. A selection committee comprising a representative from each State Party, along with a representative from the Secretariat, is subsequently formed. The committee drafts the terms of reference for the position and publishes them in a public bulletin following the GMC's approval. At the end of the application period, the selection committee produces a short-list of no more than ten candidates, which is shared with the States Parties. The candidates are then required to pass a written exam and report for an interview at their own expense. The highest-ranking candidate(s) would be hired for an initial term of one year (as a

[268] GMC Resolution 06/04 of June 25, 2004 ("General Rules Relating to Secretariat Staff"), Chapter 4 ("Staff Duties and Obligations") and Chapter 7 ("Privilege, Immunities and Exceptions").

[269] CMC Decision 05/09 of July 24, 2009.

probation period), after which the term of employment may be extended by three years at a time, subject to further renewal based on performance. Travel and relocation expenses are paid for the staff member and his or her dependants, including elderly family members.

The salary scale for Secretariat staff, set in US dollars by the GMC and updated by it from time to time, is publicly available.[270] Staff members receive an additional monthly sum of US$300 to cover any medical expenses (for themselves and for each of their dependants), in lieu of enrolment in a health insurance scheme; they are further eligible to receive a monthly education allowance for each dependent child under the age of eighteen (in the sum of US$70, for up to four children), and, if relocating to Montevideo, a rent allowance for the first three months of their employment. An annual bonus, equivalent to one month's salary, is paid to each staff member as well. Staff members are also entitled, annually, to twenty-one days of paid leave that may be accumulated for no more than two years, in addition to eleven official days off. Five days of paid leave are granted on the occasion of marriage or the death of a close relative, and up to ten days of leave may be taken each year by staff members enrolled in higher education programs and taking examinations. Paid maternity

[270] As of 2009, salaries (per month) were set as follows: Director, US$7,456; Coordinator, US$4,588; Technical Advisors, US$3,441; Technicians, US$2,008; Technical Assistants, US$1,205; Support staff, US$689. Staff of the FOCEM Technical Unit have a separate salary scale, according to which Senior Technicians receive US$3,441 per month, and Technical Assistants receive US$1,205 (see GMC Resolution 68/08 of November 28, 2008 ("General Norms Relating to Secretariat Staff")).

leave is set at twelve weeks, and breastfeeding mothers are entitled to work only six hours each day for the first three months upon their return to office; paternity leave is capped at five business days. The Director may authorize paid medical leave of up to fifteen days a year in the event of illness or physical incapacity, and these may be extended in exceptional cases to no more than sixty-three days annually; a second extension by another sixty-three days on half-pay is available as well, yet the return to work of a staff member who took such extended leave requires the authorization of a medical committee set up by the Director for making that decision.[271]

Performance evaluation for all staff (except the Director) is carried out on an annual basis against minimum efficiency standards established for each position and any other criteria identified by the Director. The evaluation is shared with each concerned staff member for the sake of transparency and objectivity of the process, and the latter has a right to object to it in writing within ten business days. Copies of the evaluations are placed in the personnel files of staff members, which are kept at the Administration Department.[272]

Retirement of all staff members (except the Director) is mandatory at the age of sixty-five, yet the GMC may

[271] GMC Resolution 06/04 of June 25, 2004, Chapter 5 ("Attendance, Absence and Leave"); the Staff Rules stipulate that "staff on leave due to illness must generally be at home."

[272] The performance of the Coordinator and Technical Advisors, as senior officials of the Secretariat, is evaluated by the Director, who may not delegate this authority.

resolve, in exceptional cases, to continue employing an individual past that age. As a general rule, the end of term for Secretariat staff may not coincide with the end date of the Director's mandate. Upon termination of employment, each staff member is entitled to his or her share of a pension fund that comprises monthly contributions by the staff member (equal to 7 percent of the monthly salary) and by the Secretariat (equal to 14 percent of the monthly salary), as well as to a *pro rata* share of any investment income accrued thereon.[273] Staff members (or their beneficiaries) have a right to benefits in the event of death, prolonged illness or an elimination of the staff member's position that brings the employment relationship to an end.

Disciplinary action may be taken against staff members who fail to comply with the Staff Rules, or who improperly fulfill their official duties, or behave, even in a private capacity, in a manner that might publicly reflect upon or harm the Secretariat (including by exploiting their position for private or third-party gains). Such misconduct may lead to oral or written admonition, or, in serious cases, to suspension or dismissal. Decisions by the Coordinator or Technical Advisors to impose such sanctions must be based on a full report on the relevant misconduct (to which the relevant staff member is entitled to respond), and are communicated through the head of the Administration Department to the Director for approval. A staff member who is found to have caused damage to the Secretariat by failing intentionally or

[273] Money in the Fund may be invested by the Secretariat.

negligently to abide by the Staff Rules could also be required to repair any such harm, or to pay monetary restitution in an amount sufficient to indemnify the Secretariat against any cost of the misconduct.

All employment disputes between staff members and the Secretariat are heard by the MERCOSUR Administrative-Labor Tribunal, if a resolution of such disputes could not be first reached through the administrative channels of the Secretariat. The Tribunal is composed of five jurists (preferably experienced in administrative/employment law), one from each of the (now five) States Parties, who are appointed by the GMC for a period of two years that may be renewed for similar periods, and must act independently. The President of the Tribunal is selected by raffle. Hearings are held at the Secretariat premises, with the Director designating a staff member to provide the Tribunal with administrative support. The Tribunal is required to render its decision (including reasoning) within thirty days; the decision cannot be appealed, and is to be communicated by the Secretariat to the GMC as well. While it is regularly the Secretariat that bears the travel and allowance expenses of members of the Tribunal, the Tribunal may order such expenses to be paid by the staff member who was party to the proceeding if he or she loses and is found to have acted in bad faith.[274]

[274] The powers of and procedures for the Tribunal are specified in GMC Resolution 54/03 of December 10, 2003 ("Administrative-Labor Tribunal of MERCOSUR"); see also Chapter 12 ("Final Provisions") of the Staff Rules.

VI.V *Budget*

The Protocol of Ouro Preto provides that the Secretariat of MERCOSUR "shall have a budget to cover its operating expenses and the expenses authorized by the Common Market Group. This budget shall be financed in equal shares by contributions from the States Parties."[275] As one author has observed, equal contributions by Member States – particularly in a bloc characterized by sharp asymmetries among these States – "means in practice that the budget is limited to the capacity of the financially weakest member, and . . . also highlights the equality of Member States and the absence of any pretension to supranationality."[276] The budget remained below US$1 million per annum until 2007, when the high-level *ad hoc* group created by the CMC to propose institutional reforms in MERCOSUR recommended that the Secretariat be given greater financial resources to meet its expanded tasks and structure. Currently set at approximately US$4 million annually (of which approximately 20 percent is set aside as a contingency to guarantee financial liquidity), it is widely considered as adequate given the limited size and mandate of the Secretariat.

The annual budget, prepared by the Secretariat, is approved by the GMC. The States Parties are then required to pay their contributions during the first trimester of the financial year. MERCOSUR's Parliament may receive and debate an annual report regarding the budget, but is not empowered to make any alterations to it.

[275] Protocol of Ouro Preto, Article 45.

[276] L. O. Baptista, "MERCOSUR, Its Institutions and Juridical Structure" (available at http://ctrc.sice.oas.org/geograph/south/mstit2_e.pdf), p. 5.

Table s.7 *The MERCOSUR Secretariat's annual budget, 1997–2013 (in US$ million)*

1997–2007	0.9
2008	1.1
2009	1.6
2010	2.0
2011	2.2
2012	2.4
2013	4.2[a]

Note

[a] The dramatic increase in 2013 stems from the acceptance in 2012 of Venezuela as a full MERCOSUR member, which is now required to pay an equal share of the Secretariat's budget. This growth in budget resources made the establishment of a Contingency Fund possible.

VII The North American Free Trade Agreement (NAFTA) Secretariat

While international agreements that set up a permanent secretariat commonly opt for a single multinational structure, the Secretariat of the 1992 North American Free Trade Agreement (NAFTA) – a comprehensive treaty between Canada, Mexico and the United States, creating a trilateral trade bloc in North America – is effectively decentralized, comprising three national sections that are to work together in administering specified provisions of the Agreement.[277] These

[277] For a general background on NAFTA and its historical context, see G. C. Hufbauer and J. J. Schott, *NAFTA Revisited: Achievements and Challenges* (Washington, DC: Institute for International Economics, 2005), pp. 1–8; F. W. Mayer, *Interpreting NAFTA* (New York: Columbia

offices, located in the respective capital cities and referred to as "mirror-images" of one another, are to be overseen by the Free Trade Commission – an annual meeting of "cabinet-level representatives of the Parties or their designees" that operates by consensus and is responsible for political oversight of the Agreement's implementation and further elaboration, as well as resolving disputes that may arise regarding its interpretation or application.[278] Known as the Canada Section, Mexico Section and United States Section, each office is headed by a Secretary appointed as a career position within the national bureaucracies of the States Parties, with no single secretary general or comparable post directing the Secretariat as a whole. The national Sections are each funded separately by the respective State Party, which is charged by the Agreement with responsibility for "the operation and costs of its

University Press, 1998); M. A. Cameron and B. W. Tomlin, *The Making of NAFTA: How the Deal Was Done* (Ithaca, NY: Cornell University Press, 2000); *Fact Sheet: Top US Export Markets: Free Trade Agreements and Country Fact Sheets* (Washington, DC: US Department of Commerce, 2008).

[278] NAFTA, Article 2001 ("The Free Trade Commission"). The Commission is further charged with supervision of all committees and working groups established under the Agreement, and with considering "any other matter that may affect the operation of this Agreement." The Commission may furthermore "establish, and delegate responsibilities to, *ad hoc* or standing committees, working groups or expert groups; seek the advice of non-governmental persons or groups; and take such other action in the exercise of its functions as the Parties may agree." It is to convene "at least once a year in regular session," chaired successively by each Party; traditionally, its members are the Mexican Secretary of the Economy, the Canadian Minister for International Trade and the US Trade Representative.

Section."[279] It is against the prevalent model of international secretariats that one author has observed that "[t]he NAFTA Secretariat, then, is a fiction; far from a supranational organ, it is a loose collection of coordinating offices in the three countries."[280]

The unusual institutional set-up established by NAFTA has been attributed to the determination of its framers "not to create even inchoate trilateral institutions that could mature into a supranational" structure,[281] and their

[279] NAFTA, Article 2002(2)(b)(i).

[280] S. Zamore, "Rethinking North America: Why NAFTA's Laissez Faire Approach to Integration Is Flawed, and What to Do About It," 56 *Villanova Law Review* 631 (2011), p. 638.

[281] *Ibid.*, p. 632; see also F. M. Abbott, *Law and Policy of Regional Integration: The NAFTA and Western Hemispheric Integration in the World Trade Organization System* (Dordrecht: Martinus Nijhoff Publishers, 1995), pp. 1–2: "The framers of the NAFTA assiduously avoided granting to regional institutions the power to make decisions which would directly bind the Parties. These framers were operating in a political and historical environment far removed from that in which the framers of the European Economic Community operated in the 1950s, and these NAFTA framers doubtless perceived little enthusiasm in the body politic of any of the Parties for a transfer of governmental authority to a regional center"; T. D. Zweifel, *International Organizations and Democracy: Accountability, Politics, and Power* (Boulder, CO: Lynne Rienner Publishers, 2006), p. 164: "NAFTA was formed as a vehicle to facilitate trade between three nations in North America. The few organizations it spawned are composed of members of national bureaucracies that serve directly under their executive branches. Only the dispute panels enjoy some independence, but not much: the member governments, through their NAFTA secretariats, control the list of eligible panelists"; D. P. Steger, "The Search for North American Institutions," in T. J. Courchene, D. J. Savoie and

preference for organs "designed to coordinate the activities of the Parties and not to make decisions on their behalf."[282] It has also been suggested that NAFTA's thin institutionalism "should be seen against the background of NAFTA being a rather complete contract, a long and detailed treaty that requires less *ex post* implementation,"[283] yet the very choice of such a contractual design may itself reflect a wish to avoid central common institutions. In this same spirit, NAFTA's supplementary agreements of 1993 – the North American Agreement on Labor Cooperation (NAALC) and the North American Agreement on Environmental Cooperation (NAAEC) – have each established a separate trinational

D. Schwanen (eds.), *Thinking North America*, vol. I (Montreal: Institute for Research and Public Policy, 2005), p. 79: "NAFTA was deliberately designed to not have central institutions or a unified dispute-settlement system because the negotiators thought it would be best to allow maximum flexibility and creativity, relying on diplomacy to further develop the rules and resolve dispute."

282 F. M. Abbott, *Law and Policy of Regional Integration: The NAFTA and Western Hemispheric Integration in the World Trade Organization System* (Dordrecht: Martinus Nijhoff Publishers, 1995), p. 23.

283 F. Laursen, "Comparative Regional Integration and the EU Model: How to Achieve Credible Commitments (NAFTA and MERCOSUR)," in J. Roy (ed.), *The State of the Union(s): The Eurozone Crisis, Comparative Regional Integration and the EU Model* (Miami, FL: University of Miami, 2012), p. 163. See also F. M. Abbott, "NAFTA and the Legalization of World Politics: A Case Study," 54 *International Organization* 519–547 (2000); L. Kanthak, "Explaining Differences in the Institutional Design of ASEAN and NAFTA," in T. A. Börzel, L. Goltermann, M. Lohaus and K. Striebinger (eds.), *Roads to Regionalism: Genesis, Design, and Effects of Regional Organizations* (Farnham: Ashgate, 2012), pp. 82–99.

secretariat to facilitate cooperation limited to their respective fields, rather than assign those functions to the already agreed-upon NAFTA Secretariat.[284] An initiative of the Free Trade Commission at its first meeting in 1994, to establish a

[284] The NAALC Secretariat, whose staff is drawn equally from the three NAALC countries, supports the Council of Ministers of the Commission for Labor Cooperation, the latter being "an international organization created under the North American Agreement on Labor Cooperation," made up of a Council of Ministers, a cabinet-level body in charge of policy-setting and decision-making consisting of the three labor ministers or their representatives, and the trinational Secretariat. Located in Washington, it "includes labor economists, labor lawyers and other professionals with wide experience in labor affairs in the region ... [who] work in the three official languages of the NAALC ... in a unique multinational institution devoted to advancing labor rights and labor standards as an integral part of expanding trade relations." The NAALC Secretariat "also undertakes labor-related research and public information, and assists the member countries with their cooperative activities" (see http://new.naalc.org/commission/secretariat.htm). The Secretariat established under the NAAEC, located in Montreal, with a liaison office in Mexico City, "provides technical, administrative and operational support to the [Commission for Environmental Cooperation's] Council, and other support, including to working groups as the Council may direct ... [It] submits for Council approval the annual program and budget of the Commission, including proposed cooperative activities ... periodically prepares independent reports on important environmental matters and provides information on the state of the environment throughout North America ... [and] also has special responsibilities to consider submissions from any non-governmental organization or citizen that a Party is failing to effectively enforce its environmental law." It is headed by an Executive Director appointed by the Council, and employs professional staff from Canada, Mexico, and the United States (see www.cec.org/Page.asp?PageID=1226&SiteNodeID=206).

trinational NAFTA "coordinating secretariat" that would assist in technical matters and serve as a clearinghouse and repository of documents alongside the national sections,[285] has never found sufficient political support to materialize. Recommendations in the academic literature for developing an enhanced North American institutional architecture, including a strengthened common secretariat, which would enable the deepening of regional integration, even if only with regard to free trade,[286] have thus far met a similar fate.

The Secretariat began operating in 1994, with NAFTA's entry into force. Its United States and Canada Sections had already existed prior to that time as the national sections of the Binational Secretariat operating under the Canada–United States Free Trade Agreement (that was superseded by NAFTA), and were simply renamed; Mexico

[285] See J. A. McKinney, *Created from NAFTA: The Structure, Function, and Significance of the Treaty's Related Institutions* (Armonk, NY: M. E. Sharpe Publishing, 2000), p. 25: "Plans were made to locate this organization in Naucalpan, a suburb of Mexico City . . . with an American as executive director."

[286] See, for example, D. P. Steger, "The Search for North American Institutions," in T. J. Courchene, D. J. Savoie and D. Schwanen (eds.), *Thinking North America*, vol. I (Montreal: Institute for Research and Public Policy, 2005), pp. 77–89; I. Morales, *Post-NAFTA North America: Reshaping the Economic and Political Governance of a Changing Region* (Basingstoke: Palgrave Macmillan, 2008), pp. 69–73; R. D. Knutson and R. M. A. Loyns, "A Policy Leadership Commission for NAFTA," in R. M. A. Loyns, K. Meilke, R. D. Knutson and A. Yúnez-Naude (eds.), *Keeping the Borders Open: Proceedings of the Eighth Agricultural and Food Policy Systems Information Workshop* (Guelph, ON: University of Guelph, 2004), pp. 430–435.

established its national Section pursuant to the Agreement. In the two decades since then, the Secretariat has not undergone any institutional reform.

VII.i *Role and functions*

The administrative and institutional provisions of NAFTA's chapter on "Institutional Arrangements and Dispute Settlement Procedures" call for the establishment of a Secretariat that is charged by the Agreement with an essentially administrative function: "provide assistance to the Commission"; "provide administrative assistance to panels and committees" put in place under the Agreement's trade dispute settlement procedures; and, "as the Commission may direct," support the work of other committees and groups created under the Agreement, as well as "otherwise facilitate" the Agreement's operation.[287] Despite the potential afforded by this language for a wide interpretation of its mandate and, consequently, a far broader array of tasks, the Secretariat has remained consistently circumscribed by the limited mandate envisioned for it, with "the role of [its national Sections being] not proactive and ... limited to trade dispute referrals after the relevant [domestic trade remedy laws] have taken their course."[288]

[287] NAFTA, Article 2002(3).

[288] R. D. Knutson and R. M. A. Loyns, "A Policy Leadership Commission for NAFTA," in R. M. A. Loyns, K. Meilke, R. D. Knutson and A. Yúnez-Naude (eds.), *Keeping the Borders Open: Proceedings of the Eighth Agricultural and Food Policy Systems Information Workshop* (Guelph, ON: University of Guelph, 2004), p. 431. One author had observed at the time of NAFTA's signing that "[t]he main institutional

Such referrals relate, in short, to disputes between private industries with regard to anti-dumping and countervailing duties (NAFTA's Chapter 19), and to disputes between the States Parties on the interpretation and application of the Agreement (Chapter 20).[289] The Secretariat is to maintain a neutral position as administrator of such proceedings in order to ensure the independence and impartiality of the dispute resolution processes: in the words of a former Secretary, "[a]s inappropriate as it is to talk about Frisbee in terms of winning and losing, so too the [NAFTA] Secretariat is not about winning and losing. It is about achieving a better process for dealing with differences."[290]

change created by the NAFTA [as compared with the Canada–United States Free Trade Agreement] is to upgrade the role and importance of the Secretariat" that under the latter "essentially performed a court registrar's function" – but this was not to be: see G. R. Winham, "Dispute Settlement in the NAFTA and the FTA," in S. Globerman and M. Walker (eds.), *Assessing NAFTA: A Trinational Analysis* (Vancouver: The Fraser Institute, 1993), pp. 251 and 257.

289 A minor role is reserved for the Secretariat under Chapter 11 ("Investment") as well. For a general overview of NAFTA's dispute settlement processes, see D. Gantz, "The United States and Dispute Settlement under the North American Free Trade Agreement: Ambivalence, Frustration, and Occasional Defiance," in C. P. R. Romano (ed.), *The Sword and the Scales: The United States and International Courts and Tribunals* (New York: Cambridge University Press, 2009), pp. 357–394.

290 C. Beehan (former Canadian Secretary of the NAFTA Secretariat, Canadian Section), "Mexico and the NAFTA: A Secretariat Perspective," 3 *Southwestern Journal of Law and Trade in the Americas* 415 (1996), p. 416.

Performing an essentially court registrar's function within the strict framework of NAFTA's dispute resolution provisions, the Secretariat provides administrative and logistical support to the relevant panels and committees established to adjudicate the disputes, working "to ensure that the Rules are adhered to and that, to the extent possible, the prescribed time periods are respected, by both the participants and the panelists."[291] With regard to Chapter 19 disputes in particular, it registers complaints (assigning a case number and notifying the involved parties, including through publication in the relevant country's official gazette); receives, copies and distributes all relevant documents; organizes the hearings (including pre- and post-hearing meetings); and issues (and translates) the decisions. Such tasks are carried out jointly by the relevant national Sections (that is, those whose government or nationals are a party to the dispute), with the Section in which the proceeding is held (as determined by the rules of procedure) responsible for the lion's share. All general costs of the proceedings, however, such as the remuneration of panelists or committee members and their travel and lodging expenses, are borne by the relevant Sections in equal parts.[292] The Sections are required to file and share with one another all documents pertaining to proceedings, while carefully protecting all confidential and

[291] F. Raynauld, "Trade Dispute Settlement Procedures in the NAFTA," in R. M. A. Loyns, K. Meilke, R. D. Knutson and A. Yúnez-Naude (eds.), *Keeping the Borders Open: Proceedings of the Eighth Agricultural and Food Policy Systems Information Workshop* (Guelph, ON: University of Guelph, 2004), pp. 221 and 225.

[292] NAFTA, Annex 2002.2 ("Remuneration and Payment of Expenses").

proprietary information associated with the cases. The Secretary of the Section that hosts a proceeding prepares and preserves in original copy a record of that proceeding.[293]

The Secretariat furthermore provides assistance to the Free Trade Commission when (seldom) required to do so, and supports the Chapter 19 Working Group that meets annually or biannually to review the adequacy of the Agreement's rules of procedure for dispute settlement relating to anti-dumping and countervailing duties. It also provides limited information to the public on NAFTA's dispute settlement proceedings, mainly through the NAFTA Secretariat website that is a joint endeavor of the three national Sections.

With the Secretariat's role as a supportive agency confined to such administrative tasks, NAFTA has no "standing bureaucracy responsible for developing policy ideas and managing the relationship";[294] in these present circumstances, the style of NAFTA's governance has been described as "*laissez faire*, reactive, and legalistic: Problems are defined by plaintiffs and settled by litigation. There is no mechanism

[293] For a more detailed account of the Secretariat's work, see F. Raynauld, "Trade Dispute Settlement Procedures in the NAFTA," in R. M. A. Loyns, K. Meilke, R. D. Knutson and A. Yúnez-Naude (eds.), *Keeping the Borders Open: Proceedings of the Eighth Agricultural and Food Policy Systems Information Workshop* (Guelph, ON: University of Guelph, 2004), pp. 220–231.

[294] D. P. Steger, "The Search for North American Institutions," in T. J. Courchene, D. J. Savoie and D. Schwanen (eds.), *Thinking North America*, vol. I (Montreal: Institute for Research and Public Policy, 2005), p. 79.

for defining problems in a proactive way or addressing them from a continental perspective."[295]

VII.ii Organizational structure

NAFTA provided its States Parties with wide discretion in setting up the permanent offices of their Sections. In particular, it does not define under which national authorities the Sections are to operate, what their internal organizational structure should be or how they are to work together as one Secretariat. Each State Party is merely required in this respect to "notify the Commission of the location of its Section's office," and to create therein a division "to facilitate the operation" of Chapter 19.[296] At present, the US Section, established by a presidential Executive Order, works within the Market Access and Compliance Division of the International Trade Administration of the US Department of Commerce; the Canadian Section works under the Trade Policy and Negotiations Branch of the Canadian Department of Foreign Affairs and International Trade; and the Mexican Section works under the Ministry of the Economy (formerly Ministry of Commerce and Industrial Development). Each has its own (albeit similar) mission statement and guiding principles, as well as internal procedures of operation; and all handle not

[295] R. A. Pastor, *Toward a North American Community: Lessons from the Old World to the New* (Washington, DC: Peterson Institute, 2001), p. 30.

[296] NAFTA, Articles 2002(2)(d) and 1908(1).

just the NAFTA, but also other free trade agreements to which their country is a party.

Although the Secretariat refers to itself as "an independent agency ... accountable to the Free Trade Commission,"[297] it is in fact more accurate to recognize that each Section routinely reports, and to a great extent owes its allegiance, to the national bureaucracy in which it operates. Funded directly by taxpayer funds in the three States Parties, the Sections are often required to demonstrate their value or loyalty, as it were, to the respective countries rather than to the trilateral organization – especially as the mission of the national ministries in which they are housed is to advance and protect each State Party's own commercial interests and champion its domestic commerce and labor force. It is only rarely that the Sections address the Commission. In administering the dispute settlement processes, the national Sections are to remain at arm's length from the investigating authorities and policy units working alongside them within the national ministries, as it is the decisions of these entities that could ultimately be challenged through the NAFTA procedures. Setting up "Chinese walls" is crucial to the function of the Sections as neutral administrators of the dispute settlement procedure, since "[n]ational executive branches act as both NAFTA's principals (using it as their agent and keeping an eye on its officials) and its agents (implementing NAFTA and keeping their promises) [with] [t]hese mixed

297 "What Is the NAFTA Secretariat?," in the Frequently Asked Questions page on the NAFTA Secretariat website (see www.nafta-sec-alena.org/en/view.aspx?x=283).

roles lead[ing] to conflicts of interest and to fuzzy chains of command."[298] There is no legal department operating under the NAFTA Secretariat, as such a unit does not appear necessary for the fulfillment of the Secretariat's current mandate.[299]

The relationship between the three national Sections is considered "fundamental to [their] effective performance" as the NAFTA Secretariat:[300] in the words of the former Secretary of the Canadian Section, "[t]he three Secretaries must always reach a consensus on any problem requiring resolution, since none of the Secretaries has authority over the others. We have to work together to implement the terms and conditions of the Agreement on the matters with which we are concerned."[301] Collaboration between the three Sections surrounds panel-related activities and proceedings;

298 T. D. Zweifel, *International Organizations and Democracy: Accountability, Politics, and Power* (Boulder, CO: Lynne Rienner Publishers, 2006), p. 163.

299 On the possible need for a legal department within the Secretariat in the event that it becomes a "Policy Leadership Commission" of some sort, see F. Raynauld, "A Policy Leadership Commission for NAFTA," in R. M. A. Loyns, K. Meilke, R. D. Knutson and A. Yúnez-Naude (eds.), *Keeping the Borders Open: Proceedings of the Eighth Agricultural and Food Policy Systems Information Workshop* (Guelph, ON: University of Guelph, 2004), pp. 436–437.

300 *NAFTA Secretariat – Canadian Section, Departmental Performance Report for the Period Ending March 31, 2009*, p. 5.

301 F. Raynauld, "Trade Dispute Settlement Procedures in the NAFTA," in R. M. A. Loyns, K. Meilke, R. D. Knutson and A. Yúnez-Naude (eds.), *Keeping the Borders Open: Proceedings of the Eighth Agricultural and Food Policy Systems Information Workshop* (Guelph, ON: University of Guelph, 2004), p. 220.

Figure s.6 NAFTA Secretariat organizational structure

cost-sharing for cases; occasional updating of the NAFTA Secretariat website and the Integrated Registry Information System (both managed by the Canadian Section); harmonizing records management and registry practices; and participation – alongside other representatives of the States Parties – in meetings of the Chapter 19 Working Group. The three Secretaries maintain regular contact through phone and email, and may meet during panel proceedings or a convening of the Working Group; there is no fixed mechanism for bringing them together for periodic designated meetings.

The Canadian Section's primary objective is "to maintain a high level of impartial and independent service in the administration of the dispute settlement provisions of the North American Free Trade Agreement, pursuant to Article 2002, in order to help preserve the benefits of free trade for all stakeholders,"[302] but responsibility for similar provisions under the Canada–Chile, Canada–Israel and Canada–Costa Rica free trade agreements falls within its mandate as well. The Section operates under comprehensive government standards of transparency and performance management that mandate regular reporting on its resources,

[302] The mission statement of the Canadian Section is available on its website (see www.nafta-alena.gc.ca/en/view.aspx?x=291).

activities and outcomes, all available to the public. Eight public service employees work under its Secretary: an Executive Assistant to the Secretary, a Financial Analyst, a Registrar and Deputy Registrar, three Trade Policy Officers, and a Deputy Director. It furthermore houses and manages a NAFTA library and reference center.

The Mexican Section supports the NAFTA and the free trade agreements signed by Mexico with other Latin American countries. Aiming to be "a National Section that satisfies the requirements of our users, with a quality level that brings national and international recognition,"[303] it currently employs seven government officials, including its Secretary, an Administrative Support Assistant to Panelists, a Deputy dedicated to NAFTA Disputes, and an Assistant Director for Information Technology and Quality.

The US Section is also known as the "Trade Agreements Secretariat," mandated within the International Trade Administration of the Department of Commerce as the office that would handle the panel review process for each of the free trade agreements the United States is a party to (to date, however, it has only done so with respect to NAFTA-related cases). It currently has five full-time employees, including its Secretary. The Section's formally independent status within the Department excludes it from any obligations for transparency under the US Freedom of Information Act.

303 Website of the NAFTA Secretariat – Mexican Section (see http://sec-tlcan-mex.org/en/view.aspx?x=377).

VII.iii *Staff and budget*

The NAFTA does not spell out any requirements or procedures with regard to the appointment of officials of the Secretariat, which, again, is left to the discretion of the States Parties, who are each responsible, as mentioned above, "for the operation and costs of its Section." This includes the appointment of the national Secretaries, whom the Agreement designates as "responsible for [the] administration and management" of the Sections that they head.[304] For the United States Section, the Secretary is appointed from within the ranks of the Department of Commerce, with the position advertised as an opportunity to "assist US businesses [to] compete globally," and "create opportunities for US workers and firms by promoting international trade and fostering a level playing field for American business." He or she is to be "an expert in international trade policy," and is expected to "lead a team responsible for coordinating with both the Mexican and Canadian sections to carry out the terms of the NAFTA agreement"; to "serve on both inter-agency and inter-government work groups to enhance and streamline the [dispute settlement] process"; to brief senior officials on the trade agreement; and to manage the office, including overseeing the budget and disbursement of funds.[305]

The expenditure profile of the national Sections "can vary from year-to-year and future spending trends are

[304] NAFTA, Article 2002(2)(c).

[305] Language of the 2011 advertisement for the opening of the position of head of the US Section (copy available at the US Department of Commerce).

difficult to predict. This is because the costs associated with delivery of [their] program[s] fluctuate with the number of dispute settlement cases that are filed."[306] Budget is generally not a concern for the national Sections, in light of their assurance that the governments in which they operate are mandated by the NAFTA to maintain the dispute settlement system and do not wish to violate this specific international obligation; it should also be borne in mind that per the NAFTA, the case work is a reimbursable cost shared equally by the involved countries.

The Canadian Section was funded until recently by Parliament through a program expenditures vote, and reported to Parliament, for financial accountability purposes, through the Minister of International Trade. In 2010, however, the Canadian Section was integrated into the Trade Policy and Negotiations Branch of the Department of Foreign Affairs and International Trade (DFAIT), and through this transfer, its reference levels of approximately C$3 million per fiscal year were integrated into DFAIT's reference levels. In the United States, NAFTA Public Law 103–182, Section 105(b) authorizes appropriations to the Department of Commerce, for each fiscal year after 1993, of US$2 million or less as may be necessary, for the establishment and operations of the US Section, and for payment of the US share of expenses of panels and committees convened pursuant to the dispute settlement proceedings. The US Section may retain and use funds provided by the Canadian and Mexican Sections

[306] *NAFTA Secretariat – Canadian Section, Departmental Performance Report for the Period Ending March 31, 2009*, p. 5.

for payment of their share of such expenses. The Mexico Section's budget, which varies more significantly each year, was set in 2013 at approximately 3,125,000 Mexican pesos.

VIII Concluding observations

Conclusions based on a limited array of case studies are inherently tentative, and, in some respects, the international secretariats under review might seem to defy comparison, having each been created in a distinct set of circumstances.[307] Yet from the preceding detailed examination, and from the parallels of operating experiences, emerge several interesting patterns; thus the lessons learned in these pages, which traverse the experience of six secretariats, lead us to a set of general observations that could perhaps inform policy-makers puzzling over similar issues of institutional management, architecture and reform.

VIII.i To lead or to support?

In discussing the role of international secretariats, scholars have generally drawn an analytical distinction between passive

[307] On the difficulties associated with comparative regionalism studies in general, see P. De Lombaerde, "Comparing Regionalisms: Methodological Aspects and Considerations," in T. M. Shaw, J. A. Grant and S. Cornelissen (eds.), *The Ashgate Research Companion to Regionalisms* (Farnham: Ashgate, 2011), pp. 31–50; P. De Lombaerde, F. Söderbaum, L. Van Langenhove and F. Baert, "Problems and Divides in Comparative Regionalism," in F. Laursen (ed.), *Comparative Regional Integration: Europe and Beyond* (Farnham: Ashgate, 2010), pp. 21–39.

or "cautious" secretariats on the one hand, and activist or "maximalist" secretariats on the other.[308] Such distinctions can obstruct a clear examination of the actual mission assigned to a secretariat or, worse, give rise to labeling that might carry with it unhelpful baggage; in particular, to use the term "activist" in describing secretariat design can trigger deep concern over loss of control and subordination of sovereignty.[309]

[308] See R. Sandford, "International Environmental Treaty Secretariats: Stage-Hands or Actors?," in H. O. Bergesen and G. Parmann (eds.), *Green Globe Yearbook of International Co-operation on Environment and Development* (Oxford University Press, 1994), p. 17; S. Andersen and J. B. Skjærseth, "Can International Environmental Secretariats Promote Effective Co-Operation?" (paper presented at the United Nations University's International Conference on Synergies and Co-ordination between Multilateral Environmental Agreements, Tokyo, Japan, July 1999) (available at http://archive.unu.edu/interlinkages/1999/docs/Andresen.PDF), p. 7.

[309] One author has suggested that, in any case, "there is no such thing as a passive secretariat ... even those secretariats that would describe themselves as passive are not *that* passive that they would not interfere with the political processes relevant to the treaty they serve ... Thus, it is preferable to talk of cautious rather than passive secretariats" (S. Bauer, "Does Bureaucracy Really Matter? The Authority of Intergovernmental Treaty Secretariats in Global Environmental Politics," 6:1 *Global Environmental Politics* 23 (2006), p. 32). Other scholars have argued that the administration versus policy dichotomy is unhelpful, as even a "seemingly innocuous or neutral role ... may involve a bureaucracy, or an international secretariat, in making decisions that will substantially ... affect the final [policy] decision that will be made" (see, for example, R. I. McLaren, *Civil Servants and Public Policy: A Comparative Study of International Secretariats* (Waterloo, ON: Wilfrid Laurier University Press, 1980), p. 34); P. B. Potter, "What International Administrations Actually Do," 30 *Iowa Law Review* 544 (1970), pp. 545–546.

It may thus be more useful to differentiate, for our purposes, between *facilitative* and *policy-shaping* secretariats. Facilitative secretariats are best described as those which adhere to the traditional function: serving as a supportive administrative apparatus, one that mostly assists and liaises with Member States, mobilizes information, monitors the implementation of the relevant enabling agreement and possibly carries out technical assistance activities as well. In essence, such secretariats operate in a narrow bandwidth, authorized to facilitate the inter-State project without much (or any) independence or discretion. They have no autonomous political voice in the political process that they serve, and their very access to it is severely limited. By contrast, the policy-shaping secretariat is defined as any of those international bureaus entrusted with a far more substantial role in carrying out an international mandate from Member States. Rather than serve as passive automatons, wired to implement mechanistically only those policies as transmitted from above, such secretariats play a meaningful role in crafting policy under mandates that can range from narrow to very broad, and act as agents, not mere structures. Empowered to articulate and advance an international perspective that is distinctly broader in outlook than that espoused by any single Member State, they build and acquire policy-relevant expertise, act with a strong degree of autonomy, promote commonly shared values and influence the inter-State discourse.

In reality, as the preceding case studies illustrate, international secretariats may defy such a strict binary classification. More accurately, secretariats can be arrayed across a spectrum whose metrics measure varying degrees of autonomy

Table s.8 *Facilitative versus policy-shaping international secretariats*

	Facilitative secretariats	**Policy-shaping secretariats**
Functions	Core administrative (and possibly technical) tasks only	Core administrative and technical as well as policy-shaping (and possibly political) tasks
Latitude and discretion	Highly constrained	Greater and generally encouraged
Substantive role in the overarching political process	No	Yes

or involvement in the policy processes of the international organization which they serve. Each secretariat, in this respect, is unique. Each arises from a specific need among a particular set of sovereign actors with different national goals, and its role in realizing a given international political project reflects that distinct set of circumstances. Above all, the decision as to what the secretariat is empowered to do (and, more importantly at times, what it *should not* do) is a political one, made by the relevant States at the bargaining table.

While a wider study is surely required in order to validate the following hypothesis, it appears that the facilitative secretariat model would be appealing, first and foremost, to States who set out a detailed and rigid plan of action for their international organization, rather than general or aspirational goals. Where the enabling agreement encapsulates in precise terms what the Member States wish to achieve (NAFTA is an example in point), policy has in fact already been determined and the Member States need only a bureaucracy to operate in administrative management mode, mostly to monitor implementation of the agreement and perform custodial and informational tasks. A facilitative secretariat may also be preferable for an international organization that would aim to advance a single and relatively narrow mandate, in particular a technical one where States already possess the relevant expertise. Here, national representatives and bureaucracies may cooperate rather easily in devising policy themselves, requiring primarily administrative services that would facilitate the multilateral exchange. In some cases, however, the top priority is to adamantly safeguard sovereignty. Thus, whatever the impetus for regional cooperation, States most concerned about control will invariably opt for a facilitative secretariat. Wishing not to "shift their loyalties, expectations, and political activities towards a new center,"[310] such States typically resolve to enhance international cooperation rather than embark on a process of regional integration, and would therefore prefer a secretariat that functions at the end of the spectrum featuring maximum restraint. Finally, a facilitative secretariat is likely to be found where "regionalism is a foreign policy resource used to achieve other ends such as international visibility, regional stability and regime legitimacy, as well as to please domestic and foreign audiences and mobilize support for the incumbent administrations."[311] In other words, where Member States

[310] E. B. Haas, *The Uniting of Europe: Political, Social, and Economic Forces 1950–1957* (Stanford, CA: Stanford University Press, 1958), p. 16.

[311] A. Malamud and G. L. Gardini, "Has Regionalism Peaked? The Latin American Quagmire and its Lessons," 47 *The International Spectator: Italian Journal of International Affairs* 116 (2012), p. 130.

(or several of them, in particular the bigger and more influential ones) are not genuinely interested in breathing much life into their international project, they will favor a secretariat with no significant power for policy formation or innovation – one that would not be able to promote change by itself.

In all such cases, as the experiences of MERCOSUR, APEC and NAFTA demonstrate, choosing a facilitative secretariat and making sure it remains constrained to that role may indeed guarantee that any significant development of the common agenda would depend solely on the States concerned. This gives the States tighter control over their international organization, as well as predictability, and places a greater weight on their national interests. But such a choice may also lead to stagnation of the political project, a perpetuation of power asymmetries, and only a limited possibility for creating an institution whose value and impact are greater than the sum of participating member nations.

By contrast, Member States are likely to show enthusiasm for a policy-shaping secretariat when a high degree of political consensus exists among them, at least with regard to the relevant regional project on which they are focused. A policy-shaping secretariat is likely to be found, moreover, where States lack the necessary expertise required to deal with the problem that their organization is put in place to solve, or where progress is sought in several fields (including in the political sphere, and especially where security comes into play), rather than within a single field. Finally, policy-shaping secretariats may be preferable where a supranational rather than international regime is adopted, and where the international organization is ultimately set up both for symbolic value and for synergistic gains.

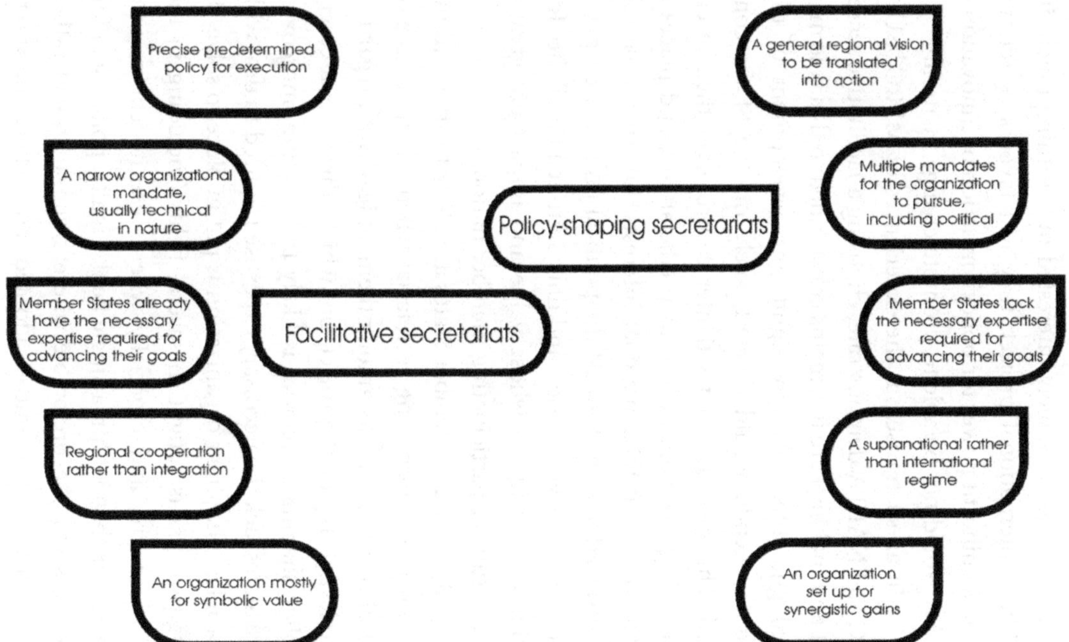

Figure s.7 Which secretariat model when?

VIII.ii *Allowing international secretariats to succeed*

Whatever their mission, some international secretariats perform better than others in terms of fulfilling their respective mandates and ultimately proving effective. The capacity of secretariats to do so appears to depend on several factors, chief among them the *political will of their masters (the Member States)*. Here, political will is like oxygen: the unswerving commitment of the organization's sovereign patrons to the secretariat function – as well as to the relevant international cause more broadly – is critical for the ability of international secretariats to provide the added value for which they were established. As elaborated below, it is this commitment that nourishes the other main factors that are required for well-functioning secretariats, and the strength of these attributes is a good barometer of the depth of that commitment. Political will is particularly important when it comes to the organization's larger and most influential Member States. The diminished position of the OAS General Secretariat since the election of Chilean José Miguel Insulza, as the first Secretary General who was not endorsed by the United States, is one example. In another example, the inability of MERCOSUR's Technical Secretariat to fulfill even the modest policy-shaping role allocated to it arose primarily from the lack of interest of two of the largest Member States, Brazil and Argentina.

Of the other factors affecting the power of international secretariats to deliver on their mandates, *trust in the secretariat among the organization's political organs* ranks

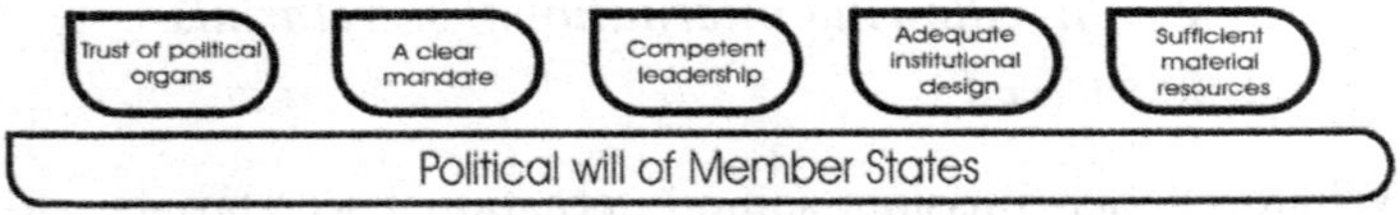

Figure s.8 What secretariats need to function effectively

first. While the external political climate plays a significant role in this context, the organs to which the secretariat is answerable must themselves perceive the secretariat to be constructive, useful and apolitical, lest they choose to sidestep it and, ultimately, mobilize to narrow its power or mandate.[312] Such trust could be maintained through enlightened political oversight that aims to ensure that the secretariat neither encroaches on sovereignty nor fails to carry out its duties by falling prey to inefficiencies or to dysfunction, the two central concerns commonly voiced by Member States. And, as we have seen, Member States may employ a variety of control mechanisms in order to keep the secretariat in check, from annual reporting requirements and the collective power of the purse to more intrusive measures. Examples of the latter may be found in the highly restrictive control exercised by MERCOSUR's political bodies over the decision-making power of the Technical Secretariat's Director, and, even more

[312] As one author has warned, secretariats must bear in mind that "[a]s bureaucratic authority is a delicate good, even minor misdemeanors of a treaty secretariat – or what is perceived as such by its parties – can seriously reduce and ultimately result in a total loss of its authority" (S. Bauer, "Does Bureaucracy Really Matter? The Authority of Intergovernmental Treaty Secretariats in Global Environmental Politics," 6:1 *Global Environmental Politics* 23 (2006), p. 32).

so, in the *de facto* subordination of NAFTA's Secretaries to national ministries. Aside from such collective controls, there are also ways for individual States to address particular concerns over a potential loss of control to which they feel especially vulnerable. One such example is the informal agreement in the OAS that secures for the United States oversight of the Finance and Administration arm of the General Secretariat,[313] and another is the separate governance arrangement put in place for APEC's Policy Support Unit. Notwithstanding efforts to fortify the means for political oversight of the secretariat, Member States must strike a balance in order to ensure that supervision does not result in curtailing the secretariat's very ability to perform its functions.

To function effectively, an international secretariat also needs *a clear mandate*. This does not necessarily mean a legal-constituent text that expressly enumerates its tasks and position. Several of the case studies (EFTA in particular) confirm what a number of political scientists who have studied international organizations have already reported: that charters, treaties and enabling documentation might not fully account for what secretariats actually do.[314] More important is

[313] On informal arrangements between Member States of international organizations for control of specific bureaucratic divisions by certain Member States who are politically vulnerable to a loss of control relating to the work carried out by such divisions, see M. Kleine, "Trading Control: National Fiefdoms in International Organizations," 5 *International Theory* 321–346 (2013).

[314] In EFTA, we see most clearly that a secretariat's core responsibilities – let alone its existence – do not have to be enshrined in any way in the constitutive documents of the regional scheme for it to take its place as a

that, whatever the form, a shared understanding must exist among all relevant actors as to the precise nature of the boundaries within which the secretariat may operate. Such a common perspective buttresses secretariat action with legitimacy, and enables secretariats to play their part without constant battles over turf (which they are in any case rarely in a position to win). This is particularly important for policy-shaping secretariats, whose measure of discretionary power and policy entrepreneurship can provoke reflexive opposition by national bureaucracies. It must also be clear that the secretariat belongs "to all [member] nations and to none,"[315] meaning that it must function neutrally and owe its loyalty to the organization alone. It is not infrequent that this basic principle comes under considerable strain in practice, and the result can severely hinder the smooth functioning of the secretariat.

Third, like any organization, secretariats require *competent leadership*. In a secretariat, however, the top person is just as much a chief executive officer as he or she is the face

central permanent organ. In fact, it just might be that the lack of such a rigid framework, the change of which often requires a cumbersome process of amendment, was what enabled the EFTA Secretariat to quickly realign its work when the institution's political condition and goals were dramatically changed. At the same time, the experience of other secretariats, such as those of ECOWAS, MERCOSUR and the OAS, suggests that a formal decision of the highest political level might indeed be helpful (although far from sufficient) in bringing about a significant change in the status and role of a secretariat.

[315] J. Lorimer, *The Institutes of the Law of Nations*, vol. II (1884), p. 266 (quoted in H. G. Schermers and N. M. Blokker, *International Institutional Law: Unity Within Diversity* (Leiden: Martinus Nijhoff, 5th edn., 2011), p. 346).

of the overarching organization and a crucial link to its Member States. Given the unique challenges that come with such a role, the importance of having an able, principled and diplomatic person serving as the head of the secretariat cannot be overemphasized. It is up to Member States to ensure that national claims to the post (especially when it rotates among them) do not jeopardize the appointment of a person who possesses the necessary qualifications, and they ought to keep in mind that "[t]op staff should not be seen in isolation but rather at the apex of a complex bureaucratic pyramid."[316] In order to enhance the stature of the secretariat in its policy-related role, it is important that Member States reserve a seat for the top secretariat official in the deliberations of political bodies, and that the voice of the secretariat is heard in such fora. The top executive, for his or her part, must epitomize the impartial character of international civil service, cultivate a culture of productivity and dynamism, and skillfully perform leadership tasks while appearing "as not exercising power but instead serving others."[317]

[316] T. G. Weiss, "International Bureaucracy: The Myth and Reality of the International Civil Service," 58 *International Affairs* 287 (1982), p. 299. On executive leadership in international organizations, see also C. Winchmore, "The Secretariat: Retrospect and Prospect," 19 *International Organization* 622–639 (1965); R. W. Cox, "The Executive Head: An Essay on Leadership in International Organization," 23 *International Organization* 205–230 (1969); and J. Mathiason, *Invisible Governance: International Secretariats in Global Affairs* (Bloomfield, CT: Kumarian Press, 2007), pp. 69–85.

[317] M. Barnett and M. Finnemore, *Rules for the World: International Organizations in Global Politics* (Ithaca, NY: Cornell University Press, 2004), p. 21 (referring more broadly to secretariats).

Table s.9 *Illustrative secretariat design factors*

Variables of institutional design	Facilitative secretariats	Policy-shaping secretariats
Organizational structure	Relatively flat	More complex
Term of service for secretariat head	Relatively short, non-renewable	Longer and usually renewable
Staff size	Generally smaller	Generally larger
Professional staff tenure	Shorter and limited	Longer (possibly indefinite)
Dedicated policy advisory unit(s)	No (or highly constrained)	Yes
Existence of a legal department	Usually no	Yes
Other similar permanent organs in the overarching organization	Possibly	No
National affinity discouraged	Usually not a top priority	Generally yes

Fourth, the effective performance of secretariats is directly linked to *adequate institutional design*. The preceding narrative illustrates the great extent to which elements of institutional design, particularly in the aggregate, may have a bearing on a secretariat's ability to carry out its mission. Determined for the most part by the political bargain among Member States, such formal attributes (examples of which are set out in Table s.9) may be utilized to either constrain the role of international secretariats or, alternatively, encourage them to take a more active part in a given regional project. Either way, they should correlate to the secretariat's mission.

These attributes are shaped by "deliberations and struggles over organizational forms but also over symbols, legitimacy, and the ethos and identity of public administration," and indeed must ultimately be understood as such.[318]

As Table s.9 illustrates (against the backdrop of the data provided in earlier chapters), Member States may choose from a diverse set of variables when setting up their organization's secretariat. To ensure the role of APEC's Secretariat remains highly circumscribed to technical-clerical tasks, for example, its sovereign creators initially opted for a relatively small and fairly flat structure, where the director and professional staff had very short terms of office that significantly constrained their ability to achieve any significant policy-shaping impact. Some of these elements, as in the cases of ECOWAS and MERCOSUR, came up for reconsideration when the secretariat's mission was expanded.

Institutional design may likewise be utilized to discourage or encourage the national affinities of secretariat staff. Member States eager to create an atmosphere in which staff members do not internalize a truly regional perspective may, as in the case of APEC, retain professional secretariat staff on short-term loan from their respective governments (which also pay their salaries), therefore giving the staff members little incentive to develop a regional *esprit de corps*. A similar disincentive manifests itself in NAFTA, where the secretariat's professional positions were designated as career

[318] J. P. Olsen, "Maybe It Is Time to Rediscover Bureaucracy," 16 *Journal of Public Administration Research and Theory* 1 (2004), p. 19.

positions within national ministries of the Member States, and in MERCOSUR, where strains of national loyalty among the Technical Secretariat's staff are accentuated through a recruitment system that emphasizes national background in achieving "equal representation" of the staff. This is markedly different from the design of the secretariats of the OAS, ECOWAS and EFTA, whose staff members can more strongly (if not exclusively) identify themselves as international civil servants.[319]

In a similar vein, the absence of a legal department (or a critical mass of lawyers who operate as such) in an international secretariat would likely also limit its policy-shaping capability. As Max Weber argued, legitimate modern authority of bureaucracies is largely invested in legalities, rules and procedures,[320] and it is highly likely that Member States,

[319] See in this context, C. Winchmore, "The Secretariat: Retrospect and Prospect," 19 *International Organization* 622–639 (1965), pp. 628–629: "The justification of the international secretariat must depend in the long run on its ability to serve purposes which can be discharged neither by any national civil service nor by a service composed of civil servants seconded from their national governments. The international civil servant is called upon to display qualities of mind and character, and indeed of intellect, which are inseparable from his calling and which are likely to be developed only as a result of long acclimatization to the service of an international organization."

[320] M. Weber, *Theory of Social and Economic Organization* (New York: Oxford University Press, 1947); see also M. N. Barnett and M. Finnemore, "The Politics, Power and Pathologies of International Organizations," 53 *International Organization* 707–710 (1999); S. Bauer, "Does Bureaucracy Really Matter? The Authority of Intergovernmental Treaty Secretariats in Global Environmental Politics," 6:1 *Global Environmental Politics* 23 (2006), pp. 30–31.

when setting up a secretariat that is meant to implement policy rather than to shape it, would wish to prevent precisely such authority from developing. The secretariats of EFTA, ECOWAS and the OAS all have lawyers playing a key role in shaping policy; in APEC, MERCOSUR and the NAFTA, however, despite recurring legal needs (from drawing up employment contracts and information policies, through monitoring the actions of Member States, to interpreting relevant legal documents) the secretariats are prevented from building an infrastructure of legal expertise. These secretariats are made to rely, instead, on outside counsel, sometimes from the Member States themselves.

The power and standing of the secretariat can also be diminished by diluting its executive authority within the international organization through the creation of additional permanent executive bodies that report independently to the political organs. In NAFTA and in MERCOSUR, the Member States have done just that. In both cases, they rejected the option of enhancing the structure and mandate of their existing secretariat, preferring instead to create additional permanent bodies, dedicated to new tasks and reporting in separate channels. In APEC, the peculiar position of the Secretariat's Policy Support Unit derives in part from similar considerations. Through this type of institutional design, secretariats are prevented from amassing, at least exclusively, the technical expertise and information which Weber identified as a second source of autonomous bureaucratic authority.[321]

[321] M. Weber, *Theory of Social and Economic Organization* (New York: Oxford University Press, 1947).

Finally, in order to provide real value, secretariats require *sufficient material resources*. Adequate funding is particularly essential for sustaining a competitive level of remuneration that would allow the secretariat to recruit and retain sufficient competent staff who are, undoubtedly, invaluable to an optimal implementation of its mandate. Such continuous availability of resources may be achieved through a variety of means, from Member States contributions, through special taxation programs (such as the ECOWAS Community levy), to allowing secretariats to raise revenue directly.[322] In any case, budgetary penury of secretariats ultimately reflects a lack of political commitment from Member States. As the preceding narrative illustrates, when Member States are committed to pushing their international agenda forward, they quickly arm their secretariats with greater resources so that they can execute their mission robustly.

VIII.iii *A structured evolution*

The foregoing narrative points to yet another general observation: that secretariats may indeed be viewed as organizations

[322] It is indeed worthwhile to consider as well that "stability and predictability in income may be more important than the level of funding," or at least as important (see S. Andersen and J. B. Skjærseth, "Can International Environmental Secretariats Promote Effective Co-Operation?," paper presented at the United Nations University's International Conference on Synergies and Co-ordination between Multilateral Environmental Agreements, Tokyo, Japan, July 1999 (available at http://archive.unu.edu/inter-linkages/1999/docs/Andresen.PDF), p. 8).

in and of themselves and may evolve as such, embodying the organizational theory that institutions created for specific purposes can acquire an ever greater range of functions within their original mandates, but also beyond, as those mandates tend to expand.[323] The secretariats of MERCOSUR, EFTA, APEC, ECOWAS and the OAS all exemplify this point, having each undergone considerable changes over time, taking on different organizational structures and adapting their missions and goals. (NAFTA's Secretariat stands as the stark exception here; its disjointed structure raises the question of whether it qualifies as an organization at all). It is worth highlighting, however, that despite the pervasive concern among States that international secretariats will run rough-shod over national sensibilities and, "[l]ike Frankenstein's monster ... behave differently from the way [their creators] ... expected [them] to,"[324] such organizational growth did not, for the most part, emanate from the secretariats themselves. Secretariats appear to understand very clearly that the political support of Member States is crucial for their effective operation, and that they exist to

[323] See, for example, G. D. Ness and S. R. Brechin, "Bridging the Gap: International Organizations as Organizations," 42 *International Organization* 245–273 (1988); D. C. Ellis, "The Organizational Turn in International Organization Theory," 1 *Journal of International Organizations Studies* 11–28 (2010). On the need for proper adaptation of both the structure and principles of action of secretariats to their expanding roles, see also W. Morawiecki, "Some Problems Connected with the Organs of International Organizations," 19 *International Organization* 913 (1965), pp. 915–916.

[324] A. Guzman, "International Organizations and the Frankenstein Problem," 24 *European Journal of International Law* 999 (2013), p. 1000.

serve their masters. It was rather the Member States, whose conception as to how the secretariat should serve their regional agenda has changed over time (in particular in the face of a crisis or poor performance of their organization as a whole), who welcomed or decided to implement reforms and reorganization. Indeed, when Member States want to give greater impetus to their regional project, one of the first things they consider, and ultimately vote in favor of, is an enhancement of the secretariat. Whatever the specific theme that the sovereign stakeholders wish to promote at the regional level, secretariats are viewed as drivers of processes, as machineries for execution and as a potential source of leadership. While scholars may still disagree on whether or not secretariats are vital to the effectiveness of international regimes, the six case studies make clear that States do believe the answer is in the affirmative.

States formalize their cooperative relations with the aim of providing, together, certain public goods that they cannot provide in isolation. The range of these goods is greatly varied, encompassing security, identity and religion; and development, infrastructure and regulatory frameworks for trade, labor or air transport, for instance. To this end, States accept to be bound by formal arrangements whereby they commit to deliver these goods, but also to respect the agreements concluded. Formal institutions respond precisely to these needs for provision and commitment.

Globalization has underlined the inability of States to provide goods in isolation and has hence accelerated legal integration at international and supranational levels: the number of international institutions – now over 60,000 – began growing after the Second World War and is still rising; the relations between State administrations and international institutions are becoming ever more numerous; forms of regional organization have been spreading; new forms of global networks and global "administrations" have been developing. As a consequence, scholars worldwide have devoted themselves to studying global governance, international organizations and regionalism. From these various perspectives, what has emerged clearly is that a mono-disciplinary approach is not capable of capturing all the implications related to these issues, which means that it becomes crucial to combine different fields of research. In this context, the use of concepts derived from both political science and law has turned out to be extremely effective, such as in the case of regime theory being used to explain the formation of global regulatory systems. This is why this book presents these two perspectives jointly, in its endeavor to define models of international and supranational legal integration.

Our aim, therefore, is threefold. First, we map and outline models of regional integration by studying their institutional design and processes of governance. Second, we extend our analysis to IOs and other international regimes, to identify which techniques are capable of governing complex global legal systems. Third, we offer a toolbox of institutional processes and legal mechanisms, which may be adopted by current or new projects of international and supranational integration, such as ASEAN. We address these aims in two chapters, both based on the idea of integration as a formal process.

Chapter 1 assesses the empirical models of formalization, based on a large sample of existing organizations across all continents. The chapter unveils the structure of formal commitments used in integration and other international organizations. It focuses on the formal mechanisms that secure "credible commitments". Credible commitments result from institutional design which comprises a number of instruments: the regulation of membership; the institutional structure of integration organizations; the decision-making procedure; the nature of derived norms and the mechanisms for their incorporation into national orders; and the mechanisms of jurisdictional control, supervision and scrutiny. Each of these serves to "lock" participants into integration schemes, and restricts their freedom to withdraw from accepted commitments. The chapter does not explore the causality link between informal/formal integration, nor does it "measure" informal integration or consider the achievements gained under informal integration. The chapter examines the structure of formalized institutional commitments by looking at the organs for decision-making, the procedures for taking decisions and the model of derived norms. It also provides a classification of the different integration schemes by examining the relationship between an integration organization's objectives and the formal instruments available to it for generating credible commitments. As the thesis of this chapter is that the objectives of regional integration organizations inspire a given institutional structure, it will also examine the kind of objectives existing within integration organizations. A data set comprising the institutional features of eighty-five integration and/or international organizations provides the empirical evidence underlying the arguments of this chapter. The analysis will show that States entering regional (and other) organizations accept formal commitments to achieve their goals with the expectation that other participant States will reciprocate, and it will also examine how this happens.

Chapter 2 focuses on the legal mechanisms and instruments that drive the development of international regimes, their institutional features and their functioning. To outline and critically describe the typology of international organizations and their regimes, and to identify the main legal techniques of governance, the analysis will cover most of the eighty-five international and regional organizations examined in Chapter 1 (such as the EU, ECOWAS, MERCOSUR and ASEAN), as well as other international institutions of both intergovernmental and hybrid public–private nature (such as the ISO and ICANN). In this chapter, the perspective adopted is essentially a "managerial" one, which seeks to avoid bias connected to any given political objective. International regimes have increasingly been using accountability mechanisms, but principally to ensure their own efficiency and effectiveness rather than to address any democratic gaps. In other words, the need to enhance the legitimacy and accountability of IOs has a functional reason; this is confirmed by the fact that all regimes tend to adopt similar mechanisms, regardless of the degree of "democracy" they may present. The focus will therefore be on a classification of IOs, and on the common threads in the development of international regimes and their mechanisms for ensuring accountability: the increasing differentiation and separation of functions – the "legislative" (norm-making), "judicial" (dispute settlement) and executive-administrative ones; the emergence of intra- and inter-IO institutional pluralism; the growing degree of proceduralization; the need for multiple forms of legitimacy and the adoption of different mechanisms for accountability. These threads may not all occur simultaneously in every regime, and there are many asymmetries. One thread may be more common than another. See, for example, the different ways in which international administrations emerge: these are stronger in global private regimes or in political unions (such as the EU), but weaker in free trade areas. This analysis will enable the main techniques of governance and models of legal integration beyond the State to be identified: indirect rule, role-splitting and normative supremacy. All these techniques can be productively adopted at various levels, in the pursuit of international and supranational legal integration.

The Study gives a detailed comparative overview of the design and role of secretariats serving selected regional organizations. Secretariats are the organ to which supra-State delegation happens (when it actually happens), and in trying to understand the potential and constraints of institutionalized international cooperation, their role should not be overlooked. The detailed parallels of operating experiences provided in the study offer a wealth of empirical evidence, and some general observations, to consider together with the thesis presented in Chapters 1 and 2.

The book offers the first comprehensive overview and conceptualization of different models of international and supranational integration. It illustrates which governance processes and institutional choices – and how and why – are developed by regional organizations. It also displays which legal instruments – regulatory, organizational, procedural – are adopted to achieve integration. It explains how different objectives can influence institutional design and the integration model: for example, a free trade area could insist only on supremacy and refrain from adopting instruments for indirect rule, while a political union would rather engage with all available techniques in all their possible declinations: from the most sophisticated (such as preliminary ruling by domestic judges) to the most effective (such as "higher law" clauses).

Finally, this book aims to provide academics and practitioners with a toolbox of concepts that may be fruitfully used, regardless of whether the "pendulum" – as Mauro Cappelletti observed in the 1980s – swings towards "nationalism" or "transnationalism, federalism, or [a] broad grouping of States."

INDEX

Made in the USA
Monee, IL
13 September 2026

62976471R00292